ACC BASKETBALL

The Story of the Rivalries, Traditions,
and Scandals of the First Two Decades of
the Atlantic Coast Conference

ACC BASKETBALL

J. SAMUEL WALKER

THE UNIVERSITY OF NORTH CAROLINA PRESS
CHAPEL HILL

This book was published with the assistance of the
BLYTHE FAMILY FUND
of the University of North Carolina Press.

The paper in this book meets the guidelines for permanence and
durability of the Committee on Production Guidelines for Book Longevity
of the Council on Library Resources. The University of North Carolina Press
has been a member of the Green Press Initiative since 2003.

Library of Congress Cataloging-in-Publication Data
ACC basketball: the story of the rivalries, traditions, and scandals of the first
two decades of the Atlantic Coast Conference / J. Samuel Walker.
p. cm.
Includes index.
ISBN 978-0-8078-3503-6 (alk. paper)
1. Atlantic Coast Conference — History. 2. College sports —
Southern States — History. I. Title.
GV351.3.S684 W35 2011
796.04/30975
2011015088

15 14 13 12   5 4 3 2

To the memory of

RACHAEL SMITH WALKER (1915–2009)

and to the arrival of

CHARLOTTE RACHAEL BURKHOLDER

CONTENTS

ILLUSTRATIONS

PREFACE

I became a passionate fan of Atlantic Coast Conference (ACC) basketball when I began graduate school in history at the University of Maryland in 1969. I arrived at Maryland in the same year as its new coach, Lefty Driesell, though with considerably less fanfare. For three years, I cheered for Maryland and reviled its opponents, especially its ACC rivals. My loyalties shifted dramatically in 1972, when my brother Wally enrolled at the University of Virginia on a basketball scholarship. For four years, I rooted fanatically for Virginia while defaming its opponents. I had the disheartening experience of watching Virginia lose every game in Wally's career at Maryland's Cole Field House, while the home fans at my own school jeered my brother and disparaged his team. I gained a measure, make that a great deal, of satisfaction, along with bragging rights, when Virginia defeated Maryland in the 1976 ACC Tournament and went on to win the conference championship.

After Wally graduated, I remained an interested, though less fervent, ACC fan. I cheered for both Virginia and Maryland (and, of course, vilified their opponents). In 2006, after following ACC basketball for nearly four decades, I decided it would make a good topic for a book. At that time, I was looking for an enjoyable research project to work on when I retired in the not-too-distant future. During my career as a professional historian, I had published several books on subjects that included President Truman's decision to use the atomic bomb against Japan and the Three Mile Island nuclear power plant accident. I was pleased with the reception of the books I wrote, but I wanted to do something different in retirement.

One day, in a bolt out of the blue, I came up with the idea of writing a book on the early history of ACC basketball. It seemed like a fun topic that would also necessarily cover serious issues relating to the role of sports in educational institutions. Once I discovered that the university archives of schools that were members of the ACC during the 1950s and 1960s contained a wealth of useful and fascinating documentary material, I was on my way. And in fact, the topic turned out to be so enjoyable that I could not wait until retirement to write it. When I began this project, I knew little about ACC basketball in the period before I started graduate school, and working on the book was a voyage of discovery about the colorful history of the conference and about the brilliant coaches and players who made it into a basketball powerhouse.

I brought a set of divided loyalties to the subject of ACC basketball. In addition to attending Maryland while my brother played at Virginia, in later years my daughter, Mary Beth, graduated from Virginia and Duke Law School, and my son, Dan, earned a master's degree at Wake Forest. The University of North Carolina Press published not only this book but also my earlier study of Truman and the bomb. I learned in the course of doing research on the ACC that there is also much to admire about the schools with which I have no direct or even distant connection. I hope that my first-hand, or at least secondhand, acquaintance with the universities that were members of the conference in the years covered by this book have enabled me to write a balanced and nonpartisan, though not uncritical, history. I attempted to capture the impressive progress made on both academic and athletic fronts without blinking when discussing more unsavory aspects of early ACC basketball.

Even books that are fun to write are not easy to write, and I am indebted to the many people who offered me invaluable assistance. I am exceedingly grateful to archivists at every institution at which I conducted research for their knowledge, guidance, and professionalism. I owe special thanks to Anne Turkos, University Archivist at the University of Maryland. She was exceedingly helpful in guiding me to a bonanza of useful material that got me started on this project and in putting me in touch with several people who knew much more about the history of Maryland basketball than I did. Best of all, she shared my enthusiasm for this topic. I am also greatly appreciative for the prompt, able, and friendly assistance of Tom Harkins of Duke University; Faye Haskins of the D.C. Public Library; Vicki Johnson of Wake Forest University; Liz Novara of the University of Maryland; Regina Rush of the University of Virginia; Sarah Rice Scott of North Carolina State University; Dennis Taylor of Clemson University; Matt Turi of the University of North Carolina; Elizabeth West of the University of South Carolina; and Gina Woodward, then of the College of William and Mary.

Jim Daves and Rich Murray of Media Relations in the University of Virginia Athletic Department provided access to a rich collection of clippings and media publications. Brian Morrison, assistant commissioner for media relations of the Atlantic Coast Conference, delivered the bad news that the conference had not kept correspondence and other primary sources from the period about which I was writing, but I benefited from the clippings files that he made available to me. During the several visits I made to the North Carolina State Archives, Kim Cumber, nontextual materials archivist, dug out thousands of strips of negatives on ACC basketball from the splendid photograph collection donated by the *Raleigh News and Observer*. She responded to my many requests cheerfully and knowledgably and on more than one occasion dropped what she was doing to help find a photo of a particular subject or a game on a particular date. Keith Longiotti of the University of North Carolina was similarly of great assistance in my research in the excellent photographs that are part of the North Carolina Collection.

The subject of ACC basketball was a departure from my previous record of research and publication, and I have benefited from comments on my drafts by well-versed scholars. Phil Cantelon read draft chapters with a sympathetic, discerning, and appropriately critical eye. Pamela Grundy and Randy Roberts read the prospectus and the completed manuscript of this book for UNC Press. They offered thoughtful, constructive, and deeply informed comments that led to substantial improvements. Chuck Grench of UNC Press provided strong support for this project from its early stages, valuable suggestions on how to organize a potentially unwieldy subject, a few lunches, and unfailing encouragement.

My wife, Pat, and other members of my family have been, as always, wonderfully supportive, tolerant of my absences (mental and physical), and reassuring on occasions when I expressed doubts about my progress or my performance on this project. My granddaughter Charlotte is still too young to care about ACC basketball, but if she follows the example of her great-grandmother, she will eventually become an astute and more than slightly partisan fan.

University Park, Maryland
November 2010

ACC BASKETBALL

PROLOGUE

On December 2, 1953, the University of Maryland Terrapins met the University of South Carolina Gamecocks in the first basketball game ever played in the recently formed Atlantic Coast Conference (ACC). Maryland, a legitimate contender for the league title, was favored to win and the matchup generated little anticipation or excitement. A "near capacity crowd" of about 3,000 attended the game at South Carolina's University Field House in Columbia; the cost of a ticket was $1.50 for adults and $.50 for children. The fans watched Maryland pull out a hard-fought 53–49 victory. After South Carolina tied the score at 49, Maryland froze the ball for about two minutes before forward Tom Young hit the go-ahead shot with 15 seconds remaining. All-American candidate Gene Shue led Maryland with 19 points, tying him for game honors with South Carolina's Joe Smith.[1]

The outcome of the game attracted slight notice. The Washington, D.C., and Baltimore newspapers that covered Maryland as a home team provided only brief accounts. The *Evening Star*, Washington's leading newspaper, ran its story on the third sports page. South Carolina's hometown paper, *The State*, offered a somewhat longer but hardly exhaustive review. The featured stories on the sports pages in both areas described in detail developments in college football, horse racing, and the pension plan for major league baseball. Although some press reports mentioned in passing that the Maryland–South Carolina game inaugurated ACC basketball, they did not treat it as an especially noteworthy milestone.[2]

Slightly more than seventeen years later, on January 9, 1971, the same schools met at Maryland's Cole Field House in College Park. The stakes of the game and the attention it commanded were dramatically different than in 1953. South Carolina, coached by the legendary Frank McGuire, who had led the University of North Carolina to a national championship in 1957, was ranked as the number two team in the nation. Maryland was coached by flamboyant Charles G. "Lefty" Driesell, who had guided tiny Davidson College in North Carolina to national prominence before moving to College Park. In his second season at Maryland, he was anxious to show that his team was on its way to becoming a formidable power in the ACC.

The matchup between a highly ranked team and a highly ambitious program would have produced excitement and tension under any circumstances. But in this case the buildup for the contest took on elevated proportions because of a brawl that had occurred when the teams had played in Columbia the previous month. On December 16, 1970, South Carolina was cruising to an easy victory when, with 4:52 remaining in the game, two players got into a shoving and elbow-throwing skirmish. Both benches rushed to the aid of their teammates, and a slugfest broke out. As Driesell tried to separate players and stop the melee, he was struck twice in the face by South Carolina forward John Ribock. The fracas continued for about four minutes before police managed to halt the fighting and the referees decided to end the game. "In my 20 years of officiating," referee George Conley reported to acting ACC commissioner Norvall Neve, "I have never seen every player so involved in a fight." The final score was 96–70.[3]

After Maryland left the floor, Driesell was informed that South Carolina athletic director Paul F. Dietzel had banned reporters from the visitors' locker room. With bruises on his lip and cheek clearly visible, Driesell defiantly held an informal press conference. Speaking with evident emotion, he called the altercation "a disgrace" and accused McGuire of smiling while "they were going wild out there." He added, "If I was Frank McGuire, I would not bring my team to College Park." McGuire responded with his own provocative statements. "I don't care what Lefty has to say. There are a million Lefty Driesells in the world," he commented. "You won't see the day I'm afraid of him." The following day, Driesell repeated his warning and announced that he might protest the game to try to nullify the outcome. "Hell, there was five minutes left," he said. "We might have caught them." More than a month later, long after the ACC declared the shortened game official, Dreisell urged Maryland athletic director James H. Kehoe "to work on getting the South Carolina game, at Columbia, to be judged as no-contest."[4]

While the coaches traded barbs, the top administrators of both universities sought to prevent any lasting damage. South Carolina president Thomas F. Jones wired Maryland president Wilson H. Elkins that he "deeply regretted" the incident because "we cherish our fine relationship with the University of Maryland at all levels." Elkins expressed his hope that the relationship between the two schools "which has existed for many years will continue in a manner which will reflect credit on the institutions."[5]

Despite Jones's conciliatory telegram, South Carolina officials took Driesell's warnings seriously and petitioned the ACC to cancel the upcoming game in College Park. In a hand-delivered letter, T. Eston Marchant, chairman of the university's Board of Trustees, told Acting Commissioner Neve that Driesell's "inflammatory remarks" had created such a "dangerous situation" that the game should be called off. Kehoe, who believed that "the incident has been exaggerated out of all proportion to its real importance," responded that South Carolina's concerns about safety were "ill founded" and that "all necessary protection" would be provided. Neve accepted Kehoe's assurances and ruled that South Carolina must play the game. If it refused, he threatened to disqualify the team from participating in postseason tournaments. In light of Neve's ruling, South Carolina unhappily agreed that "under these circumstances and conditions" it would make the trip to College Park.[6]

In the days leading up to the rematch, Maryland administrators and students pleaded for civility and good behavior from local fans. "We treat our guests with hospitality," Kehoe declared. "And I certainly don't think in view of all the things that have been said that any student would want to give South Carolina a chance to say 'I told you so.'" The student newspaper, the *Diamondback*, commented in an editorial, "The way is open for University students and fans to administer a telling blow to USC and to coach McGuire in particular. The method of revenge that would be most effective would be the restriction of fan reaction to nonviolent means." The game and the possibility of another free-for-all generated a great deal of attention from the news media. A contingent of 48 reporters and broadcasters—more than for any previous regular-season game in Maryland basketball history—and live coverage on local television were indications of the extraordinary interest the rematch created.[7]

On the evening of January 9, 1971, an impassioned crowd of 14,312 packed Cole Field House. In addition to following customary security procedures, Kehoe stationed beefy Maryland students in seats on the floor to guard players and coaches from the possibility of unruly acts by fans. Also ringing the court, in a more conspicuous and lighthearted presence, were members of the Maryland Medieval Mercenary Militia, a student group that occasionally staged mock battles on campus. Dressed in more or less medieval-type costumes, they perhaps helped to ease the tension that pervaded the building. Although McGuire had boasted after the fight in Columbia that he was not afraid of Driesell, he apparently was wary of what other Maryland partisans might do. He wore a bullet-proof vest under his tailored suit.

As the arena filled to capacity, the electricity in the air was fueled by the Maryland pep band. It repeatedly performed "East Side, West Side," a not-too-subtle reference to the fact that several members of the South Carolina team came from New York City, including guard John Roche, the reigning ACC Player of the Year. Roche had just been featured in a cover story in *Sports Illustrated* that called him "the best of some New York transplants who are mean enough to take South Carolina to the NCAA title." When the South Carolina team emerged from its locker room to warm up, the Maryland fans, in response to earlier advice from student leaders and to appeals that spread informally through the stands, suddenly became completely silent. The eerie quiet continued until the Maryland players made their appearance to a thunderous eruption of cheers. Driesell walked to the bench a few minutes later, and the noise reached epic dimensions after he greeted the crowd by flashing a "V" sign.[8]

Once the game began, it offered less drama than the crowd had anticipated. South Carolina normally played an effective 2-3 defense, and Driesell did not believe that Maryland could win against the zone. Therefore, he instructed his guards to employ stalling tactics to force the Gamecocks into man-to-man coverage. McGuire refused to adjust, however, and Maryland's offensive strategy turned into an impromptu freeze. Its players simply held the ball, lobbed it back and forth, or dribbled in place. While fans at the arena clapped in unison to support their team, outraged television viewers called the local station that carried the game to protest. In the broadcast booth, announcers Steve Gilmartin and Sonny Jurgensen read selections from the *Canterbury Tales* and the U.S. Constitution. When the first half ended, Maryland had hit both shots it attempted and clung to a 4–3 lead.

The second half was, by comparison, a high-scoring affair, in part because South Carolina used a man-to-man defense. The score was tied, 23–23, at the end of regulation play. South Carolina took a 30–25 lead in overtime with just 24 seconds left in the game, but Maryland scored three quick baskets on an uncontested layup and two steals of in-bounds passes thrown by Roche. Jim O'Brien hit the winning shot with 2 seconds on the clock. Pandemonium reigned in Cole Field House. As the pep band played "Amen," Maryland fans dashed to the floor to celebrate an improbable victory. An elated Driesell told the press that the "Good Lord had to be with us, the way we did it."[9]

The game received banner headlines and extensive coverage in local media as well as considerable national attention. Maryland won accolades not only for the performance of its team but also for the conduct of its fans. Dietzel told Kehoe that "your students, your fans, and all of your support people deserve our gratitude." He expressed confidence that "we

Maryland's Jim O'Brien holds the ball as teammate Sparky Still looks on.
South Carolina's Tom Riker (51) yawns, Kevin Joyce (43) scowls, and John Ribock (41)
converses with fans. (© Bettmann/CORBIS)

have closed a *short*, unfortunate chapter in our *long* book of most pleasant
and cordial relationships between two excellent Institutions." Some South
Carolina supporters, however, were much more critical of the crowd's behavior. An article in the *Charleston News and Courier* by "Ashley Cooper"
(a pseudonym for columnist Frank B. Gilbreth) charged that the Maryland
fans were "unsportsmanlike, nasty, and violent." He reported that "huge
signs were displayed using one of the most inexcusable of the four-letter
Anglo-Saxon monosyllables—the one which means coupling." Gilbreth
complained that "the displayers of the signs were neither reprimanded nor
expelled." The Columbia [S.C.] Decent Literature Committee made similar
claims and urged that in the future the University of South Carolina "just
walk off the court when these signs are displayed."[10]

Norvall Neve, who had attended the game, was surprised by the indict-
ments of the Maryland crowd. He told Kehoe that he had only seen one

Maryland players, fans, and coaches erupt after last-second victory.
Assistant coach George Raveling is at center and Coach Lefty Driesell is at right.
A dejected Tom Owens walks through the celebration. (Star Collection, reprinted
by permission of the DC Public Library: © Washington Post)

sign that "was even suggestive." Kehoe replied that he also had noticed only
one sign that could have been offensive and disclosed that he had delib-
erately refrained from making an issue of posters that showed poor taste.
His principal concern was to prevent more serious fan misconduct, such
as rushing the court or hurling objects at players or referees. "Our security people felt . . . that to challenge the displaying of posters by arresting
or removing the students from the arena could precipitate a real crisis," he
explained, and "it was decided not to make any move in this direction."
Kehoe, a former Marine, advised another correspondent that vulgar displays at football and basketball games were a sign of the times. He lamented
"calls and comments" that were "rude, and crude and obscene—a type of
thing that would have been unbelievable and unheard of just a few years
ago." To his regret, students, administrators, and courts "refused to take any
positive action" to curb such behavior.[11]

Even by the standards of ACC basketball, the buildup for and outcome of the Maryland–South Carolina game at Cole Field House were unusual. But they highlighted in particularly sharp relief the changes that had occurred between the ho-hum contest of 1953 and the spectacle of 1971. During that period, basketball became the ACC's premier attraction. The conference was founded with football in the forefront of the minds of university administrators. But by the early 1970s it won national acclaim in basketball, both for the quality of its play and the competitive balance of its teams. In March 1970, Curry Kirkpatrick, the leading writer on college basketball for *Sports Illustrated*, called the ACC "the country's strongest league."[12] From the time it was established, the conference had featured excellent teams, colorful coaches, and intense rivalries. But in its early years the league was divided between schools that consistently fielded good teams and those that did not. By 1972, the traditionally weaker members had upgraded their programs to the point that ACC games commonly became much-anticipated contests between peers, or at least near-equals. As the Maryland–South Carolina matchup of 1971 vividly demonstrated, ACC basketball teams, much more often than in 1953, drew large, raucous crowds. In a related development, the game was a striking example of the growth of media coverage, in newspapers and on television, of college basketball during the late 1950s and 1960s.

The contrast between the 1953 and 1971 games also reflected economic, cultural, and social trends in the South. The ACC was very much a southern institution — in addition to Maryland (the northernmost member) and South Carolina, the schools that belonged to the conference were the University of Virginia (Charlottesville), the University of North Carolina (Chapel Hill), North Carolina State University (Raleigh), Duke University (Durham, North Carolina), Wake Forest University (after 1956, Winston-Salem, North Carolina), and Clemson University (Clemson, South Carolina). Before World War II, the South had been by any standard the poorest region in the United States. After the war, it experienced remarkable economic growth that provided unprecedented prosperity to a significant percentage of its population. One result was that southerners had more disposable income and more leisure time, and they used some of both to support college basketball. Every ACC school except Duke and NC State, which already had large basketball stadiums, built modern arenas during the 1950s and 1960s. Boisterous and highly partisan fans jammed the new facilities, at least when their teams were competitive with league rivals.

Cultural changes in the South and throughout the United States were evident in the comments about fan behavior at the 1971 game at College Park. The student rebellions, severe generational divisions, and cultural shifts of the 1960s inevitably affected events at athletic arenas. In 1953, a dean at Duke announced that he was "seriously perturbed by the poor sportsmanship" shown by Duke fans at basketball games, particularly "the uncalled for booing when an opponent is on the foul line or the referee's decision seems unjust." By 1971, such concerns seemed quaint. The previous spring, student protests had effectively shut down the University of Maryland and Governor Marvin Mandel had called out the National Guard to maintain order. In the atmosphere that prevailed at campuses across the nation, including ACC schools, Kehoe and his counterparts had to worry about the appropriate response to fan misdeeds that were considerably more serious than booing foul shooters.[13]

ACC basketball between 1953 and 1972 was profoundly influenced by the most urgent and momentous social issue of the time — the movement for racial justice and civil rights. When the ACC was founded, no member school had a black player on its roster in basketball or any other sport. Nevertheless, administrators and coaches of conference schools deliberated over a series of racial questions, including segregated seating at games, playing against teams with African American players, and recruiting blacks for their own programs. The racial integration of the conference was a gradual and painfully slow process, and it did not occur without abusive behavior by some fans. In 1965, Billy Jones, a sophomore at Maryland, made the first appearance by a black player on an ACC varsity basketball team, and not until 1971 had all eight ACC schools followed suit. George Raveling became the first African American assistant coach in the conference when he was hired by Lefty Driesell in 1969. The presence of black players and a black coach in the Maryland–South Carolina matchup of 1971 was a momentous contrast with the racial norms that prevailed during the ACC's inaugural game in 1953.

Despite the important changes in the competitive fabric and cultural terrain of ACC basketball between 1953 and 1972, one crucial aspect remained a constant. Administrators of conference schools were deeply concerned about maintaining a proper balance between academic principles and athletic achievements. The goal of producing winning teams without sacrificing academic integrity was a critical issue when the ACC was established, and it was still a major source of vigilance, debate, and frustration throughout the conference two decades later. Indeed, an extended and acrimonious controversy over academic standards for athletes caused the University of South Carolina to leave the ACC in 1971. The departure of a charter member of the conference was a milestone that ended what should be regarded as the formative years of ACC basketball.

1

THE CRISIS
IN COLLEGE SPORTS,
1951

John E. Hocutt, the dean of men at the College of William and Mary in Williamsburg, Virginia, customarily met individually with all male students near the end of their sophomore year to review their records and evaluate their progress toward graduation. William and Mary was a state-supported institution with an enviable academic reputation. In the spring of 1949, Hocutt, a gruff, no-nonsense administrator, informed a member of the college's football team that an introductory Spanish course he had passed would not count toward his degree. Hocutt explained that since the student had taken two years of Spanish in high school he could not receive credit for freshman Spanish at William and Mary. The student protested that he had never taken Spanish in high school and the transcript that showed his having done so was incorrect. Hocutt reported those claims to J. Wilfred Lambert, the dean of students, who checked with the principal of the football player's high school. The principal confirmed the student's story and also called attention to other discrepancies in the high school transcript that was on record at William and Mary. It was apparent that the college's copy of the transcript had been altered.

Lambert conducted a careful search of student records and found more evidence of tampering. Eventually, he determined that several transcripts had been changed in the athletic office at the direction of the football coach, Reuben McCray. McCray had led William and Mary to gridiron glory during the previous few years. The college's team won the Southern Conference championship in 1947 and ranked 13th in the nation. It played in a bowl game that season and again in 1949. McCray's achievements received enthusiastic support from the college's governing body, the Board of Visitors, which was fully committed to a strong athletic program. Lambert's findings suggested that McCray's success depended in no small measure on altering high school transcripts of players who would not otherwise have qualified for admission to William and Mary. Further investigation by Nelson Marshall, dean of the college, revealed a series of other abuses by the athletic department, including changing grades, offering credit for physical education courses that lacked academic rigor, pressuring faculty members to keep players eligible, and violating the college's honor system.

Dean Marshall reported the unsavory results of his inquiry to the president of William and Mary, John E. Pomfret. During his tenure, Pomfret had tried to reduce financial assistance to athletes and de-emphasize the school's commitment to intercollegiate sports, but the Board of Visitors had overruled him. When he learned of the offenses that Lambert and Marshall uncovered, he sought to avoid a confrontation that would embarrass the college. In July 1951, McCray and assistant football coach Bernard Wilson agreed to resign after the upcoming season. When information about the football situation began to circulate and attract press attention, however, the two coaches suddenly quit. For the first time, Pomfret informed the Board of Visitors about the nature and extent of the coaches' transgressions. The board immediately reasserted its support for big-time football and blamed Pomfret for failing to prevent the scandal. Within a short time, Pomfret accepted an appointment as director of the Huntington Library in California, which, he pointedly affirmed, had "no alumni, no football team, and a very small and distinguished board of trustees."[1]

While Pomfret gladly departed for California, most members of the William and Mary faculty made clear that they deplored the scandal he left behind. Unlike the Board of Visitors, they did not implicate Pomfret.

Rather they fixed responsibility for the abuses in the football program on "an athletic policy" that "has proceeded to the point of obscuring and corrupting the real purposes of an institution of higher learning." At a meeting on September 17, 1951, 91 members of the faculty of 112 agreed on a statement of their views, which the press soon dubbed the "Williamsburg Manifesto." The faculty bitterly complained that the intercollegiate athletic program threatened to destroy "the very integrity of the College." Rather than serving as "a healthy and indispensable extracurricular activity," it had "become a commercial enterprise demanding winning teams at any cost, even the cost of dishonest academic practice." To correct the abuses, the faculty pledged action to ensure that athletic programs took their "rightful place as a beneficial but distinctly subordinate activity of the College."

The faculty's manifesto won favorable reviews in and beyond Virginia. Hocutt, whose name appeared first on the list of signers, commented that the "enthusiastic acceptance of our statement of policy by the press and by the public generally has exceeded our fondest hopes." It was the subject of a front-page story in the *New York Times* and received editorial support from the *New York Herald Tribune*. The *Richmond News Leader* called it the "first heartening development to come from a scandal that has shocked and sickened the State." The *Richmond Times-Dispatch* hoped that the statement would "prove a landmark in the history of modern education." The William and Mary scandal was a graphic demonstration of the tensions that often existed between athletic and academic objectives in American higher education. It testified to the difficulty of determining and enforcing the proper place of athletics in academic institutions. And the infractions in the football program at William and Mary played an important, if indirect, role in the formation of the Atlantic Coast Conference in 1953.[2]

The NCAA and the Reform Impasse

The popularity and problems of intercollegiate athletics first became apparent in football, which commanded more attention by far than other college sports. Within a short time after Rutgers defeated Princeton in what is usually regarded as the first intercollegiate football game in 1869, the sport generated keen interest among students and alumni of many schools. Games between top-drawer rivals attracted large crowds, inspired raucous cheers, and received prominent press coverage. The growth of college football also caused increasing controversy. The primary source of concern was the violence that was common on the gridiron, some of which was inherent in the rules of the game and some of which was wanton brutality. Critics pointed to the severe injuries and occasional deaths that occurred during games.

In December 1905, delegates from about 60 colleges with football teams met in New York. They agreed to establish a new organization, the Inter Collegiate Athletic Association (ICAA), to revise the rules to make college football less violent. The formation of the ICAA was an important step toward reform but was not enough in itself to correct abuses effectively. Many colleges that were most influential and successful in football did not join the ICAA and some adamantly opposed rules changes. The organization had no enforcement powers to achieve its objectives. Nevertheless, within a short time, the ICAA adopted a series of new rules that revolutionized the game. It also condemned in principle practices that members regarded as inappropriate for competition among academic institutions, such as recruiting, providing scholarships and other financial inducements to athletes, and using players who were not enrolled at the school they represented. Gradually more colleges joined the ICAA, especially after a highly publicized increase in the number of football deaths in 1908. The ICAA further refined its football rules to reduce brutality and, in 1910, took another enduring action by changing its name to the National Collegiate Athletic Association (NCAA).[3]

During the 1920s, public interest in college football rose to unprecedented levels and fans flocked to games in record numbers. The growth in college football's popularity contributed substantially to already ample pressures to win. This, in turn, heightened concerns about the impact of big-time sports on academic institutions and about the means that colleges used to field successful teams. In 1926, the Carnegie Foundation for the Advancement of Teaching, which had published highly regarded studies of medical and legal training, public schools, and other topics, decided to conduct a survey of college sports in the United States and Canada. Staff members of the foundation visited 130 schools, where they examined documents and interviewed administrators, coaches, students, and alumni. The organization released their findings in a 383-page bulletin in 1929. Henry S. Pritchett, president of the foundation, told readers that the investigation had not been undertaken in a "captious or faultfinding spirit" and that "there is a legitimate place in the secondary school and in the college for organized sports." Nevertheless, the report was sharply critical of practices at many colleges. It denounced recruiting athletes and subsidizing their participation in sports through jobs, scholarships, and direct payments. This was, Pritchett declared, "the most disgraceful phase of recent inter-collegiate athletics." The staff members who wrote the report, led by Howard J. Savage, found only 28 schools that did not provide subsidies in one form or another to its athletes, though the level of assistance varied greatly. They argued that the primacy of commercial considerations and the emphasis on winning conflicted with the educational mission and intellectual quality of American colleges. "The good repute which a university attains through high academic standards and their honest enforcement is priceless," they commented, "and it is not to be compared with the cheap and ephemeral notoriety that winning teams may bring."

The authors of the Carnegie review insisted that "neither subsidizing nor recruiting is essential to college sport" and that the effects of "these evils" on American higher education were "profoundly deleterious." They contended that outlawing those practices would preserve the virtues of sports programs and remove the corrupting influence of commercialism. The Carnegie Foundation report suggested that the abuses in college athletics, especially football, could only be eliminated if college presidents made a steadfast and courageous commitment to reform. Although the study identified a series of problems in college sports, it did not offer particularly bold or persuasive solutions. It received a great deal of attention when it was published, but its long-term impact proved to be slight. Some college presidents denied that their schools were guilty of the offenses the report cited, and others did not regard the existing system with the same level of alarm.[4]

One prominent college president who strongly agreed with the complaints of the Carnegie report was Frank Porter Graham of the Consolidated University of North Carolina, which included the campus in Chapel Hill, North Carolina State College of Agriculture and Engineering in Raleigh, and the North Carolina College for Women in Greensboro. Both UNC–Chapel Hill and "State College," as it was commonly known, were members of the Southern Conference. By November 1935, Graham had concluded that dishonorable practices in college sports had increased since the publication of the Carnegie Foundation study. He drafted a plan that he hoped would win the approval of the Southern Conference and then gain support in other leagues across the country. It included a strict prohibition on recruiting players or providing athletes with financial assistance in any form. In early 1936, members of the Southern Conference narrowly adopted Graham's proposals. But they soon reconsidered.

The Graham plan aroused strong objections from several conference schools. It also suffered harsh attacks from coaches, fans, students, and alumni of the University of North Carolina, who feared that its requirements would place them at a serious disadvantage in competing with their archrival, Duke, and other opponents. The Southern Conference soon backed off its endorsement of Graham's proposals. In December 1936 it approved the consideration of athletic ability in decisions on granting scholarships to students. A year later, it went even further by allowing conference schools to award athletic scholarships as long as they were funded by outside organizations. The defeat of Graham's campaign to forbid subsidies in college sports underscored the difficulty, if not the impossibility, of carrying out the recommendations of the Carnegie Foundation report of 1929.[5]

The NCAA and the Sanity Code

Although the National Collegiate Athletic Association endorsed the objectives of the Carnegie Foundation investigation and the Graham plan, it was too weak to provide effective support. In 1935, the NCAA, citing a "real emergency," appointed a committee to study the effects of recruiting and financial aid on college sports. The committee reported that those practices were "of such importance in scope as to bring about the downfall of intercollegiate athletics." But the NCAA lacked enforcement powers to redress the problems. The authority for correcting abuses remained firmly in the hands of individual institutions and conferences. In 1939, the NCAA passed new restrictions on recruiting and subsidies, and it established, for the first time, penalties against violators. Institutions that broke the rules could be expelled from the association by a two-thirds vote of the membership.[6]

Shortly after World War II, the NCAA sought to clarify its position on recruiting and subsidies, codify its rules, and toughen its enforcement procedures. In 1946, it laid the foundations for taking action by sending a questionnaire to more than four hundred institutions to solicit opinions on a set of principles it had drafted. It then prepared regulations on the key issues of recruiting and offering subsidies to athletes. In what soon came to be known as the "Sanity Code," the NCAA in 1947 proposed that athletes could be awarded, at most, only the cost of tuition and fees. Such aid could be delivered only on the basis of need and had to be provided by the college itself rather than by alumni or boosters. An exception was made for players who were good students. The need-based scholarship requirement did not apply to athletes who ranked in the top 25 percent of their high school classes or who achieved a "B" grade average in college. The Sanity Code allowed athletes to hold jobs to pay their college expenses, but only if they received compensation in amounts "commensurate with the services rendered." The code was approved overwhelmingly at the NCAA's 1948 convention. Although it was an attempt to exercise control over activities that were widely condemned, the Sanity Code also for the first time officially sanctioned, under specified conditions, financial aid for athletes. In that regard, it was a major departure from the reform objectives of the 1930s.[7]

The Sanity Code, despite the acclaim it received at the NCAA's convention in 1948, soon triggered strong dissent. The opposition came largely, though not exclusively, from schools in the South that offered athletic scholarships. They regarded the Sanity Code's requirement that financial assistance to athletes be based on need to be both disingenuous and discriminatory. They argued that although prominent schools in other sections of the country did not allow athletic scholarships, they provided or arranged for jobs for their athletes. In at least some cases, football players and others received pay for work that was notoriously undemanding. Southern schools complained that the pretense of prohibiting athletic scholarships while subsidizing players with jobs was especially common among members of the Big Ten conference in the Midwest. The two institutions that spearheaded the campaign against the Sanity Code were the University of Virginia and the University of Maryland. Their approaches to and attitudes toward the role of sports in academic institutions differed sharply, but they joined forces in challenging the NCAA's new rules.[8]

In July 1949, Virginia declared that it would not observe the provisions of the Sanity Code, even at the risk of expulsion from the NCAA. Its position was unexpected because it seemed an unlikely candidate to defy the new rules. The university was not, as *Washington Evening Star* columnist Francis Stann pointed out, "one of the football factories of the South." The Carnegie Foundation had reported in 1929 that it was one of 28 schools that did not give subsidies to athletes. In the wake of the debates over the Graham plan, however, Virginia quit the Southern Conference and began to award athletic scholarships funded by alumni. The university had initially supported Graham's proposals, but it changed its position in part because it suspected that other Southern Conference schools, including the University of North Carolina, violated the rules they had approved. Administrators at Virginia also cited their concern that the university's cherished honor system would be undermined if, in accordance with existing Southern Conference requirements, team members had to sign a statement that falsely affirmed that they had not received scholarships or other subsidies for their athletic skills. After Virginia changed its policies on awards to athletes, its football fortunes improved and it consistently fielded competitive, though not dominant, teams.[9]

The president of the University of Virginia when the NCAA approved the Sanity Code, Colgate W. Darden Jr., was hardly a big football fan. He commented after his retirement that he "got so tired of football" that "nothing suited me better" than missing games. Nevertheless, he made clear that he opposed rules that prohibited athletic scholarships but permitted schools to provide jobs for players. An unidentified Virginia spokesman explained to the *Washington Post* that it was "impossible for the school to abide by the code." He argued that a student could not participate in sports and hold a job "without sacrificing his academic career—the very thing he came here to get in the first place." Virginia favored revising the Sanity Code to make it "realistic" by allowing colleges to offer financial aid, regardless of need, that enabled students to play sports and earn their degrees.[10]

In contrast to Darden, the president of the University of Maryland, Harry Clifton "Curley" Byrd, was, by any standard, a football enthusiast. He supported Darden's position on the Sanity Code, but his priorities were quite different. Byrd had starred in football, as well as in baseball and track, as an undergraduate at Maryland between 1905 and 1908. He returned to his alma mater in 1912 as an instructor of English and football coach. He built a successful football program at Maryland, and while still coaching, turned his attention to administration. In 1936, the Board of Regents selected Byrd as president of the university. Although he lacked an advanced academic degree, he earned affection and respect with his personal magnetism, superb political skills, and dedication to the university. Byrd believed that the university could gain recognition by playing winning football on a national stage, and after World War II, Maryland accomplished that goal. Under coaches Paul "Bear" Bryant and Jim Tatum, the university became a powerhouse. It recruited players aggressively and provided them scholarships, though Byrd denied that financial aid was given solely on the basis of athletic prowess.[11]

The Sanity Code threatened Maryland's winning ways and Byrd's vision of achieving greatness for the university, and he fought the NCAA's rules with force and flair. Like Virginia and other opponents of the code, Byrd thought the rules encouraged underhanded tactics and hypocrisy. "When a Maryland boy . . . tells us that he wants to enter the University of Maryland," he wrote Clarence P. Houston, chairman of the NCAA's compliance committee, "but that he cannot afford financially to do so because a big school in the so-called Ivy League is offering him a much better scholarship than the University of Maryland can offer him, and without any consideration of scholastic achievement, then I . . . have some reason for certain reservations." On January 12, 1950, the council of the NCAA proposed that Virginia, Maryland, and five other schools that admittedly or allegedly violated the Sanity Code be expelled from the organization. Curley Byrd assumed the leadership of the so-called "Seven Sinners" in lobbying against the council's recommendation at an NCAA meeting in New York. "I understand that Ohio State University has what we'll call unusual jobs for its athletes," he told delegates to the conference. "The compliance committee looked into the situation and found that it conformed with the code. I'll accept it. But I would like an answer to this: 'Does Ohio State want to vote for expulsion of Virginia when Ohio State has facilities to take care of four to five times as many athletes as Virginia?'"[12]

The arguments of Byrd and representatives of the other "Seven Sinners" carried the day. The council's recommendation required the approval of two-thirds of the membership (136 votes). When the delegates were polled on January 14, 1950, 111 schools favored expulsion and 93, from the North as well as the South, opposed it. The vote indicated that a large minority of the NCAA's membership agreed with the view expressed by Robert Neyland, the football coach and athletic director at the University of Tennessee. "None of us can conscientiously vote against Virginia or any of the others on the carpet," he said. "How can we vote to expel them when all of us are guilty ourselves?" Before the meeting to decide on punishing the culprits, Karl Leib, president of the NCAA, had suggested that the decision would be "the most important in the history of college athletics." He contended that the stakes were so high because "if we aren't able to show the sanity code has teeth, then the code is dead and so is the NCAA as a regulatory body." Leib's concerns were well founded. The failure to banish the "Seven Sinners" left the NCAA without a credible policy governing recruitment of and financial aid for athletes.[13]

After years of debate and the demise of the Sanity Code, the NCAA resolved its position on the scholarship issue in 1956. It voted to allow its members to provide financial aid to athletes without regard to financial need in accordance with the rules of individual schools and the conferences to which they belonged. The following year it defined the level of assistance its members could offer as room, board, tuition, fees, books, and $15 per month for "incidental expenses." The NCAA, to avoid the implication that scholarship recipients were professionals and the possibility of member institutions becoming liable for workers compensation for their athletic "employees," soon began to use and insist that others use the term "student-athlete" to describe those who represented their schools in sports competition.[14]

The Growth of College Basketball

Throughout the first half of the twentieth century, college basketball was a distant second to football in exposure and popularity. Nevertheless, the game of basketball expanded in that time from humble beginnings to highly visible national and international stages. At the college level, it faced the same issues surrounding recruiting and financial aid that caused so much controversy in football. In 1951, the importance of those issues was magnified by a series of scandals that shook college sports and shocked the nation. For the first time, the most grievous offenses occurred in college basketball, which was perhaps a perverse indication of its growing popularity.

James A. Naismith invented basketball in 1891 as a means of keeping restless, energetic students at a Young Men's Christian Association (YMCA) training school in Springfield, Massachusetts, occupied during winter months. His game quickly won the favor of players and fans. Within a short time after basketball began in Springfield, YMCAs in cities across the country were playing one another and drawing enthusiastic crowds. Colleges took up the game gradually; a contest between Yale and the University of Pennsylvania on March 20, 1897, is widely, though not indisputably, regarded as the first intercollegiate competition between five-man squads. Basketball was an immediate favorite among women, who formed teams both in high schools and colleges and initially played by the same rules as men. "By the turn of the century," historian Pamela Grundy has written, "basketball had become the most popular pastime at women's schools from Maine to California."[15]

As his game gained in popularity, Naismith accepted a faculty position in the Department of Physical Education at the University of Kansas. He was firmly committed to the principle of amateurism in college sports and continued to regard the game he invented primarily as a means of indoor exercise and recreation. As basketball coach at Kansas between 1898 and 1907, he demonstrated a decidedly casual attitude toward winning. He stood apart from his successors at the school as the only coach to compile a losing lifetime record (55 wins, 60 losses). Naismith's low-key approach soon gave way to a strong emphasis on winning, at Kansas and elsewhere. His replacement at Kansas was one of his former players, Forrest C. "Phog" Allen, who had won more games than any other college coach by the time he retired in 1956. Allen's total was later surpassed by two of his own players, Adolph Rupp at the University of Kentucky and Dean Smith at North Carolina. Allen and other leading coaches across the country, in contrast to Naismith, used strategy, conditioning, and recruiting to build consistently successful programs. Their goal was to win games and championships, and they followed a pattern already well-established in football. The quest for dominance in basketball led to familiar questions about recruiting and financial aid for athletes and about commercialism in college sports.[16]

During the 1930s, college basketball reached new heights of popularity. One reason was that rule changes made the game faster, more fluid, and more exciting. In 1932, the NCAA adopted a rule that forced a team on offense to move the ball across the center line within ten seconds of gaining possession. Five years later it took an even larger step by abolishing the center jump after every made shot. The effect was to transform basketball from a sluggish game that featured a great deal of passing and not much scoring. One writer, Frank Fitzpatrick, has described this style of basketball as an "aesthetic nightmare"; in 1936, for example, college players scored on only 18 percent of their field-goal attempts. The pace of the game was also accelerated by the increasing prevalence of a one-handed shot taken while jumping or moving, which gradually replaced the traditional two-handed set shot. Angelo "Hank" Luisetti of Stanford was not the first to use a one-handed shot, but he proved its superiority with his offensive genius. In 1938, at a time when low-scoring contests were still the norm, he set a college record by tallying 50 points in a single game.[17]

As college basketball became more appealing for spectators, it emerged as a major attraction across the country. Several coaches who later became legends developed highly successful programs, including Allen at Kansas, Rupp at Kentucky, Hank Iba at Oklahoma A&M, Branch McCracken at Indiana, Ward "Piggy" Lambert at Purdue, and Eddie Cameron at Duke. Schools normally played games in small gymnasiums, but during the 1930s, several built arenas that seated more than 10,000 fans. In 1939, the NCAA held its first national championship tournament at Northwestern University. It was a three-round competition in which one team from each of the organization's eight districts participated. The winner of the tournament was the University of Oregon, which defeated Ohio State, 46–33, before a crowd of 5,000. During the next ten years, the location of the schools that earned the NCAA championship clearly demonstrated the national scope of college basketball: Indiana (1940), Wisconsin (1941), Stanford (1942), Wyoming (1943), Utah (1944), Oklahoma A&M (1945, 1946), Holy Cross (1947), and Kentucky (1948, 1949). The tournament drew enough support to provide the NCAA with its single largest source of income. In 1940, it cleared a $10,000 profit, which compared favorably with its second largest source of income, the $25 annual dues it collected from each of the colleges that were members.[18]

As the popularity of college basketball surged around the country, the unrivaled center of interest and attention during the 1930s and 1940s was New York City. This occurred largely as a result of the efforts of a sportswriter named Ned Irish. In 1931, Irish was a part of a group of reporters who, at the request of New York mayor Jimmy Walker, set up a basketball tripleheader with local colleges at Madison Square Garden to raise money for unemployment relief. The event drew a capacity crowd, and later matchups using a similar format proved to be equally big attractions. Irish was so confident in the drawing power of college basketball that he left his job with the *New York World-Telegram* to become a full-time promoter. In the first doubleheader he arranged at Madison Square Garden in December 1934, a crowd of more than 16,000 watched New York University (NYU) defeat Notre Dame and tiny Westminster College in Pennsylvania stun St. John's University.

Within a short time, Irish was staging several doubleheaders per season at Madison Square Garden and in other cities in the East. The games provided an unprecedented opportunity for intersectional matchups, and coaches from the best teams across the United States coveted an invitation to Irish's events. In one particularly memorable contest at the Garden in 1936, Stanford's Hank Luisetti dazzled fans with his one-handed shots and led his team to a victory over Long Island University (LIU), a nationally ranked squad that had won 43 games in a row. With several excellent local teams and a procession of out-of-town national powers playing at the Garden, New York was the focal point of intercollegiate competition. Its status as "the basketball capital of the nation" was further enhanced in 1938 when a group of sportswriters organized the postseason National Invitational Tournament (NIT), which selected a field of elite teams to participate. The NCAA established its own tournament a year later, but the NIT remained more prestigious and more glamorous for more than a decade. "Intersectional competition, stimulated by the Garden doubleheaders and the National Invitation [sic] Tournament," the Associated Press reported in 1951, "sent interest sky-rocketing and started basketball dollars flowing to college athletic coffers formerly fed only by football receipts."[19]

The Point-Shaving Scandal

Among the several outstanding college basketball programs in the New York area during the 1930s and 1940s, two stood out: the City College of New York (CCNY), coached by Nat Holman, and Long Island University, coached by Clair Bee. Holman was an innovative and demanding coach who made CCNY the dominant team among his formidable competition in New York. His achievements were a great source of pride at City College, a highly selective and academically rigorous institution. Holman was also well known for his arrogance, which was evident in his appropriation of the terms "The Master" and "Mr. Basketball" to describe himself. But he backed his claims with performance; in 1950, CCNY accomplished for the first and only time the remarkable feat of winning both the NIT and the NCAA championships.[20]

Holman's chief challenger for supremacy in New York was Clair Bee, who made LIU into a basketball powerhouse within a short time after taking over as basketball coach in 1932. LIU, in contrast to CCNY, did not have a strong academic reputation or even a campus. It held classes, as Bee later recalled, "in a bleak factory building, adjacent lofts and even over a bowling alley in the industrial section of Brooklyn." LIU wanted Bee to produce winning teams to gain visibility and improve student morale. He was a keen student of the game, an excellent motivator, and an effective recruiter. In January 1951, *Time* magazine described him as a "50-year-old dynamo" who served not only as basketball coach but also as athletic director and assistant to the president of LIU. In addition, Bee wrote several manuals on basketball coaching, a regular newspaper column, and a series of books on sports for young people. The hero of his fictional books was Chip Hilton, a gifted athlete and student who was a model of hard work, clean living, and fair play.[21]

Shortly after *Time* applauded Bee's achievements at LIU, the empire of New York basketball came crashing down. On January 11, 1951, Junius Kellogg, the leading scorer for Manhattan College's basketball squad, was approached by a former teammate, Hank Poppe, who offered him $1,000 to shave points in an upcoming game. Kellogg, the first African American to play at Manhattan, came from a poor family in Virginia, and apparently gamblers believed he would be likely to cooperate with them. But he reported Poppe's overture to authorities immediately and then participated in setting a trap for the fixers. After Kellogg feigned acceptance of the deal and Poppe explained how he could "control the margin of victory" to provide a pay-off for gamblers, police arrested Poppe and several of his co-conspirators. The *New York Journal-American* broke the story on January 18, and the problem of gambling in college basketball received headline treatment and outraged condemnation in and beyond New York. Further investigation by New York district attorney Frank S. Hogan soon revealed that point shaving was a distressingly common practice.[22]

The corruption of college basketball by criminal elements was not a recent development. Within a short time after Ned Irish began to put on doubleheaders at Madison Square Garden, interest in the games was clearly fueled by gambling activities. The growth of gambling on college basketball went hand-in-hand with the growth in the sport's popularity. The prevalence of gambling on basketball was greatly assisted by the innovation of the "point spread." Instead of giving odds on the outcome of a game, the point spread allowed bookies to accept bets and make money even on games that were probable routs. In this system, the result of the contest mattered little; the pay-off depended on whether the winning team covered the spread. And this, in turn, led directly to bribing players to manage the final score to suit betting interests.[23]

The role of gambling in college basketball caused a great deal of concern among some prominent figures in the game. Shortly before the NCAA championship game of 1944 between Utah and Dartmouth, a shamelessly bold fixer asked Utah coach Vadal Peterson how much he would expect to be paid to allow Dartmouth to win. Peterson made his answer clear either by landing a punch on the man's jaw, as eyewitnesses reported, or by slamming the door of his hotel room in the gambler's face, as the coach later recalled. Utah won the game in a huge upset, 42–40. Phog Allen warned his coaching colleagues later the same year that the behavior of professional gamblers could cause a scandal that would "stink to high heaven." He called for actions to limit the opportunities for gamblers to reach players, but his proposals were dismissed by most of his fellow coaches and by the NCAA.[24]

The problem could no longer be disregarded, however, after District Attorney Hogan blew it wide open with his investigation of point shaving in 1951. In the wake of the scandal that Junius Kellogg exposed, Hogan soon learned that many players from local and out-of-town schools were taking money from gamblers. On February 18, 1951, police arrested three CCNY players, who quickly confessed to accepting bribes from fixers. Two days later, three LIU players admitted to shaving points during the previous (1949–50) and the current (1950–51) seasons. The most prominent of them was Sherman White, who had the best scoring average in the country and had just been named national Player of the Year by the *Sporting News*. Both Nat Holman and Clair Bee expressed acute disappointment and profound shock, though some informed observers suggested that the two coaches should have known that their players were manipulating the scores of games or that they did know and chose not to do anything.[25]

The anguish that the dumping scandal caused CCNY and LIU was compounded by revelations that Holman and Bee had compromised academic standards in their efforts to build winning teams. Although CCNY's players had been hailed as exemplary athletes and students, it became clear after the point-shaving arrests that the basketball office had altered high school transcripts to make certain that the talent the coaches courted was admitted to the school. "All Nat wanted was ballplayers," one recruit commented. "He didn't care how he got them." Bee provided tuition, books, and fees on the basis of athletic ability (he could not include room and board because, for most of his coaching tenure, LIU had no dormitories or dining halls). He also supplied small cash subsidies and jobs to his team members. One of the arrested players, Leroy Smith, told prosecutors that the job he was assigned did not interfere with his basketball activities. He reported "that it was not necessary to put in time at the job, and if he had given a good athletic performance that week his pay slip would be marked extra hours and he would receive an additional five or ten dollars." The requirements that basketball prospects had to meet for admission to and eligibility at LIU were outlandishly lax.

Holman always fixed the blame for the point-shaving scandals on others, but Bee took a share of the responsibility for creating an atmosphere that led to illegal activities. "I was a "win-'em-all coach who . . . helped to create the emotional climate that led to the worst scandal in the history of sports," he lamented in the *Saturday Evening Post* in 1952. "I . . . was so absorbed in the victory grail that I lost sight of the educational purposes of athletics." Bee admitted that he gave athletic scholarships and that he was guilty of "overemphasizing the importance of sports." But he insisted that the payments to players were loans that he expected them to repay, and he countered charges about academic abuses by pointing out that some of his prized recruits had flunked out of school.[26]

On the same day that the LIU players confessed to accepting bribes, the university's Board of Trustees declared that the "shocking and unimpeachable evidence of gross corruption" demonstrated that "an undue emphasis has been placed upon basketball and perhaps on other intercollegiate sports." Therefore, it announced that it would immediately cancel "all intercollegiate athletic activities" and reduce LIU's athletic programs to the "status of intra-mural competition." A short time later, the New York City Board of Higher Education took action to remove its four municipal colleges, including CCNY, from big-time sports. It stressed the need to "restore sanity to intercollegiate basketball" and to make clear that members of its teams should be "students who play and not players who register." The board prohibited its schools from playing games at Madison Square Garden or other arenas outside of "educational control." It also banned recruiting of players and offers of "special privileges or scholarships" to "outstanding athletes."[27]

While LIU and CCNY suffered through the humiliation of the point-shaving scandal, some eminent figures in college basketball rubbed salt on their wounds by suggesting that the gambling problem was peculiar to New York. "Out here in the Midwest these scandalous conditions, of course, do not exist," commented Phog Allen. "But in the East, the boys . . . are thrown into an environment which cannot help but breed the evil which more and more is coming to light." His protégé Adolph Rupp remarked that gamblers "couldn't reach my boys with a ten-foot pole." But District Attorney Hogan's continuing investigations soon demonstrated that Allen, Rupp, and others who shared their views were woefully mistaken. In July 1951, Hogan announced that players from the University of Toledo and Bradley University in Peoria, Illinois, had taken money from gamblers to shave points. Both schools had traditions of excellent teams; Toledo had finished the 1950–51 season ranked 14th in the nation, and Bradley had been ranked number one in 1949–50 before losing in the finals of the NIT and NCAA tournaments to CCNY.

In October 1951, two former greats from Kentucky, Alex Groza and Ralph Beard, confessed to accepting bribes for fixing games during their college careers. Groza and Beard had led Kentucky to NCAA championships in 1948 and 1949. The exposure of the corruption in the programs at Toledo, Bradley, and Kentucky showed beyond doubt that gambling influences on college basketball extended far beyond Madison Square Garden. It also highlighted the overemphasis on sports that prevailed at some prominent colleges and universities. When one unnamed college official expressed disbelief that players had conspired with gamblers, a reporter replied: "You paid them for campus jobs they didn't work at; you gave them passing grades for classes they didn't attend. You bribed them to play for you; the gamblers bribed them not to play too well. What's the difference?"[28]

Judge Saul S. Streit of New York pulled no punches in criticizing the "evil system of commercialism" in college sports when he handed down sentences in the point-shaving scandal. He gave prison terms to three gamblers and sent four players to jail for shorter periods. The other players received suspended sentences. Streit denounced the coaches and administrators whom he held responsible for creating the conditions that produced the point-shaving scandal. "The naivete, the equivocation, and the denials of the coaches and their assistants concerning their knowledge of gambling, recruiting and subsidizing," he wrote of CCNY and LIU, "would be comical if it were not so despicable." The judge's complaints echoed the position of the Carnegie Foundation in 1929 and subsequent advocates of reform. The solutions he offered were similar to earlier proposals; he called for dedicated efforts by college presidents and faculties to control athletic programs and a stronger regulatory role for the NCAA. "The time has come to act," Streit admonished, "to eliminate commercialism and overemphasis and the evils that it breeds."[29]

The impact of the revelations of serious gambling and governance problems in college basketball was soon magnified when the United States Military Academy announced that 90 cadets, including most of the football team, had confessed to violating West Point's honor code. They were guilty of sharing information about tests or of knowing about the misconduct and not notifying authorities. This was sufficient grounds for dismissal from the academy. To make matters worse, the investigation of the "cribbing" scandal revealed that Army football coach Earl H. "Red" Blaik had held special tutoring sessions for promising players to enable them to meet the rigorous academic requirements for attending West Point. He had also sought to circumvent admission procedures in his recruiting efforts. The news of the offenses at West Point, even though they were far less serious than taking money from gamblers, set off a barrage of criticism of the ill effects of college sports on academic standards. President Harry S. Truman was so disturbed that on August 9, 1951, he ordered a "full investigation" of athletic programs at West Point and the United States Naval Academy to determine whether they were placing too much emphasis on sports, especially football.[30]

Against the backdrop of the outcry over point shaving in basketball and infractions at West Point, the abuses by the football coaches at the College of William and Mary that hit the headlines in September 1951 received wide attention. They seemed to offer further evidence of disturbing trends in college sports that threatened to undermine the purposes and the integrity of even prestigious academic institutions. The reports about the misdeeds in the football program at William and Mary were not only an embarrassment to the college but also a call to action for other schools in the Southern Conference.

The series of scandals in college sports in 1951 inspired a great deal of commentary about the need to strike a reasonable balance between athletic and academic objectives. Harold E. Stassen, president of the University of Pennsylvania and a strong proponent of playing big-time football at his school, declared in response to the point-shaving disclosures: "The athletic scandals should cause our entire educational system to take a careful look in the mirror and take stock not only of its athletic programs, but also of its moral and ethical teaching of the youth of the nation." The *Saturday Evening Post* suggested in an editorial on point shaving that "so long as academic honesty is perverted in the name of sport, so long can we expect 'fixes' and all the other nauseous by-products of overemphasis." The *New York Times* ran a six-part story in March 1951 on the "impact of athletics in education." It concluded that the "most serious effects of semi-professionalism and big money in intercollegiate sports are the establishment of false values, impairment of democracy in education, and a lowering in some cases of academic standards and cheapening of college degrees."[31]

To many observers, the scandals of 1951 were a culmination of the growth of big-time college sports during the previous half-century and the failure to exercise control of athletic programs. Amid a pervasive sense of crisis, college officials and other observers embraced the view that something had to be done. But there was little agreement on how to resolve the problems that had become so apparent and how to determine the proper place of athletics in educational institutions. Most college administrators and other authorities recognized the need for reform but did not favor the elimination of, or a drastic reduction in, intercollegiate competition. When President Truman called for an investigation of overemphasis of football at West Point and Annapolis, he made clear that he "was trying to find a remedy without killing the patient." A. Whitney Griswold, president of Yale University, declared: "Amateur athletics have a vital role in American education." But, he added, "Professionalized big-time athletics are the bane of its existence."

Proponents of college sports often cited the advantages that competition provided both for individuals and for institutions. For students, participation in sports, at its best, built character, encouraged teamwork, and taught fairness in high-pressure situations. For institutions, athletic programs, at least potentially, provided visibility, fostered a sense of community, improved student morale, and attracted alumni support. Further, football and basketball raised money that paid for student participation in sports that were not popular or self-supporting. The benefits that athletic programs could and often did deliver were worthy and laudable. But, as the scandals of 1951 made abundantly plain, the individual and institutional value of sports could be badly tarnished, if not irredeemably fouled, if the pressures to win lurched out of control. Clair Bee drew on bitter experience when he wrote in 1952: "The net result of the conniving and insane competition is an athletic program infested with so many abuses that the entire structure must be rebuilt from scratch."[32]

The question, then, was how to gain the benefits of college athletics without endangering the other goals and standards to which academic institutions aspired. This was the fundamental issue that had stood at the center of the controversy over the role of athletics for decades. Although the crisis of 1951 pointed up the problem in sharp relief, it did not provide obvious solutions. In important respects, colleges were no closer to finding their footing in resolving conflicts between athletic and academic objectives than they had been after the Carnegie Foundation report highlighted a multitude of ills in 1929. The NCAA remained a weak regulator that was too short of money and power to effectively police the conduct of college sports. The failure of the Sanity Code had prevented it from instituting strong enforcement procedures, and, as the opponents demonstrated, the code was neither a fair nor an effective means of controlling abuses in college athletics. The NCAA was not deeply or visibly involved in responding to the point-shaving scandal. Although it cancelled intercollegiate basketball at Kentucky for an entire year, its success in imposing the penalty was due more to the courage and rectitude of the university's NCAA representatives than to the authority of the organization.[33] Despite the condemnation of the Carnegie Foundation and later reformers, recruiting of and financial aid for athletes were well-established practices that the NCAA eventually sanctioned. Sharp differences remained, however, over what restrictions, if any, should be placed on recruiting, and what rules, if any, should apply to the granting of athletic scholarships. Addressing those issues would be the key to balancing educational and athletic ambitions and to determining the proper role of sports in an academic environment. In a setting of controversy, crisis, and uncertainty over those critical questions, the Atlantic Coast Conference was created.

2

THE
FOUNDING OF
THE ACC

The disclosures of point shaving in college basketball and the violations of academic standards by football coaches at the College of William and Mary were sources of immense concern to presidents of the members of the Southern Conference. Soon after the William and Mary scandal became public knowledge, they held a meeting to consider actions to maintain a healthy balance between academic and athletic goals. The presidents agreed on several measures that they hoped would prevent overemphasis on sports, the most visible and controversial of which was to prohibit participation by Southern Conference football teams in bowl games. This recommendation, which was later formally adopted as conference policy, aroused the opposition of a few members. Led by the University of Maryland's Harry C. "Curley" Byrd, the dissenters began to weigh the possibility of abandoning the Southern Conference and establishing a new league.

At the same time, some presidents of Southern Conference schools who strongly supported the ban on playing in bowls increasingly looked with favor on the idea of forming a new conference as a means of asserting better control of athletic programs. Their most prominent spokesman was Gordon Gray, president of the Consolidated University of North Carolina. Between fall 1951 and spring 1953, proposals to organize a new conference gathered momentum. Officials who held differing and sometimes contradictory motives for taking this step operated on separate but parallel tracks. The eventual result was the creation of the Atlantic Coast Conference.

"A Man Truly to Be Pitied"

In the aftermath of the highly publicized discrepancies between academic integrity and the practices of football coaches at William and Mary, a disinterested but well-informed observer provided his thoughts on the difficulties that faced college presidents in dealing with athletic issues. Charles J. Smith, former president of Roanoke College in Virginia, published an article in the *Roanoke Times* that described "an undeclared war between college football and college faculties." One side was made up of "students, alumni, coaches, sportswriters, the smokeshop boys, many boards of trustees, and most powerful of all, the millions of dollars taken in at the gate." On the other side, "the poor little college professor stands almost alone." Smith detailed the plight of the professor. "He has spent long years preparing to teach. He has great respect for the dignity of his calling, and he thinks of a college as being primarily interested in intellectual, spiritual, and moral values. He resents its being turned into a football factory."

Smith then explained the dilemma that faced administrators who tried to arbitrate the conflict. The college president was, he wrote, "a man truly to be pitied." In Smith's view, the "cards are stacked against him. . . . If he sides with the professors he sacrifices his job. If he lines up with the football crowd he sacrifices his integrity." Smith had no easy solutions to offer. He suggested that pleas for "de-emphasis" of athletics were unlikely to succeed because, like disarmament agreements, such a process required the cooperation of all parties and "constant inspection." Nevertheless, he argued that football and faculty interests could achieve a "long peace" if presidents and boards of trustees would take corrective action against the "more glaring evils" of the system. He added that this would call for "integrity and courage" that authorities had "so generally lacked in the past."[1]

Smith's comments on academic-athletic tensions were an apt summary of the predicament that confronted Southern Conference presidents in the fall of 1951. They sought ways to avoid overemphasis on winning and the attendant risks of suffering the problems that had afflicted William and Mary. At the same time, they did not want to surrender the benefits of their athletic programs. The members of the Southern Conference at that time were: The Citadel (Charleston, South Carolina), Clemson, Davidson College (Davidson, North Carolina), Duke, Furman University (Greenville, South Carolina), George Washington University (Washington, D.C.), Maryland, North Carolina, North Carolina State, the University of Richmond (Richmond, Virginia), South Carolina, Virginia Military Institute (Lexington, Virginia), Virginia Polytechnic Institute (Blacksburg, Virginia), Wake Forest, Washington and Lee University (Lexington, Virginia), the University of West Virginia (Morgantown, West Virginia), and William and Mary.

The Consolidated University of North Carolina

The administrator who took the initiative in spurring the conference's efforts to control but not cripple athletic programs was Gordon Gray. Gray had succeeded Frank Porter Graham as the president of the Consolidated University of North Carolina in 1950. At the age of 41, he had already compiled a remarkable record of achievement. He grew up in wealth and privilege; his father was the president of the R. J. Reynolds Tobacco Company of Winston-Salem. Gray graduated first in his class at Chapel Hill and received a law degree at Yale. He practiced law in New York for a time and then returned to his hometown. He purchased and served as the president of the Piedmont Publishing Company, which owned two newspapers and a radio station in Winston-Salem. In 1938, Gray was elected to the North Carolina Senate. After Pearl Harbor, he refused a commission, enlisted as an infantry private, and rose to the rank of captain. In 1947, President Truman appointed him assistant secretary of the army, and two years later, secretary of the army. When he accepted the post of president of the Consolidated University, he commented, "I have decided to devote the rest of my life to public service, and I would rather do it in North Carolina than anywhere else."

Despite Gray's talents and dedication, he was not particularly well-suited to running a university. He was reserved, formal, and unfamiliar with campus institutions and politics. He did not seem comfortable in dealing with either students or faculty and showed little ability to reach out to

Gordon Gray. (Photo by Hugh Morton, North Carolina Collection, University of North Carolina Library at Chapel Hill)

either. Gray once commented that his positions as secretary of the army and president of the university were "somewhat alike," except that in the case of the university, the "faculty had no one below the rank of general." Nevertheless, he was committed to promoting the interests and the reputations of the three schools that made up the Consolidated University, and he was determined not to allow athletic problems to undermine those priorities. While he sought "to preserve both the integrity of American higher education and the undoubted values of intercollegiate athletics," he worried that "troubles arise" when "the basic values to be had in team sports . . . are obscured and forgotten in an overwhelming desire to have winning teams at any cost."[2]

The Consolidated University over which Gray presided had been created as an administrative unit in 1931. Each of the three campuses had its own chancellor, and the lines of authority and division of labor between the president and the chancellors were, in many respects, ill-defined. Gray tried to clarify one important area of ambiguity in 1954 by making the chancellors responsible for managing intercollegiate sports at their own institutions. But, despite his preferences, Gray could not remove himself from athletic issues in the big-time programs at Chapel Hill and State College. "Intercollegiate athletics," he lamented in December 1954, "is the biggest problem I have."[3]

The University of North Carolina at Chapel Hill prided itself on both its academic distinction and athletic achievements. The governor of North Carolina and several other dignitaries launched America's first state university on January 15, 1795, though the first student did not show up for two weeks and others arrived some time later. It struggled to attract students and pay its bills during most of the nineteenth century and was forced to close for a few years during Reconstruction. By the early part of the twentieth century, however, the university had grown in enrollment and gained national stature. One indication of its elevated academic standing was that it was awarded a chapter of the renowned honor society Phi Beta Kappa in 1904. In 1922, it joined the University of Virginia as the only members from the South of the selective Association of American Universities, which sought to promote the interests of research universities in the United States. By midcentury, UNC–Chapel Hill had expanded its programs, developed prestigious professional schools, hired eminent professors, and further enhanced its reputation. Students, faculty, and alumni, in addition to their appreciation of the university's growing academic prominence, were shamelessly and justifiably boastful about the exceptional beauty of its campus.

Athletic programs were an important part of student life at, and alumni support for, the University of North Carolina. It enjoyed considerable, though uneven, success in football, by far the most popular sport. The glory years of North Carolina football came between 1946 and 1949 when Charlie "Choo Choo" Justice led the team to two Southern Conference championships and appearances in three bowl games. The university was even more successful in basketball. It won eight conference championships, and in 1946, coach Ben Carnevale led UNC to the final game of the NCAA tournament, which it lost to Oklahoma A&M by the score of 46–43. When Carnevale departed to take the head coaching job at the U.S. Naval Academy, Tom Scott took over. He continued the winning tradition at first, but resigned in 1952 after two consecutive losing seasons. By that time, fans and supporters were grumbling about the decline of North Carolina basketball, which was all the more galling because of fifteen straight losses to their much-disdained partner in the Consolidated University, North Carolina State.[4]

State College was established by the North Carolina legislature in 1887 as the "farmers' college" of the state. Its original name was the North Carolina College of Agriculture and Mechanic Arts. It soon adopted a series of requirements that followed patterns of military schools. Students wore uniforms, marched to chapel and the dining hall, and received demerits for misconduct. As the culture and the academic focus of the college evolved, it de-emphasized military conventions and changed its name to the North Carolina College of Agriculture and Engineering in 1917. During the 1920s, it expanded what became highly respected courses of study in textiles and forestry, upgraded its engineering programs, created a school of education, placed greater emphasis on research by faculty, and admitted women. The curriculum at State College remained largely oriented toward its specialties in agriculture and engineering, and in those fields it gradually strengthened its academic reputation. It did not begin to award degrees in the liberal arts until the 1960s.

Although UNC–Chapel Hill and State College were parts of the same institution under a single president after 1931, their relationship was often strained and sometimes hostile. A certain amount of ill will was inevitable. Chapel Hill had long tradition, academic prestige, and a leafy campus in a bucolic setting. Even its name sounded romantic. State College was a newer "cow college" that was still seeking to establish its academic reputation when consolidation took place. It was built in the heart of Raleigh and was physically divided by mainline railroad tracks that ran through the middle of campus. Officials at State believed that Consolidated University decisions on the allocation of resources too often favored UNC. They were keenly aware that the president's office was located on the Chapel Hill campus and that the first president of the system, Frank Porter Graham, had headed UNC. The resentment that many State College administrators, faculty members, and students felt toward Chapel Hill extended to athletic competition. In 1958, after NC State was placed on NCAA probation for recruiting violations, Athletic Director Roy B. Clogston complained: "Some of our people have a strong feeling that UNC can and has done some very questionable things as far as ethics is concerned and always seem[s] to get away with it. On the other hand we feel that we always get short changed."[5]

State College football and basketball teams achieved only occasional success against North Carolina and other Southern Conference opponents during the 1920s and 1930s. In football, it won the Southern Conference championship in 1927, but generally fared poorly. It had only five winning seasons between 1924 and 1944, and its record against North Carolina was

3 victories, 15 losses, and 2 ties. State College did better in basketball. It won the Southern Conference in 1929, and it compiled a winning record 15 times between 1922 and 1946. However, it won just 10 games against North Carolina while dropping 43 during that period. Between 1940 and 1946, it had only one winning season, and the program appeared to be heading in the wrong direction. NC State turned its basketball fortunes around when it hired Everett Case as coach in 1946.[6]

The Southern Conference and the Problem of Overemphasis

On September 28, 1951, the presidents of the schools that were members of the Southern Conference or their representatives gathered in Chapel Hill to discuss athletic issues. The meeting was arranged by Gordon Gray. This was not the first such conference; Gray had presided over a similar convocation the previous March "to demonstrate the interest and responsibilities of the presidents of the member institutions in all athletic matters." The September meeting had been scheduled far in advance, but by the time the presidents arrived in Chapel Hill, the football scandals at West Point and William and Mary had drawn national attention. In welcoming his colleagues, Gray emphasized that "this group was considering problems concerning athletics prior to the scandals" and that "this particular meeting was not called to act as a fire alarm squadron." Nevertheless, the shadow of the point-shaving debacle and, perhaps more ominously, the misconduct of football coaches at one of their own members loomed large among the attendees. Lee W. Milford, the chairman of the faculty Athletic Council at Clemson, asserted that "the basketball bribery which took place at Madison Square Garden in New York has caused a general feeling of fear on the part of several college presidents in the Southern Conference."[7]

Acting out of a combination of long-standing concerns, as Gray insisted, and recently triggered fears, as Milford suggested, the Southern Conference presidents recommended a series of measures to combat the ills of overemphasis on athletics in their institutions. Among other things, they agreed to limit or eliminate out-of-season practices, to ban freshmen from participating in varsity sports, and to establish uniform admissions standards for athletes. Their most audacious decision was to prohibit Southern Conference football teams from playing in bowl games as of January 1, 1952. This proposal was overwhelmingly approved by a vote of 13–1 with 3 abstentions and would apply to the season that was already under way. Those recommendations were not binding until they were formally approved by conference representatives at their regular meeting in December 1951. But there was little doubt that the presidents' views would carry a great deal of weight. The actions the presidents took were a clear indication of their distress over the recent scandals in college sports and their determination to place athletic programs in a suitable perspective.[8]

The proposed ban on participation in bowl games was consistent with the position of Gordon Gray. "Our experience with bowl games has convinced us that they are a non-educational distraction for students, both players and otherwise," he commented. "As primarily commercial ventures they command much spectator interest but contribute little to the underlying values of intercollegiate athletics." Many of his colleagues among Southern Conference presidents felt the same way, as their vote at the September 28 meeting demonstrated. A. Hollis Edens, president of Duke, which had a highly successful football program and had played in the Rose Bowl in 1939 and 1942, pointed out that bowl games were "sponsored by promoters, by interests completely divorced from educational institutions." He believed that the "commercialism of college sport . . . has made certain phases of college athletics wholly incompatible with the aims of higher education." Harold W. Tribble, president of Wake Forest, offered similar complaints. He asserted that bowl games "contribute definitely to the trend toward commercialism of college athletics," and added: "I am in favor of doing everything we can to restore inter-collegiate athletics to the status of general student activities."[9]

Clemson College and the Bowl Ban

The burden of the prospective Southern Conference policy of barring participation of its members in bowl games fell hardest on Clemson and Maryland. Both had excellent football teams in the fall of 1951 and hoped to receive invitations to postseason bowls. Clemson College (it became a university in 1964) cast the only vote against the ban at the presidents' meeting on September 28.

Clemson was located on land bequeathed to the state of South Carolina by Thomas G. Clemson, a prosperous mining engineer, diplomat, scientific farmer, and son-in-law of John C. Calhoun. He died in 1888, and his will designated that the school placed on his property should be named the Clemson Agricultural College of South Carolina. Like State College in North Carolina, Clemson specialized in agriculture and engineering and struggled to build an academic reputation. It fared well in competing with the University of South Carolina in perennial legislative contests over budget allocations. But in a poor state that habitually underfunded education, Clemson, like other public colleges in South Carolina, did not receive the resources required to establish programs that ranked with the leading academic institutions in the South. From the time that it was founded, Clemson enforced military procedures and discipline. Its all-male student body wore uniforms, received military instruction, marched to classes and meals, and was subject to rigorous rules of conduct. The military aspects of student life at Clemson continued until 1955, when military customs were abolished and replaced by civilian norms. Women were first admitted the same year.[10]

Intercollegiate sports, especially football, inspired intense pride and fervent loyalty at Clemson. The college began playing football shortly after it opened and quickly achieved success. The team went undefeated in 1900 under the coaching of John W. Heisman, for whom the award for the best player in college football was later named. Clemson's chief rival, in football as in budget battles, was South Carolina, and for many years the annual matchup drew boisterous capacity crowds during Fair Week at the state fairgrounds in Columbia. Frank Howard, who became head coach in 1940, guided Clemson to six bowl games before retiring in 1969. The basketball program generally lacked the fan following or the institutional support that football received, and it had just ten winning seasons between 1922 and 1953. It captured its only Southern Conference championship in 1939, led by its first basketball All-American, Banks McFadden. McFadden, regarded as "Clemson's best athlete ever," was also the school's first consensus All-American football player in 1939, when he was the star running back on a team that appeared in the Cotton Bowl.[11]

The president of Clemson in 1951, Robert Franklin Poole, sharply disagreed with his Southern Conference counterparts on the benefits of a ban on bowl appearances. After graduating from Clemson in 1916, Poole had earned a Ph.D. at Rutgers University and pursued a career in plant pathology. He joined the faculty at North Carolina State College in 1926 and stayed until offered the presidency of Clemson in 1940. He joked that when he moved to Clemson from State College, he improved the intellectual quality of both institutions. Poole sought to elevate Clemson's academic reputation by increasing the number of professors with advanced degrees and by encouraging the faculty to conduct original research. Having played end on the football team as an undergraduate, he was a strong supporter of Clemson's athletic programs. He believed that the proposal to prohibit participation in bowl games by conference schools was misguided. While he disapproved of "unethical practices and low moral standards" that caused "loss of institutional integrity," he denied that a bowl ban would solve the problem. On the contrary, he declared that he was "in favor of more bowl games." Poole argued that in "these uncertain times, we should use good, clean American sports of all kinds as a means of building up the morale of our people." For those reasons, he had opposed the recommendation on bowl games that the conference presidents adopted at the meeting of September 28, 1951.[12]

The University of Maryland and the Bowl Ban

Although Maryland had voted "pass" on the bowl game issue at the presidents' meeting, Curley Byrd, like Poole, regarded the ban as unpalatable and unnecessary. As Maryland marched toward an undefeated season and the Southern Conference championship in the fall of 1951, Byrd commented that despite abuses at some schools, "in the great majority of institutions, football is being kept on a safe and sane basis." He added that "we believe we are doing that here." *Washington Post* columnist Shirley Povich reported that if the Southern Conference blocked Maryland's bowl ambitions, Byrd might "give a thought to kissing the conference good-bye."[13]

If Byrd believed that football was administered on a "safe and sane basis" at Maryland, others were doubtful. The university made great strides after he became president in 1936, but by the early 1950s it had gained a reputation as a "football factory." When Byrd took over the presidency, the University of Maryland was a modest-sized, underfunded, and undistinguished institution. He set out to elevate its stature and heighten its visibility. He applied his formidable powers of persuasion to win unprecedented levels of support from the state legislature. He also secured large amounts of funding from the New Deal programs of the federal government for campus buildings and professional schools. Between 1935 and 1954, the enrollment at Maryland rose from 3,400 to more than 15,000, its annual budget increased from about $3 million to more than $20 million, and the value of the physical plant surged from $5 million to $65 million.

Byrd's manner and appearance exuded self-confidence, warmth, and glamour, and he charmed legislators, corporate donors, alumni, and students. But neither his personality nor his achievements impressed most members of the University of Maryland's faculty. Byrd, who was a dominant presence in almost any social or political setting, was seldom if ever comfortable in dealing with his own faculty. He had, at best, a limited understanding of faculty concerns or the importance of research and scholarship as a path to prestige for the university. He held honorary doctorates from Dickinson College in Pennsylvania and Western Maryland College, and he used the title of "Dr. Byrd" in his formal communications. But he showed little respect for Maryland professors and tended to regard them as "hired hands." Faculty members resented low salaries, heavy teaching loads, and the lack of appreciation for scholarly activities. They were also deeply offended by Byrd's dictatorial style. "Regarding salary and promotion increases," he once commented, "I do not usually consult with department heads at all." There were no clear guidelines for tenure, no faculty organization, and no general faculty meetings. In 1948, Phi Beta Kappa denied membership to Maryland in significant part because of Byrd's "autocratic powers" and the fact that the faculty "does not function at all as an academic body."[14]

By the end of World War II, Byrd had decided to promote the name of the university by making it a national football power. "We want the biggest and best of everything," he declared, "including our football team." In his first decade as president, Byrd had maintained his interest in the football team but had not placed great emphasis on its performance. Maryland achieved only moderate success and did not consistently rank among the best teams in the Southern Conference. In 1944, it won only a single game. In 1945, Byrd hired a young coach named Paul "Bear" Bryant on the recommendation of George Preston Marshall, the owner of the Washington Redskins. In his first and only season, Bryant led Maryland to a 6–2–1 record. But the euphoria ran out when Bryant discovered that Byrd, without his knowledge, had fired one of his assistants and given a player a second chance after the coach dismissed him from the team. Bryant promptly departed College Park to take the coaching job at the University of Kentucky.[15]

After a losing season in 1946, Byrd hired Jim Tatum, head coach at the University of Oklahoma, who fulfilled his ambitions for gridiron excellence. Maryland appeared in the Gator Bowl in 1947 and 1949 and had an even stronger team in 1951. While the top priority for Byrd and Tatum, who also served as athletic director, clearly was football, they also sought to improve Maryland basketball, which had recently suffered through a series of dismal seasons. In 1950, they brought in Herman A. "Bud" Millikan as head coach, and he immediately made Maryland a strong competitor in the Southern Conference.

Curley Byrd (left), Jim Tatum, and members of the University of Maryland football
team, 1951. (Special Collections, University of Maryland Libraries)

Although Byrd was gratified by Maryland's rapid and widely noted
progress in its athletic programs, he was distressed by criticism that the
university overemphasized football. The charges arose in part from the high
percentage of available scholarships that went to football players and other
benefits for athletes. But they focused on the university's heavy expenditures on sports while glaring academic needs were not addressed. In 1951,
the university opened its new million-dollar football stadium, which was,
appropriately enough, named for Byrd. A short time later it began work on
a new indoor coliseum that would be the second largest arena in the East,
after Madison Square Garden. The projected price of this building was $2.7
million. Byrd's desire for "the biggest and best of everything" did not extend to the school's library, which the student newspaper described in 1954
as not "even reasonably close to being adequate." It had only limited seating
for students and its collections were woefully sparse. Byrd adamantly denied that his "only concern" was "producing a winning football team" and

asserted that "educational authorities almost everywhere have looked upon the progress of the University of Maryland in the last few years as one of the outstanding developments in American education." It appeared to a growing body of observers, however, that the balance of athletic and academic goals had shifted to an overemphasis on football in the late 1940s.[16]

In light of the strong connection that Byrd saw between the fortunes of the Maryland football team and the reputation of the university, his opposition to the recommendation of Southern Conference presidents to ban participation in bowl games was predictable. By the time that the conference held its regular annual meeting on December 14–15, 1951, both Maryland and Clemson had accepted invitations to bowl games. In defiance of the proposals the presidents had adopted in September, Maryland agreed to play in the Sugar Bowl and Clemson in the Gator Bowl on New Year's Day, 1952. At the December meeting, Byrd asked the conference representatives to approve Maryland's bowl appearance. He affirmed that he supported actions that could discourage athletic abuses at conference schools, including higher standards of eligibility and tougher recruiting restrictions. But he argued that the ban on bowls was not an effective means of "eliminating evils." After listening to his appeal, the conference rejected it by a vote of 14–3. Then, by a margin of 12–5, the delegates placed both Maryland and Clemson on probation for one year, which meant that they could not play any conference member in football, except one another, during the 1952 season. Gordon Gray suggested that the penalty was necessary "for the integrity of the Conference in the eyes not only of the sports world but of the educational world as well."[17]

The University of South Carolina and the Formation of a New Conference

After Maryland's victory over top-ranked Tennessee in the Sugar Bowl, Byrd remained disgruntled with the actions of the Southern Conference. "Confidentially, I met with the Presidents and they were perfectly frank in saying that they had to do something to save face," he told Southeastern Conference commissioner Bernie Moore. Byrd's annoyance quickened his interest in forming a new conference. This was not a new idea; in June 1951, he had advised Gray that "we should have a more closely knit organization . . . in which there would only be institutions of similar resources and interests." The bowl ban and probation, however, seemed to spur his determination to investigate the advantages of abandoning the Southern Conference. In May 1952, he invited the presidents of North Carolina, Duke, South Carolina, Clemson, and the University of Virginia, which was not a conference member, to a dinner to discuss "our specific future in intercollegiate athletics." He did not explicitly mention the option of establishing a new league, but he raised the possibility of making "a far reaching decision." He acknowledged that "it may be that it would seem more advantageous to continue our present status," but he clearly was trying to gain support for a change. There is no indication that Byrd's dinner ever took place.[18]

Clemson, which was equally displeased with the penalties imposed by the Southern Conference, shared his views on the need for change. Athletic council chairman Milford found it "really pathetic to see some of the weak, young presidents who had gotten caught in the North Carolina–Duke web." President Poole believed that the presidents were "on a limb for having ignored lack of morals and unethical practices in some of the conference schools." He told Byrd that "more and more it seems to me one of the ways to correct the thinking in the Southern Conference is to match teams on the basis of their ability to play relatively equal teams under the same conditions."[19]

Another conference member that lined up with Maryland and Clemson was the University of South Carolina. At the December 1951 meeting, it was the only school to join them in voting to approve Byrd's request for permission to play in the Sugar Bowl. South Carolina's position on the bowl ban reflected is disaffection with the Southern Conference. Rex Enright, the university's football coach and athletic director, played a leading role in pressing for the formation of a new league. During an NCAA meeting in January 1952, he met informally with a few other athletic directors to discuss the difficulties in scheduling that were inherent in the makeup of the Southern Conference. Among the other attendees at the meeting, which was neither officially authorized nor publicized, were Jim Tatum, Eddie Cameron of Duke, and Chuck Erickson of North Carolina. All were former football players and were either coaching football at the time or had done so in the past. It is likely that they stood together in opposing the conference's policy on bowl games. In any event, they informally agreed at their meeting to approach the presidents of their universities about establishing a new conference.

The fundamental problem with competition in the Southern Conference was the large number of schools and their differences in size. The larger members of the conference were reluctant to play the schools with small student bodies and limited seating in their stadiums. And with 17 colleges in the conference, it was impossible to play every other member in a season. In 1950, Washington and Lee won the conference title with a 6–0 record and received an invitation to the Gator Bowl. But its schedule did not include Clemson, which had a 3–0 record in conference play, or any of the other larger schools in the conference. The same kind of issue arose in basketball. The conference champion was decided in a postseason tournament, but only eight teams qualified. For those reasons, the athletic directors of the big-time athletic schools who met in January 1952 supported the creation of a conference with fewer members and greater uniformity in size and resources. Their top priority was to improve the level of competition and the financial well-being of their football programs. The accord among the athletic directors of several schools was an important step in that direction. But they recognized that the departure from the Southern Conference they advocated would not take place without the approval of the presidents of the prospective members of a new league. The ban on bowls was critical in persuading Presidents Byrd and Poole that the time had come to form a new conference.[20]

The leadership of the University of South Carolina (USC) gradually moved toward the same conclusion. Although the university had voted against placing Maryland and Clemson on probation in December 1951, the school's president, Norman M. Smith, told Byrd the following month that "bowl games are a growing abuse." The ineffective Smith was a lame duck by that time, and his successor, Donald S. Russell, took a more favorable view of the role of athletic programs in gaining recognition for the university. He assured Byrd in November 1952 that South Carolina "will be happy to support a modification of the rule . . . banning participation in bowl games." Russell was a highly popular choice to replace Smith and to deal with a series of severe problems the university was facing. He was a close friend and former law partner of South Carolina governor James F. Byrnes. When Russell took over as president of South Carolina in September 1952, he vowed to make it a "great university" that would soon be "as good as" the University of North Carolina.[21]

The University of South Carolina was founded in 1801 under the name of South Carolina College, and for the first six decades of its existence it achieved distinction as one of the leading institutions of higher learning in the South. The Civil War was a devastating blow to the college. It closed for a time and after it reopened it sought in vain to recover its previous status. It made out poorly in competing with Clemson and other state colleges for the limited funds that the legislature provided. By the time that the United

States entered World War II, historian Henry H. Lesesne has written, USC "was a racially segregated, small, sleepy southern college" that "ranked well behind the leading public universities in other southeastern states." Conditions became even worse after the war ended. Even as enrollment boomed, the state reduced the university's appropriations, which placed it in dire financial straits. In the late 1940s, USC was threatened with a loss of accreditation because of the meagerness of the state's support and the weakness of its libraries and graduate programs. Faculty salaries were the lowest among southern state universities, and in 1948–49, only 19 percent of the faculty held Ph.D.s.[22]

South Carolina's athletics, underwritten by private funding from boosters, were well-off compared to academic programs. But the university failed to win any Southern Conference championships in football and only one in basketball (in 1933). Its performance in those sports was respectable, though hardly dominant, in the immediate postwar period. Enright led the football team to winning seasons in 1946, 1947, and 1951. Under the guidance of Frank Johnson, the basketball team was competitive and compiled winning records in five years between 1946 and 1953. When Donald Russell assumed the presidency of USC in 1952, he took important measures to improve academic quality, upgrade the faculty, and elevate the university's reputation. As a part of his campaign to make South Carolina a "great university," he favored, in Lesesne's words "a successful, well-rounded athletic program that was fully integrated into campus life." Russell held Rex Enright in high regard, and he apparently endorsed the athletic director's views on abandoning the Southern Conference and organizing a new league.[23]

By some point in 1952, then, the presidents of three Southern Conference schools — Maryland, Clemson, and South Carolina — had concluded, along with a group of athletic directors, that they should establish a new conference. Their position was based largely on their opposition to the ban on participation in bowls and their judgment that a league of like-minded schools with similar resources would be beneficial to their football programs. It remained unclear, however, whether other conference members who fit that category and whose presidents were far less interested in football would support the same objective.

The Big Four and the Formation of a New Conference

Once a football faction that included several presidents and athletic directors decided to work for the formation of a new conference, the success of their campaign depended on the support of the "Big Four" in North Carolina. The schools that made up the Big Four—UNC, State College, Duke, and Wake Forest—were located within a 30-mile radius of Raleigh. The title of "Big Four" seems to have been a journalistic invention that had caught on in the local area. It had nothing to do with the size of the schools in the early 1950s; UNC was the biggest of the Big Four with about 7,500 students, State College and Duke were relatively large with about 5,000 students, and Wake Forest was by far the smallest with about 2,200 students. But the name was a convenient short-hand for the keen and tenacious nature of their rivalry.[24]

The presidents of the Big Four schools regarded sports as a legitimate and, if well-controlled, beneficial part of their educational mission. "Big-time football," Gordon Gray wrote in January 1952, "keeps the persons, the appearance, and the general nature of the institution before a large section of the public and gives a wholesome emotional catharsis to the students themselves." His counterparts at Duke, Hollis Edens, and at Wake Forest, Harold Tribble, took the same position. But they also were deeply concerned about the abuses that arose from an overemphasis on winning, and they found that athletic issues too often detracted from matters of greater importance in academic institutions. On balance, they seemed to regard sports as a necessary and frequently annoying nuisance, and they worried that the Southern Conference and some of its members were not adequately governing athletic programs. "We believe that a sane program of intercollegiate athletics is a constructive influence in the life of a college or university," Edens commented. "It becomes our duty to make every effort to preserve that which is good." But, he added, "we are administering to a sick patient."[25]

Gray, Edens, and Tribble gradually came to regard withdrawing from the Southern Conference and forming a smaller, more manageable league as the best way to deal with a "sick patient." They were not sympathetic to the motives that drove the football faction to the same conclusion, and indeed, do not appear to have known about the secession efforts of their counterparts in other conference schools at the time. They determined that a new conference would advance their goals of asserting control over athletics and avoiding overemphasis on winning. Gray told a friend in September 1952 that unless the Southern Conference "mends its ways we will pull out." He was particularly unhappy that the conference had not banned freshman participation in varsity sports, but he was concerned about other issues as well. Gray's position represented a separate, parallel track toward a new conference from that followed by Byrd and his supporters. One track focused on football ambitions while the other emphasized the primacy of academic goals. Gray worked with Tribble and more closely with Edens to carry out their vision of balance and discipline in athletic programs through the formation of a new conference.[26]

Edens had become president of Duke University in 1949. He had spent almost his entire career in college administration, first at Emory University, his alma mater, and then as the vice-chancellor of the University System of Georgia. He had recently accepted a job as associate director of the Rockefeller Foundation's General Education Board when the Duke trustees elected him the third president of their institution. Edens delayed taking over at Duke until he completed the requirements for a Ph.D. by writing his dissertation in political science at Harvard. During his rapid rise through the ranks of college administration he had earned a reputation as a personable, talented, and ambitious leader, though his limited scholarly credentials were a concern to the Duke faculty.

At the time that Edens arrived, Duke was a well-regarded private university that aspired to join the top echelons of American higher education. Duke had been established as a result of the vision and wealth of James Buchanan "Buck" Duke. He had made his fortune in the tobacco and electrical power industries, and in 1924, he set up the Duke Endowment to provide support to the Methodist Church in North Carolina, hospitals and orphanages for black and white citizens in North and South Carolina, and educational institutions. In addition, 32 percent of the endowment was designated to create a new university that was named for his family. Duke University was built as an elaborate and carefully planned extension of Trinity College in Durham, to which the Duke family had offered generous financial assistance for years. J. B. Duke wanted the faculty of the new university to "insure its attaining and maintaining a place of real leadership in the educational world."

Duke University gradually carried out the wishes of its founder. It expanded its academic programs, recruited faculty, and established graduate and professional schools. In 1938, it was admitted, with effective support from the University of North Carolina, to the Association of American Universities, a key indication of its growing stature as a research university. Although in its early years it suffered from a reputation as a refuge for, in *Time* magazine's phrase, "well-heeled Joe Colleges," it became increasingly selective in its admission policies. By 1949, Duke had the 14th largest university library in the country, the second largest university hospital in the South, and a strong academic reputation. Edens was committed to further improving Duke's academic standing and its contributions to southern society.[27]

From the time that Duke was founded, athletics were an important part of campus life. The school's first president, William P. Few, commented in 1939 that sports "contribute greatly to the physical well-being and pleasure of the students" and had been "conducted in full cooperation with the University's educational purposes." The football team played in a 35,000-seat stadium built along with other new campus structures, and after Duke lured an outstanding coach, Wallace Wade, from the University of Alabama, it became a leading power in the Southern Conference. It won six conference titles under Wade and played twice in the Rose Bowl. The 1942 Rose Bowl was played before a throng of 56,000 in Durham after the seating capacity of the stadium was temporarily expanded. The game took place outside Pasadena, California, for the only time in its history because of a prohibition on large public events on the west coast in the wake of the Japanese attack on Pearl Harbor. When Wade joined the military, he was replaced for the duration of the war by assistant coach Eddie Cameron, who led the team to three conference championships and Duke's first bowl game victory in the 1945 Sugar Bowl.

Before taking over for Wade, Cameron had coached Duke's basketball team to Southern Conference championships in 1938, 1941, and 1942, and a record of 226–99 between 1929 and 1942. During that time, he extended Duke's recruiting, scheduling, and renown well beyond North Carolina. He was also instrumental in the construction of Duke Indoor Stadium, which could seat more fans than any basketball arena south of Philadelphia. The initial funds for the facility came from Duke's participation in the 1939 Rose Bowl. When the arena opened on January 6, 1940, a crowd of about 8,000, the largest attendance ever for a basketball game in the South, turned out to watch Duke defeat Princeton. Shortly after Wade returned from the war, Cameron was appointed Duke's athletic director, and he remained at that post until 1972. Duke's sterling performance in football and basketball during the first quarter-century after its founding continued to demonstrate what President Few had called "full cooperation with the University's educational purposes." In March 1951, the *New York Times*, in a series of investigative articles on college sports after the point-shaving scandals came to light, concluded that Duke "holds its athletes to high academic standards." Edens was determined to carry on that tradition. "I would not want the alumni," he once wrote when declining an invitation to an out-of-town Duke football game, "to get the idea that I take the game as seriously as they do."[28]

Harold Tribble, the president of Wake Forest College (it became a university in 1967), agreed with Gray and Edens on the desirability of sponsoring competitive athletic programs without overemphasizing them. The problems he faced in achieving that goal were in many ways more difficult than those of administrators at UNC, State College, and Duke. The school that became Wake Forest was established in 1834 by the North Carolina Baptist Convention to train ministers. It was located in Wake County a few miles north of Raleigh in an area known as the Forest of Wake. The town of Wake Forest gradually developed around the college to provide homes, dining services, and entertainment to students and faculty. Both the college and the town remained small; the enrollment at the school in 1919 was 534 and in 1943 it was 458. The Baptist Convention exercised great influence over the governance and the culture of Wake Forest College. It required all students to participate in chapel services every day for many years, though by the 1940s, the rule for compulsory attendance had been reduced to three days a week. In 1937, the Convention prohibited dancing on campus on the grounds that it was "demoralizing and . . . tends toward immorality." Women were first admitted as students to Wake Forest in 1942, in part to maintain the college's enrollment with so many men serving in the military.[29]

Wake Forest's faculty focused on teaching rather than on research and publication. The college was proud of the rigor of its academic programs, but it did not rank with Duke and North Carolina among the prestigious institutions of higher learning in the South. Wake had only a small endowment and faced chronic financial uncertainties. In 1946, it received an irresistible offer that eventually brought about profound changes for the small college and the town that supported it. The Z. Smith Reynolds Foundation, named for the son of the founder of the R. J. Reynolds Tobacco Company, pledged an annual contribution of $350,000 in perpetuity to the college if it would move 110 miles west to Winston-Salem, the second largest city in North Carolina. The gift caused both excitement over the improvements it would make possible and consternation over the prospect of leaving the town of Wake Forest. After much deliberation, the trustees of the college and the Baptist Convention decided to accept the grant and make the move. The first task was to raise a great deal of money for the costs of relocation and the construction of a new campus. The Reynolds family provided indispensable support for those efforts with additional funds and with the donation of a 300-acre tract of prime land for the new campus.

The burden of fund-raising and of dealing with the myriad problems that the move to Winston-Salem created fell on Harold Tribble. Tribble was serving as president of the Andover-Newton Theological School in Massachusetts when he was elected as president of Wake Forest by the Board of Trustees in May 1950. He was an ordained Baptist minister who held a doctorate in theology and had published three books on Christian doctrine. When Tribble interviewed for the Wake presidency, he announced that he was impressed with the "vital religious atmosphere" at the school and that he was "enthusiastic about Wake Forest." In light of the daunting challenges he faced, he needed all the enthusiasm he could muster. The board's first choice for president had turned down the job in part because he doubted that Wake could raise the money it needed to move to Winston-Salem and build a new campus.

Tribble took on the task with dedication and skill. The upheaval and uncertainties that the change of location caused for students, faculty, and residents of the town of Wake Forest required both tact and toughness. Tribble earned much respect, along with some criticism, for the manner in which he managed the move, and won affection from many for his warmth and kindness. He was very much a hands-on administrator who was interested in every aspect of Wake Forest's educational, religious, and social activities. His goal was to build the college's reputation along with its new campus without sacrificing its traditions. He was ever mindful that the college had been founded and supported for over a century to advance the purposes of the Baptist Convention. In seeking his objectives, he displayed an administrative style that could be "uncompromising and sometimes dictatorial," in the words of college historian Bynum Shaw. In 1954, for example, he offended Gordon Gray, who had close ties with Winston-Salem and with the R. J. Reynolds Tobacco Company. After a fight broke out during a football game between Wake and North Carolina, Tribble accused UNC of "a very unfortunate display of bad sportsmanship." Films of the game did not show conclusively who was to blame for starting the brawl, and Gray said only that he was "very sorry it happened." Even after administrators of both schools met to resolve their differences, Tribble complained to Gray about North Carolina's behavior. He suggested that its representatives had failed to "demonstrate clear moral and ethical discernment and trustworthiness."[30]

Tribble believed that athletic programs could contribute to the welfare of Wake Forest College if they did not receive inordinate attention or emphasis. "It is our earnest desire and firm resolve," he wrote in 1953, "to maintain the high scholastic and moral standards that are essential in a well-balanced program of Christian education and a wholesome program of such activities as athletics, intramural sports, debating, gymnastics, dramatics, glee club, and other phases of school life." As the smallest and poorest of the Big Four schools, Wake struggled to remain competitive with its local rivals. It was remarkably successful in fielding good teams. After Wake Forest joined the Southern Conference in 1936, football coach Douglas "Peahead" Walker led his teams to a record of 77–51 and two bowl appearances over 14 seasons. He resigned as coach in 1951 after a salary dispute with Tribble, who refused to pay him more than senior faculty members made. Walker's departure caused much dismay among Wake fans, who viewed it as evidence that Tribble was not committed to strong support for athletics. In basketball, coach Murray Greason led Wake to the regular season championship of the Southern Conference in 1938–39. Although the team lost in the conference tournament, which decided the league championship, it received a bid to play in the first NCAA tournament. During World War II, basketball was suspended from 1941 to 1944, and after the war, Greason had to rebuild the program. In 1953, Wake won its only Southern Conference championship by defeating powerful NC State in the tournament finals by the score of 71–70.[31]

The Creation of the ACC

In the early part of 1953, the idea of forming a new conference picked up momentum. It gained the support of the two groups, representing seven schools, who favored withdrawing from the Southern Conference for quite different reasons. The football faction regarded this step as the best means to achieve their scheduling and bowl objectives. The academic faction viewed a smaller and more cohesive league as the most promising way to gain better control over athletic programs. In a new conference with fewer schools, the Big Four by itself would have enough votes to establish policies on which its members agreed. Gradually, the two separate tracks converged. Gray, who had spearheaded the ban on participation in bowl games, softened his position in late 1952. Although he personally continued to oppose bowl appearances, he was no longer certain that the best policy was a conference ban. He preferred to allow individual schools to make their own decisions about playing in bowls. For their part, the football partisans did not dispute the need to enforce academic standards and stricter control of eligibility and recruiting. Byrd had stated this clearly when he appealed to the conference meeting in December 1951 for permission to play in the Sugar Bowl. Eddie Cameron favored a "high academic standing requirement" for athletes and suggested that scholarship awards be limited to those who placed "in the upper three quarters of [their] graduating class."[32]

Gray conversed frequently by telephone with Edens about plans for a new conference, and administrators from all of the prospective members presumably contacted one another informally to discuss the topic. The *Washington Post* reported that UNC athletic director Chuck Erickson "spent several days at College Park going over plans for the secession" with Byrd, though Gray apparently was not aware of the meeting. By early May 1953, the presidents of seven schools—the Big Four plus Maryland, Clemson, and South Carolina—had agreed on establishing the new league, subject to the approval of their governing bodies. Gray told the Committee on Athletic Relationships of the Board of Trustees for the Consolidated University on May 6 about the arrangements and received their tentative endorsement. Curiously, he included the University of Virginia among the prospective members of the conference. There is no evidence that Virginia had been approached about joining, but its academic reputation and priorities fit well with Gray's own goals.[33]

On May 7, 1953, the eve of the regular meeting of the Southern Conference, representatives from the schools that planned to make up the new league met in Greensboro. Most of those in attendance were athletic directors and faculty chairmen; Tribble was the only president to participate. They agreed, without dissent, on their intention to "separate from the present Southern Conference and form a new working organization." They proposed that in "view of the increasing problems in intercollegiate athletics . . . the formation of a smaller conference is desirable." The seven seceding schools acted out of a coincidence of interests, and that is how Byrd and Gray, who were at the opposite poles of the bowl game debate in 1951, wound up on the same side in working for a new conference. Everyone concurred, with varying levels of enthusiasm, on seeking to maintain a balance between academics and athletics and on allowing individual members of the new league to decide on bowl game appearances. Some unidentified administrators had already contacted Sugar Bowl and Orange Bowl officials about the possibility of signing a contract that would extend an automatic invitation to the champion of the new conference.[34]

After the seven colleges agreed among themselves to establish a new conference, they appointed three representatives to advise Max Farrington of George Washington University, president of the Southern Conference, of their action. He accepted their suggestion that at the regular Southern Conference meeting the next day, he would order an executive session that included only official representatives of the 17 schools. On the morning of May 8, 1953, James T. Penney, faculty chairman at the University of South Carolina, informed the executive session that seven members were leaving the conference. He disclosed that this idea had been "under consideration" for some time and that it "was crystallized at a meeting last night." Penney added that the decision to form a new league "was taken with mixed feelings" but with the "belief that this action will be best for all concerned." The ten remaining members of the Southern Conference were surprised but gracious, and the rest of the day's activities were devoted to working out a series of administrative details to carry out the separation. After the breakup was announced, Dick Herbert, the highly respected sports columnist for the *Raleigh News and Observer*, commented that although rumors about "a division of the unwieldy Southern Conference" had circulated "for years," it had occurred with "a minimum of acrimony" and with a "suddenness" that was "startling." When Eddie Cameron was asked if he had expected the new league to emerge from the Southern Conference meeting, he responded, "Frankly, I did not."[35]

After determining to depart from the Southern Conference, the members of the new league faced a variety of organizational issues. The first was the selection of a name. Among the possibilities mentioned were Mid-Atlantic, South Atlantic, Seaboard, Dixie, Mid-South, Tobacco, Rebel, and Cotton. When league representatives gathered on June 14, 1953, to take up questions relating to administration and governance, they unanimously adopted the recommendation of the athletic directors that the name be "The Atlantic Coast Conference."[36]

The ACC immediately considered questions of greater substance, including the two that had led to the founding of the conference: the balance between academic and athletic programs, and participation by conference schools in bowl games. The new conference approved a set of by-laws on August 7, 1953, that were in large part drawn word-for-word from the by-laws of the Southern Conference. But there were a few significant differences that reflected the priorities of Gray, Edens, and Tribble. The most prominent was that the ACC specifically prohibited freshmen from playing on varsity teams. The failure of the Southern Conference to take this action had been a major disappointment for Gray and one of the primary reasons he supported the formation of a new conference. The ACC also added to its by-laws a requirement that athletes must "be enrolled in an academic program leading to a recognized degree, and should be making normal progress, both quantitatively and qualitatively, toward the degree." Otherwise, the ACC's rules for eligibility and financial assistance for athletes were the same as those of the Southern Conference. Athletes who were awarded scholarships could receive only "actual institutional expenses" plus $15 per month.[37]

The ACC's regulations were similar in many ways to guidelines that the NCAA had adopted in 1951. But, unlike the NCAA's non-binding recommendations, the ACC's requirements carried sanctions, including the threat that any contest in which an ineligible player participated would be forfeited. ACC members clearly indicated, however, that they would not support academic requirements that they viewed as unreasonably strict. Duke University pushed for acceptance of Cameron's proposal that students who placed in the "lowest quartile" of their high school graduating class could not be granted athletic scholarships or other financial assistance. This motion was defeated by a wide margin on the grounds that the quality of secondary schools varied so much that class rank was not a fair measure of a student's ability. Even UNC and State College voted against Duke on this matter.[38]

Despite Duke's setback on the class standing issue, Gray and his associates succeeded in achieving the fundamental academic goals they had sought in favoring a new conference. The football faction also won support for its objectives of allowing members to play in bowl games and easing scheduling difficulties. The football scheduling problem was quickly resolved at the June 14 meeting with an agreement that by the 1956 season, ACC members would play at least five other conference schools. The bowl issue was also settled without major contention. In November 1953, the ACC signed a two-year contract to send its best team to the Orange Bowl for a guaranteed payment of at least $110,600. The ACC adopted a policy that allocated 50 percent of the bowl receipts to the participating school and divided the remainder among the other league members and the conference.[39]

Another important issue that the ACC addressed shortly after its founding was the status of its basketball tournament. Football coaches and their concerns had played a key role in the formation of the conference, but basketball questions were at best secondary considerations. Basketball coaches were not deeply involved in the breakup of the Southern Conference and in at least some cases were not even consulted. Maryland's Bud Millikan recalled that the ACC was "originally formed as a football league" and that he had not been asked for his views on the impact it would have on his program. The Southern Conference was the only league in the nation to select its champion in a postseason tournament, and the ACC's policy on this matter was initially unclear.

A few days after the announcement about the creation of the new conference, NC State's Everett Case called for a meeting of basketball coaches. He wanted to revise schedules for the upcoming season to drop games with former Southern Conference rivals that would "not mean a great deal" and to make arrangements that would "maintain interest in our new league." He was also anxious to achieve a consensus on determining the basketball champion and deciding who would represent the conference in the NCAA tournament. On June 14, 1953, the ACC voted to follow the Southern Conference's example by designating the tournament titlist as the league's NCAA representative. It did not, however, formally declare the team that won the tournament as the "conference champion" until 1961. With a smaller conference, the ACC tournament would include every team, who would be seeded by the regular season standings. The tournament, along with receipts from bowl games, was expected to provide most of the operating expenses for the conference. The most recent Southern Conference basketball tournament had turned a profit of about $53,000, and the old league retained its total assets of about $150,000 after the new conference was formed. The ACC did not begin with a large reserve. Each of the seven charter members paid an initial assessment of $200, and at the conference meeting in December 1953, the league's balance sheets showed that it was $14 in the red.[40]

The Eighth Member

When plans for the new conference were announced in May 1953, many observers speculated that an eighth member would be added in the near future. At that point, the seven original members had not decided whether to invite another school to join the conference. The principal advantage would be that an eight-team league would make better pairings and presumably generate greater interest in the conference basketball tournament. The three schools that were prominently mentioned as a possible eighth member that would fit the academic and athletic profile of the ACC were

Virginia, West Virginia, and Virginia Tech. Virginia appeared to have the inside track, and its academic distinction made it especially appealing to North Carolina and Duke. Some members, however, complained that Virginia "had never done anything for the Southern Conference but withdrawn from it." West Virginia was anxious to join if invited, but it was hampered by the difficulty of traveling to Morgantown. Virginia Tech was a long shot, largely because, as Dick Herbert explained, it "has had trouble for years producing strong football teams." The charter members were not inclined to expand beyond an eight-team league; one of the main purposes of forming the ACC was to keep it relatively small. At their meeting on June 14, 1953, they agreed to invite Virginia to join the conference. A motion to make the same offer to West Virginia and Virginia Tech failed for lack of a second.[41]

It was far from certain that Virginia would accept the ACC's invitation. The final decision would be made by its governing body, the Board of Visitors, and its members were sharply divided on whether joining the conference would be beneficial to the university. The University of Virginia, famously, had been founded by Thomas Jefferson, who purchased the land, designed the buildings, and planned the curriculum for his "academical village" in the last years of his life. It was chartered by the Commonwealth of Virginia in 1819 and opened six years later. The stately Rotunda, modeled after the Pantheon in Rome, and the elegant pavilions that flanked the "Lawn" that Jefferson laid out, were the symbol and the pride of the university.

By the time that the university celebrated its centennial, its academic quality did not measure up to the splendor of its architecture. "Entrance requirements at the university in the 1920s were extremely low," historian Virginius Dabney wrote. "The university had been plagued for many years by the presence of mediocre undergraduates. . . . Frequently they were flunk-outs from Ivy League colleges or they had been rejected by one or more of those institutions." The graduate school was lackluster and few of the faculty produced notable publications. The library ranked low among research institutions in numbers of and expenditures on books. Support for the university from the state was limited to "meager allotments," both in absolute and comparative terms. Presidents of the university worked hard to improve academic programs and to increase state appropriations, with mixed success. During the early years of the twentieth century, Virginia's academics had been strong enough to gain membership in two organizations that were emblems of prestige, Phi Beta Kappa and the Association of American Universities. In later years, it still qualified as a leading institution of higher learning in the South, but its performance fell short of its own aspirations and the prerequisites of lofty national stature.[42]

While Virginia struggled to uphold high academic standards, it remained rich in traditions that had developed over the years. Its student body took enormous pride in an honor system that effectively guarded against cheating and other offenses. The all-male enrollment wore jackets and ties to class and to practically any other school function. Students and alumni had their own vocabulary. The university did not have a campus, it had "the Grounds." New students were not freshmen but "first-years," and so on until they graduated as "fourth-years." They often referred to their school not as the University of Virginia but as "The University." Above all, Virginia had a long-standing tradition as a party school of staggering proportions. Its reputation for world-class revelry was exaggerated but nevertheless based in fact. "The University has been regarded since the 1920s as a center of hard drinking rather than studying," *Holiday* magazine reported in 1961, "a kind of lower-case Ivy League playground for Southern snobs and rich Northern boys who couldn't make the tougher scholastic hurdles at Princeton or Harvard."[43]

When Colgate Darden became president of the University of Virginia in 1947, he sought to extend the academic improvements his predecessors had set in motion and to combat the school's image as a "playground" for casual students. The son of working-class parents, Darden had graduated from Virginia in 1922 and gone on to a career in politics. A conservative Democrat, he served as a member of the Virginia House of Delegates and the U.S. House of Representatives and as governor of the Commonwealth of Virginia during World War II. When he took over at the university, he was committed to enlarging its budget and upgrading its programs by using his political skills and experience in dealing with the state legislature. One of his primary goals was to put into effect a policy of admitting fewer students from private preparatory schools and more from public schools in Virginia. During the 1950–51 school year, the university's student body included students from only 54 of 352 high schools in the commonwealth. "I have always felt that Jefferson intended that the University would be the capstone of a great public school system in Virginia," Darden remarked. He also campaigned to assert more control over fraternities as a way to change the perception of Virginia as a party school.[44]

Darden's position on athletics reflected the priority he attached to academic issues. Although he had no desire to "downplay" athletics, he wanted to avoid placing undue emphasis on them. "As a matter of fact, athletics constitutes one of the lesser problems at this University," he commented in 1951. "There are many other things that need looking after and need it more than athletics." Nevertheless, he could not avoid a series of important matters involving athletic policies and programs. One was his opposition to the NCAA's "Sanity Code." Another was the attitude of the faculty toward the role of sports at the university. In October 1951, a faculty committee complained that Virginia was guilty of overemphasis of athletics. The committee was chaired by Robert K. Gooch, a professor of political science and a star quarterback during his undergraduate days at Virginia. He was also a longtime friend of Darden, with whom he had shared a "great adventure" as volunteer ambulance drivers during World War I. The Gooch committee recommended that Virginia eliminate athletic scholarships and assign control of athletic policies to the faculty, particularly in applying "strict rules of eligibility." It argued that "the detrimental effects that can come from too much emphasis on athletics in colleges and universities" were evident in the recent scandals at West Point, William and Mary, and elsewhere.

The Gooch panel's proposals won the endorsement of the faculty of the College of Arts and Sciences, but other faculty members were less enthusiastic and alumni supporters of Virginia sports were outraged. Virginia's football teams under Art Guepe compiled a record of 39–15–2 between 1946 and 1951, and its basketball teams had seven consecutive winning seasons between 1944 and 1950. Darden defended the football program by pointing out that the graduation rate for players was only slightly lower than the student body as a whole. But he was sympathetic to the Gooch report's warnings about the dangers of big-time sports.[45]

Under those conditions, Virginia's acceptance of the invitation to join the ACC was doubtful, and it generated a great deal of debate within the university community. The advisability of joining the new conference was first considered by the Athletic Council, a committee composed of faculty members, alumni, and students that played a key role in determining athletic policies at Virginia. On May 30, 1953, Athletic Director Gus Tebell urged the council to support membership in the ACC. He was concerned that if Virginia remained an independent, it would face unprecedented difficulties in finding opponents to schedule and in raising adequate funding to support its teams. He also suggested that the new conference would "help provide . . . sane rules which everyone can live up to." The council was convinced and voted unanimously in favor of membership. At its next meeting on September 25, 1953, the council asked Tebell to list potential disadvantages of affiliation with the ACC. In response, he expressed concern that Maryland, Wake Forest, and Duke would be so powerful that they would force Virginia to make changes that were "out of character" or face the likelihood of assuming "a door-mat role." Tebell also expressed doubt that Virginia had much "in common" with Maryland, NC State, Wake, and Clemson. He feared that some members of the ACC, whom he did not name, would violate the rules of the conference. "They did it in the old Southern," he remarked, "and they can't be trusted now." The council deliberated at length over the pros and cons of joining the ACC and then unanimously agreed that, on balance, the advantages of membership outweighed the drawbacks.[46]

The final decision was in the hands of the Board of Visitors, and it discussed the issue for about four hours at a meeting on October 9, 1953. Barron F. Black, the rector of the board, asked Tebell about his comment to the Athletic Council that Virginia had little in common with some members of the ACC. Tebell explained that the "feeling against Maryland results from their recent ruthless attitude in building a football team." But he added that "we play them in all other sports, and relations are good." He believed that Maryland and Wake, which had a "fine president," would "fall in line" with conference rules. He confessed that he knew little about Clemson. Darden announced that he opposed joining the ACC, in part because it would separate the university from its traditional rivals in the state of Virginia. He also worried that the ACC's rule for the number of courses an athlete had to pass to be eligible for competition, which was stricter than Virginia's standard, would discourage players from public high schools in the state from enrolling at the university. After several members recited conflicting views, the board concluded that joining the ACC was both necessary to sustain the competitive and financial viability of the athletic program and desirable as a way of balancing the university's athletic and academic commitments. It was a close call; the board decided in favor of affiliating with the ACC by a vote of 6–4. At its meeting on December 4, 1953, the ACC voted unanimously to admit Virginia to the conference. On the same day, it declined to extend invitations for membership to West Virginia and Virginia Tech.[47]

Commissioner Weaver

After the ACC settled the question of membership, it turned to the important task of appointing a commissioner, who would be the administrative officer of the conference. Duke's Wallace Wade, the commissioner of the Southern Conference, also served as the interim commissioner of the ACC while it was getting organized. On May 6–7, 1954, the ACC agreed on a series of duties and powers that it vested in the commissioner. They included routine matters such as preparing an annual budget, purchasing trophies, and selecting game officials. They also included a broad range of responsibilities for interpreting and enforcing conference rules. They were similar to the duties of the commissioner of the Southern Conference, but the ACC granted greater discretion and independent authority to its executive officer. For example, the commissioner could, on his own initiative, investigate possible violations (neither the conference's minutes nor its expectations were gender neutral). If he found that rules had been broken, he could impose fines, reprimands, penalties, and even "order severance of athletic relations with the offending institution subject to action of the Conference." The Southern Conference had not explicitly provided its commissioner with such sweeping jurisdiction. The ACC, in another departure from its predecessor, also directed the commissioner to "study athletic problems of the Conference, offer advice and assistance in their solution and encourage and promote friendly relations which should exist among the member institutions, their students and alumni."

At a special meeting on May 28, 1954, the ACC chose James H. Weaver as its commissioner. He had been athletic director at Wake Forest since 1937, and during that time had earned the affection and respect of his colleagues and adversaries in the Southern Conference. Weaver was the son of a Methodist minister and college president, and he grew up in Emory, Virginia. He attended Trinity College in Durham for a time, but an incident in which he and several others provided freshmen with involuntary swimming lessons led to his abrupt departure. He then went to Centenary College in Louisiana, where he played football, basketball, and baseball and was elected vice-president of the student body. After graduating in 1924, Weaver got into coaching and wound up as head football coach at Wake Forest. When Wake joined the Southern Conference, he became its first athletic director. In that capacity, he produced consistently successful teams that at least held their own and often excelled in the Big Four. Weaver was calm, levelheaded, and slow to anger. He clearly displayed his wrath, however, when coaches or administrators took actions that he thought undermined the principles of the conference. "Jim Weaver wanted [the ACC] to be admired for its integrity," commented Gene Corrigan, who worked for Weaver as assistant commissioner for a time in the 1960s and later became the commissioner of the conference. "The NCAA wasn't a factor then. Conferences took care

Jim Weaver, shown here presenting the ACC Tournament championship trophy to North Carolina State's Dave Gotkin, 1955. (Courtesy The North Carolina State Archives; reprinted by permission of *The News and Observer* of Raleigh, North Carolina)

of all penalties. He had a very, very difficult job." Weaver began his job with the ACC on July 1, 1954; he performed his duties in a suite in the King Cotton Hotel in Greensboro. Until he hired Corrigan in 1967, he and his secretary were the entire administrative staff of the ACC.[48]

With the appointment of Weaver, the ACC completed its organizational framework. The founding of the conference was a direct result of the severe problems in college sports that emerged with such fanfare in 1951. The point-shaving scandal and the transgressions at William and Mary motivated Southern Conference presidents to take actions that they hoped would prevent similar difficulties in the future. The ban on bowl appearances that they favored, in turn, led Curley Byrd and others to conclude that forming a new league would be the best way to accomplish the goals they sought in their athletic programs, especially football. Meanwhile, Gordon Gray and his allies decided that a new conference was the most likely means to assert the primacy of academic programs and to avoid overemphasis on winning. With the exception of the rule prohibiting freshman participation in varsity sports, the ACC's rules on eligibility and scholarship assistance were much the same as those of the Southern Conference. But the size of the new conference and the compatibility of its members were a substantial departure from previous arrangements. Gray and his supporters believed that those attributes would enable better control of conference policies and reduce the risk of athletic infractions that embarrassed member institutions. The ACC was established, then, with a commitment to academic integrity that went hand-in-hand with its aspirations for athletic excellence. The dual purposes of encouraging competition between well-matched rivals while also promoting an appropriate balance of academic and athletic programs were the critical considerations that led to its founding. It soon became evident that those goals, however desirable, were not easily achievable. Within two months after its creation, the ACC had to deal with the issue of overemphasis on winning when allegations of serious violations of NCAA and conference rules by one of its own members came to light.

3

THE MAN WHO MADE
ACC BASKETBALL

The approach of the Dixie Classic of 1958, the tenth anniversary of an event that had become a cherished institution among basketball fans in North Carolina, generated even more excitement and anticipation than usual. The tournament, a three-day affair held between Christmas and New Year's Day, pitted the Big Four schools against powers from other parts of the country. In 1958, the participants included four teams ranked nationally in the top 10. In the Associated Press poll, the University of Cincinnati, led by Oscar Robertson, was second, North Carolina was third, NC State was sixth, and Michigan State, featuring John "Jumpin' Johnny" Green, was ninth. In the United Press International ratings, Cincinnati was first, Michigan State fourth, North Carolina fifth, and NC State sixth. NC State coach Everett Case, who had been most responsible for establishing the Dixie Classic, considered the field the "greatest ever," and advance ticket sales were a record 71,000 for six sessions of basketball. The Classic was not an elimination tournament; each of the eight teams played three games, and the winners of their first two games played for the championship.[1]

The Dixie Classic grew out of a conversation between Case and Dick Herbert of the *Raleigh News and Observer* in 1949. When Case complained about the hardships of traveling to out-of-town holiday tournaments, Herbert suggested that NC State hold its own tournament in its new William Neal Reynolds Coliseum, which seated 12,400 fans. By inviting top teams from other sections to compete against the Big Four, the tournament could not only heighten interest in the Raleigh area in the local rivalries but also earn greater respect in the national press for basketball in North Carolina. Case immediately realized that the tournament could offer major benefits in winning recognition and making money for his program. He also liked the name of "Dixie Classic" that his assistant coach, George "Butter" Anderson, proposed. The other Big Four schools, despite the reluctance of coaches to potentially play another tough game against their local competition, agreed with Case's position. "You needed the recognition and you sure needed the money," recalled Vic Bubas, who was an assistant to Case from 1951 to 1959 and then head coach at Duke. In 1958, for example, each of the eight teams that played in the Classic received about $9,000 beyond expenses. NC State took an extra share plus profits from concessions, and its additional income caused considerable grumbling among the other participants.[2]

The Dixie Classic, as Case hoped, soon became an extraordinarily popular drawing card. In 1949, the first year it was held, it attracted more than 54,000 fans, who paid $7.50 for the best seats and $4.50 for end zone tickets for twelve games. The following year, 11,000 fans ignored warnings to stay off ice-covered roads in order to attend the games on the first night of the tournament. The intensity of the competition and the taut atmosphere at Reynolds Coliseum made the Classic a consistently memorable event. "People used to line up their vacations to make sure they could go," Horace A. "Bones" McKinney, who coached at Wake Forest during the 1950s and early 1960s, later recalled. "Reynolds was packed, the basketball was tremendous. Nothing was as big as the Dixie Classic." William C. Friday, former president of the University of North Carolina system, commented in 1994: "When people talk about the euphoria of the [NCAA] Final Four these days, I tell them, 'You never saw the Dixie Classic.'"[3]

When the 1958 Dixie Classic opened on December 29, it was covered by 70 writers, 30 photographers, 9 radio stations, and 5 television channels (though the games were not shown live on TV). In addition to the ranked squads, the tournament included Duke, Wake Forest, Louisville, and Yale. Duke (2–4) and Wake (3–3) were struggling, Yale's best player was injured, and Louisville, which came in with a record of 4–4, was talented enough to make the NCAA tournament's final rounds at the end of the season. Cincinnati was a slight favorite to win the Classic, a feat that had never been accomplished by a team from outside the Big Four. Dick Herbert even suggested that "before teams around the country get the idea it is impossible to win here it might be well for a visitor to take the title."[4]

At a time of growing racial tensions in the South, the possibility of discrimination against black players was a source of concern for administrators from integrated schools who participated in the Dixie Classic. In January 1958, M. Charles Mileham, director of physical education and athletics at the University of Cincinnati, contacted NC State athletic director Roy Clogston to make certain that Oscar Robertson would suffer "no discrimination of any kind" when he played in the Classic at the end of the year. Clogston replied that "many colored boys" had played against NC State in regular season games and in the Dixie Classic without "one complaint about discrimination." He added that "it is true that we cannot house teams that have colored boys in the down town hotels," where teams with all white rosters were lodged. But he assured Mileham that State College had special facilities near its campus that were "ideal for athletic teams." Bill Guthridge, who stayed in those facilities as a player for Kansas State in 1959, likened them more to an out-of-the-way "infirmary" than to the "ideal" accommodations that Clogston described. Clogston told his counterpart at Cincinnati that "N. C. State College will do everything in its power to see that there is no discrimination of any kind to the participants" in the Dixie Classic. Nevertheless, Robertson later recalled that the grand wizard of the Ku Klux Klan had sent him a letter with a warning: "Don't Ever Come to the South." He resented the University of Cincinnati's acceptance of separate accommodations, especially since members of the school's Board of Trustees stayed in a downtown hotel that denied service to their team.[5]

Although the extensive newspaper coverage of the 1958 Dixie Classic did not emphasize racial concerns, an awareness of the possibility of racial incidents, despite appeals for civility, was clearly present. As things turned out, race was less of an issue during the tournament than it was in making arrangements for accommodations for integrated teams. Partisan fans jeered Robertson boisterously when he competed against Big Four squads. But according to informed observers who attended the games, they did not, for the most part, stoop to racial insults. In an opening round contest between Cincinnati and Wake Forest, tempers flared briefly but fell short of a serious racial confrontation. Dave Budd, Wake's outstanding 6'6" center, tangled with Robertson in a scramble for a rebound and both players landed on the floor. Budd cocked his fists as though he intended to slug his opponent before officials and coaches intervened. Budd commented after the game: "I could have hit him but I didn't. I happened to think about his race, and knew if I hit him, it would cause a lot of trouble . . . and look bad for this section." He also denied that race was a factor in his battle with Robertson. Budd's home was in New Jersey, where, he said, "my best buddy in high school was a colored boy." The scuffles between Budd and Robertson had little impact on the outcome of the game, which Cincinnati won easily, 94–70. As Robertson left the game with a short time remaining, he received a smattering of boos that were drowned out by cheers from fans who appreciated his exceptional talent. Despite the general absence of overt racial animosities, some observers suggested that the discord between Budd and Robertson introduced racial tensions to the Dixie Classic. "Negro players have appeared in the Classic before," Hugh Germino wrote in his column in the *Durham Sun*, "but this is believed to be the first time in the 10-year history of the event that a racial rhubarb took place."[6]

There were no more flare-ups between players that could be attributed to racial friction during the remainder of the 1958 Classic. The focus of attention was the competition between highly ranked basketball teams. NC State edged Louisville in its first-round game, setting up a much-anticipated matchup with Robertson, generally regarded as the best player in college basketball, and his Cincinnati teammates. With Governor Luther Hodges and a packed Reynolds Coliseum watching what the *News and Observer* called "one of the Dixie Classic's all-time thrilling games," NC State won a 69–60 victory that was closer than the final score indicated. By using zone defenses that shifted along with Robertson's position on the floor, it managed to limit the Cincinnati star to 29 points, 9 below his average. State center John Richter scored 26 points and collected 15 rebounds. When the game ended, the jubilant NC State players carried Case off the floor on their shoulders. In the other semifinal game, Michigan State led North Carolina by only 4 points with 1:20 left to play, but pulled away to earn a 75–58 victory.[7]

In the title game, NC State faced an undefeated opponent with a highly talented star for the second day in a row. "Jumpin' Johnny" Green did not have the all-around scoring, rebounding, and passing skills that made Robertson so spectacular. But he was a superb athlete, 6'5" tall, with astonishing leaping abilities. Duke's Doug Kistler, who stood 6'9", commented after his team's opening round loss to Michigan State, "It gets sorta disheartening when you jump as high as you can and see you are just up to John Green's elbows." NC State effectively executed zone defenses that kept Green away from the basket and limited him to 4 points and 6 rebounds. It won by a score of 70–61. Guard Lou Pucillo controlled the pace of the game and scored 22 points. Case got another ride on his players' shoulders, and although he could barely talk because of hoarseness, he called the game the "greatest tournament triumph" of his coaching career. NC State's win came after the crowd was treated to an electrifying contest for third place in which North Carolina's Lee Shaffer made a 3-point play with 30 seconds remaining to defeat Cincinnati, 90–88.[8]

The 1958 Dixie Classic ended on a familiar note. Visiting powerhouses fell to Big Four opponents, the home team won the championship, and the fans enjoyed three days of highly entertaining basketball. Jack Horner, a columnist for the *Durham Morning Herald*, suggested that the outcome of the tournament signaled the superiority of basketball in North Carolina. "The way our Big Four basketballers manhandled the visitors focused national attention on this section," he wrote, "and proved to the Doubting Thomases that the greatest college basketball in the nation is played right here in Tobaccoland." NC State's title reaffirmed the excellence of the program that Everett Case had built. But it also highlighted the fact that the team was ineligible to play for the national championship because in 1956 the NCAA had placed State College on probation for four years.[9]

The Old Gray Fox

The Dixie Classic was only one of many innovations that Everett Case introduced during his coaching career at North Carolina State. He had been hired in 1946 with no head coaching experience at the college level but with an exceptional record as a high school coach in Indiana, a breeding ground of basketball mania. Born in 1900, Case grew up in Anderson, Indiana, and although he did not play basketball in high school, he showed a precocious interest in and knack for coaching the game. He did not have enough money to attend college, but at age 18, he landed a job as a high school teacher and assistant coach. He then moved on to brief and successful stints as head coach at other high schools. In 1922, Case was hired to coach the "Hot Dogs" of Frankfort High School, whom he led to ten consecutive appearances in the Indiana state tournament and to championships in 1925 and 1929. After he went back to Anderson to coach, the state athletic association suspended the school from competition for one year for illegal recruiting practices, the most flagrant of which was bringing a semi-pro player from Ohio to play for his team.

By that time, Case had earned a bachelor's degree, and he left Indiana in a huff to attend graduate school at the University of Southern California. He served as freshman coach at the university and wrote a master's thesis in which he analyzed various methods for shooting free throws. He decided that the underhanded shot was the most effective technique. The Frankfort Hot Dogs, whose basketball fortunes had declined after Case's departure, persuaded him to return, and he won two more state titles in 1936 and 1939. An article in *Collier's* magazine later reported that the Hot Dogs were not well liked in Indiana. Case's teams, it said, were "respected yet detested for their near perfection" and "were chased out of practically every Indiana town large enough to work up a barrage of rotten eggs, stones, or overripe vegetables." Case continued to display his coaching talents as a U.S. Navy officer during World War II, guiding teams at training bases where he was stationed to outstanding records against tough competition.[10]

While Case was compiling an enviable coaching record, NC State was looking for a way to improve its athletic programs. Its administrators first considered replacing their decrepit football stadium as a means of competing with North Carolina and Duke. But the costs far exceeded their limited resources. Further, they knew it would be difficult to recruit enough football players who were interested in or qualified for the academic majors — engineering, agriculture, textiles, and forestry — that State offered as a part of the Consolidated University. Therefore, shortly before World War II, State College officials decided to focus their efforts on basketball. They realized that a strong basketball program required fewer players and less money than football and, if successful, could offer the same benefits. They took the first step by making plans for a new arena that would seat about 9,000 fans. A fund-raising campaign produced enough money to break ground and to put up the steel framework for the building in 1943. The most generous donor was Mary Reynolds Babcock, a member of the Reynolds Tobacco Company family, who gave a gift of $100,000 to honor her uncle, William Neal Reynolds, a longtime supporter of State College. A short time later, wartime exigencies forced the suspension of construction of the coliseum.[11]

When the war ended, NC State began its search for a coach to carry out its quest for basketball supremacy. At the suggestion of Dick Herbert, H. A. Fisher, a professor of mathematics and chairman of the athletic council, consulted with Chuck Taylor, who conducted basketball clinics around

Everett Case, shown here with two of his star players, Mel Thompson (left) and Ronnie Shavlik, 1954. (Courtesy The North Carolina State Archives; reprinted by permission of *The News and Observer* of Raleigh, North Carolina)

the country as a means of selling sneakers for the Converse athletic shoe company. Taylor had played for Case in high school in Indiana, and he advised Fisher that the "best basketball coach in the country is a lieutenant commander in the Navy" and that "if you want him you'd better not waste any time." Fisher and colleagues met with Case a short time later and soon offered him the job. Case was undecided about accepting until he made a trip to Raleigh and saw the steel skeleton of the new arena. The prospects of playing in a large, modern coliseum prevailed over his reservations about coaching at a school with little basketball tradition that was far from his home. When Fisher asked about his salary requirements, Case replied that he had done well with his investments and that "money isn't the big consideration." They agreed on $5,000 a year. Case arrived in Raleigh on July 1, 1946, to begin his college coaching career.[12]

Case immediately guided State College to the top of the Southern Conference and to national prominence. His 1946–47 team included an outstanding guard, Leo Katkaveck, who returned to State after serving in the military, and talented players, many from Indiana, whom Case and his assistant, Butter Anderson, recruited. Among them were Dick Dickey, a future All-American, and Norm Sloan, a future coach at NC State. Within the short time available, Case managed to mold a group that had never played together into an excellent unit. The "Red Terrors," as State's teams were then named, commanded attention and respect with wins over quality opponents, highlighted by an overtime victory over North Carolina in Chapel Hill. They also drew overflow crowds to tiny Frank Thompson Gym, which had a seating capacity of about 1,200. For the final home game, a rematch against North Carolina, some 4,000 fans crawled through windows and beat down a door to squeeze into the arena. Raleigh's fire chief, W. R. Butts, after issuing a warning about overcrowding that the fans ignored, decided to cancel the game because the size of the throng created "both a fire hazard and a structural hazard." The crowd booed angrily and some disappointed spectators pelted Butts's car with stones as they left the arena. Despite this setback, State went on to win the Southern Conference Tournament and to earn an invitation to the NIT for the first time in the school's history. It finished third in the NIT and wound up the season with a record of 26–5.[13]

After this impressive debut, Case built on his success. He imported more talent from the Midwest, notably center Paul Horvath from Chicago and guards Vic Bubas and Sammy Ranzino from Gary, Indiana. In 1947–48, the "Wolfpack," a name the school adopted to replace "Red Terrors," won 16 games in a row at one point, ranked first in the country for a time, and finished with a record of 29–3. It went undefeated in the Southern Conference and rolled over William and Mary, North Carolina, and Duke for the tournament title. Nevertheless, it did not receive an invitation to compete for the NCAA championship. The NCAA at that time took only one team from each of its geographical sections, and it chose Kentucky over NC State. The selection was partly due to the power of Kentucky coach Adolph Rupp and partly due to the fact that State played three freshmen. Although the Southern Conference allowed freshmen to participate in varsity sports, the NCAA did not allow them to play in events it sponsored. NC State went to the NIT, where it lost in the opening round to a DePaul squad led by George Mikan.[14]

State College's performance in Case's first two seasons established a pattern of dominance of both the Southern Conference and the Big Four. It captured the conference title every year from 1947 through 1952. It won the Dixie Classic championship every year from 1949 through 1952. After Case's arrival, State beat North Carolina 15 times in a row, often in routs.

It defeated Duke in 12 of the first 14 games played under Case and Wake 13 times out of 15. Case's success was in no small part a result of the up-tempo style he employed. He was a master at teaching his players to run a fast break without turning the ball over and to press relentlessly on defense. Although he was not the first to use a running game, it was still fairly rare in college basketball. When he became coach at NC State, the center jump after every made field goal had been abolished only nine years earlier. Lou Bello, who officiated many of NC State's games in both the Southern Conference and the ACC, once commented on Case's approach: "Not only did he bring in the fast break, the one-hand shot, and speed, speed, speed, [the] next thing he came in with was the pressing defense. . . . Coach Case was so far ahead of everybody else." Case cited another reason for accelerating the pace of play: "Our boys want to run. They love this race horse game."[15]

NC State fans felt the same way. They packed and occasionally overflowed Thompson Gym, even after the college expanded its seating capacity. State then shifted its home games to Raleigh's Memorial Auditorium, which seated 3,900 and was not much of an improvement. Meanwhile, construction of Reynolds Coliseum steadily progressed. When Case first arrived at State, he insisted on a substantial increase in its size. He wanted it to exceed the capacity of Duke Indoor Stadium, and therefore, become the largest arena in the South. Because the steel frame had already been erected, the only way to expand the coliseum at an acceptable cost was to add seats in the end zone areas. The result, wrote Alwyn Featherston, who covered the ACC for the *Durham Herald-Sun* for many years, was an arena that looked "like an elongated shoebox with a handful of excellent seats on the sidelines and thousands of bad seats in the end zone." Nevertheless, fans jammed the new coliseum when it opened in 1949 and kept on coming. NC State led the nation in on-campus attendance for basketball games for ten consecutive years. The grandeur of Reynolds Coliseum and the aura of excitement, prestige, and success that it conveyed, combined with State's winning ways under Case, instilled enormous pride in students, alumni, and other fans throughout North Carolina. The new arena, commented Smith Barrier, sports editor of the *Greensboro Daily News* and the *Greensboro Record*, made Raleigh the "basketball capital of the world."[16]

In addition to Case's ability as a coach, he was a gifted promoter. He made the game more enjoyable for fans by bringing to NC State practices that he had used to good effect in Indiana, such as spotlighting players during pregame introductions and cutting down the nets to celebrate an important victory. He sought to encourage vocal fan support for his team by installing a noise meter in Reynolds Coliseum. Case and Butter Anderson traveled around the state to offer clinics and to talk to civic groups and schools about basketball and about NC State. The *Raleigh News and Observer* reported in 1951 that after Case's arrival, interest in basketball in North Carolina had grown noticeably. It affirmed that "all across the State" attendance at high school games had increased, and "makeshift goals have been erected in the most unlikely places—on trees, on the sides of barns, in tobacco warehouses—where budding collegiate stars spend their weekends working to perfect their basket [*sic*] technique." Case did not create widespread love of basketball in North Carolina. Shortly after the game was invented, it gained great popularity in schools, mills, and factories and among blacks and whites, men and women. Case built on existing foundations to elevate basketball to new levels of pride and passion. Although the other Big Four schools had fielded some outstanding teams in previous years, Case produced what an article in the *Saturday Evening Post* in 1951 called the first "consistent major-league outfit" in the Southern Conference. As a result of State's success, it concluded, "big-time basketball has come to North Carolina to stay."[17]

Within a short time after Case began coaching at NC State, the college's supporters treated him as a hero, if not a deity. In 1951, they showed the depth of their gratitude for his achievements by presenting him with a new Cadillac (assistant coach Anderson received a new Oldsmobile). While Case's coaching record impressed fans, his considerate demeanor enhanced his stature with reporters and even opposing coaches. The writers who covered NC State appreciated his unfailing willingness to talk with them and his courtesy in returning their phone calls. Maryland coach Bud Millikan called Case a "great man." Early in Millikan's coaching tenure, Maryland defeated NC State in a closely contested game in College Park. The next day, Case called to congratulate Millikan and to tell him that he was doing a good job with the Maryland program.[18]

Case was a bachelor whose only interest outside of basketball was collecting furniture for his home, located a few blocks from the State College campus. He was normally friendly and gracious, though he could turn nasty, especially with reporters who wrote stories he did not like, when he had too much to drink. "He could get bombed," commented Bill Hensley, who was State's sports information director during the late 1950s. "He loved his booze." Norm Sloan described Case as a "small man" who had "worlds of nervous energy." He "never looked tired . . . and was full of life, always going in high gear." His high energy levels were partly a result of his ritual of taking a nap every afternoon.[19]

Case was a hard-driving and intensely competitive coach. During games, *Collier's* reported, he played "harder on the side line than any of his panting North Carolina State athletes." Case called himself "a leaner, a twister, and a scroocher." He explained his demonstrative manner on the bench: "I shoot for every one of my boys. If it looks like they're gonna miss, I try to lean, twist or scrooch 'em in." Case was tough and demanding with his players, but they responded to his coaching methods. "It was easy to play for him because he was a winner and demanded a lot," remarked Bubas. "He didn't want to be second best." In order to gain an edge over opponents, he made meticulous preparations for games. He was among the first to study game films to devise strategies. To get ready for a fast-breaking opponent, he ran scrimmages in which the starters had to defend against six reserves. He practiced for an upcoming game against a 7′0″ center by having a second-string player stand on a chair in front of the basket. Another key to Case's success was the talent and dedication of his assistant coaches. Anderson, Bubas, and Lee Terrill, who had played for Case and who became an assistant in 1955 when Anderson resigned, were better bench coaches than Case, who was not especially strong at drawing up plays or making adjustments during games. The trials of recruiting fell principally on the assistants; they sacrificed time with their families to spend long periods on the road selling the NC State program to prospects.[20]

Case's nickname was the "Old Gray Fox." The "gray" part of the moniker referred to the color of his hair; the "fox" part was a tribute to the craft he used to win games. Winning was an obsession, and his single-minded commitment enabled him to achieve enormous success at State College. But it was also a burden to bear. "He won too much," commented Lou Pucillo, one of State's stars in the late 1950s. "He had a fear of losing." That fear apparently led him to disregard NCAA and conference recruiting rules in his determination to stay on top, and his program suffered severe penalties for what the NCAA and ACC found to be serious violations.[21]

The ACC Competition

When the ACC was established in 1953, NC State's chief competitors in basketball were the other members of the Big Four, though Maryland was improving. Wake Forest, Duke, and North Carolina had strong programs and traditions, and they quickly tired of losing so consistently to Case's teams. Within the constraints of the resources available to them, they sought ways to challenge State's dominance.

Wake Forest lacked the means to take major steps, but good coaching and some good fortune helped it to break State's string of consecutive championships under Case. After Wake suspended basketball during World War II, Murray Greason rebuilt the program and made it competitive. But it was not a serious contender for the Southern Conference championship, and its record in the 1951–52 season slipped to 10–19. In the fall of 1952, assistant coach Harold Barrow left to attend graduate school, and Greason decided to invite Bones McKinney to serve as his assistant. McKinney, who stood 6'6" and had been an outstanding high school, college, and professional basketball player, was delighted to accept. He acquired his nickname either because of his role in a high school play or because of his slender frame (he once described himself as "muscled up like a clothes line"). Either way, he much preferred "Bones" to his given name of "Horace." When Greason approached him about becoming assistant coach, he was a student at the Southeastern Baptist Theological Seminary, which the Southern Baptist Convention established in Wake Forest after the college decided to move to Winston-Salem.

McKinney grew up in Durham, where he was the star center on his high school teams that won 69 games in a row and three state championships. He enrolled at NC State and topped the Southern Conference in scoring as a sophomore. After serving in the army, he decided to move to the University of North Carolina because of his high regard for its coach, Ben Carnevale. McKinney led a talented UNC squad to the NCAA finals in 1946, which it lost in a close game with Oklahoma A&M. By that time, he had a family to support, and he could not afford to stay in college. After working briefly in the personnel office at Hanes Hosiery in Winston-Salem, he joined the Washington Capitols of the Basketball Association of America, which was a predecessor of the National Basketball Association. Playing for coach Arnold "Red" Auerbach, he was an all-pro selection. When Auerbach quit the Capitols, McKinney filled in as the team's player-coach for part of a season. He wound up his professional career in 1952 as a member of Auerbach's Boston Celtics.[22]

McKinney was well-known to fans not only for his skills but also for his antics as a player. In high school, he indulged in such capers as sitting on the lap of a rival coach, leading cheers, and performing yo-yo tricks on the sideline. In one tournament, the crowd erupted in cheers and laughter when he sank to his knees to plead after he was charged with a foul. By the time the referee turned around to check on the commotion, McKinney was busily tying his sneakers. In an exhibition game with the Capitols, he helped himself to a handful of popcorn from a container held by a fan in the first row as he dribbled down the court. After practicing foul shots with his back to the basket and becoming quite proficient, he decided to try it in a game in which the Capitols had a big lead. "I stepped to the foul line, turned around and threw the ball backwards over my head," he later recalled. "I missed the shot, was thrown out of the game, and was almost thrown out of the league." [23]

After his professional basketball career ended, McKinney decided to attend the Baptist seminary in Wake Forest. By that time, he was the father of four children, and money for his growing family needs was in short supply. To earn a little cash, he delivered newspapers. When Murray Greason asked him to become Wake's assistant basketball coach, he thought the "Lord must have heard my prayers." His hopes of making a salary of $3,000 to $5,000 that would allow him to quit his paper route, however, were soon dashed. When he went to see Jim Weaver, then Wake's athletic director, about how much he would be paid, he got the bad news. Weaver disclosed that he had no funds available in his lean "Baptist budget" but that he could "scrape up $750." The following year, McKinney received a raise to $3,300, which enabled him to terminate his career as a 33-year-old paper boy. He continued his seminary studies while serving as assistant coach. [24]

After signing on with Greason in November 1952, McKinney quickly proved his ability as a coach. Despite his well-deserved reputation for clowning, he was an intense competitor and very serious about winning. When he went to his first practice as assistant coach, he immediately focused his attention on one player, Ned Dixon "Dickie" Hemric. Hemric was a solidly built 6'6" sophomore center who had, in McKinney's words, "legs like tree trunks." Although Case had not been impressed enough with his skills to offer him a scholarship at NC State, he received a full ride at Wake and averaged 22.4 points as a freshman on a varsity team that won only ten games. McKinney promptly determined that Hemric had the potential to become even better if he worked to correct his weaknesses. "Dickie couldn't make a left-handed hook shot or a free throw to save his life," he later wrote.

Day after day, McKinney stayed after practice to play one-on-one and to teach Hemric to shoot with either hand, to draw fouls, and to hit free throws. "Dickie learned more in thirty days than anyone I ever saw," he re-

Dickie Hemric, 1955. (Courtesy The North Carolina State Archives; reprinted by permission of *The News and Observer* of Raleigh, North Carolina)

called. "His accomplishments during the next three years were phenomenal." Hemric not only excelled as a scorer but also as a shot-blocker and rebounder. During his sophomore year, he increased his scoring average to 24.9 points per game and led the Southern Conference in rebounding. The culmination of the season was a stirring 71–70 victory over NC State in the 1953 Southern Conference Tournament, the first time that Case was denied the league title. Hemric went on to win recognition as ACC Player of the Year in 1954 and 1955 and to set career conference records in both scoring and rebounding. Greason was named Southern Conference Coach of the Year in 1953. But McKinney had clearly demonstrated his passion and his coaching prowess, and within a short time he assumed, without objections from Greason, the status of de facto head coach. Jack Murdock, who played at Wake in the mid-1950s and made the All-Conference team in

1957, later commented: "Case brought big-time basketball to the ACC but Bones McKinney brought big-time coaching."[25]

Although Duke did not duplicate Wake's feat of winning a conference championship during the decade after Case's arrival at NC State, it fielded teams that were good enough to compete with and occasionally triumph over the Wolfpack. When Eddie Cameron stepped down as Duke's basketball coach in 1942, he was replaced by his assistant, Kenneth C. "Gerry" Gerard. In eight years as head coach, Gerard compiled a record of 131–78 and won the Southern Conference championship in 1944 and 1946. In early 1949, he was diagnosed with cancer, and although he fought the disease well enough to work during the 1949–50 season, by the fall of 1950 his declining health forced him to take a leave of absence. He died at age 47 in January 1951. In light of Gerard's health problems, Cameron had hired Red Auerbach in the summer of 1949, ostensibly as a physical education instructor but in fact as a coach-in-waiting. Auerbach never felt comfortable in "a job where I was supposed to sit around and wait for Gerry to die." He left within a few months to return to professional basketball.[26]

When Gerard gave up coaching, the opening of the 1950–51 season was only a few weeks away, and Cameron had to find a replacement quickly. He soon hired Harold "Hal" Bradley, who had coached Hartwick College in Oneonta, New York, to a record of 50–18 over three years and earned a reputation as one of the best small-college coaches in the country. Cameron was impressed by Bradley's statement in a letter of application that he did not worry about dealing with the pressure that would come with the Duke job. He favored a running style of play that Cameron might have hoped would enable Duke to compete more effectively with the fast-paced game that Case used at NC State. In contrast to many of his coaching rivals, Bradley was composed and calm, even during games. Duke's student newspaper commented in 1959 that Bradley's "quiet manner and gentlemanly appearance both on and off the basketball court is a refreshing change from the crying-towel coaches who dominate the present day basketball scene."

Bradley was a little-known newcomer to the Big Four and the Southern Conference, but he benefited from inheriting a roster that included a superb junior guard, Dick Groat. During Bradley's first season, Groat averaged 25.2 points, led the nation in total points scored, and became the first Duke player to score 1,000 career points. Duke finished the season with a 20–13 record after falling to NC State in the Southern Conference semifinals. Groat was even more productive during his senior year. His scoring average increased to 26 points per game, he was second in the country in both scoring and assists, and he was named national Player of the Year. Duke's record of 24–6 included a decisive victory over NC State during the regular season, but it lost to State in the finals of the conference tournament. The following season, without Groat, Duke went 18–8. Although Duke did not win a conference title under Bradley, he proved his ability as a coach who provided tough competition for NC State. "In the days when Everett Case's State teams were beating every Dixie team in sight," Jack Williams of the *Durham Morning Herald* wrote in 1959, "Bradley didn't roll over and play dead. He didn't beat Case often, but he did it enough to make the series interesting."[27]

Duke and Wake Forest did not resort to drastic measures to try to keep pace with NC State, but the coaching of McKinney and Bradley and the talents of Hemric, Groat, and their less-heralded teammates enabled them to compete with, and sometimes defeat, Case's powerhouses. By contrast, the University of North Carolina, which had suffered greater indignities at the hands of its institutional sibling, took a major step that was clearly intended to elevate its program to State's level. In August 1952, it hired Frank McGuire, who had coached St. John's University to the finals of the NCAA Tournament the previous season. North Carolina was coming off two consecutive losing seasons during which its teams had failed even to qualify for the Southern Conference Tournament. When Tom Scott resigned as head coach, UNC supporters wanted a replacement who would challenge NC State and recapture the glory days of Tar Heel basketball. William D. "Billy" Carmichael Jr., vice president and controller of the Consolidated University, thought he knew just the man. Carmichael had been a star basketball player at North Carolina in the 1920s. He was a highly regarded administrator who had been instrumental in the selection of Gordon Gray as president and served as a close adviser. He attended the 1952 NCAA regional playoffs at Reynolds Coliseum and watched McGuire's St. John's squad upset both NC State and top-ranked Kentucky. After Scott decided to take another job, Carmichael called McGuire and told him that North Carolina "needed a coach who could compete with Everett Case" and that he believed McGuire "was the coach that could do it."[28]

Frank McGuire had lifelong roots in New York. His father, a city policeman, died when McGuire was only two years old, and he grew up in a large family where the children began working at young ages to pay the bills. He went to St. John's on a basketball scholarship and played in the first of Ned Irish's Madison Square Garden doubleheaders in 1934. After graduation, he taught English and coached basketball at St. Xavier High School, his alma

Frank McGuire (left) and Hal Bradley, 1956. (North Carolina Collection,
University of North Carolina Library at Chapel Hill)

mater, where he compiled a record of 126–39 over 11 years. In 1947, he was
unexpectedly offered the head coaching job at St. John's, where his salary
of $7,500 per year was the highest in the country. McGuire soon proved his
ability to win at the college level; his teams finished with top-10 rankings in
1950 and 1951 and played for the national championship in 1952. When approached about the North Carolina job, his initial reaction was, "Why leave
New York?" But he had been stationed in Chapel Hill during World War II
and liked the area. He also thought that living in North Carolina might provide a better environment for his son Frankie, who was born with cerebral
palsy.

With those considerations in mind, McGuire, accompanied by his
close friend Harry Gotkin, traveled to Chapel Hill for an interview. His
talks with top administrators went well, and he quickly emerged as the
leading candidate. UNC chancellor Robert B. House and Gordon Gray
had different ideas about the priorities for a new coach than Billy Car-

michael and others who hoped to break NC State's dominance. House told McGuire that "we are not out to exploit basketball." Gray was "very much impressed with [McGuire's] apparent sincerity and integrity." He was persuaded that McGuire agreed with him that "whereas we wish to have a creditable team, we are not interested in moving into bigtime, pressure basketball." The basis for Gray's misreading of McGuire's ambitions is not clear, but it smoothed the way for North Carolina to offer him the job at a salary of $9,500. McGuire soon justified the confidence that Carmichael had showed in him; he went 17–10 in his first season. More important, in his first game against Case in January 1953, North Carolina broke its 15-game losing streak against NC State with a 70–69 victory at Reynolds Coliseum. State easily won the next two games, including an 86–54 debacle in the Southern Conference Tournament. But North Carolina's improvement under McGuire's direction soon made it a formidable opponent for NC State. "I've declared open war against State College," McGuire announced in January 1954. Throughout the remainder of the 1950s, the intensity of his rivalry with Case measured up to the belligerence of his rhetoric.[29]

The only team beyond the borders of North Carolina that threatened the Big Four's ascendancy in the early years of ACC basketball was the University of Maryland. After taking over as coach in 1950, Bud Millikan turned a struggling program into a consistent winner. He had been an All-American player under Henry Iba at Oklahoma A&M, and he brought what he learned from his legendary mentor to College Park. Millikan, like Iba, emphasized disciplined offense and tenacious defense as the keys to success; he did not favor the running style of play that Case had made so popular in North Carolina. Millikan went directly from coaching a high school team in Iowa to coaching at Maryland after Iba recommended him to Athletic Director Jim Tatum. When Tatum called to invite him for an interview, Millikan had to consult an atlas to find out exactly where College Park was located. He impressed both Tatum and Curley Byrd with his assurances that he could make Maryland basketball competitive in the Southern Conference, and they offered him the job.

Millikan immediately carried out his promise. In his first season, he coached a team that had stumbled to a 7–18 record the previous year to a surprising 16–11 finish. The following season, Maryland compiled a 13–9 record and featured an outstanding sophomore guard, Gene Shue. Shue, who played high school basketball in Baltimore, had stirred little interest among college coaches and decided to attend Maryland only after his first choice, Georgetown University, declined to provide a scholarship. Millikan had no scholarships to offer, but Shue, who needed financial assistance to attend college, worked at various jobs on campus, including sweeping the floor of the basketball arena at night, to pay his way. He was such a gifted offensive player that Millikan instructed his teammates to feed him the ball. In his career at Maryland, he scored 1,386 points, a school record that stood for 20 years. He also excelled as a defender; his teammate Tom Young later recalled that when matched up against Dick Groat, Shue "gave him fits." Shue led Maryland to a 15–8 record his junior year. The following year, he averaged 21.8 points per game and was named to the All-Conference team in the ACC's inaugural season. Maryland won 23 of 30 games and was ranked in the top 20 for the first time in its history.[30]

The other three members of the ACC had some outstanding players but lacked the depth of talent to achieve parity with the Big Four and Maryland. The University of Virginia struggled to compete in the ACC. Its basketball program was hampered by limited resources, indifferent support from students and the Darden administration, and, as the Gooch report of 1951 had made clear, an abiding concern about overemphasis on athletics. Coach Evan "Bus" Male commented that playing in the ACC was like "bear hunting with a switch." Virginia joined the ACC too late to play a full conference schedule in 1953–54; it went 1–4 against league rivals and fell to Duke by the score of 96–68 in the first round of the tournament. The following season it won just 5 of 14 conference games but made a good showing in the tournament. It defeated Maryland in the first round and took Duke to overtime before losing in the semifinals. Virginia achieved a measure of respectability in the first two years of ACC competition largely because of the exceptional talent of 6′2″ guard Richard "Buzz" Wilkinson. Wilkinson used his quickness and ball-handling ability to set up a dazzling array of shots, which he made with remarkable consistency. "When you play him man-to-man, you just can't stop him and that's all there is to it," commented Gene Shue. Wilkinson averaged 30.1 points per game as a junior and 32.1 as a senior, and during his three-year varsity career scored a total of 2,233 points. He also drew sell-out crowds to Virginia home games. But his achievements could take Virginia only so far. "Despite Buzzy," *Sports Illustrated* commented, "Virginia is still way out of its class in basketball." After he graduated, both fans and victories were in short supply for many years.[31]

The University of South Carolina and Clemson College, like Virginia, found that keeping pace with the strong teams in the ACC was, at best, an imposing challenge. Although South Carolina had performed creditably

Buzz Wilkinson, 1955. (Courtesy The North Carolina State Archives; reprinted by permission of *The News and Observer* of Raleigh, North Carolina)

in its final few years in the Southern Conference, it did not fare nearly as well in the ACC. In the first three years of ACC play, its conference record was 7–31. It climbed to 5–9 in the conference and 17–12 overall in 1956–57 and advanced to the tournament finals. The major contributor to its sudden and temporary improvement was 6′4″ sharpshooter Grady Wallace. Wallace was a native of the coal mining regions of eastern Kentucky. He considered playing for Adolph Rupp but decided that he did not want to attend college in a town as large as Lexington. He wound up spending two years at nearby Pikeville Junior College, where he averaged 32.4 points per game in his second season. When his coach, Walt Hambrick, was hired as the assistant to Frank Johnson at South Carolina, Wallace enrolled at the university along with five of his teammates. During his first season, he was second in the ACC in scoring with an average of 23.9 points per game. The next year, his average of 31.2 points was the best not only in the ACC but in the entire nation. He also led the conference in rebounding. "Sure he has a

Grady Wallace shooting over Duke defenders, 1957. (Courtesy The North
Carolina State Archives; reprinted by permission of *The News and Observer*
of Raleigh, North Carolina)

weakness," observed Norm Sloan, then coaching at The Citadel. "I noticed
that he doesn't dribble too well with his left foot."[32]

Clemson athletic director and football coach Frank Howard provided
little support for the basketball program, and the results were apparent. It
lost its first 26 games after the ACC was founded and did not win for the
first time in the conference until it beat Virginia in 1956. Its overall record
in the ACC from 1953 until the end of the 1955–56 season was 1–36. The
bright spot in Clemson's disastrous ACC debut was the play of guard Bill
Yarborough. The 6′0″ guard used a set shot from long range and a running
one-hander to score an average of 28.3 points per game, second in the con-

ference to Wilkinson, in 1954–55 and 18.7 the following season. He made second team All-ACC each time. He received support from Vince Yockel, who averaged 20.9 in 1955–56 and 19.8 in 1956–57. But their efforts were not enough to lift Clemson from the depths of the ACC.[33]

Despite the increasingly fierce challenges it faced from Big Four rivals and Maryland, NC State remained the team to beat. It won the conference championship in each of the first three years of ACC competition. It finished fourth in the regular season standings during the ACC's inaugural campaign but captured the tournament by edging North Carolina and Duke and then defeating Wake Forest in overtime in the finals. Its star players were senior forward Mel Thompson (a first-team All-ACC selection), sophomore center Ronnie Shavlik, and sophomore guard Vic Molodet. Thompson, who averaged 18.6 points and used his thickset frame to grab 9.6 rebounds per game during the season, was once described by Case as the "most competitive player I ever coached." He led State with 29 points when it outlasted Wake in the tournament finals. An emotional Case told reporters: "Anytime you take on the Big Four in three successive days and win, you've done something. They're the toughest." The Wolfpack finished third in the NCAA eastern regionals after beating George Washington and falling to eventual national champion LaSalle.[34]

The following year, a deep and talented NC State team, led by Molodet and Shavlik, won both the regular season and the ACC Tournament championships. Molodet was one of many outstanding players that Case lured from Indiana. He stood 5'10" and used his extraordinary speed to attack the basket with a variety of offensive moves, ranging from a set shot from outside to drives and runners on the inside. He also had an effective hook shot, an unusual weapon for a guard. While Molodet was a small man with big-man shots, the 6'7" Shavlik was a center with the skills of a guard. He was a quick, agile big man who was an excellent passer and ran the floor exceptionally well. Shavlik grew up in Denver, where he attracted the attention of college coaches after leading his high school to two state championships and playing well against older, more experienced opponents in the national Amateur Athletic Union tournament in 1952. Bubas prevailed on a skeptical Case, who doubted that anyone from Denver would come to NC State, to recruit him. Shavlik turned down Adolph Rupp and decided on State because of Kentucky's involvement in the point-shaving scandal. During the 1954–55 season, Shavlik averaged 22.1 points and 18.1 rebounds per game, including an astonishing performance against a very good Villanova team in which he scored 49 points and pulled down 35 rebounds. State swept through the ACC Tournament with victories over Clemson, Wake Forest, and Duke. But it could not play in the NCAA tournament because it was on probation for recruiting violations. Duke represented the ACC in the national tournament and lost to Villanova in the first round.[35]

NC State's probation had ended when the 1955–56 season began, and Case's squad was rich in ability and experience. It rolled to a regular season record of 21–3 to win the conference. Shavlik broke his wrist in the final game against Wake Forest, but, even wearing a cast, managed to rebound effectively during the ACC Tournament. Molodet and the other starting guard, John Maglio, often called the "M Twins," took up the scoring slack. Maglio put up 65 points in the three games and Molodet topped him with 79. Every Big Four team was ranked in the top 20 in the country when the tournament began, but State, after struggling against Clemson, handily defeated Duke and Wake to take the title. It went to the NCAA Tournament with a ranking of number two in the country and high hopes of contending for the national championship. Instead, it suffered a shocking loss to lightly regarded Canisius College in quadruple overtime in the first round, despite Shavlik's 25 points and 17 rebounds in his final game. It was, Case said, "my greatest disappointment in 36 years in basketball."[36]

NC State and Illegal Tryouts

The loss to Canisius, however painful in the short term, was less of a blow to NC State's basketball program than severe penalties that the NCAA imposed for violations of recruiting rules. In 1954, the NCAA placed State College on probation for one year, and in 1956, it stiffened the punishment to four years of probation. As a result, the game against Canisius turned out to be State's last appearance in the NCAA Tournament during Case's coaching career.

In the wake of the point-shaving scandals and other problems that made headlines in 1951, the NCAA stepped up its enforcement activities. It did so partly in response to the revelations of serious abuses in college sports and partly in response to recommendations of the American Council on Education, an organization that represented college presidents. The council offered a series of proposals to improve control over athletic programs that were similar to the NCAA's recently scrapped Sanity Code. The NCAA, in an effort to head off the challenge to its authority, responded by announcing that it would place much greater emphasis on enforcement of its rules by investigating alleged misconduct and penalizing offenders. Unlike its earlier approach, which dictated that schools guilty of violations faced expulsion from the organization, the NCAA adopted more flexible disciplinary measures. The NCAA's Committee on Infractions had only a limited budget and a small staff, but the organization hoped that it would provide an effective and credible way of policing college athletics.[37]

On June 1, 1953, Walter Byers, the NCAA's executive director, informed Gordon Gray that there was "considerable evidence" that North Carolina State College had violated NCAA rules. He cited allegations that Case and his assistants had paid travel costs to bring high school players to visit the State College campus and had conducted tryouts for fifteen prospects. If true, those practices broke NCAA regulations approved the previous year that prohibited offering travel expenses to potential recruits and holding tryouts "at which one or more prospective students reveal, demonstrate or display their abilities in any branch of sport." In addition, Byers told Gray of accusations that State College had taken illegal steps to recruit Ronnie Shavlik, including paying his way to Raleigh for a tryout in the spring of 1952, promising to provide him three round-trips per year to his home in Denver, and supplying him with new golf clubs and golf privileges at a local country club. Byers requested Gray's "cooperation and assistance to the end that the complete facts can be developed" by answering a list of questions about the charges.[38]

Gray was dismayed but not surprised by the NCAA's investigation. "I have feared for a long time that we were sitting on top of a powder keg with respect to the basketball situation at State College," he told Billy Carmichael, "and now it appears that the fears are justified." Gray insisted that the NCAA's "very serious allegations" be promptly evaluated. "I am sure that it is unnecessary to point out to you that we must as a matter of integrity make a full disclosure of the facts," he instructed J. W. Harrelson, chancellor at State College. "I am hoping, of course, that they will not be embarrassing to us." Gray's hopes were not fulfilled. During a meeting of top administrators at State College that Harrelson called to discuss the report to the NCAA, H. A. Fisher, chairman of the faculty athletic committee, declared that with respect to paying travel expenses to prospects and holding tryouts, "we are guilty as hell." The only encouraging news was that Ronnie Shavlik forcefully denied the charges against him. He insisted that the college had not paid for his visit in 1952, that no one had held a tryout for him, and that he and his parents had borne the costs of his travel between Raleigh and Denver. He disputed the claim that he had been given golf clubs and golf privileges and revealed that he had not even played a round of golf since enrolling at State College.[39]

Case's response to the NCAA's inquiry left no doubt that he had violated rules on tryouts. He explained that State College had brought prospects to Raleigh for campus visits and scrimmages before he had taken over as coach, and that he had continued well-established practices with the knowledge and consent of the athletic council. Although alumni often provided transportation expenses, which was allowed, the college at times had paid the costs. Further, Case admitted that his assistants conducted scrimmages with players who visited campus while he "sat in the Coliseum stands and observed." Therefore, he stated, "we must candidly admit that we have not been in complete compliance with . . . the regulations of the N.C.A.A." As soon as Gray received this information, he passed it along to Byers. He also required that the coaching staffs at State College and Chapel Hill furnish their athletic directors with a monthly certification that they were acting in "complete compliance" with the rules of the ACC and the NCAA. In turn, the chancellors of each institution had to deliver the same assurances to the president of the Consolidated University. Gray made clear the importance that he attached to full compliance by stipulating that any coach who "willfully violated" conference or NCAA regulations would be "dismissed immediately."[40]

The investigation of the charges against NC State occurred as the ACC was being established, and it presented the conference with an unwelcome dilemma. On the one hand, other members of the conference also had held tryouts, and consequently, they were reluctant to punish State College for the same transgressions they had committed. On the other hand, they realized that this was a test case of the ACC's enforcement procedures. The conference had just been founded in large part as a means to provide better administrative control of athletic programs. At a meeting on August 7, 1953, representatives of ACC schools, including those from State College, agreed that there was "sufficient evidence" to show that Case had violated conference and NCAA rules on tryouts, though they did not find proof that Shavlik had received illegal inducements. Giving State College a pass for its offenses would set a bad precedent and undercut the conference's own objectives. Therefore, ACC members decided to prohibit any of the players who participated in tryouts in May 1953 from ever playing for NC State. To encourage correction of the illegal practices, they placed the college on probation for one year. This decision seemed to show that the ACC was serious about adherence to its rules without inflicting severe damage on the guilty member. Athletic Director Clogston commented that he doubted that the ACC's sanctions would "hurt us much." The NCAA concluded that the ACC's action was too lenient. In May 1954, it supported the conference's ruling that players who tried out would not be eligible at NC State, and it also placed the college on probation for one year. This meant that State could not participate in the NCAA basketball tournament in 1955. The NCAA's penalty was an unexpected blow to State College, but Gray believed that "we were dealt with very generously in this matter."[41]

The Jackie Moreland Affair

Two years later, when the NCAA again placed NC State on probation for recruiting violations, no one suggested that the college had been treated "generously." This time, the evidence against Case was much less conclusive. On October 12, 1956, the NCAA informed Carey H. Bostian, chancellor at State College, that it was conducting an investigation of offenses allegedly committed in the recruiting of Jackie Moreland, an outstanding prospect from Minden, Louisiana. Moreland was an ambidextrous 6'8" center with exceptional range, court sense, and shooting ability; he would be an ideal replacement for Ronnie Shavlik. He was an excellent student with an interest in engineering, but he had trouble deciding among the many schools that sought his talents. His decision to attend NC State was a recruiting triumph for Case and his staff. Unfortunately for them, Moreland also signed letters of intent to enroll at the University of Kentucky and at Texas A&M and made an oral commitment to attend Centenary College, which was near his home.

The NCAA requested that NC State respond to allegations that assistant coach Vic Bubas, assistant athletic director and swimming coach Willis Casey, and Harry Stewart, director of the Wolfpack Club, a booster organization, violated recruiting regulations during a trip to Moreland's home in August 1956. The NCAA claimed that the State College representatives promised Moreland $200 per year to purchase clothing, a cash payment of $1,000 per year while he was a student, and a scholarship for five years. It also charged that Moreland's girlfriend, Betty Claire Rhea, was told that the college would provide free transportation to visit Jackie and would also pay her education costs for seven years so that she could attend medical school in the Raleigh area. Finally, the NCAA accused Bubas of giving Moreland $80 so that he could travel to Raleigh to register for classes. The NCAA did not reveal its reasons for undertaking the investigation in the first place, but NC State officials believed that it resulted from a complaint by Adolph Rupp, who was resentful that Moreland had spurned his overtures. The NCAA built its case by interviewing, among others, Betty Rhea and Moreland. Walter Byers and Jim Weaver, who participated because the charges against State would also violate ACC rules, talked to Moreland in a hotel room in Raleigh on September 24, 1956, a few weeks after he enrolled at NC State. He supported some of the allegations against State College, including the most astonishing part of the indictment—the purported offer to finance a medical education for Betty Rhea. He said that he thought that Casey or Stewart, but definitely not Bubas, "told Betty that they would 'help her' attend medical school at a college near Raleigh."[42]

Bostian, who had taken over as chancellor at State College in 1954, set out immediately to determine whether the NCAA's charges were true. He was a geneticist who had joined the faculty at State in 1930. He had risen through academic ranks and was serving as the director of instruction in the School of Agriculture when he reluctantly accepted the post of chancellor. Bostian was literally a down-to-earth administrator; he was a dedicated gardener who returned to his own home to tend to his plants, fruit trees, and chickens even after moving to his official residence on campus. He was a popular figure among students and his colleagues at State College, and his priorities as chancellor were to encourage original research by the faculty and improve the school's academic standing. Bostian had lettered in track as an undergraduate, served on the athletic council at State College for five years, and supported the college's sports programs. He told Case after the loss to Canisius in 1956 that he "personally shared this grief" and that "it should be our goal to have another team as good as the one this year." But he had no illusions about the seamier side of intercollegiate athletics, especially "how corrupt recruiting was," and he was committed to finding out what had happened in State's efforts to land Jackie Moreland.[43]

Bubas, Casey, and Stewart denied the NCAA's charges. In a memorandum to Bostian, they provided a detailed account of their trip to Louisiana to recruit Moreland. The purpose of their trip was to persuade Moreland to enroll at NC State rather than the other schools to which he had made commitments. When the three men visited the Moreland home in Minden on August 29, 1956, Jackie and his parents agreed that he would attend State College. Bubas, Casey, and Stewart told Bostian that they made no promises "in the way of excess aid, travel, clothes, unrestricted scholarships, money, or any other illicit offers." The following morning, to their exasperation, Moreland and Betty Rhea came to their hotel and announced that "Jackie was not going to N. C. State College." Rhea then talked at length about "their love affair, her plans, Jackie's future, and her feelings on where Jackie should attend school." She wanted Jackie to attend Centenary, where she was going. When the dumfounded NC State representatives made another visit to Moreland's home, his mother was "very disturbed, and very apologetic." Later that day, Jackie and his family once again decided that he would attend State, and they "were all of the opinion that the sooner he left the better." He flew to Raleigh the next day to take an entrance examination, and Bubas insisted that he had not provided money for plane fare. He and his colleagues emphasized that they made no illegal offers of aid to Moreland and no promises of a scholarship, financial aid, clothes, or travel expenses to Betty Rhea.[44]

On October 18, 1956, Moreland, by that time a student at NC State, supported the account of Bubas, Casey, and Stewart in an interview with Bostian. He signed a statement in which he affirmed that neither he nor, "to his knowledge," Rhea were promised gifts or illegal incentives. He was aware that his statements "might not exactly coincide" with what he had told Byers and Weaver three weeks earlier. Moreland explained that when he met with them, he had not had lunch or dinner and in his haste to end the interview, "initialed several pages of which I cannot definitely recall the contents in full." He added: "I was very tired at the time and would have signed anything to get away from the Hotel and the type of questioning that I was being subjected to." Based on the testimony he received from the principal participants in the Moreland case, Bostian told the NCAA that it "is our belief that North Carolina State College has not violated any regulations of the Atlantic Coast Conference and/or the NCAA."[45]

The NCAA was not convinced. On November 13, 1956, it announced that NC State would be placed on probation for four years, the stiffest punishment it had ever imposed on any member. The unprecedented magnitude of the penalty reflected not only the NCAA's findings in the Moreland case but also the fact the State College had only recently gotten off its previous probation. To make matters worse, the newly ordered probation applied not only to basketball but to every other sport. This meant that State's football team could not play in bowl games and that athletes in so-called minor sports could not compete in NCAA events. Dick Fadgen, for example, an All-American swimmer who had won NCAA titles in two events in 1956, would be ineligible to defend his championships or to have any records that he might set in ACC meets recognized by the NCAA. The harshness and sweeping scope of the NCAA's action came as a stunning blow to administrators, athletes, and fans. William Friday, who had replaced Gray as president of the Consolidated University, issued a statement in which he reminded the NCAA that it had "commended the College for its directness and forthrightness" in responding to the charges against Case two years earlier. But this time the college's own inquiry had produced no evidence of violations, and therefore, "on the basis of the information furnished to us by the NCAA to date we cannot understand the probation decision."[46]

The shock of the NCAA's action was compounded in December 1956 when the ACC decided to impose its own penalties. Bostian had requested that the conference perform an investigation of the charges as a means of resolving the wide discrepancies between the NCAA's findings and his own conclusions. The NCAA refused to provide the evidence that it used to establish NC State's guilt without conditions that Bostian and Friday regarded as unacceptable. Byers said that Friday could examine the files on the Moreland case if he traveled to NCAA headquarters in Kansas City and agreed to keep the information he collected confidential. The stand-off between the NCAA and State College placed Bostian and Friday in an extremely awkward position. In 1953, in response to Case's violations of recruiting restrictions, Gordon Gray had decided that any staff member who "clearly" broke NCAA or ACC rules would be fired. Bostian did not believe that State College's guilt in the Moreland affair had been categorically demonstrated, and he apparently hoped that the ACC would offer support for his views. The conference, however, rejected his arguments. On December 15, 1956, Commissioner Weaver, drawing on interviews with Moreland, Bubas, Casey, and Stewart, wired Bostian that he and the faculty representatives of other ACC schools had determined that NC State had violated league regulations. Therefore, he declared that Moreland was ineligible to play at State, prohibited the basketball staff from contacting "any prospective athlete" for one year, and fined the college $5,000, the maximum allowed by the conference.[47]

Weaver based his decision on two alleged infractions: (1) that Moreland received $80 for transportation from his home to Raleigh, and (2) that Bubas had promised him a fifth year of scholarship assistance if he needed the extra time to graduate. Bostian told Friday that both charges were fallacious. He explained that the $80 was given to Moreland by an NC State supporter to take an admission test, which was permissible, and not to enroll as a student, which was forbidden. Further, he denied that Bubas had made an offer of a five-year scholarship. Bostian conceded that Moreland might have inferred this from a conversation in which Bubas told him that some athletes were granted financial assistance for an additional year if they were enrolled in demanding academic programs that took longer to complete. But he had made no commitments. Further, this conversation had taken place after Moreland registered at State College, and not, as the NCAA maintained, as an inducement for him to attend. Consequently, Bostian appealed Weaver's decision and requested that the ACC conduct "an independent and complete investigation." In February 1957, the faculty chairmen who considered the appeal reaffirmed their earlier decision, though they reduced the fine to $2,500. Bostian announced that he was "deeply disappointed," but that in the absence of conclusive evidence, he would not make a "sacrificial offering" of the accused staff members in order to placate the NCAA and the ACC.[48]

After the ACC made its final ruling, NC State had no further recourse and had to accept, however grudgingly, the decisions of the conference and the NCAA. But the important question that remained to be resolved was whether the staff members whom the two organizations had found guilty of serious offenses should be fired. This was an issue that Bostian and Friday did not take lightly. They had not seen clear evidence of wrongdoing on the part of the staff members directly involved in the Moreland affair or Case, who was one step removed from the accusations but still was an unindicted presence in the deliberations. At one point, the NCAA had offered to reduce the penalties against State College if Case were dismissed. Bostian and Friday recognized that, despite their own assessment of the charges, the NCAA's committee on infractions and the ACC's faculty representatives had determined, presumably in a fair way, that NC State had committed violations that justified severe penalties.

The efforts by Bostian and Friday to reach a proper, or at least a defensible, decision were made more difficult by contradictory statements from Betty Rhea and Moreland. In December 1956, Rhea, who was a freshman at Centenary, publicly supported one of the NCAA's principal accusations. She told the *News and Observer* that Willis Casey had offered her a "seven-year medical education" during the trip that he made with Bubas and Stewart the previous August. She added that she had turned down the offer "because I wouldn't take anything like that. If I want to go to medical school, my parents can send me." A short time later, Moreland gave a sworn statement that was dramatically different from Rhea's comments. He testified that the NC State representatives had not offered Rhea a medical education or made any other promises of illegal assistance during their visit to

Louisiana. Two weeks later, however, Moreland changed his story. On February 10, 1957, he advised Walter Byers that his original statements to the NCAA had been correct. He claimed that he had supplied conflicting information that denied illegal inducements after Bubas and Casey suggested that this could "get me eligible and get [NC State] off probation and I could play ball." By that time, Moreland had transferred to the Louisiana Polytechnic Institute near Shreveport. The school's athletic director, Joe Aillet, accompanied him on his visit to Byers, perhaps to pave the way for the NCAA to restore Moreland's eligibility.[49]

The final decision on the fate of the NC State coaches rested with President Friday. He had been selected as president of the Consolidated University on October 18, 1956, at the age of 36. Friday grew up in Dallas, North Carolina, near Gastonia, where he was an outstanding student and a star catcher in highly competitive baseball leagues that textile mills in the area sponsored. His father was a salesman and later an executive in the textile machinery business, and as a result of the Great Depression, his family's income had declined drastically during the 1930s. With the assistance of a $50 scholarship, Friday enrolled at Wake Forest College in 1937. He stayed for only one year and then transferred to NC State, where, at the urging of his father, he majored in textiles. He did not particularly enjoy his textiles courses, and he found the many extracurricular activities in which he participated much more satisfying. He was sports editor of the school newspaper and president of his class during his senior year. He was well-known and well-liked by the student body at State College for his efforts to improve campus life and for his genuine friendliness, good judgment, and unassuming manner.

Friday joined the U.S. Navy shortly after Pearl Harbor and spent most of the war as the plant operations manager of a munitions factory near Norfolk, Virginia. After the war, he attended law school at the University of North Carolina. When he finished in 1948, he planned to combine his undergraduate training and his law degree to work in the textiles industry. Instead, he accepted a job as assistant dean of students at Chapel Hill, which he was offered on the strong recommendation of a former mentor at State College. In that position, he earned the admiration of top administrators of the Consolidated University, including Billy Carmichael and Frank Porter Graham. After Graham resigned as president, Carmichael urged his replacement, Gordon Gray, to hire Friday as his administrative assistant. Although at first Friday carried out largely routine duties, he gradually gained Gray's respect and took on increasing responsibilities. Friday was viewed throughout the university as the "friendly side" of the president's office. His warmth contrasted with Gray's stiff and formal manner, and Friday was the one "who met the people at the front door." A few months after Gray resigned in 1955, Friday became acting president, largely because Carmichael was ill and the first person selected was ineffective. He did not expect to be chosen to succeed Gray, but as acting president he won favorable recognition for handling some delicate problems with skill and tact. The Board of Trustees, despite reservations about his lack of experience and scholarly credentials, eventually decided to award him the job. Friday was named president just as the Jackie Moreland investigation was emerging as an issue of major importance for NC State and the Consolidated University.[50]

Before the Moreland case, Friday later commented, "I had never in my life . . . gotten into anything that was as perplexing, and as bothersome to me as that episode. Simply because I couldn't find out the truth." He was forced to make a decision on a matter in which the stakes were high and the evidence available to him was ambiguous. It came down to a question of whether to believe Moreland, who had provided conflicting accounts, and Betty Rhea, who wanted Jackie to stay in Louisiana, or whether to believe the State College staff members whose jobs and perhaps careers were on the line. Friday was enormously frustrated that the NCAA would not provide him with the evidence it had collected on an unconditional basis so that he could make an informed judgment. "The NCAA acted as judge, jury, prosecutor, and that was it," he later complained. "You had to abide by what they said." At one point during the Moreland proceedings, an NCAA investigator who happened to be in Chapel Hill called Friday and asked to meet him clandestinely on Franklin Street at the edge of campus. The individual reported in a very brief conversation that Friday "was not being told the truth" by the State College coaches. But he provided nothing conclusive.

Friday took the warnings of the NCAA official seriously and viewed the charges against NC State as plausible. He was surely aware of Gray's suspicions that Case's practices over the years had placed NC State and the Consolidated University "on top of a powder keg." But he refused to fire Case or the others without more substantive documentation than the NCAA and the ACC supplied. He reached this position in part because he objected to the NCAA's procedures and in part because he knew that discharging Case would arouse the ire of NC State supporters and probably some members of the Board of Trustees. Removing a popular and successful coach would be an improbable step for any college president to take without persuasive evidence and even more so for one who had not yet been officially installed. Friday later recalled that he asked Byers, "How do you expect me to fire somebody, if all I can say is, 'I hear from the NCAA you've done these things.'" Therefore, in February 1957, he endorsed Bostian's recommendation that "we consider the Moreland case closed . . . and begin our efforts to maintain our athletic programs under the handicaps imposed upon us by the NCAA and our own Conference." The Board of Trustees supported this decision a short time later.[51]

After months of controversy, the Moreland affair came to an inconclusive and generally unsatisfactory end. Friday, who spent "weeks, and weeks, and weeks, almost all of the time I had, trying to straighten this thing out," finally threw up his hands. "I got a bucket of whitewash, painted over the whole mess, and called it concluded," he later lamented. Both he and Bostian regarded the NCAA's penalties as a serious blemish on State College's reputation. The sanctions sent a message "all over the country," Friday remarked, "that here was a problem campus." Bostian told a correspondent that "great harm has . . . been done to our prestige."[52]

Case, Bubas, and Casey presumably were relieved not to be fired, but the basketball program suffered a major setback. The loss of Moreland, whom Case described as "one of the greatest prospects [he had] ever seen," was hard to accept. "I'm getting damn tired of all the charges," Case grumbled. "They're splitting hairs, grasping at technicalities." Even after suffering the wrath of the NCAA, Case exhibited a cavalier attitude toward the Consolidated University's requirement that coaches certify that they fully complied with NCAA and ACC regulations. In 1959, to Bostian's irritation, Case noted on the form he signed: "Have not read all of the rules and regulations [of] the NCAA and ACC, and do not understand all the rules and regulations." Bostian instructed Athletic Director Clogston to make certain that Case learned all the rules "so that there can be no doubt about our complying" with them.[53]

Moreland made one appearance in an NC State uniform before he was declared ineligible and memorably displayed his talents. In an annual matchup between the freshman team and the varsity, he scorched the upper classmen for 30 points in limited playing time. Moreland was a victim, though not necessarily an entirely innocent one, of the recruiting battles to win his talents. As Dick Herbert suggested in his column in the *News and Observer*, "If anyone has been made the 'goat' of the case it has been Moreland. He has now been portrayed to the nation as a young man who plays loosely with the truth." In an article published in *Sport* magazine in

1957, Furman Bisher, a prominent sportswriter, contended that "there will always be a mental asterisk after Jackie's name. . . . It's an unjust destiny for the boy, for he is a by-product of the harsh mill of college recruiting." Bisher observed, however, that Moreland had quickly "picked up some pretty worldly advice on the matter of how to be recruited." Texas A&M coach Ken Loeffler reported that Moreland had asked what rewards he could expect, such as "an automobile, or something like that," if he agreed to attend the school. Shortly after departing from NC State and returning to Louisiana, Moreland and Betty Rhea broke up. He became a star at Louisiana Tech and made small college All-American teams. He did not receive the same level of recognition as players in big-time programs, but he won the attention of professional scouts. He was the fourth player selected in the first round of the 1960 National Basketball Association draft, and he went on to have a solid career in eight years as a professional.[54]

Case's Last Championship

After Moreland left NC State, the outlook for Case's team became even gloomier when two other prize recruits transferred to schools that were not saddled with four years of probation. "We sure have taken a beating in this Moreland case," Clogston confided to a friend in February 1957. "Basketball is at a low ebb." But he also suggested that "our material is not quite as bad as many would think." Clogston's appraisal proved to be correct. State had finished the 1956–57 season with a 15–11 record, the worst showing since Case arrived. The prospects did not look good the following year; Case described his 1957–58 squad as "thin as a dime and about as tall as a Shetland pony." To make matters worse, Whitey Bell, the team's only senior starter and its leading scorer, was tossed out of school during the season for cheating on a test. Nevertheless, State's team, led by juniors John Richter and Lou Pucillo, finished with a record of 10–4 in the ACC and 18–6 overall.[55]

Richter, a 6′8″ center from Philadelphia, was a rugged rebounder and an effective inside scorer. He was second in the ACC with 10.8 rebounds per game and averaged 12.3 points during the 1957–58 season. Richter was a hardworking student who excelled in nuclear engineering. Pucillo, the other half of what *Life* magazine called a "Mutt-and-Jeff pair," had a different kind of game. He was a 5′9″ guard, the shortest player Case ever signed to a scholarship, who delighted fans and flustered opponents with his dribbling and passing skills. *Sports Illustrated* described him as "one of the smallest men . . . in college ball and one of the best." He also had "every

Lou Pucillo (20) passes behind his back to a waiting John Richter as North Carolina's Lee Shaffer (12) and Doug Moe (35) watch with what appears to be amazement, 1959. (Courtesy The North Carolina State Archives; reprinted by permission of *The News and Observer* of Raleigh, North Carolina)

shot in the book" and averaged 15.7 points per game in 1957–58, fourth highest in the conference.[56]

Before enrolling at State, Pucillo had not been a highly touted prospect. He had been cut from his high school team in Philadelphia as a freshman and a sophomore and had been so discouraged that he did not try out as a junior. He made the team as a senior but was not a starter and averaged about 4 points per game. After Pucillo graduated, he took some courses at a local prep school where his father taught and joined its basketball team. He demonstrated enough ability and flair that Bubas, on an extended recruiting trip to Philadelphia, heard about his talents. He attended a game in which the opponent was the Philadelphia School for the Deaf and Mute, and liked what he saw. Bubas called Case and told him that he thought that they could sign Pucillo because none of the colleges in the Philadelphia area were interested. He also suggested that Pucillo's skills would force

Case to change his coaching philosophy, which did not favor guards who threw flashy passes. Case was skeptical. "Let me get something straight," he queried. "You saw this Pucillo [play] against a deaf and mute team — and nobody in Philadelphia wants him, and you want me to take him?" Bubas replied, "That's right." Case continued: "You're telling me that [Pucillo] dribbles behind his back, throws fancy, blind passes, and you want me to change the way I coach?" This sounded so farfetched that he followed with what seemed a reasonable question: "Bubas, have you been drinking?" But Case relented. "Okay, I'll take him," he said, "but Bubas, you better be right."[57]

Bubas turned out to be right. After his outstanding performance as a junior, Pucillo topped it as a senior. He averaged 14.7 points per game and, among other awards, was named ACC Player of the Year. Richter led the conference in both scoring and rebounding and finished second to Pucillo in the voting for Player of the Year. During the 1958–59 season, NC State won the celebrated Dixie Classic of 1958 and tied North Carolina for first place in the regular ACC season with a 12–2 record. It then defeated South Carolina, Virginia, and heavily favored North Carolina in an 80–56 rout to win the tournament championship. The outcome was bittersweet because State could not advance to the NCAA Tournament, but it was a remarkable achievement nevertheless. In the wake of the demoralizing four-year probation and loss of talent after the Moreland affair, State's players and coaches rallied against the odds to extend a championship tradition. In that regard, Case's last championship was his most satisfying. Before the tournament finals, he told Dick Herbert that if State upset North Carolina, "this will be the greatest season I ever had."[58]

From the first championship that Case won at NC State in 1947 until his final conference title in 1959, his success increased fan interest, intensified rivalries, and elevated the caliber of competition in the Southern Conference and then the ACC. He laid the foundations for sustained excellence and bitter contention that made ACC basketball a riveting spectacle from the time the conference was founded. Case's promotional genius, aggressive recruiting, and winning traditions forced his Big Four counterparts to respond. The efforts of Duke, Wake Forest, and especially North Carolina to keep up with NC State commanded rapt attention among local fans and media, and increasingly, among a wider audience as well. The growing parity among Big Four rivals and their aspirations for national recognition also created more pressure to win. One regrettable result was that Case's violations of NCAA and ACC rules, both admitted and alleged, tarnished his program and damaged the reputation of the school he represented. Unfortunately, NC State's woes did not end with the probation it endured in the late 1950s, and, along with archrival North Carolina, it soon faced even more harrowing trials. Case's powerful influence on the development of ACC basketball was a mixed blessing; it brought the excitement and glamour of big-time basketball to North Carolina, but it also brought greater incentive to win at any cost.

4

A CHAMPIONSHIP WON,
A CLASSIC LOST

On March 1, 1957, after defeating Duke in Durham, Frank McGuire's North Carolina Tar Heels finished their regular season schedule unbeaten and ranked number one in the country. But their record did not assure them of a chance to play for the NCAA championship because they still had to win the ACC Tournament. McGuire was outspoken in objecting to the ACC's method of choosing its NCAA representative. He described it as a "ridiculous" system because "the regular season games in this conference are meaningless." McGuire's views were shared by other conference coaches; Maryland's Bud Millikan called the ACC's rule on the primacy of the tournament a "farce." He contended that the regular season winner should go to the NCAA Tournament because "after struggling through the 14-game conference schedule," it was "more representative as the conference champion." Those arguments did not persuade conference officials or athletic directors to change the system by awarding the automatic NCAA berth to the regular season champion, as most coaches preferred. Nevertheless, North Carolina's dominance of the regular conference season in

1956–57 made the dissenting position more prominent, and for many, more sensible. Dick Pierce, sports editor of the *Charlotte Observer*, put the matter in stark terms when he wrote in March 1957 that the ACC sponsored "the basketball tournament which has everything—except a convincing reason for existence." The 1957 tournament highlighted the excitement, intensity, pressures, animosities, and virtuosity of ACC basketball. In the end, despite McGuire's complaints, it launched North Carolina on the road to a national championship.[1]

When the ACC was formed in 1953, it had continued, without a great deal of discussion, the Southern Conference's tradition of holding a postseason tournament to determine the league champion. The ACC's bylaws specified that the tournament champion would "be nominated for the NCAA tournament"; they did not officially designate the team that swept the ACC Tournament as the "conference champion" until 1961. But the tournament winner was regarded as the ACC champion, even without the formal declaration, from the time the league was established. The tournament was played at Reynolds Coliseum from 1954 through 1966, and although it was a well-attended event from the outset, it was not a complete sellout before 1965. The first tournament in 1954 drew a total attendance of 39,200 for four sessions and only the semifinals attracted a capacity crowd. Fans paid either $9 or $6 for a seat at all the games. The tournament appealed to fans not only for the high stakes in the competition between bitter rivals but also for the social events that were a popular complement to the games.[2]

Supporters of the tournament acknowledged that it could deny deserving teams an NCAA berth, but they emphasized both its financial and competitive advantages. NC State athletic director Roy Clogston pointed out that the tournament cleared enough profit to cover the annual expenses of the conference; in 1956, for example, it contributed about $80,000 to the league's treasury. He might have added that this money would otherwise have come from assessments of member schools. He insisted that "it would be foolish to think of changing the present tournament format." Duke athletic director Eddie Cameron agreed with Clogston and stressed the excitement the tournament created among fans. He told ACC sportswriters on March 8, 1957, that the "tournament has built up basketball in our area; we want to keep it going up." Bones McKinney, one of the few coaches who spoke in favor of the tournament, cited the opportunity it provided for conference teams to redeem a disappointing regular season. "They all have a chance of winning," he said, "even after they may have had a bad season."[3]

Most ACC coaches were not convinced by those arguments. The *Char-*

lotte Observer's Pierce reported that when McGuire aired his complaints about the tournament, "six other ACC skippers will echo the sentiment when money-conscious athletic directors are out of earshot." Millikan asserted that the rigors of winning the conference title hurt the chances of ACC teams to perform at their peak ability in the NCAA Tournament. "Take the last two years as an example," he said in March 1957. "State, which won the tournament last year, was a much better team than they showed in losing to Canisius and two years ago Duke was a much better team than it demonstrated in losing to Villanova. Both were tired from the three games in the [ACC] tournament."[4]

In the midst of a serious but low-key debate in 1957 about the merits of the ACC's system, North Carolina sought to preserve its unblemished record and advance to the NCAA Tournament. It was heavily favored to win the title, but its coaches, players, and fans were keenly aware that one bad game could shatter their hopes for NCAA glory. North Carolina had survived several close calls against conference opponents during the regular season, including an overtime victory over South Carolina in Columbia, a double overtime triumph over Maryland in College Park, and a two-point win over Duke in Chapel Hill. It was especially wary of Wake Forest, the only other ACC team ranked in the top 20, whom it had beaten three times in tight games (once in the Dixie Classic and twice during the regular season). For Wake, competing against North Carolina was a labor of hate; its players made no secret of their intense antipathy toward McGuire's squad. Their attitude reflected the feelings of their head coach, Murray Greason, who had run up the score in routing North Carolina by 21 points during the semifinals of the 1956 tournament. When assistant coach McKinney had suggested resting the starters for the finals after the outcome was assured, Greason, who normally displayed little emotion on the bench, allowed his ill will toward McGuire to cloud his judgment. He exclaimed, "I've got that SOB where I want him and I'm going to beat the hell out of him!"[5]

The first round of the 1957 ACC Tournament went according to expectations, with one exception. South Carolina, led by Grady Wallace's 41 points, pulled off a mild surprise by upsetting Duke. North Carolina dismissed Clemson, and Maryland edged Virginia. Wake defeated NC State, 66–57, the first loss that Everett Case had ever suffered in an ACC Tournament game. The *News and Observer* reported that "except for creating an impression of over-joviality, Case appeared adjusted to his strange role." The results of the opening day's action produced a second-round matchup between North Carolina and Wake Forest.[6]

Wake brought an overall record of 18–8 to the tournament, but it was seeded fourth because it was only 7–7 in the conference. Its coaches and players welcomed another shot at North Carolina, and in view of the near-misses of the first three games, believed they had a good chance of ending their rival's season. Wake had a veteran team led by seniors Jack Williams, Jim Gilley, Ernie Wiggins, and Jack Murdock. Williams, a 6'3" forward who had returned to the team as a junior after spending two years in the army, was the top scorer (16.2 points per game) and rebounder (8.2 per game). Gilley was a 6'6" center who averaged 13.1 points and 8.0 boards per game. Wiggins was a 6'0" guard who averaged 12.8 points per game and led the nation with a foul-shooting percentage of .877. He worked so well with Murdock, who played the other guard position, that McKinney called them "Karo" and "Syrup." Murdock, who stood 5'10", scored 15.3 points per game and finished second in the nation to Wiggins with a free-throw percentage of .875. McKinney later described Murdock as "one of the greatest competitors I had ever seen." He added: "Jack just never made a mistake on the basketball court. He passed the ball to the right person, moved the ball well, never took a bad shot, and was always at the right spot on the court."[7]

While Wake's coaches and players looked forward to battling North Carolina again, McGuire fretted about the difficulty of defeating them for a fourth time. He recognized that a "bounce of the ball" had determined the outcome in at least two of the previous games, and he worried that the ball would bounce the wrong way in the fourth meeting. North Carolina's starters were a group of tough and talented New Yorkers who were among the first recruits to emigrate to Chapel Hill on McGuire's "underground railroad." One guard, 5'10" Tommy Kearns, had been an offensive standout in high school who gradually accepted McGuire's admonitions to look to pass before shooting. The other guard was 6'4" Bob Cunningham, who was exceptionally tall for his position and used his height to excel as a defender and a rebounder. He was not a consistent offensive threat, in part because of an injury to his hand that limited his ability to grip the ball. The team's center was Joe Quigg, who stood 6'9" and averaged 10.3 points and 8.6 rebounds. He had been one of the top high school players in New York, and his decision to attend UNC was a key to convincing several of his future teammates to sign with McGuire. One forward was 6'6" Pete Brennan, who had a deadly shot from the corner and posted an average of 14.7 points and 10.4 rebounds. The star of the team was 6'5" Lennie Rosenbluth, who was a superb scorer with an all-but-unstoppable hook shot and a delicate touch on jumpers or set shots out to 20 feet. During the 1956–57 season, he scored

28 points per game and collected an average of 8.8 rebounds. When North Carolina needed a basket in a tight game, McGuire's strategy was usually quite simple and predictable: "Get the ball to Rosie." The team's most glaring weakness was a lack of depth, and McGuire used his bench sparingly.[8]

Before the tournament game between North Carolina and Wake, neither coach felt that a fiery pep talk was required to inspire his players. McGuire was a masterful motivator, but his squad needed no reminder of the beating they had taken from Wake in the 1956 tournament. Both teams were keenly aware of the stakes involved in their fourth meeting. When McKinney walked out on the floor, he felt as if he "had been through a wringer . . . and the game hadn't even started." He had concocted a special 1–1–3 defense in which he put one man between Rosenbluth and the ball, one man in front of him, and one man behind him. The purpose was "to deny Rosenbluth the ball at all times."

Once the game began, it turned into the intensely hard-fought contest that the sell-out crowd of 12,400 anticipated. North Carolina rushed to a 22–11 lead, but Wake, behind Williams and Murdock, narrowed the gap to 33–29 by halftime. McGuire made an important adjustment in the second half by assigning Cunningham to cover Murdock, and he kept the Wake guard from scoring any field goals in the final twenty minutes. The game remained close throughout the half. While Greason watched with ostensible calm, McKinney was a "whirling dervish" who "jumped, ran, tossed towels, and sweated off [his] customary ten pounds." The 1–1–3 zone was fairly effective against Rosenbluth, but it placed Wake at a severe rebounding disadvantage. During the second half, after Wake switched to a man-to-man defense, Rosenbluth hit several shots from outside and wound up with 23 points for the game. With 2:17 remaining, North Carolina led 58–53. Wake responded with two quick baskets, and a charging foul on Cunningham put center Jim Gilley on the line. As he was preparing to shoot, McKinney told Murdock to go back to the 1–1–3, and Murdock passed the word to all his teammates on the floor except Gilley. Wake's practice was to avoid distracting a teammate who was shooting free throws, and these were shots that could make or break its season. Gilley, who hit 72.5 percent of his foul shots during the year, sank both ends of the one-and-one to put Wake ahead 59–58 with 55 seconds to go.

With the fans standing and roaring, Wake fell back into its zone, but Gilley stayed with his own man. This left Rosenbluth open to receive a pass around the key, and his teammates found him immediately. Wake reserve Wendell Carr recognized what had happened and moved quickly to pick

Tommy Kearns drives against Jack Murdock in the ACC Tournament semifinal game between North Carolina and Wake Forest, 1957. (North Carolina Collection, University of North Carolina Library at Chapel Hill)

up Rosenbluth. In an instant, Rosenbluth took a dribble, put up a hook shot from the foul line, and collided with Carr. A whistle blew as the ball swished cleanly through the net. Referee Jim Mills had a very tough call that could have gone either way. If he ruled that Rosenbluth had charged, Wake had the ball and the lead. If he called a block on Carr, the basket counted and Rosenbluth went to the line. As the crowd grew silent and each team held its breath, Mills signaled a foul on Carr. Rosenbluth made the free throw, and Ernie Wiggins missed a shot that would have tied the game. Final score: North Carolina 61, Wake Forest 59. It was, wrote Dick Herbert, "one of the great tournament games of them all."[9]

The next evening, North Carolina faced South Carolina, which had followed up on its first win ever in an ACC Tournament with a victory over

Maryland in the semifinals. The Tar Heels won easily, 95–75, and Rosen-bluth outscored fellow All-American Grady Wallace, 38–28. The 1957 ACC Tournament strongly reinforced the arguments that supporters had made in the debate over the conference's method of choosing its NCAA representative. The tournament drew about 46,000 fans, who witnessed several exciting games and the nail-biting classic between North Carolina and Wake. It cleared a tidy profit for the league's coffers. It provided an opportunity for an underdog to advance to the finals, offer its fans unaccustomed thrills, and take satisfaction in its performance. South Carolina coach Frank Johnson commented after the loss to North Carolina: "I think my team has done very well this season. We had no idea in December we'd even get to the finals of the ACC tournament." Despite the complaints of many coaches about the drawbacks of the ACC Tournament, the best team in the conference earned the league's NCAA bid. And McGuire expressed confidence that the burdens of winning the ACC Tournament would not harm his team's prospects in competing for the national championship. "Good athletes never get tired," he said after capturing the title. "They could play another game right now if they had to."[10]

McGuire and His Underground Railroad

By his fourth season as head coach at North Carolina, McGuire, as Billy Carmichael had hoped, had achieved at least parity with Everett Case. Indeed, as Case was suffering through the Jackie Moreland investigations in 1956–57 and facing four years of NCAA probation, North Carolina was dominating the ACC. McGuire gained the gratitude and affection of UNC students and fans, who raised money for and presented him with a new blue-and-white Cadillac in February 1957, even before his team captured the ACC championship. The gift won the approval of the *Charlotte News*, which did not "begrudge Mr. McGuire a single cylinder of his prize" but regretted that faculty members did not receive similar recognition. "We are just stuffy enough to believe that the social sciences, say, are every bit as important as dribbling and free throws," it commented. McGuire's success at North Carolina, *Sports Illustrated* observed in December 1957, made him "Dixie's favorite Yankee."[11]

McGuire brought a lot of other Yankees to Chapel Hill to play basketball. As soon as he arrived at North Carolina, he began to attract talented players from northern New Jersey and New York City. "I knew all of the high school coaches in New York and the style of play they coached—which was similar to mine," McGuire said in explaining his recruiting success in the New York area. "I use five or six scholarships each year. I make sure the kids receiving them are topnotchers. If they come from New York, well, they come from New York." He was convinced that he knew how to capitalize on the skills of the players he recruited from his hometown, many of whom were Roman Catholic or Jewish. "There are ways to motivate Jewish players and Italian players," he commented. "I know how to get them mad and how to get the most out of them." McGuire had no illusions that "boys from the City can run any faster or jump any higher than others." But, he added, "I understand them better, and what is even more important is they understand me." The path from New York to Chapel Hill quickly became known as McGuire's "underground railroad." The *New York World Telegram and Sun* ran a cartoon showing basketball players emerging from the New York subway at a station on the University of North Carolina campus.[12]

McGuire's efforts to recruit in New York benefited greatly from the assistance of his old friend Harry Gotkin. Gotkin was one of several self-appointed talent scouts who offered information to college coaches about promising high school players in the New York area. He was a baby bonnet manufacturer who spent much of his spare time at high school games and all-star tournaments. He was a knowledgeable judge of talent who loved basketball and admired Frank McGuire. He was not paid by the University of North Carolina for his labors, though McGuire provided entertainment expenses that Gotkin accrued while talking to potential recruits. Gotkin had once performed similar services for Everett Case, but he switched allegiances because of his loyalty to McGuire and because he thought that Case had underestimated the ability of his nephew, Dave Gotkin, who played two seasons at NC State. Harry Gotkin denied that he made any illicit offers to prospective players. "Look, I just speak to a kid. I talk North Carolina to him," he said. "I arrange for the kid to see Carolina's campus at Chapel Hill. . . . Somebody takes him over to Raleigh to see North Carolina State's campus with the railroad running through it. That makes up the kid's mind."[13]

Gotkin was instrumental in a train of events that led Lennie Rosenbluth to North Carolina. Rosenbluth had been a late bloomer as a high school player in New York. He failed tryouts for his school's basketball team as a sophomore and again as a junior. He made the squad as a senior, but the season was cut short by a coaches' strike that lasted for two years. Rosenbluth developed his skills on playgrounds and as a member of an outstanding YMCA team coached by Gotkin's cousin Hy. When he com-

peted against professional and college players in a summer league in Catskill Mountain resorts, he impressed college scouts and other observers with
his offensive talents.

By that time, Rosenbluth had attracted the attention of Harry Gotkin,
who advised him to attend NC State. In April 1952, Rosenbluth traveled to
Raleigh for a campus visit. To his surprise, he found himself in a tryout with
about one hundred other prospects, and he did not perform well. Case told
Rosenbluth that he did not want to "waste" his one remaining scholarship
on him. There were also academic problems that interfered with Rosenbluth's interest in State. Case examined Rosenbluth's transcript and determined that "it would be impossible for him to gain entrance" at NC State,
partly because his grades were low and partly because he had not graduated
from high school.[14]

After Case's brush-off, Gotkin contacted McGuire, who was still at St.
John's and who was much impressed with Rosenbluth's potential. McGuire
was then considering leaving St. Johns, and Rosenbluth liked him so well
that he told him: "No matter where you go, I'll go with you." Rosenbluth attended the Staunton Military Academy in Virginia for a year to earn his di-
ploma and improve his academic qualifications. He arrived at North Carolina in 1953 as a 20-year-old freshman who was, as McGuire put it, "like
a man playing among boys." His circuitous path to playing for McGuire
instead of Case proved to be a major turning point in North Carolina's
efforts to challenge NC State's control of the ACC. McGuire later remarked
that "Rosenbluth was the first big recruit in our building program." His
skills and the addition of a strong recruiting class the following year provided "the depth and quality of talent we needed to take our team to the
next level," McGuire said. "And that level was to move us ahead of State in
the ACC."[15]

Gotkin and McGuire were an effective combination in recruiting players
for North Carolina. Gotkin laid the foundations by selling prospects on the
advantages of the university and the virtues of Frank McGuire. After he
piqued their interest, McGuire used his outsized charm and charisma to
close the deal. Pete Brennan was one of the best players in New York as a
high school senior, and Gotkin made a good case for the academic and athletic benefits of attending North Carolina. But Brennan's parents were first-
generation Irish immigrants, and his father strongly favored Notre Dame.
When McGuire visited the family, dressed in an expensive suit, he exuded
charm and assured Brennan's father that he would make certain that Pete
went to mass every Sunday. Once McGuire left, Pete's father told him that

he could go to whichever college he chose. As a student at North Carolina, Brennan recalled, he went to mass every Sunday and never once saw McGuire there.[16]

McGuire's natural affability was an enormous asset in his recruiting efforts. In 1964, shortly after he accepted the coaching job at the University of South Carolina, he made his pitch to Brendan McCarthy, a highly recruited two-sport star who played basketball for Hall of Fame coach Morgan Wootten at DeMatha High School in Hyattsville, Maryland. When McGuire went to the player's home for the first time on a recruiting visit, McCarthy's mother answered the door. McGuire greeted her by saying, "Good evening, young lady. Is your mother at home?" Most coaches could not have gotten away with such a transparent ploy, but McGuire could pull it off with aplomb. McCarthy's mother, who had met scores of football and basketball coaches by that time, found McGuire so engaging that she told her son that if he wanted to play college basketball, he would do it at South Carolina (he decided to play football at Boston College instead).[17]

McGuire packaged his winning personality in sartorial splendor. "Picture a guy with an easy charm and utter confidence who appeared to have stepped out of the pages of *Esquire* magazine, and that was Frank," recalled Dean Smith, who served as his assistant coach from 1958 to 1961. McGuire was so meticulous about his appearance and wardrobe that he was included on at least one list of the best-dressed men in America. He had his tailored suits and silk ties shipped from New York and insisted that dressing well enhanced the prestige of his team, his school, and his profession. It also made him vulnerable to the derision of opposing fans and teams. McGuire had a well-noted ritual when he called time-out during a game. He stood up, adjusted his cuff links, straightened his tie, and gave the "T" sign for time-out. On one occasion, Wake Forest was handily defeating North Carolina in Chapel Hill. Toward the end of the game, Bones McKinney, who could not have been described as a fastidious dresser, stood up, adjusted his cuffs, straightened his tie, and called time. A few minutes later, he walked out on the floor and did it again as the home crowd voiced its displeasure and McGuire fumed. Several Duke students also lampooned McGuire's routine. They attended games in Durham dressed in their finest suits and silk ties, and they made a point of sitting near the visiting team's bench. Each time that McGuire stood to call time-out, they imitated each step of his ritual in unison. This annoyed McGuire enough that he once gestured to them with an ever-popular hand signal used to convey disrespect.[18]

McGuire extended his belief in the importance of appearance to his players. He required them to be clean shaven and well groomed, and they wore blue team blazers and gray slacks on road trips. For games, they donned satin warm-up jerseys and pants that buttoned down the side for quick removal when entering a game as a substitute. The teams he coached travelled in comfort. At a time when coaches often drove their players to away games in their own cars, in part because they wanted to collect compensation for mileage, McGuire hired buses to transport his teams. He also booked rooms in hotels rather than have his players sleep on cots in the host school's gymnasium, which was a common practice at the time. "He brought class to everything he did," Smith wrote. "He traveled first-class, ate at fine restaurants, and insisted that his teams have the most handsome uniforms and best equipment."[19]

Of all the traits that McGuire regarded as keys to winning basketball, he emphasized loyalty as crucial. "Loyalty on the part of a coach breeds loyalty on the part of the players," he commented. "And this pays off not only in terms of personal relationships, but also in the success of the team." McGuire showed his loyalty to individual players and assistants with well-remembered acts of kindness, empathy, and confidence. Bob Cunningham was a prime target of college recruiters before he had an accident in which he injured his hand so badly that it affected his shooting. Most coaches backed off immediately, but McGuire told Cunningham that he still had a scholarship for him. Cunningham became a valued member of the 1956–57 team, and McGuire's action had the unanticipated benefit of helping to convince Tommy Kearns to attend North Carolina. McGuire showed his loyalty above all to his former college coach, James "Buck" Freeman. Freeman had been an outstanding coach who had fallen victim to alcohol abuse. When McGuire took the job at Chapel Hill, he hired Freeman as his only assistant, even though, as *Sports Illustrated* reported, "Buck was having some lean days and had no prospects of a job anywhere." McGuire was well aware of his mentor's drinking problems but benefited from Freeman's brilliance in devising strategies and in teaching skills to players.[20]

Although McGuire was celebrated for his coaching record and his charm, he was also well-known for his toughness and belligerence. He grew up poor in rowdy Irish-Italian sections of lower Manhattan, and even after he achieved fame and prosperity, he retained some of the rough-and-tumble characteristics that enabled him to get along as a boy. He learned to box as well as to play basketball, and in both sports he earned a reputation as a fierce competitor who was always ready for a fight. For a time when he was teaching high school, he held a part-time job as a bouncer at a local tavern. Those experiences helped engender a combative attitude that sometimes astonished and often infuriated his ACC rivals. They also produced a certain nastiness that he turned on his own players. McGuire was convinced that he knew how to motivate the New Yorkers who populated his teams by making them angry. He apparently determined that a good method "to get the most out of them" was to curse them with vile epithets; one of the milder terms he used on his Jewish players was "Jew-bastard." In some cases, his insults were better disguised. On one occasion in the late 1960s, he reproached Frank Fellows, who had replaced Millikan as head coach at Maryland, before a game at Cole Field House. McGuire put his arm around Fellows and chatted with him in a way that gave the appearance of a veteran coach offering friendly advice to a younger colleague. In fact, McGuire was complaining about the demonstrative behavior of Maryland assistant coach Tom Young and instructing Fellows to exercise firmer control over his staff.[21]

McGuire adopted what he called an "us against the world" approach that he used effectively to motivate his players. But it also reflected his outlook on the challenges he faced in building and maintaining a successful basketball program. His adversaries included his own boss, North Carolina athletic director Chuck Erickson. McGuire resented Erickson's favoritism toward the football program and his complaints that basketball expenses were needlessly lavish. To make matters worse, McGuire occupied a tiny office that was barely large enough to seat visitors. He was convinced that Erickson had promised a new field house to replace the small and inadequate Woollen Gym, and he protested bitterly that nothing had been done to build an arena that could compete with Reynolds Coliseum, Cole Field House, and Duke Indoor Stadium. McGuire also carried on running battles with Duke's Eddie Cameron and ACC commissioner Jim Weaver. He claimed, among other things, that Cameron ran the conference and had a "vendetta" against his teams. He charged that Weaver was "prejudiced against me" and "out to get me."[22]

Many of McGuire's fellow ACC coaches were good friends when they were not competing, even to the point of entertaining visiting team colleagues at their homes after games. McGuire did not participate in these congenial gatherings. With the exception of Hal Bradley, he thought "the others considered me too much of a threat, because we were beating them." His chief and unchallenged coaching rival remained Everett Case. After McGuire announced in January 1954 that he had "declared open war against State College," the competition between the two coaches reached new levels of intensity, though it sometimes had the tone of schoolyard bickering. McGuire issued his declaration of war after losing to State by the score of 84–77. He grumbled that Case had taken "unfair advantage of our weakness" by using a pressing defense that capitalized on State's superior depth. "I can't sit back and be 'Genial Frank McGuire' and be stepped on forever," he said. Case responded that McGuire's comments were "the most childish thing I've ever heard of." When UNC and State played later in the year, McGuire used a "possession game" to hold the ball and slow State's offense. State won 47–44, and Case commented that a slow-down style was "not good for basketball." In February 1957, when State was suffering through its worst season under Case, McGuire pointedly retaliated for past insults by letting his starters play until the last two minutes of a game that North Carolina won, 86–57. McGuire and Case sometimes attempted to play down their differences by suggesting that their battles were mere gimmicks to fuel fan interest. But their rivalry was too real, deep, and immutable to make such a ruse convincing.[23]

McGuire's Miracle

After defeating Wake Forest to win the ACC championship in 1957, North Carolina advanced through the first three rounds of the NCAA Tournament with relative ease. Tar Heel coaches, players, and fans were well aware that Case's teams had generally fared poorly in postseason competition. But North Carolina was a road-tested squad; it had played only eight of its games at home, and it was not intimidated by unfamiliar surroundings and hostile fans. In the first round of the NCAA Tournament, held just three days after it edged Wake, it faced Yale at Madison Square Garden. Playing in New York was a thrill in itself for North Carolina; several members of the squad had grown up watching games and dreaming about performing at the Garden. Further, their families and hometown friends seldom, if ever, saw them play in the ACC, and there were no television broadcasts of their games in New York. Yale kept the contest close well into the second half, but North Carolina pulled away to claim a 90–74 victory. It followed with wins over Canisius, 87–75, and Syracuse, 67–58, in Philadelphia to earn the eastern regional title.[24]

By winning the regionals, North Carolina became the first ACC team to qualify for the NCAA's final rounds (the term "Final Four" was not yet widely used, nor were "March Madness," the "Big Dance," or other names for the NCAA Tournament that later became popular). The win over Syracuse made the Tar Heels 30–0, which broke the record for the most wins in a season by an undefeated team, set the previous year by the University of San Francisco. The other semifinalists who traveled to Kansas City to compete for the national championship threatened North Carolina's hopes in varying degrees of likelihood. The weakest contender was San Francisco, which, led by center Bill Russell, had captured the title the previous two years. Without Russell, it was unranked and came to Kansas City as a surprise winner of the western regionals. Michigan State had eight losses but was ranked number seven in the UPI poll and had decisively upset Kentucky in the mideast regional final. The most powerful opponent that North Carolina might meet in the tournament was the University of Kansas, ranked number two in the country. The unrivaled star of the Kansas team was Wilt Chamberlain, who was already a legend as a sophomore. It was not only his 7′1″ height that placed him in a class by himself but also his strength, speed, mobility, and, above all, his gift for intimidating the competition. Although Kansas had lost two close games during the regular season, its prospects in the tournament were improved by playing in Kansas City, a location that gave it a decided home-court advantage.[25]

North Carolina drew Michigan State as its opponent in the semifinals on Friday evening, March 22, 1957. The game turned into a grueling and galvanizing marathon that went into three overtime periods before the Tar Heels won. North Carolina struggled offensively for much of the game. Rosenbluth led the team with 29 points, but Michigan State's "Jumpin' Johnny" Green played him so effectively that he made only 11 of 42 shots. Bob Cunningham assumed the unaccustomed role of offensive stalwart and scored a season-high 21 points. At the end of regulation play, Michigan State's Jack Quiggle hit a last-second jump shot that appeared to decide the outcome until the officials ruled that he released the ball after the clock expired. In the first overtime, North Carolina was on the ropes again. Michigan State had a 64–62 lead with just 11 seconds left and Green on the line for a one-and-one. North Carolina's unbeaten season was in such dire jeopardy that a Michigan State player boasted to Tommy Kearns as Green prepared to shoot, "Thirty and one." But Green missed the first shot. Pete Brennan grabbed the rebound, dribbled the length of the court, pulled up at the foul line, and sank a jumper with 2 seconds remaining. North Carolina finally took command in the third overtime and prevailed by the score of 74–70. Students in Chapel Hill formed a huge celebratory conga line on Franklin Street.[26]

North Carolina had little time to savor its victory. The following evening, it took on an even more formidable challenge in Kansas, which had routed San Francisco in the other semifinal matchup, 80–56. Kansas came into the finals after an easy win with a partisan crowd on its side, and it was heavily favored to take the title. McGuire's suggestion after the ACC Tournament that "good athletes never get tired" would be severely tested. The North Carolina players were confident that they could compete with Kansas, partly because some of them had played against Chamberlain in Catskill resort summer leagues and partly because they had already won 31 consecutive games. But they had no illusions about the difficulty of the task. McGuire decided that the only strategy that offered a reasonable chance of success was to collapse defensively on Chamberlain to keep him from dominating the game and inciting the crowd with dunks. This meant that the outcome would depend in significant measure on whether the other Kansas players made the open shots that would be available to them. McGuire also instructed his team to be patient on offense.

McGuire, at the suggestion of Buck Freeman, began the game with a psychological maneuver that he hoped would give Chamberlain "a good shock." He designated Kearns to jump center against Chamberlain, who was more than a foot taller. Chamberlain could not conceal his "bewilderment and embarrassment," and although he won the tap, McGuire believed that the scheme threw him at least slightly out of balance. Whether or not that was the case, North Carolina raced to an early lead. Kansas coach Dick Harp used a box-and-one defense to contain Rosenbluth, but Kearns, Quigg, and Brennan hit open shots consistently. Kansas, in contrast, threw up bricks from outside with equal consistency. North Carolina took a 29–22 advantage to the locker room at halftime after shooting 64.7 percent. Kansas made only 27.3 percent of its field-goal attempts.

The second half was a different story. Kansas charged back to take a 40–37 lead with about 10 minutes remaining in the game. At that point, Harp committed what McGuire later called a "strategic boner." He first told his players to stall on offense and then, with about 7 minutes left, he ordered a "solid freeze." The crowd roared its approval, but the slow-down tactic allowed a weary North Carolina team to catch its breath. It came back to tie the game at 46 in regulation, despite suffering the loss of Rosenbluth on fouls at the 1:45 mark. The first two overtimes were excruciatingly tense and low-scoring; each team managed only 2 points.

By the third overtime, Kansas players looked as exhausted as their North Carolina opponents, who were playing three extra periods for the second

Lennie Rosenbluth defends against Wilt Chamberlain as Pete Brennan arrives
to help in the NCAA championship game, 1957. (© Bettmann/CORBIS)

night in a row. After the Tar Heels took a 4-point lead on a basket and two
free throws by Kearns, a 3-point play by Chamberlain and a pair of foul
shots gave Kansas a 53–52 lead with 28 seconds to go. As the clock ran down
at the other end, Quigg saw an opening for a drive. Chamberlain swat-
ted the shot away, but Quigg was fouled by another Kansas player. North
Carolina was down 1 with 6 seconds to play and Quigg, a 71.9 percent foul
shooter, at the line. At that point, McGuire called time-out. This was unusual for a team that was shooting fouls, but McGuire had a keen sense of
when he needed to talk to his players. In the huddle he instructed them to
deny Chamberlain the ball "after Joe makes these" shots. With a national
championship at stake, Quigg sank both free throws. North Carolina then
dropped back to defend Chamberlain. Unfortunately, a missed assignment
left Quigg fronting Chamberlain and no one behind him. A lob pass over
Quigg's head would mean an easy basket for Chamberlain and a Kansas
victory at the buzzer. But the pass was too low, and Quigg leaped to bat

the ball to Kearns, who threw it high in the air as time expired. Final score: North Carolina 54, Kansas 53.[27]

It was, Dick Herbert wrote, "one of the great heartstoppers in basketball history." Frank Deford, the eminent *Sports Illustrated* writer, supported that judgment 25 years later when he called it "the most exciting game in NCAA tournament history." Chamberlain was magnificent in defeat; he scored 23 points and was named the tournament's Most Valuable Player. His teammates, however, made only 9 of 34 field-goal attempts. North Carolina benefited from a balanced attack; Rosenbluth scored 20 points, Brennan and Kearns chipped in 11 each, and Quigg had 10, including the game-winning free throws. McGuire took his staff, coaching colleagues, North Carolina governor Luther Hodges, reporters, and others (but not his players) to dinner at one of Kansas City's finest restaurants, where he spent $1,500 on the meal. A short time later, UNC athletic director Erickson further impaired his already chilly relations with McGuire by refusing to pay for Roquefort dressing that was part of the tab and cost $58.[28]

The reaction in Chapel Hill and throughout the state of North Carolina to the victory over Kansas was unrestrained joy. Students spilled out of dormitories, lounges, and bars, lighted a bonfire in the middle of Franklin Street, and once again formed a gigantic conga line. As they celebrated, a car came rolling down the street with "an especially jubilant man" riding on top. The students gave a big cheer, particularly after they realized that the man who "jumped up and down and shouted and waved his arms" was Robert B. House, the popular chancellor at Chapel Hill. Similar celebrations occurred in towns across the state, where "mass hysteria" had taken hold. While bells rang, bands played, and bonfires raged, citizens danced in the streets or simply bellowed in glee. The following day, about 10,000 fans jammed Raleigh-Durham airport to welcome the national champions home.[29]

Some North Carolina supporters regarded the victory over Kansas as a source of pride for the entire South as well as for the state. UNC was the first school from a former Confederate state to win an NCAA basketball championship. The reaction in some ways was similar to what happened when the University of Alabama's football team, coached by Wallace Wade, pulled off a stunning upset over the University of Washington in the 1926 Rose Bowl. This game not only struck an important blow for the quality of college football played in the South but also for southern self-esteem. The *Atlanta Georgian* called it "the greatest victory for the South since the first battle of Bull Run."[30]

North Carolina's title did not seem to rank with Bull Run in consequence, but it carried sectional implications nevertheless. *Sports Illustrated*
reported that when the Tar Heel players arrived at the Raleigh-Durham
airport, "the roar that went up from the 10,000 fairly crackled with Dixie's
pride in its own." Fans held placards that hailed their "Rebel Yanks" and
"Confederate Yankees." As those signs suggested, the purity of the southern achievement was diluted by the fact that the coach, assistant coach,
starting five, and all but three members of the squad came from New York
or New Jersey. But sectional loyalty still was an important part of the excitement over North Carolina's championship. One follower told McGuire:
"I don't care if you guys are all Yankees. I'm ready to call you Southerners
and be damned glad I can." The sectional pride that North Carolina's victory aroused was almost certainly related in some measure to race. The Tar
Heels defeated a team led by a black man who was the biggest, best, and
most intimidating basketball player in the country. This was not a consideration that was mentioned in the local papers, but it surely played a role in
the response of some, perhaps many, North Carolina fans.[31]

The NCAA championship that North Carolina brought home elevated
the status of the entire ACC. After NC State and Duke had flamed out early
the three previous years, the national reputation of the conference had suffered. North Carolina's triumph did not eliminate doubts about the caliber
of competition in the ACC, but it was a major step toward placing conference teams among the elite of college basketball. The win over Kansas, in
the opinion of scholar and diehard fan Fred Hobson, "was the greatest in
Carolina history" because "it was the birth of the Carolina legend." Frank
Deford suggested in 1982 that the impact of capturing the title extended
even further. Before the championship weekend, he wrote, "ACC basketball was popular as a sport; after this, it was woven into the fabric of North
Carolina society."[32]

The ACC on Television

One critical reason for the impact of North Carolina's championship on
the entire state was that the games against Michigan State and Kansas, in
all their triple-overtime glory, were shown on television. This was a new
phenomenon in North Carolina, and the excitement generated by the live
broadcasts could hardly be overstated. "It was the first time that a North
Carolina team participated in a televised national event," the *News and
Observer* commented in an editorial, "and both the novelty of the event

and the sheer drama of the concluding games drew people to the television screen who ordinarily would rather be caught dead than looking at a basketball game."[33]

The scale of the coverage of the final games of the NCAA Tournament was unprecedented in North Carolina, but a few regular season games had been televised previously. On January 8, 1955, North Carolina and Wake Forest met in the first ACC basketball game to be televised. It was carried on the public television station in Chapel Hill, WUNC-TV. The following season, three more games were aired on the same station, which reached an audience within a 50-mile radius. Those broadcasts raised concerns on several grounds. One was the effect of television on attendance at games. Bones McKinney commented: "You can't convince me that TV will not hurt the attendance. It's so easy to stay home in the comfort of your own parlor to see a game." Radio stations were distressed by the prospects of competing against television. As a result, WUNC reached an agreement with radio stations to broadcast games on TV without sound. Fans could listen to the play-by-play on radio. At one point, UNC system president Friday and vice president Carmichael personally wielded hammers and chisels to knock a hole in the wall at Woollen Gym for a television camera. The vantage point that they carved out made possible the introduction of "Broadvision," which panned the entire floor of the gym while a radio announcer called the action. In addition to the potential effects on attendance and radio, there was another reservation about television broadcasts. Chancellor House found that "some people think the crowd doesn't behave good enough to go on the air."[34]

From those humble and conflicted beginnings, television coverage of ACC basketball gradually expanded. Initially, the commercial market for ACC broadcasts appeared unpromising. In 1956, the conference made arrangements for regional telecasts, but its plans failed because it "could not find a sponsor." North Carolina's run to the national championship dramatically changed the outlook for showing ACC basketball on TV. Beaming the NCAA semifinals and finals throughout the state of North Carolina was the brainstorm of a television pioneer and entrepreneur, Castleman D. Chesley. Chesley had played football at UNC and later worked as coordinator of college football broadcasts for the NBC and ABC television networks. His experience made him well acquainted with both the business and technical aspects of televising games.

When North Carolina reached the NCAA's eastern regional tournament in 1957, Chesley quickly made arrangements for TV stations in Charlotte,

Greensboro, and Durham to carry the games. After the Tar Heels won the regionals, he established a network of five stations in North Carolina to air the games from Kansas City, lined up sponsors, and hired announcers. His efforts were rewarded with two riveting contests that kept North Carolinians glued to their sets. The final game went late into the night, and Chesley feared that viewers in the East would not stay up to watch it. He need not have worried. Irwin Smallwood, who covered ACC basketball for the Greensboro papers, later remarked: "As a single event, probably nothing so mesmerized the state as that [game] did." Within a short time, the ACC accepted Chesley's proposal to broadcast a total of 12 games during the 1957–58 season "as a trial experiment." Despite the enormous success of the NCAA Tournament broadcasts, he encountered difficulty finding sponsors. But his plan gained the financial support it required when the Pilot Life Insurance Company of Greensboro bought half of the advertising time for the telecasts. The ACC game of the week, presented by the C. D. Chesley Network and prominently sponsored by Pilot Life, became a popular institution among fans and, over time, played a vital role in expanding the visibility and prestige of the conference.[35]

The American Game

A principal reason that telecasts of ACC games proved to be so successful was the growing popularity of college basketball. Although football remained the "king" of college sports during the 1950s, even in ACC territory, basketball received increasing attention and fan support. This development was largely a result of the rules changes of the 1930s that made basketball more fluid and far more fun for spectators. It was, *Sports Illustrated* commented in 1957, "colorful and exciting and full of action, and even the relatively uninformed find it an easy sport to watch, understand, and appreciate." As early as 1951, Arthur Daley, the respected sports columnist for the *New York Times*, suggested that basketball had ceased to be "an obscure college sport played in obscure college gymnasiums" and had "become a big boy, the most popular sport of them all." Daley's judgment was premature. In 1953, for example, when Kansas met Indiana for the NCAA championship, the game was carried by a Kansas City TV station only as a delayed broadcast following a live presentation of a boxing match. Nevertheless, the trend toward greater interest in and passion for college basketball was clear.

The ACC was not the only conference to telecast games to a growing number of fans. Both the Pacific Coast Conference and the Big Ten lined up regional broadcasts of selected games. By late 1957, despite continuing concerns, there were indications that television did not harm attendance at college games. During the 1956–57 season, more than 13.3 million fans attended college basketball games. This figure was fairly close to the 16.5 million who turned out to see major league baseball during the 1956 season at a time that baseball was regarded as the "national pastime." The comparisons between the two sports are imperfect. But they indicated, as *Sports Illustrated* put it, that the "American game," the only one "to have been devised in the United States with no appreciable roots in the sports of other nations," had "joined football in the collegiate athletic big time." The importance of basketball on campus was heightened by the fact that many schools eliminated their football programs during the 1940s and 1950s because of high costs. The increasing popularity of ACC basketball was not only a result of intense rivalries between conference schools but also a part of a national pattern.[36]

McGuire and the NCAA

After North Carolina won the national championship, great talent continued to arrive in Chapel Hill via the underground railroad, and McGuire's teams posted excellent records. But they did not win another ACC title under his guidance. In their only postchampionship NCAA appearance in 1959, made possible by NC State's probation, they were decisively defeated in the first round. In 1961, under the shadow of NCAA penalties and a point-shaving scandal that focused on State but extended to UNC, McGuire was forced out of his coaching position at North Carolina, just four years after the championship season.

During the 1957–58 season, North Carolina ended with a record of 19–7 after losing in the ACC Tournament finals to Maryland. Pete Brennan led the conference in scoring and rebounding and was named ACC Player of the Year. The following year, junior Lee Shaffer and sophomores York Larese and Doug Moe starred as the Tar Heels finished 20–5. The title game of the ACC Tournament caused further controversy between McGuire and Case. By making the finals, North Carolina was assured of a berth in the NCAA Tournament, and McGuire rested his starters for a good part of the game. The fans hooted their displeasure; one unhappy ticket-holder broke into a locked room at Reynolds Coliseum and turned off the lights. The arena was dark for eight minutes and remained dimly lighted for the last few minutes of the game. McGuire's decision to rest his first team in the ACC Tournament did not help its performance in the NCAA's eastern regionals, where it fell to Navy, 76–63. In 1959–60, Shaffer and Larese led North Carolina to a record of 18–6; Moe also played well but was academically ineligible for much of the season. After tying Wake Forest for the regular season championship, the team lost in an upset to Duke in the tournament. The next season, as Larese averaged 23.1 points and Moe 20.4 points and 14.0 rebounds per game, North Carolina went 19–4 and again finished in the top spot in the regular season. But it elected to withdraw from competing in the ACC Tournament when the NCAA placed it on probation for recruiting violations.[37]

The NCAA apparently began an investigation of North Carolina's recruiting practices after an article on "basketball's underground railroad" appeared in *Sports Illustrated* in February 1957. The writer, Richard J. Schaap, discussed the activities of Harry Gotkin and his rival talent scouts. Among those he interviewed was Mike Tynberg, a UNC graduate. "I'm on the North Carolina payroll," Tynberg boasted. "So is Uncle Harry [Gotkin]. We're listed as assistant coaches." The university denied that Gotkin, Tynberg, or any other scouts were on its payroll, and McGuire commented, "No one gets paid, but everybody looks out for me." A short time after publication of the article, the NCAA informed Chancellor House that it was conducting an informal investigation of unspecified allegations against the University of North Carolina.[38]

The NCAA carried out its investigation at a leisurely pace. It found little support for vague suggestions that North Carolina had provided illegal transportation to basketball players or their families and that team members had received free clothing from a shop in Chapel Hill. It fixed its attention on the activities of Harry Gotkin and uncovered potential recruiting violations. While it accepted the university's assurances that Gotkin was not paid for his scouting services, it explored the question of whether the compensation he received for entertaining potential recruits was excessive. In June 1958, Erickson informed McGuire that, effective immediately, "we are . . . not allowed to pay expenses of any talent scout, individual, or friend for recruiting activities." Nevertheless, the NCAA continued to examine the expenses that Gotkin had previously claimed and that McGuire had authorized.[39]

On January 22, 1959, Walter Byers, the NCAA's executive director, informed Erickson that the organization was conducting a "preliminary inquiry" into UNC's use of Gotkin as a "talent scout." He requested detailed information on Gotkin's relationship to the university and to McGuire. A year later, Byers notified William B. Aycock, who had replaced House as chancellor at Chapel Hill, that the NCAA's Committee on Infractions had information of "sufficient substance and reliability to warrant an official inquiry." It alleged that Gotkin had "provided excessive entertainment to prospective student-athletes" and that the University of North Carolina had violated NCAA rules by reimbursing Gotkin for those expenses. It requested that the university answer a series of questions about Gotkin's income and bank accounts and compile a list of "all checks" sent to him by the university after 1955. It also sought "copies of all expense statements submitted by members of the basketball coaching staff . . . for recruiting expenses."[40]

The burden of responding to the NCAA's charges fell on Chancellor Aycock. He had graduated from State College in 1936 and then earned a master's degree in history and political science at Chapel Hill. He taught high school history for a time and worked as an administrator for a New Deal agency, the National Youth Administration, before joining the army in 1942. He became a lieutenant colonel and served as a battalion commander under General George S. Patton. He was awarded a Silver Star for bravery and other medals for his combat leadership in the European theater. After the war, Aycock returned to Chapel Hill to attend law school, where one of his close friends was fellow law student Bill Friday. When he received his degree, he was immediately offered a faculty position in the law school of his alma mater. He remained a law professor at UNC until he was appointed chancellor in 1957.

In that position, Aycock demonstrated the same toughness and discipline that had served him so well as a combat officer. He worked punishing hours to enhance the academic stature of the University of North Carolina even as it grew rapidly. He carried out his goals in an open manner that won affection and support from both faculty members and students. One former colleague remembered that students found a "warmth, strength, and friendly energy about him" even when he disagreed with them. Aycock had reservations about the prominence of athletics at UNC. He once commented that "if I was writing on a clean slate, I am not so sure that I would be a proponent of 'Big-Time Athletics' as we know it." He recognized that there was no way to "get rid of it." But when he took over as chancellor, he was determined "to see that we abided by the rules and regulations, and that we would conduct our programs accordingly." As long as North Carolina's sports programs came under his authority as chancellor, he said, "I'll accept the responsibility . . . and I will try to do it right."[41]

Aycock was, therefore, disturbed by the NCAA's allegations that UNC's basketball program was not "doing it right." When he took immediate steps to acquire the information the NCAA requested, he discovered that little of it was available. Gotkin told Aycock that he could not provide financial records because he had "not had any type of bank account" or "written a check in the last thirteen years." He acknowledged that he had taken "prospects and their parents to nice restaurants and to games" but offered his assurances that he had "done nothing to break the rules of the N.C.A.A." McGuire's records of his recruiting expenses were equally meager. Although he clearly spent generously on dinners and entertainment, he generally paid in cash and did not keep careful accounts of what he spent. Aycock tried without great success to reconstruct an itemized list of reimbursements made to Gotkin and McGuire. "Apparently, neither Mr. Gotkin nor Coach McGuire made any effort to keep an accurate account of expenses," he told the NCAA. "I have no reason to believe that the amount of money received by either of them was in excess of the actual expenses incurred by them." He determined that the total amount paid to Gotkin between September 1, 1952, and September 1, 1958, was $4,694.69 and the amount paid to McGuire for recruiting costs between 1955 and 1959 was $13,201.48.[42]

The pivotal question was whether the NCAA regarded those expenses as "excessive," and its standard for distinguishing between legitimate and excessive costs was, at best, both ill-defined and arbitrary. In the autumn of 1960, McGuire traveled with Aycock to meet with the NCAA's Committee on Infractions. McGuire viewed the accusations as groundless if not contemptible and he made no effort to conceal his opinion. At one point during the proceedings, a committee member from Columbia University questioned McGuire's claim for a meal for three at a New York restaurant that cost $35. He remarked that he knew "many good restaurants in New York" where he could buy a good dinner for $3. McGuire's reply was, by any standard, impolitic: "I wouldn't eat where you eat."[43]

McGuire's attitude did not help North Carolina's cause. In December 1960, the Committee on Infractions concluded that the university had violated NCAA rules by providing "excessive entertainment for prospective student-athletes." It did not define what it considered "excessive," but it insisted that McGuire and Gotkin's recruiting expenses fell into that category. The committee condemned the university's failure "to maintain records with a reasonable degree of accuracy" so that recruiting costs could be traced and evaluated. The following month, Aycock appeared before the

NCAA Council to contest the findings of the Committee on Infractions. He contended that the UNC basketball program was guilty of "errors in judgment rather than . . . a deliberate violation of rules." He pledged to make certain that the university "would take every precaution to insure that its future activities adhere strictly to the rules and regulations of the N.C.A.A."[44]

Aycock's presentation impressed the council, but his arguments did not save UNC from disciplinary action. On January 10, 1961, the NCAA announced that it was placing North Carolina on probation for one year. The penalty was less severe than some North Carolina supporters had feared, presumably in part because of the flimsiness of the NCAA's case. Unlike the four-year probation imposed on NC State in 1957, UNC's punishment applied only to basketball. Dick Herbert commented that "the penalty was almost as light as the NCAA has rendered." Nevertheless, Aycock regarded the NCAA's judgment as an embarrassment to the university that required corrective measures. As a first step toward asserting control of the basketball program, he petitioned the ACC to allow UNC to withdraw from the conference tournament. Commissioner Weaver immediately granted the request. In April 1961, Aycock reminded McGuire that a decision on extending his contract would be made in 1962 (approximately one year before it expired in June 1963). Aycock suggested that he would not support its renewal if the NCAA found continuing violations during the probationary period. He also disclosed that he was "deeply concerned" that McGuire's players had been involved in bench-clearing brawls in recent years. Aycock told McGuire that his position on the coach's contract would not hinge on the "number of games won or lost during the next season." Rather, it would depend on McGuire's ability to "avoid the many mistakes which have been made this year and to have a basketball season which will reflect the highest credit on the University."[45]

The End of the Dixie Classic

By the time that Aycock delivered his warning to McGuire, a much more serious problem had overtaken his distress over North Carolina's probation. In a repeat of the scandal that rocked college basketball in 1951, one player from UNC and four from NC State admitted to participating in a widespread point-shaving scheme in which they accepted payments from gamblers. This shocking revelation, coming on top of the series of NCAA penalties that State College and UNC had incurred since 1954, persuaded Consolidated University president Friday, with the full support of Aycock and State College chancellor John T. Caldwell, to abolish the Dixie Classic.

In March 1961, New York district attorney Frank Hogan, who had uncovered the point-shaving scandal in college basketball ten years earlier, arrested two men, Aaron "the Bagman" Wagman and Joseph Hacken, for bribing players to manipulate the scores of games. In order to beat the point spread of selected games, they lined up "contact men" who were willing to approach their own teammates or make arrangements with friends on other college teams. The contact and the participating player(s) would then split the payment from the gamblers. Hogan's investigation, which began in 1959, eventually found that 49 players from 27 schools in 18 states had joined in point-shaving schemes and collected payoffs, usually in the range of $1,000 for each successfully fixed outcome, from gambling interests.[46]

One of Wagman's principal contacts was Lou Brown, a member of North Carolina's basketball team. He was, *Look* magazine reported, "more deeply involved" in point-shaving activities than any other college player. He had grown up in Jersey City, New Jersey, in a family of modest means. His ability in basketball enabled him to attend college, and although he received room, board, tuition, books, and fees, he struggled to get by on the $15 a month spending money that his scholarship provided. "I envied the kids with the Thunderbirds," Brown later wrote. "The urge for money kept growing." That urge made him receptive to an approach from Jerry Vogel, a former player at the University of Alabama. Vogel introduced Brown to Wagman, who made shaving points "sound safe and easy."

At Wagman's request, Brown tried to recruit his good friend Doug Moe to "do business" with the gamblers, but Moe refused. Nevertheless, Moe talked to Wagman and accepted a "gift" of $75 from him. Brown was more successful in lining up players at St. Joseph's College and LaSalle College, both in Philadelphia, whom he knew from summer basketball camps. The St. Joseph's player, Frank Majewski, enlisted two of his teammates, Jack Egan and Vince Kempton, who were stars on a team that beat Wake Forest in the NCAA eastern regional in 1961 and placed third in the NCAA Tournament. In this manner, the point-shaving network expanded to include dozens of players. Brown made money both from the payoffs he received on fixed games and from placing his own bets with bookies. He was not aware that New York detectives followed him, took photographs, and recorded phone conversations. When he was picked up in Chapel Hill and taken to New York in March 1961 for questioning, he quickly realized that the evidence clearly established his guilt, and he cooperated with the police to identify other participants in the point-shaving conspiracy.[47]

Aycock believed that the scandal was another serious setback for the University of North Carolina. While Brown was still providing information for Hogan's investigation, Aycock could not announce disciplinary action against him. But he quietly forced Brown to withdraw from the university "under other than honorable conditions" on March 29, 1961. Brown, who was just two months short of graduation, was informed that he would not be permitted to return without Aycock's express approval.

The chancellor also suspended Moe for an "indefinite period," a measure that was less severe than Brown's punishment. Aycock was keenly aware that Moe had rejected Brown's invitation to shave points, but he found fault with Moe's failure to report the overture. Further, on three occasions, Moe "had not made a clean breast of the whole affair" by telling the chancellor that he had accepted $75 from Wagman. Aycock lifted the suspension in September 1962, but Moe paid heavily for his marginal role in the scandal when the National Basketball Association (NBA) banned him from playing in the league.[48]

Aycock's decisions on Brown and Moe did not end the painful disclosures about point-shaving activities that shook the Consolidated University and the entire state of North Carolina. On May 13, 1961, the North Carolina State Bureau of Investigation (SBI) charged three NC State players, Anton "Dutch" Muehlbauer, Stan Niewierowski, and Terry Litchfield, with accepting bribes to fix the outcome of games. All admitted their association with gamblers, though Litchfield, who was not a starter, denied that he had actually shaved points or received payments. The arrests of the three players eventually led investigators to Don Gallagher, who had graduated with honors in 1960 but had enlisted the others to help him shave points while still in school. Gallagher had originally been approached by a gambler named Joe Green, who was associated with Wagman and Hacken. All worked in uneasy collaboration with Jack Molinas, a former standout player at Columbia University, a one-time NBA All-Star, and a compulsive high-stakes gambler. Green had initially contacted Gallagher at a summer basketball camp in the Catskills in 1959, and the player responded favorably to the prospect of easy cash because he and his wife had a baby son and very little money. Although Lou Brown and the NC State players dealt with the same group of fixers, they apparently had no contact with one another. Their misconduct ran on parallel but separate tracks.[49]

As soon as he learned of the SBI's findings and the players' admissions, State College chancellor Caldwell took disciplinary action against them. Muehlbauer and Niewierowski had been suspended a month earlier for failure to attend classes, and Caldwell announced that they would "not be permitted to return." He expelled Litchfield with the same stipulation. Caldwell had proven to be an effective and popular chancellor since arriving at NC State in 1959. A native of Mississippi, he held a Ph.D. in political science from Princeton University. He had spent much of his academic career as a college president, first at Alabama College and then at the University of Arkansas for seven years before moving to Raleigh. Caldwell's ability as an administrator won respect, and his natural friendliness and easy charm won friends. "John Caldwell," Friday once said, "radiated confidence, joy, excitement, enthusiasm, and his heart was as big as all outdoors." He was egalitarian in practice as well as principle. He treated janitors with the same courtesy that he extended to his own colleagues. He often could be seen sharing a table with students at a campus cafeteria and was well known for inviting small groups of them to dine at his home. On one occasion, he remarked that his "finest day" as chancellor came when a popular restaurant near campus began to serve blacks.

Caldwell was committed to elevating the academic programs and reputation of NC State. He strongly believed that faculty research and publication "must be supported and encouraged" in order "to produce the highest possible intellectual result in scholarship and ability to serve the next generation." Under his tenure as chancellor, the institution first began to award degrees in liberal arts and attained the status and the name of "North Carolina State University." Caldwell complained about the amount of time and attention that athletic issues consumed. He astonished a booster organization by telling its members that rather than gaining recognition from sports, he would "much prefer [an] international reputation in other departments of our educational and research enterprise." But he also wished to field teams that would "have reasonable success and occasionally the prospect of a championship." He told Everett Case that as chancellor, "I want to be proud of everything we do, including our program of sports competition." He added that "winning is not by any means the sole or even dominant consideration I feel (though one always wants to be a worthy competitor with an even chance of winning)." The desire to be both clean and competitive guided his response to the point- shaving scandal.[50]

The disclosure that his players had accepted money for corrupting college basketball games was a stunning blow for Case. Each season since the point-shaving scandal of 1951, he had invited a representative of the SBI to talk to his teams about how gamblers operated and about the consequences of doing business with them. Case had become suspicious that some of his players were involved with fixers early in the 1960–61 season and had asked the SBI to investigate. Nevertheless, the confirmation of his fears was a shock. He told his players that he was "sad and disappointed" that "three of my boys . . . conspired with gambling fixers to shave points and lose games" (Gallagher had not yet been implicated). "These boys have let down a great many people who had confidence in them," Case observed, and placed "a black mark on the great game of basketball."[51]

While acknowledging that he did not "know the answer" to preventing point shaving, Case informed columnist Smith Barrier that he assigned part of the blame to the direct or indirect New York connections of the players who accepted bribes. He proposed that in order to tone down their "vicious" rivalries, Big Four schools might have to use more players from the state of North Carolina, even at the cost of downgrading the level of competition. "Maybe the sense of values of New York boys is all screwed up," Case said. "I don't know, but the North Carolina boys would certainly be loyal." He realized that "we would not hold our ratings against outside competition" but suggested that "maybe we've been too much in the national spotlight." The irony of Case's thoughts about the drawbacks of big-time basketball was not lost on critics who taunted him in scathing terms. The *New York Herald Tribune* submitted that the "sense of values that needs looking to is that of a university which recruits young men not because they are good students, but because they are good basketball players." *Sports Illustrated* cited the Jackie Moreland case as evidence that Case's "outside-the-rules recruiting" had laid the foundations for the corruption of college athletes. "Since the current scandal broke, there has been no more arrogant, self-serving, and sanctimonious expression of opinion," it wrote of Case's comments. "It will be a great day—but don't hold your breath waiting for it to come—when coaches like Everett Case admit their own responsibility in this matter, instead of trying to shift the blame to the boys themselves, the gamblers, and, finally, the manners and mores of a whole city."[52]

Local commentators refrained from harsh attacks on Case but called for effective reforms. The *News and Observer* described the point-shaving scandal as a "sickening spectacle" and urged top administrators to "cut the cancer of materialism and win-at-any-price malignancy out of collegiate sports." The *Durham Sun* also compared the problem to a "malignant growth" and suggested that "some major surgery may be necessary." Mike

Lea, the editor-elect of State College's student newspaper, *The Technician*, blamed not only the players who took money from gamblers but also the administrators, students, reporters, and fans who placed the "pursuit of trophies" above the school's more important purposes. Jonathan Yardley, a member of the *Daily Tar Heel* staff, argued that the "lamentable story of athletics in Chapel Hill and Raleigh . . . has reached a point from which it cannot return to the 'normal' mode of operation." North Carolina governor Terry Sanford, a good friend and former law school classmate of President Friday, announced that he would support Friday "in his desire to clean up the evils of big time basketball."[53]

Amid much talk about the need for "de-emphasis" of basketball, Friday moved quickly and decisively to address the issues that the scandal raised. After becoming president of the Consolidated University, he had affirmed Gray's assignment of responsibility for athletics at each campus to its chancellor. But the magnitude of the problem reached beyond the individual schools, and Friday took the lead in dealing with it. After lengthy consultation with Chancellors Aycock and Caldwell, he had to determine the best means to correct athletic abuses, because, as Aycock later commented, "he was the one who was going to have to take the heat for it."[54]

Friday, with Aycock and Caldwell's concurrence, decided on a series of measures to establish better control of the basketball programs at NC State and UNC and to reduce the likelihood that players would get involved in fixing games. He announced his policies at a meeting of the executive committee of the university's Board of Trustees on May 22, 1961. Friday declared that over the previous five years, the NCAA's penalties against NC State and North Carolina and the point-shaving scandal had caused the Consolidated University "serious embarrassment." Therefore, he and the chancellors had considered two options. The first was to "discontinue altogether or suspend for a fixed period of time participation" in intercollegiate basketball. The second was to "move forthrightly to eliminate or correct conditions that have discredited the sport." They had chosen the second alternative "for the present."

Friday outlined three major steps that he hoped would remedy the abuses. The first was to prohibit basketball players from participating in "any organized competition of any kind over the summer months." This was done in response to reports that gamblers had contacted players who played in leagues at Catskill resorts. The second step was to limit the number of scholarships offered to players from "regions of the country distant from our State and our Conference." Friday acknowledged that recruiting

William Friday (left), William Aycock (center), and John Caldwell
announce their response to the point-shaving scandal, May 22, 1961.
(Courtesy The North Carolina State Archives; reprinted by permission
of *The News and Observer* of Raleigh, North Carolina)

players from afar "*per se*, may have nothing to do with the predicament in
which we find ourselves." But he insisted that NC State and UNC's teams
should be made up of players who were "more-or-less representative of the
normal composition of our student bodies." Therefore, no more than two
basketball scholarships could be offered at each school to students who
came from states outside of the ACC area.

Finally, in his most surprising and most controversial edict, Friday
shortened NC State and North Carolina's regular season schedules to a
total of 16 games. Since 14 of the games would be played against ACC opponents, only 2 games would be played against nonconference teams. One
result of this decision, Friday pointed out, was "the immediate discon-
tinuance of the Dixie Classic." Although investigators later discovered that
gamblers had corrupted the Dixie Classic by bribing players to fix at least
one game, this was not known at the time. Friday emphasized that he chose
to eliminate the Dixie Classic because it was a "prominent example" of the
"exploitation for public entertainment or for budgetary and commercial
purposes of a sports program which properly exists as an adjunct to col-

legiate education." He expressed his hope that the reforms he introduced would "keep an intercollegiate basketball program worthy of the aims and purposes and example of the University." He informed the trustees of his plans but did not ask them for their approval. Although this caused grumbling from some members, the executive committee voted unanimously to "express its approval and endorsement" of his actions.[55]

The stern measures that Friday imposed were an effort to reestablish a proper balance between academic purposes and athletic performance. In his view, with the agreement of Aycock and Caldwell, the scales had tipped way too far on the athletic side of the equation, and this had severely harmed the reputation of the university. Caldwell told the trustees that although "many people rejoiced" in having highly ranked basketball teams, the "real question is whether the price has been too great." In his judgment, "the price has been pretty big in the Consolidated University." Yet the actions Friday took were designed to correct abuses and not to weaken the NC State and North Carolina programs to a point that they could not compete in the ACC. He considered but decided against the elimination of basketball scholarships at the two schools. Aycock saw little inherent value in big-time athletic programs, but Friday and Caldwell took a more favorable position. Friday later declared that "intercollegiate sports [had] a terribly important role to play" in higher education because it inspired school spirit and accomplished "things that are important in the collegiate experience."

In a speech he delivered in early 1962, Caldwell reflected on the role of sports in academic institutions. He argued that despite the failures and abuses, college athletic programs were "an integral, expected part of American life." They provided "the only activity of [an academic] institution which excites the common interest of large numbers of students, large numbers of the faculty, large numbers of alumni, and large segments of the general public." This important benefit often caused "painful" problems for administrators who sought to "satisfy partially the idealism of the educator, the appetites of the sports enthusiasts, and the balance sheets of trustees and business officers." In attempting to meet the competing and sometimes incompatible demands of those constituents, Caldwell commented, he and his colleagues in leadership posts in schools across the nation had "a bear by the tail." The actions the Consolidated University took in the wake of the point-shaving scandal were intended to tame the bear without declawing it. "Our aim," Friday told reporters on May 22, 1961, "is to save athletics by de-emphasizing certain practices and removing certain influences which have been detrimental to college sports."[56]

The effort to "save athletics" received a predictably mixed response. The *News and Observer* saw it as "at least a step toward de-emphasis of the sport" that might "restore basketball to its proper role." The *Charlotte Observer* hoped that it would bring about a necessary adjustment in a "scale of values" that "may canonize some young lout who can drop an inflated skin through a net." Others were less favorably impressed with Friday's decision. Jack Horner of the *Durham Morning Herald* conceded that Friday and the chancellors had to take action to respond to the scandal but argued that they "may have cut off a leg because of bruised toe." He feared that the steps they announced "could mean the end of big-time intercollegiate basketball at State College and Carolina." NC State athletic director Clogston told a friend that the corrective measures were a "terrific shock" that he thought would "backfire." He lamented the cancellation of the Dixie Classic, in significant part because it meant a substantial loss of income for his programs. Merchants in Raleigh complained bitterly about the loss of the Classic. The tournament was a boon for local stores, restaurants, and hotels in the slack period that followed Christmas. Friday later recalled that he "couldn't go in the city of Raleigh for a good long while, without being cursed up one side and down the other." When NC State fans and Raleigh businesses made attempts to revive the tournament in subsequent years, Friday and Caldwell reminded them of the "humiliation" the Consolidated University had suffered from NCAA penalties and gambling offenses. The campaign to restore the Dixie Classic failed, and the event gradually passed into fond but distant memory.[57]

McGuire's Departure

The recruiting restrictions that Friday adopted effectively forced Frank McGuire to leave the University of North Carolina. Aycock had put him on notice that his tenure was in jeopardy after the NCAA placed UNC on probation. McGuire was "deeply upset" by Aycock's letter. He was also "stunned" by the participation of one of his players in the point-shaving scandal; he later commented that it "was like being let down by a member of your family." But he did not agree with Friday's commitment to de-emphasizing basketball. The decision to limit coaches to two scholarships for players from outside the states with ACC schools meant that the underground railroad, at least to the extent that McGuire had used it, had reached the end of the line. The major source of his talent was now largely off-limits. McGuire's alienation from UNC was aggravated by the continuing failure to replace Woollen Gym with a modern field house and by his enduring feud with Chuck Erickson. For those reasons, he was receptive to approaches for other coaching jobs.[58]

In May 1961, shortly after Friday announced his response to the "serious embarrassment" that basketball had caused the Consolidated University, McGuire acknowledged that he had "considered quitting." The NBA's New York Knicks offered him their head coaching job, but the terms were not attractive enough to lure him from college basketball. A few weeks later he accepted an opportunity he found "impossible to refuse" to become vice president and head coach of the "floundering" Philadelphia Warriors, whose star was Wilt Chamberlain. The founder and owner of the Warriors, Eddie Gottlieb, met every one of McGuire's demands and paid him $25,000, more than double his salary at North Carolina.[59]

Aycock announced that the university accepted McGuire's resignation "with regret" and added that "we are most reluctant to lose him." The regret he cited was presumably mixed with relief that the popular McGuire was departing before the question of renewing his contract could become a source of controversy. Despite Aycock's differences with McGuire, he immediately accepted the coach's recommendation for his replacement. McGuire told Aycock that Dean Smith, his assistant for three years, was ready to "fully accept the responsibilities of the Head Coach and perform the necessary duties in an excellent manner." He affirmed that he knew "of no man more capable to lead our basketball program."[60]

Aycock had already formed a high opinion of Smith. When he was preparing the university's case during the NCAA's investigation of recruiting violations, Smith, at McGuire's request, had assisted the chancellor in examining financial records to try to figure out details about expenses for entertainment of prospective players. This effort proved largely futile, but Aycock was impressed with Smith's recognition of the primary purposes of the university. Friday later commented that Aycock saw a lot of himself in Smith. He hired Smith without conducting a national search for a coach or even consulting with his athletic director, which was a cause of considerable resentment on Erickson's part. Aycock instructed Smith to "give the university a team of which it could be proud." He pledged that as long as Smith conducted the program with integrity, he would support him regardless of the number of games his teams won and lost. Smith took over the head coaching job in August 1961 for a salary of $9,200.[61]

The actions that Friday took in the wake of the point-shaving scandal marked the end of the roller coaster ride that NC State and North Carolina fans and administrators had experienced during the first eight years of the ACC. State College established a record of consistent excellence and won four conference championships. It also suffered through a total of five years of NCAA probation and the shock of the bribery scheme that its players joined. North Carolina stirred pride and jubilation across the entire state and improved the national stature of the ACC by winning the NCAA championship in 1957. But it also was penalized by the NCAA and staggered by the squalor of point shaving. As a result of the embarrassments off the court and the de-emphasis that Friday imposed, Case and McGuire lost their status as the preeminent coaches in the ACC. Four years after winning the national title, McGuire was effectively forced out as coach at North Carolina because the university's leadership believed that he had harmed the reputation of the school. In their minds, winning basketball games was a poor trade-off for this kind of damage. Case did not lose his job at NC State, but, as Smith Barrier observed, after the exposure of the bribery scandal and the withering criticism of his statements about the "values of New York boys," he "was never the same." A short time after Smith was named coach at North Carolina, Case invited him to dinner. He commented on how difficult it would be to compete in the ACC with the restrictions that both schools faced and suggested that their rivals at Duke, where Vic Bubas was head coach, and Wake Forest, where McKinney was head coach, were gleeful about recent developments. "Ole Bubas and Bones are licking their chops now," he remarked. "With the limitations we have on us, Duke and Wake will have it to themselves."[62] Indeed, at least for a time, the mantle of dominance in ACC basketball passed from NC State and North Carolina to Duke and Wake Forest.

5

THE BIG FOUR

Shortly after the NCAA placed the University of North Carolina on probation but before the point-shaving scandal broke, the Tar Heels met the Duke Blue Devils in Durham in an important ACC matchup. Duke, ranked fourth in the nation, came into the game with a record of 7–0 in the conference and 15–1 overall. UNC was ranked fifth nationally with a record of 7–0 in the ACC and 13–2 overall. Chancellor Aycock had already decided that North Carolina would not participate in the conference tournament, which meant that there would be no postseason action of any kind for its players. Therefore, the success they achieved and the satisfaction they gained would necessarily depend on their performance during the regular season. This further elevated the stakes of the contest between, in the words of *Sports Illustrated* writer Ray Cave, "two testy and contentious southern neighbors."[1]

The game, played on February 4, 1961, was a tight thriller from the opening tip-off. Both teams played exceptionally well and neither could build a lead of more than 6 points. The outcome remained in doubt until Duke's Art Heyman made two foul shots to put the Blue Devils ahead by the score of 80–75 with 15 seconds left. After more than 39 minutes of gripping drama, the game deteriorated into a bench-clearing fist fight at the end. With 9 seconds to play, North Carolina's Larry Brown drove under the basket and was intentionally fouled by Heyman. Brown responded by hurling the ball into the crowd and by punching Heyman twice in the face. North Carolina's Donnie Walsh "forcibly" pushed Heyman from behind into Brown, and as both belligerents fell to the floor, Heyman slugged Brown. Players from both benches and fans rushed to join the fray before ten guards hired specifically by Duke to police the game could restore order. The free-for-all, Dick Herbert wrote, "was a sorry ending to what had been an outstanding athletic event."[2]

ACC commissioner Jim Weaver promptly investigated the causes of the fracas and decided on punishments for those he found responsible. He disclosed the results of his review on February 16, 1961. He lamented in general terms the "inhospitable behavior" of students at ACC schools who exhibited their "total lack of maturity" by "tossing articles onto the playing floor, booing officials, booing visiting players when they are attempting foul shots, and . . . eagerly await[ing] any opportunity to rush onto the court." Weaver suggested that those conditions prevailed throughout the ACC because "spectator conduct" had "not kept pace" with the "phenomenal" improvement in the performance of conference teams over the previous decade. After issuing his indictment of overzealous fans, he announced that he was suspending the principals in the Duke–North Carolina fight for the remainder of the regular conference season. In Weaver's judgment, the actions of Heyman, Brown, and Walsh in starting and escalating the melee were unacceptable.[3]

The burden of Weaver's action fell harder on Duke. Brown and Walsh were reserves on the North Carolina squad, and it went on to win the regular season championship. Heyman was Duke's star; he was averaging 24.4 points and 11 rebounds per game when he was suspended. The Blue Devils finished the regular season by losing three conference games in Heyman's absence and winding up third in the league standings. When Weaver announced his decision, Duke officials were unhappy but withheld comment. Frank McGuire, however, declared that the suspensions of his players offered further proof that Weaver was "out to get me." He complained that "we get clobbered, and Duke comes out of it smelling like a rose."[4]

The fight that marred the Duke–North Carolina game was in part an extension of a rivalry between Brown and Heyman that had begun during their high school careers in New York (though they were friends away from the court). It was also a result of the ill will that had developed between players on both teams; Heyman and Doug Moe spent much of the game spitting at each other. But the brawl was not simply a matter of misbehavior in the heat of battle. It graphically demonstrated the growing intensity of the competition between Duke and North Carolina for supremacy in the ACC and national recognition. During the 1950s, North Carolina's most formidable and most reviled conference opponent was usually NC State. Duke fielded highly competitive teams under Hal Bradley but had never quite achieved parity with UNC and State. When Vic Bubas replaced Bradley as head coach, however, Duke quickly advanced to the top tier of the ACC. The key player in leading Duke to a consistently elite position in the conference and to unprecedented national stature was Heyman, and he had originally planned to play for Frank McGuire at North Carolina.[5]

A "Young Man with Ideas"

Bradley resigned at Duke in March 1959 to become head coach at the University of Texas. "The opportunity," he said, "was too good to pass up." He reportedly received a salary of $10,000 per year, a substantial increase over what he made at Duke and the highest amount that Texas had ever paid its basketball coach. Bradley had just been named ACC Coach of the Year after guiding a team that regularly started five sophomores to a 13–12 record and third place in the conference. In his nine years at Duke, he won 168 games and lost 77. In December 1958, he had the 12th-best career winning percentage (.708) of active coaches in the country who had won at least 200 games, ranking just behind Frank McGuire and just ahead of Indiana's Branch McCracken. The ACC was the only conference with three coaches, including Everett Case, on the list of sixteen with winning percentages of at least .700.[6]

Duke supporters appreciated Bradley's accomplishments but still hoped that his successor would elevate them to North Carolina and NC State's slightly higher plane. Athletic director Eddie Cameron received 135 applications for the position, and on May 6, 1959, he announced that he had selected Vic Bubas. Bubas was not a popular choice with some Duke fans, who grumbled that he had never been a head coach and that he was a graduate of and assistant at NC State, which they regarded as an academically inferior "basketball factory." Above all, there were misgivings about the extent to which Bubas was responsible for the severe penalties the NCAA imposed on State as a result of the Jackie Moreland affair. Cameron shared the concerns about the recruiting violations that had led to State's four-year probation, and he thoroughly investigated Bubas's role. After talking with people who were knowledgeable about the case, he was satisfied that Bubas had not made illicit offers to Moreland or his girlfriend.[7]

Despite the behind-the-scenes reservations of some observers, the hiring of Bubas was generally hailed as the right move for Duke. "Duke University not only came up with the most logical choice for the position," Jack Horner commented in the *Durham Morning Herald*, "but it filled the head coaching vacancy with one of the brightest young coaching prospects in the nation." Bubas took over at Duke at age 32 after earning an outstanding reputation for his coaching and recruiting abilities during his eight years as an assistant to Case. He was one of the first scholastic stars that Case lured from Indiana to play at State College. Bubas grew up in Gary, where his father, an immigrant from Croatia who spoke no English when he arrived penniless in the United States in 1915, ran a successful hardware store. He served in the army after graduating from high school and then enrolled at State in fall 1947. Bubas played the guard position on teams that won four Southern Conference championships and he twice received All-Conference honors. He also scored the first field goal at Reynolds Coliseum when it opened on December 2, 1949. In addition to his achievements on the court, Bubas was one of twelve State College seniors selected for the Golden Chain, an honorary society that recognized leadership and scholarship.[8]

Bubas decided that he wanted to coach basketball even before he entered NC State. Case both encouraged him to achieve his goal and appreciated the promise he showed to do it well. When Bubas graduated in 1951, Case hired him as freshman coach. In four years in that capacity, Bubas compiled a record of 64–10. Case made him the top assistant when Butter Anderson left State College in 1955, and Bubas excelled as a coach and recruiter. He was better than his mentor in devising strategies to use against particular opponents and making midcourse adjustments from the bench. As a result, Case frequently deferred to him in practices and asked him to take over during games. Bubas was an aggressive, effective, and far-reaching recruiter. Most coaches sought players from nearby areas that were accessible by automobile, though ACC schools also drew heavily from New York, New Jersey, and Pennsylvania, and Case had extended the normal boundaries of his recruiting to the Midwest. Bubas went even further. He convinced Case to go after Ronnie Shavlik from Colorado, and he was instrumental in landing Jackie Moreland from Louisiana and others from locations far removed from Raleigh.[9]

Bubas brought several strengths to the job at Duke that his friends, rivals, and players regarded as keys in his success. One was his engaging personal style. Jeff Mullins was high school player of the year in Kentucky in 1960 and was under a great deal of pressure from Adolph Rupp, Kentucky fans, and the governor of the state to attend his hometown university (he lived in Lexington). But he did not hold Rupp in high regard. The previous year, his teammate and good friend Jon Speaks had wanted to attend Kentucky but Rupp had initially rebuffed him. The coach changed his mind late in the season and then tried to bully Speaks into signing. Mullins witnessed Rupp's tactics and found them offensive. He had gotten to know Bubas, who was still at NC State and who was very much interested in Speaks. Bubas not only convinced Speaks to attend State, where he became an All-Conference player, but also won Mullins's respect with his friendly, low-key, and thoughtful manner. Mullins seriously considered other schools, including Maryland, but he signed with Duke because he was so impressed with Bubas and wished to play for a team that ran the ball. The ACC as a conference was not a drawing card in itself. Mullins later commented that he knew only a few of the teams that were members of the ACC when he committed to Duke.[10]

Another vital ingredient of Bubas's success was his work ethic. "I'll give my job 100 per cent effort," he promised when he was introduced as Duke's head coach. "And even more, if it requires it." He soon made good on his word. He shared a small office with his two assistants and asked Cameron for an air-conditioner to cool the room during the summer. When a surprised Cameron replied that no one worked at Duke Indoor Stadium during the summer months, Bubas explained that he and his staff would be doing so. He then purchased an air-conditioner himself. Bubas, like Case, was an energetic and effective promoter. He talked up Duke basketball to local businesses and to civic, fraternal, and church groups. He held basketball clinics for boys and girls. He attracted more women to Duke games by improving restrooms at the arena and by establishing a modestly priced family section in end zone seats. He won the loyalty of fans by making parking easier and assigning Duke coeds to check coats. He enhanced the home-court advantage for his teams by creating a pep band. Within a short time, Bubas's innovations helped to lift Duke basketball to new levels of visibility, popularity, and national prominence.[11]

Bubas was not alone among college basketball coaches in being agreeable and hardworking, but he was exceptional in his organizational talent. In a profession that did not place a premium on managerial skills, he demonstrated how valuable they could be. He made thoughtful plans on matters great and small and paid close attention to details on every aspect of the basketball program, from the condition of the furniture in his office to the academic prospects of potential recruits. Once he decided on his objectives, he delegated responsibility for carrying them out. He told his assistants exactly what he wanted done and then expected them to follow through. "He delegated a lot," remarked Fred Shabel, who was an assistant for Bubas from 1959 through 1963. "It was like he was the general partner and the assistants were limited partners. He was always involved, on top of it with total knowledge."[12]

Bubas's system worked effectively in significant measure because of the ability and dedication of his assistants. Shabel had played for Hal Bradley from 1951 through 1954 and joined his staff in 1957. When Cameron hired Bubas, he told him to keep Shabel and Bradley's other assistant, Whit Cobb, for at least one season. After the first year, he could decide whether he wanted to replace them. Bubas quickly realized that Shabel "was really a blessing" because he "understood Duke and would work hard." Cobb decided to leave shortly after the coaching change, and Bubas hired Bucky Waters as freshman coach. Waters had graduated from NC State in 1958 and played for Case (and Bubas).[13]

Bubas applied his various attributes to the ever-critical task of recruiting. He and his assistants carefully screened high school players from around the country not only for their basketball prowess but also for their academic qualifications. Bubas was committed to finding players who could meet Duke's admission standards and were likely to graduate. In a practice rare at the time, he tried to keep a step ahead of his competitors by evaluating high school juniors as well as seniors. After the coaches narrowed their list of prospects, they sought to sell both the educational and athletic benefits of attending Duke. Jay Buckley decided to sign with Duke in 1960 partly because of its academic reputation but mostly because he was very impressed with the way that Bubas, whom he liked, and Waters, whom he especially liked, presented the advantages of the university. In 1962, *Sports Illustrated* described Bubas as a "young man with ideas and inexhaustible energy" who "began in 1959 to corral players from everywhere." It quoted an unnamed Big Ten coach who called Bubas college basketball's "best recruiter."[14]

Bubas's mastery of the details of recruiting and his "astounding knowledge of the landscape" were evident in a conversation with another coach. The colleague provided sketchy information about high school players who were being recruited and challenged Bubas to name them. For about ten

Vic Bubas and, to his left, Bucky Waters, 1965. (Courtesy The North Carolina State Archives; reprinted by permission of *The News and Observer* of Raleigh, North Carolina)

minutes, Bubas correctly identified the players his friend described. Finally, the other coach asked the name of a prospect who stood 6'10", weighed 240 pounds, scored 32.1 points per game, and was an orphan with a gold front tooth. Bubas hesitated and then replied: "There is no such person." He was right again.[15]

Duke's Rise to the Top

The day after Bubas was introduced as Duke's coach, he flew to New York with Shabel on a recruiting trip. "We are behind in the recruiting, and it may be we are too far behind to come up with a good freshman squad this coming season," he told reporters. "But we will give it a hard try." The principal focus of the "hard try" was Art Heyman. Heyman had already signed a letter of intent to play at North Carolina, where he planned to team up with Doug Moe, Larry Brown, and other friends and rivals from the New York area. The letter of intent did not become binding until July 1, 1959. Some time after his decision was announced, Heyman and his stepfather, Bill Heyman, made a visit to Chapel Hill. In a conversation with McGuire,

Bill Heyman asked about North Carolina's academic requirements and implied that McGuire cared little about his players' performance in the classroom. McGuire took offense and the two men were soon engaged in a furious argument. Consequently, Bill Heyman decided that Art would not attend North Carolina. At about the same time, Bubas contacted Heyman. Heyman's stepfather and mother found Bubas charming and his case for Duke persuasive. They prevailed on their son to sign with Bubas despite his reservations about spurning North Carolina.[16]

Heyman's change of mind was an acute disappointment to McGuire. He told Heyman that Bubas was anti-Semitic, a charge that Shabel, whose parents were first-generation Jewish immigrants, refuted. Heyman's arrival was a turning point for the Duke program. Just as Lennie Rosenbluth's enrollment at North Carolina instead of NC State shifted the balance of power in the ACC in the mid-1950s, Heyman's decision was the crucial first step that enabled Duke to surpass UNC in the early 1960s. During his senior year in high school on Long Island, Heyman averaged more than 30 points and 25 rebounds per game. He was an aggressive player of 6'5" and 205 pounds who used his strength to find or make openings to the basket. "His best play," Ray Cave wrote, "is a power-packed rush for the basket which carries him at, on, and over anyone who is foolish enough to get in his way." Heyman's appearance could be deceptive; he shuffled his feet when he walked and leaned forward from the waist in a way that looked awkward. "The first time I saw him," Bubas joked, "I wasn't so much concerned over his basketball ability as whether or not he was going to fall down." But he never doubted Heyman's talent.[17]

In keeping with his combative style of play, Heyman was brash and emotional. Although he could be considerate and respectful, his cockiness and belligerence were usually more apparent. Roy Terrell suggested in *Sports Illustrated* in 1962 that Bubas, Shabel, and Waters "will bear scars to their dying day received in the service of helping Arthur Heyman age gracefully." Heyman's impertinence could be beneficial. When he first arrived at Duke, he was astonished that his teammates, including upper classmen, were not playing and practicing diligently in the off-season. "What's going on?" he asked Bubas. "Don't these fellows want to win?" Within a short time, Bubas recalled, Heyman "gathered everybody up prior to official practice, and next thing I knew they were going at each other like it was mid-season. . . . Art kind of opened their eyes to what it took." Heyman's boisterous arrogance could also be offensive. Novelist Pat Conroy was a player at The Citadel during the 1960s and worked at a well-known summer basketball camp near Charlottesville called Camp Wahoo. He knew Heyman from games in which the camp counselors competed. "Art's game was urban, black, big-city, kiss my ass and hold the mayo, in your face, wiseass Jewish, no-holds barred and a hot dog at Nathan's after the game," Conroy later wrote. He seemed to thrive on the "loathing" of the other players and "ran his mouth the entire game."[18]

Heyman's skill and passion as a player and the growing ferocity of Duke's rivalry with North Carolina were vividly apparent in a freshman game be-tween the "Blue Imps" and the "Tar Babies" in 1960. At that time, the fresh-man teams often played each other three times, the third at a neutral site. In a game in Siler City, North Carolina, about 45 miles from Durham, UNC players, presumably prompted by McGuire, made their animosity toward Heyman clear. As soon as the game started, they began to call him "Jew-bastard," "Christ-killer," and other anti-Semitic slurs. Their efforts to agi-tate Heyman quickly succeeded. Freshman coach Waters recognized what was happening and called time-out twice early in the game to try to calm his star. He suggested that if Heyman stayed cool and led his squad to a big win, toward the end of the game he could point to the scoreboard as a parting shot at his tormenters. Heyman kept his composure and scored 34 points as the Imps built an insurmountable lead. Waters removed Heyman from the lineup shortly before the final buzzer, and as Heyman walked past the North Carolina bench, he defiantly pointed at the scoreboard. Dieter Krause, a brawny 6′5″ UNC player, took umbrage and blindsided Heyman with a blow to the face that required six stitches. This set off a fierce fight between the teams; Waters was so angry that he took hold of North Caro-lina freshman coach Ken Rosemond's lapels and shoved him hard against the scorer's table. Afterward, Waters worried that the brawl could finish his college coaching career at age 23, but Cameron and Bubas stuck by him. They advised him, however, not to use the point-at-the-scoreboard routine again.[19]

While the Blue Imps previewed Duke's bright future, Bubas's varsity en-countered difficulties during his first season as coach. Bubas had inherited a group of talented juniors, led by 6′3″ guard-forward Howard Hurt, 6′9″ forward Doug Kistler, and 6′6″ center Carroll Youngkin. The team finished the 1959–60 regular season with a disappointing 12–10 overall record and placed fourth in the conference with a 7–7 record. It lost three times to North Carolina, twice in the regular season and again in the Dixie Classic, by 22, 26, and 25 points. North Carolina and Wake Forest tied for the regu-lar season championship with 12–2 records.[20]

Duke then seized the conference championship by pulling off the greatest upset in the history of the ACC Tournament to that time. After opening with a win against South Carolina, it rode Youngkin's 30 points to a shocking 71–69 victory over North Carolina. The next evening, the Blue Devils faced Wake, which had defeated them by margins of 19 and 17 points during the regular season. In another stunning performance, Duke prevailed, 63–59, to win the ACC championship. Kistler scored 22 points, and the team held Wake to shooting less than 34 percent from the field. An ecstatic Bubas told reporters that the ACC titles he had won as an assistant at NC State "felt mighty good," but "this one is all mine." Duke followed its conference championship by beating Princeton and St. Joseph's in the NCAA Tournament before falling to New York University in the regional finals.[21]

The following season, Heyman moved up from the freshman team to play for the conference champions. He showed no deference to his senior teammates. He called them by decidedly irreverent nicknames, and they responded with a fitting label for him: "The Pest." The team played exceedingly well until it faltered at the end of the season after the fight with North Carolina and Heyman's suspension. It lost badly to Wake Forest in the ACC Tournament finals. Duke received a national ranking of 10th in the final AP poll, which equaled its highest position ever.

Despite the high ranking, the outcome of the season was a disappointment that was compounded when Duke's top recruit decided at the last moment to attend another school. Bill Bradley of Crystal River, Missouri, was one of the best high school players in the nation, and the Duke coaches were elated when he signed a letter of intent with them. It was such a "profound happening," Waters recalled, that they closed the basketball office and indulged in pizza and beer as they drew up plays on napkins with Bradley, Heyman, and Jeff Mullins on the same court. Bradley opted for Duke in part because of its academic programs but mostly because he thought it had an excellent chance to win a national title. During the summer of 1961, he made a trip to England that changed his priorities. He visited Oxford University and "fell in love with the place." Therefore, he chose to go to Princeton because it had turned out more Rhodes scholars, who studied at Oxford, than any other school. The Ivy League did not recognize letters of intent, and to Bubas's acute distress, he lost his star recruit.[22]

When the 1961–62 season rolled around, the key players on the 1960 championship team were gone, but Heyman was joined by outstanding sophomores Mullins, Buckley, and Buzzy Harrison. Even with the departures, the *Durham Sun* predicted that Duke's "hoopsters will pack trouble

Art Heyman goes up for shot as Jay Buckley watches, 1962. The Clemson players are Mike Bohonak (14) and Jim Brennan (20). (Courtesy The North Carolina State Archives; reprinted by permission of *The News and Observer* of Raleigh, North Carolina)

galore." The 6'4" Mullins was a "silky-smooth" offensive player who scored on a dazzling variety of jump shots, drives, and put-backs after rebounds. During his sophomore season he averaged 21.2 points and 10.4 rebounds per game. When he went to the foul line, he always bounced the ball 13 times before shooting, and Duke fans offered their assistance by counting each dribble in unison. *Sports Illustrated* noted that Mullins was "not as exciting as Heyman—which is probably just as well." But the volatile Heyman and the levelheaded Mullins got along well and gave Duke the best combination of forwards in the country. Buckley was a 6'10" center who was not aggressive on offense, nor did he need to be on a team that featured Heyman and Mullins. He was, however, dangerous with a hook shot from either hand, and he scored on 48 percent of his field-goal attempts. He also set picks, rebounded, and played excellent defense. Harrison was an exceptionally quick guard who shot 51.8 percent from the field and averaged 9.6 points per game.[23]

Duke's size, speed, shooting accuracy, and strong defense more than compensated for its youth during the 1961–62 season. The team finished the regular season with a 19–4 overall record, and its 11–3 conference record was good for second place behind Wake Forest. It defeated Maryland in the first round of the tournament and faced in the second round, to everyone's surprise, Clemson. Clemson had placed sixth in the conference standings with a 4–10 record, but it routed NC State in the first round, 67–46. This was not only Clemson's first victory ever at Reynolds Coliseum but also the first postseason game it had won since Banks McFadden led it to the Southern Conference championship in 1939. Duke looked ahead to a matchup with Wake in the finals and did not take Clemson seriously. This turned out to be a mistake. It fell to Clemson, 77–72, and its season came to a painfully premature end.[24]

The loss to Clemson was a shattering lesson that Duke learned well. The following season was Heyman's last, and he finished with a flourish. He led the ACC in scoring with a 24.9 average, became the first conference player to be a unanimous All-Conference selection three consecutive years, and was named national Player of the Year. Duke went undefeated in the regular conference season and then swept the ACC Tournament. It won the NCAA eastern regionals, but it lost to Loyola of Chicago, the eventual titlist, by the score of 94–75 in the national semifinals. Loyola jumped out to a big lead before Duke closed the margin to 3 points with 4:20 left. At that point, Heyman fouled out, and Loyola stretched its lead to win by a wide margin.[25]

Despite Heyman's departure, Duke's 1963–64 squad was loaded with

Jeff Mullins, 1964. (Courtesy The North Carolina State Archives; reprinted by permission of *The News and Observer* of Raleigh, North Carolina)

talent. Mullins, Buckley, and Harrison were seniors. They were comple-
mented with Hack Tison, a 6'10" junior who made a formidable tandem
in the middle with Buckley, and sophomores Jack Marin and Steve Vacendak. The team was exceptional not only for its ability on the court but
also for its achievements off the court. Mullins was president of both his
junior and senior classes. Buckley was a dean's list student in physics and
earned a fellowship from the National Aeronautics and Space Administration to work on physics projects during the summer of 1963. Harrison
and the other backcourt starter, Danny Ferguson, were Dean's List scholars, and Harrison was president of the Duke chapter of the Fellowship of
Christian Athletes. Marin also made the Dean's List, and he, Tison, and
Vacendak were enrolled in the university's premedical curriculum. Those
accomplishments were a source of pride for Bubas, who was committed to
signing players who were good students and good citizens. "It would be a
great thing for basketball," he said, "if this group could go all the way."[26]

They came very close. Duke romped through the regular season with a
conference record of 13–1 and then won the tournament in three lopsided
games, including an 80–59 victory over second-place Wake in the finals.
Mullins was named ACC Player of the Year and averaged 24.2 points and
8.9 rebounds per game. Duke reached the final rounds of the NCAA Tournament after beating Villanova, 87–73, behind Mullins's 43 points, and the
University of Connecticut, coached by Fred Shabel, 101–54. Duke went up
against more powerful competition in the national semifinals. Its opponent
was the University of Michigan, led by Cazzie Russell, which had pounded
Duke by the score of 83–67 earlier in the season. Buckley had played such
a poor game that one writer called him Duke's "weak link," after which
his teammates jokingly called him "Link." Buckley, who had improved
his offensive skills and averaged 13.8 points and 9.0 rebounds as a senior,
scored 25 points and collected 14 rebounds as Duke avenged its previous
loss, 91–80.[27]

Duke's opponent in the championship game was undefeated UCLA,
coached by John Wooden. UCLA had little size—none of its starters was
taller than 6'5". But it used a devastating zone press that created general
havoc, caused turnovers, and set up easy baskets. Duke was not well-
prepared to face UCLA, in part because the final game was the night after
the semifinals and in part because the coaches and players did not know
much about teams from California. National television coverage of college
basketball was rare, and Buckley later recalled that he had the impression
that West Coast teams were not that good. The title game was close for

much of the first half. Duke held a 30–27 advantage when UCLA launched a "Bruin Blitz" like those that had demoralized its competition throughout the season. It scored 16 points in a row in the space of two and a half minutes to take a lead it never surrendered. UCLA forced 29 Duke turnovers and coasted to a 98–83 victory that provided Wooden with his first national championship. "We just lost our poise against their pressure defense and went to pieces," Bubas lamented.[28]

Duke's 1964–65 team was short on experience after the graduation of the senior stalwarts of the previous season, but it still went 18–4 overall and placed first in the regular season ACC standings with a record of 11–3. Marin, whom Bubas once called the "most complete basketball player I've ever coached," and Vacendak, a tough, hustling guard, stepped up to become stars as juniors. They were joined by sophomore Bob Verga, one of the best pure shooters in ACC basketball history. The team was an offensive juggernaut; it ran so effectively that it averaged a school-record 92.4 points per game. Verga led the way with 21.4 points per game, Marin followed closely at 19.1, and Vacendak added 16.2. The season came to a ruefully abrupt end when NC State, which tied for second in the conference, defeated Duke in the ACC Tournament finals.

With the nucleus of the team back for the 1965–66 season, Duke once again led the ACC. It finished 12–2 to win the regular season. Overall, its 23–3 record included two smashing victories over UCLA. Duke was ready for UCLA's press and Vacendek showed "extreme coolness . . . under pressure." The Blue Devils won the ACC Tournament, but only after a harrowing semifinal matchup with North Carolina. UNC coach Dean Smith decided that his best chance to win was to slow down the game, and Duke barely came out on top, 21–20, after sophomore center Mike Lewis hit a foul shot with four seconds left. Duke then beat NC State for the league title. Its stars once again were Marin, Verga, and Vacendak. Lewis, who hailed from Montana, was also a major contributor; he averaged 13.5 points and led the ACC in rebounding with 11 per game. Vacendak performed so well in the tournament that he was named ACC Player of the Year—the only time in ACC history a player received this award after making second-team rather than first-team All-Conference. Duke won the eastern regionals in the NCAA Tournament by defeating St. Joseph's and Syracuse. Verga, who was named Most Valuable Player in the regionals, spent several days in the hospital with a high fever and flu before the national semifinal contest against Kentucky. He played in the game but was not close to full strength. He scored only 4 points as Kentucky edged the Blue Devils, 83–79. Kentucky went on to lose the finals to Texas Western in one of the legendary games of NCAA Tournament history. Had Duke won over Kentucky, its all-white squad would have met the Texas Western team that started five blacks and, symbolically at least, changed the face of college basketball.[29]

Between 1960 and 1966, Duke's performance exceeded NC State's mastery of the ACC during the 1950s. Duke captured four ACC championships in that period, which matched the number that NC State won between 1954 and 1959. Duke performed better than State in NCAA Tournaments, making the final rounds on three occasions and the championship game in 1964. It received consistently high rankings in national polls and commanded a great deal of attention and respect in the national media. Bubas continued to sign outstanding recruits who built on a strong tradition of excellence. After the 1965–66 season, however, observers suggested that while Duke remained the team to beat, its dominance could no longer be assumed. In its forecast of the 1966–67 season, *The State* of Columbia, South Carolina, summarized this way of thinking with a headline: "Duke Still Favored, But No Longer a Sure Thing."[30]

Glory for the Demon Deacons

Duke's chief competitor in the early 1960s was Wake Forest. The teams met in the ACC Tournament finals every year between 1960 and 1964 except 1962, when Clemson ousted Duke in the semifinals. The architect of Wake Forest teams that challenged Duke's supremacy and that won league titles in 1961 and 1962 was Bones McKinney. Even in a conference prominently inhabited by brilliant and colorful coaches, he was in a class by himself.

McKinney was named Wake's head coach in March 1957. Murray Greason became assistant director of athletics, a job in which he was responsible for helping coaches in all sports to recruit and coordinating public relations programs. Wake Forest president Harold Tribble was worried about losing McKinney, who had been courted by Clemson the previous year and who was seriously considering an offer to become head coach at Appalachian State Teachers College in Boone, North Carolina. He agreed to take over at Wake only after checking with Greason to make certain the change was "what he really wanted." McKinney insisted that it be "made very clear that Greason is resigning of his own accord" and that he was "being offered the position as his successor with pleasant relations and in good faith." On that basis, McKinney happily accepted the promotion.

Greason retired from coaching after 23 years in which he compiled a record of 276 wins and 227 losses.[31]

By the time that McKinney was appointed head coach, he had completed his seminary studies and had been ordained as a Baptist minister. His coaching salary was supplemented by income for serving as Wake Forest's assistant campus chaplain. In 1960, he received a salary of $8,000 for coaching and another $3,000 in pay and a housing allowance as assistant chaplain. The combined total placed him in the same salary range as Case and McGuire, though they were not expected to minister to the spiritual needs of students and faculty. Tribble told McKinney how pleased he was "in having in one person an excellent Head Basketball Coach and a devout and capable Assistant Chaplain." He suggested, however, that McKinney allocate more time to "the actual work of the Chaplain's office." Even if the time he spent on his chaplain duties was limited, McKinney took his ministerial responsibilities seriously. He had entered seminary in 1952 after making up his "mind to abandon those things I knew to be wrong," and he told one audience that "if all I ever could be at Wake Forest is a basketball coach, I would not be there." He was much in demand as a preacher. He drove all over the state of North Carolina delivering hellfire-and-brimstone sermons to enthralled Baptist congregations. Billy Packer, who was a star player on Wake's outstanding teams in the early 1960s, often went along on the trips at McKinney's request. He was always impressed that without notes or preparation, the coach could speak in a cohesive and stirring manner and, even more remarkably, give talks that were invariably different than previous ones.[32]

When McKinney took over as head coach, four starters from the team that narrowly lost to North Carolina in the 1957 ACC Tournament had graduated and he faced a major rebuilding job. Nevertheless, he had already gained a reputation, according to *Sports Illustrated*, of being "as good a coach of basketball as any league can boast of." His effectiveness in part reflected his ability as a teacher of skills, as his tutoring of Dickie Hemric had demonstrated so vividly. Wake usually had less depth to draw on than its Big Four rivals, but McKinney was an excellent tactician who devised innovative ways to match up against specific opponents and a resourceful bench coach who made adroit adjustments during games. "The Wake Forest formula in recent years has been making the most of what is available," Dick Herbert commented. "Greason and McKinney showed it does not take a lot of super stars from which to form a sound basketball team."[33]

Bones McKinney, 1962. To his right is assistant coach Jack Murdock and to his left is assistant coach Charlie Bryant. (Courtesy The North Carolina State Archives; reprinted by permission of *The News and Observer* of Raleigh, North Carolina)

Despite the recognition he received for his coaching savvy, McKinney readily conceded that the key to winning was to "have the horses." He gradually found the horses he needed to compete successfully in the ACC. He suffered through his first season with a squad that went 6–17 overall and finished in a tie for last place in the conference with South Carolina. McKinney lacked the recruiting resources available to coaches of other Big Four schools, and he was not a master of organizational detail like Bubas. But he soon managed to bring talented players to Wake Forest. On one occasion, he found out about some likely prospects with the inadvertent assistance of Hal Bradley. During a visit with the Duke coach in Durham, McKinney had to make a personal phone call. Bradley offered the use of his office, and while placing the call, McKinney noticed a blackboard with the names of players Duke wanted to recruit. He decided that those players must be worthy of attention and went after some of them himself. Two of the players on Bradley's list, Packer and Len Chappell, enrolled at Wake Forest and were instrumental in its dramatic improvement.[34]

Packer was a native of Bethlehem, Pennsylvania, where his father coached the basketball and baseball teams at Lehigh University. Packer knew little about the ACC, but he was convinced that he wanted to attend Duke. He aspired to follow the example of Dick Groat, by then a star short-stop for the Pittsburgh Pirates, who had excelled at both basketball and baseball as a student at Duke. Bradley was interested in Packer but had not decided whether to offer him a scholarship. Packer had never heard of Wake Forest, and McKinney would never have recruited him, especially in a location as distant as Bethlehem, had he not seen the list in Bradley's office. When McKinney showed up at one of Packer's games, he stood out in the crowd. "You couldn't miss him," Packer said later. "A tall, gangly guy wearing goofy-looking red socks." When Packer made a visit to Wake, he liked the school, the coach, and the other prospects he met. He still favored Duke until he learned that Bradley remained uncertain about giving him a scholarship. He immediately decided to sign with Wake, in part to gain vengeance when he competed against Duke.[35]

Meanwhile, McKinney was making a series of eleven-hour drives each way to recruit Len Chappell in the western Pennsylvania town of Port-age. Chappell was considering many other schools, including Duke, Vir-ginia, and North Carolina. But he was much taken with McKinney, who told him that he had the ability to play a leading role in Wake's revival. During McKinney's "do-or-die visit" to Portage, he convinced Chappell's recently widowed mother that Wake was the right choice. She told him

Billy Packer (left), Len Chappell (center), and Dave Budd, 1960. (Courtesy The North Carolina State Archives; reprinted by permission of *The News and Observer* of Raleigh, North Carolina)

that another school had offered her son a scholarship plus one hundred dollars per month. McKinney responded that he could provide only what the NCAA allowed and added, "If that school is going to break that rule now, how many more are they going to break when Lenny gets there?" Mrs. Chappell found McKinney's case persuasive and told her son he was going to Wake Forest. As a result, McKinney later wrote, "'Old Bones . . . and Wake Forest had them a new 'Chappell.'" Despite the success that he and assistant coaches Charlie Bryant and Al DePorter achieved in landing good players, McKinney did not enjoy the recruiting process. "Recruiting," he complained, "is what makes coaches grow old in a hurry."[36]

The arrival of Packer and Chappell, who teamed as sophomores with talented veterans Dave Budd and George Ritchie, restored Wake Forest to the top ranks of the ACC by the 1959–60 season, McKinney's third as head coach. The team's promise was so great, McKinney remarked, that opponents "no longer waited for us at the city limits with bands playing." Wake demonstrated its ability early in the season by defeating North Carolina to win the Dixie Classic for the first and only time. Packer, an accomplished playmaker who made "breath-taking passes" and a dangerous scoring threat, was named Most Valuable Player, the only sophomore to be so honored. The team finished the regular season with a 19–6 record and tied for first place, but lost in an upset to Duke in the ACC Tournament finals. Chappell was second in the conference in scoring with an average of 17.4 points and third in rebounding with 12.5 per game. He was a rugged 6'8" and 255 pounds with a strong inside game. "If you think of the history of the league," Packer later commented, "there probably hasn't been a more powerful interior player than Lenny Chappell." He was not only an excellent rebounder with sure hands but also difficult to guard because he was an accurate jump shooter with exceptional range.[37]

Expectations were high for the 1960–61 season, and Wake Forest, after a slow start, placed second in the regular season conference standings with a record of 11–3 and then routed Duke in the tournament finals. Chappell led the league in scoring at 26.6 points per game and rebounding with 14 per game. Packer scored 17.2 points per game and joined Chappell on the All-Conference first team. In the NCAA Tournament, Wake defeated St. John's and St. Bonaventure, both highly ranked, and then fell to St. Joseph's in the regional finals. A few weeks later, three members of the St. Joseph's team admitted to point shaving, and, to his astonishment, Packer was summoned by the New York District Attorney's Office for questioning about the scandal. At first, an incredulous Packer found the suggestions that he had fixed games to be ludicrous. But he gradually became worried about the investigators' conviction that he was guilty, which they shared with McKinney and Tribble. He was enormously grateful that both his coach and Wake's president accepted his assurances that he was innocent of the charges and issued a public statement of support. The unpleasant episode ended when the evidence against Packer turned out to be a case of mistaken identity. The investigators confused a hometown acquaintance who visited Packer after a game in New York with the notorious gambler Jack Molinas, whom Packer's friend resembled.[38]

Four of Wake's starters returned for the 1961–62 campaign, and the team was ranked third in the nation in the AP's preseason poll, behind Ohio State and Cincinnati. Once again, the team got off to a slow start; fans grumbled as it lost 8 of its first 17 games. One of the defeats was an 84–62 thumping by Ohio State, led by Jerry Lucas and John Havlicek, which occurred at home before a disappointed sell-out crowd. In the last month of the season, Wake got hot. It rolled to six consecutive wins, including a 97–79 victory over Duke, to place first the ACC regular season standings with a 12–2 record. It earned the tournament championship with a win over upstart Clemson. Chappell again led the league in scoring with an average of 30.1 points and in rebounding with 15.2 per game. After being snubbed the previous year, he was named a first-team All-American by AP and second-team by UPI.

In the NCAA Tournament, Wake survived close games against Yale and St. Joseph's and then won the eastern regionals with a 79–69 triumph over Villanova. This set up a rematch with Ohio State in the NCAA's final four; Wake was the first ACC team to advance that far since North Carolina in 1957. It had been hoping for another shot at Ohio State after the embarrassing defeat earlier in the season, but Havlicek scored 25 points and held Chappell to making just 10 of 24 shots as the Buckeyes dominated again, 84–68. The losers of the semifinal games then met in a consolation game for third place. Wake's opponent was UCLA, which fell to Cincinnati, the eventual national champion, in its first appearance in the NCAA's final rounds. Like most coaches, McKinney "hated consolation games," and he placed little importance on the outcome. But he changed his attitude after a conversation with Everett Case. "Bonesy," Case said, "you've got the whole ACC riding with you. If you win this game, we get the bye next year." At that time, the NCAA picked 25 teams for the tournament, including 15 conference champions. The conferences with the best winning percentages during the history of the tournament received a bye in the first round. "All of a sudden this 'nothing' game," McKinney recalled, "became one of the most important ones in my life. We didn't want to let the conference down." Wake narrowly defeated UCLA, 82–80, the last NCAA Tournament game the Bruins lost until 1974. "This was the first time a consolation game had given me any consolation," McKinney commented. "We were [a] preseason pick for third place and that's where we ended up."[39]

"Mr. Bones"

While Bones McKinney was widely respected for his coaching ability, he was also beloved by fans, players, and even rivals for the passion and hilarity that he brought to college basketball. During games, he was wired with nervous energy. "I used to have anxiety as a player before the game started.

But once it began, I lost it," he said. "Now I never lose it as a coach." A feature profile that *Life* magazine published in February 1960 described him as a coach "with his own private volcano." Eventually, it added, "the moment arrives when 'Mr. Bones' erupts dramatically . . . , looking like a dead ringer for Ichabod Crane." Wearing red socks for good luck, McKinney paced the sidelines, drank large volumes of water from a cooler, directed his team, protested calls, tossed towels, heaved his jacket, and occasionally exchanged barbs with opposing fans. In a game at Clemson in 1960, someone in the crowd hurled a cup of ice at him. When he turned around and demanded to know who had thrown the ice, a "giant of a football player" shouted, "I did." McKinney quickly sized up the situation and opted for discretion by replying, "I hope you're enjoying the game." On more than one occasion, McKinney became so disgusted by his team's poor performance that he left the bench and sat in the stands.

In perhaps the most famous incident of McKinney's storied career of sideline antics, he briefly wore a safety belt attached to his seat on the bench. During the 1959–60 season, ACC commissioner Weaver tried to prevent coaches from charging up and down the sidelines to harass referees. He issued an edict that prohibited coaches from leaving the bench to protest calls. "I'm not sure," McKinney later wrote, "but I think Jim was thinking about me when he announced this new policy." To his surprise, a group of fans installed a seat belt on the bench before the next game. When he walked out of the locker room, he strapped himself in as the fans roared their approval and photographers took pictures that appeared in newspapers around the country. The experiment was short-lived. McKinney stayed in his seat for about ten minutes after the game began and then returned to form. "Sometimes I hate myself for all those antics on the bench," he told *Life*. "Some people think I rehearse them, but if that were so I'd be in Hollywood. I just want to win." An article on McKinney in the *Sporting News* in 1964 concluded, "As a player, coach, and man, there will never be another like him."[40]

After Chappell and Packer graduated, Wake was a weakened but still formidable power in the ACC. In 1962–63, it finished second in the regular season with a conference record of 11–3 and bowed to Duke in the tournament finals. The following season, it repeated the same pattern, placing second in the regular season and then making the tournament finals before losing in a rout to Duke, 80–59. Those teams were led by several outstanding players—Dave Wiedeman, Frank Christie, Butch Hassell, Ronny Watts, and Bob Leonard—all of whom made first- or second-team All-

Conference during their careers. Despite its continuing success in the ACC, Wake's basketball program was increasingly troubled by serious personal problems that afflicted McKinney. At the same time that he guided Wake to national prominence and won enormous popularity, he was fighting a losing battle with alcohol and amphetamines. McKinney managed to keep his dependencies largely a secret for a long time, in part because his normal behavior was so frenetic and unpredictable. But those who were closest to him knew. At one point during the 1961–62 season, assistant coach Charlie Bryant became drowsy while watching game films late at night. McKinney offered him one of the pills he was taking. Bryant reluctantly swallowed it and then found that he could not sleep the entire weekend. McKinney was taking the same pills "by the handful," and when he could not sleep, popping sleeping pills. Billy Packer later commented that he had no clue about McKinney's addictions when he was playing, but it "turned out that by our senior year he was totally out of control in his personal life with drugs and alcohol."[41]

McKinney's abuse of alcohol and pills apparently was a result of his impossibly demanding schedule. When he decided to attend seminary in 1952, he had given up drinking and become a teetotaler. Bill Hensley, at that time director of sports information at Wake, was McKinney's roommate on road trips and never saw him touch alcohol. But McKinney fell off the wagon after he became head coach and the pressures on him greatly intensified. He coached a highly ranked team, made frequent recruiting trips, and appeared on a weekly television program. He served as the college's assistant chaplain. He preached at Baptist churches and revival meetings. He was much in demand as a luncheon and after-dinner speaker. He talked at summer basketball camps. And he was the father of six children. A physician acquaintance gave him amphetamines to combat fatigue, with disastrous results. Some friends also thought that discrepancies between his preaching and his behavior contributed to the tensions that led to his addictions. McKinney's language and conduct were sometimes incompatible with Baptist standards and could be crude enough to surprise his players. "It occurred to us that although coach was a minister," Packer later remarked, "he'd had quite a past and it wasn't completely out of him."[42]

During the 1963–64 season, McKinney's problems became more apparent and his actions more objectionable. His driving habits, which never had been good, became noticeably worse. He hit a parked car on the wrong side of the street and then left the scene without reporting the accident. In February 1964, he ran across a median strip at high speed and barely avoided serious injury. He sometimes missed speaking engagements. He failed to show up at several practice sessions before important games and before the ACC Tournament. He annoyed reporters by informing them that he intended to resign and then denying that he had made such statements. McKinney had always been a favorite of reporters not only because he was so quotable but also because he was so considerate. He treated Mary Garber, who endured a great deal of discrimination as a pioneering female sports writer for the *Winston-Salem Journal*, with the respect that her talent merited. Once he realized that holding press conferences after games in the team's locker room excluded her from attending, he met with reporters in places where she could be present. But McKinney's behavior in early 1964 eroded the goodwill he had earned with the press.[43]

Growing doubts about McKinney's stability reached a critical point in April 1964 when he suddenly fired his two highly regarded assistant coaches, Bryant and Jack Murdock, who had joined the staff in 1960. "The firing of the popular young assistants created a furor that started Bones on a downhill slide from which he never recovered," the *Winston-Salem Journal* later commented. Bryant and Murdock were shocked, and the reasons McKinney provided for his decision were vague. "We have not reached the potential in basketball that I believe available and necessary," he said. Neither Tribble nor recently hired athletic director Gene Hooks, a former baseball star at Wake, offered any clarification. The basis for McKinney's action stirred speculation, and the *Raleigh News and Observer* addressed the issue in a lighthearted but critical way when it proposed a number of awards modeled after Hollywood's Oscars that the ACC could give. It suggested that the "best foreign language production" be presented to Wake Forest for its "explanation of why basketball aides Charlie Bryant and Jackie Murdock will not be asked back next year," which "fans are still trying to translate."[44]

McKinney's dismissal of his assistants raised so many questions that the editors of Wake's student newspaper, the *Old Gold and Black*, decided to undertake an investigation. Its staff interviewed team members, former players, and others and learned about McKinney's abuse of alcohol and pills. It prepared a hard-hitting report on the coach's behavior, but because it lacked hard evidence, did not mention his addictions. Hooks knew what the paper had found, and although he preferred that no article be published, he told the editors that he would not take action to kill it. Hooks advised them, however, that it would doom his efforts to persuade McKinney to retain Murdock. The *Old Gold and Black* elected to publish an editorial that, on the one hand, cited McKinney's "erratic behavior" and, on the other hand, suggested that his "contributions . . . far out-weigh any temporary harm or embarrassment he may have brought to the school." It also ran an interview with McKinney in which it asked him about criticisms of his behavior. McKinney attributed his problems to exhaustion from too many commitments. "I've created a monster," he said. "It's been the tail wagging the dog, and I must eliminate that monster." A few days later, he rehired Murdock, claiming that the assistant's dismissal had been "a little misunderstanding." Bryant was soon offered a job as an assistant at NC State.[45]

In early May 1964, McKinney sought to deal with his "monster" by entering Appalachian Hall near Asheville, North Carolina, a hospital that specialized in treating mental health disorders and alcohol and drug dependencies. Wake Forest announced that he would stay in a hospital, which was not identified, for "two to four weeks of rest for exhaustion." Tribble, who had strongly supported McKinney "as a basketball coach, as an inspiring leader of students, and as a valuable representative of the College in public relations," told a friend that "Bones is ill, and has been for some time." He confided that after "a period of treatment and rest," McKinney's schedule would be tightly controlled so that he could remain at Wake "for a long time to come." McKinney returned to coaching in fall 1964. The team performed respectably, finishing with a 12–15 overall record, but it was a significant decline from the previous five seasons. Wake Forest students expressed their dissatisfaction by hanging their coach in effigy.[46]

Worse, McKinney's health again became a source of growing concern. In September 1965, Hooks advised Tribble to immediately request McKinney's resignation. He reported that although "McKinney's conduct was acceptable for a while and he did a presentable job as coach" the previous season, he appeared to be reverting to the erratic behavior that had led him to Appalachian Hall. He wrecked his car. He charged the college for dubious expenses in a "flagrant mismanagement of funds." His "recruiting efforts were poorly organized [and] poorly handled." After making optimistic statements about landing top prospects, he signed only one player. Hooks concluded that McKinney was "a sick man" who was "an embarrassment to the school." He urged Tribble to replace the coach before "he does something else that will further endanger the reputation of the school, and while there is still time to salvage something from our present basketball program." Tribble needed little convincing. He acted immediately on Hooks's recommendation, doubtlessly with a heavy heart. On September 27, 1965, McKinney submitted his resignation and declared that his health "simply makes it impossible for me to continue as coach and at the same time be fair to the college and to the team."[47]

McKinney's resignation was greeted with an outpouring of regret and affection. Mary Garber declared that "Wake Forest basketball will never be the same" without his "color, showmanship and spirit of fun and competition." Dick Pavlis, sports editor of the *Old Gold and Black*, lamented the departure of McKinney's "intangible something that brought a much needed spark of enjoyment and excitement to the sports scene." Everett Case commented that McKinney "contributed a great deal to the ACC and to basketball in general . . . Basketball just lost something great." Wake Forest paid McKinney's salary through January 1966 to ease his transition to the new job he accepted with an insurance company. In 1969, he returned to basketball as the head coach of the Carolina Cougars of the American Basketball Association. After McKinney's resignation, Murdock was named Wake's "acting head coach." One of his assistants was Billy Packer, who was hired shortly before the coaching change. After the turmoil of the previous two years, they faced a tough challenge to keep Wake competitive in the ACC.[48]

A "Heck of a Coach" at North Carolina

While Duke and Wake Forest were thriving during the early 1960s, North Carolina and NC State were struggling with the consequences of the point-shaving scandal. Dean Smith took over as North Carolina's head coach at age 30 in August 1961 under trying conditions. His team would play only 16 games, all but 2 against conference opponents. The leading scorers from the previous season, York Larese and Doug Moe, were gone, and two other players he counted on for big contributions, Ken McComb and Yogi Poteet, were declared academically ineligible. The outlook for the future was dimmed by the restrictions on recruiting that President Friday had imposed, and Smith agreed to place further barriers on the underground railroad. In a meeting with Chancellor Aycock and Athletic Director Erickson, he "was strongly advised that it would be best" if Harry Gotkin was not "connected in any way to the University's basketball program." Although Gotkin had not directly contacted or entertained prospects on behalf of the university for three years, Smith informed him that he could no longer even recommend players that North Carolina coaches should recruit.[49]

Smith inevitably faced unfavorable comparisons with the legend he replaced. In contrast to the outgoing, charismatic McGuire, he was reserved and guarded. "The successor to Frank McGuire, one of the most dynamic men in sports, is not overpowering in personality," commented George Cunningham of the *Charlotte Observer* when Smith was introduced as North Carolina's head coach. "But he hits you right between the eyes with sincerity and forthrightness." Curry Kirkpatrick, who was a freshman at North Carolina in 1961 and later covered college basketball for *Sports Illustrated*, once described his reaction to Smith's appointment. "He seemed at the time, so uncool," he recalled. "I was very disappointed that the ultra-cool, sophisticated, great-dressing Frank McGuire was gone."[50]

Others who felt the same way were probably not aware of why McGuire had hired Smith in the first place and then recommended that he be made head coach. In his short career as an assistant at two schools, Smith had earned the respect of his bosses for abilities that he had demonstrated even in his youth in Kansas. Growing up in Emporia and Topeka, he excelled in baseball, football, and basketball. Smith's father, who coached Emporia High School to the state basketball championship in 1934, sparked his interest in coaching and taught him the importance of teamwork and discipline. Smith was offered a partial basketball scholarship at Kansas State but had his heart set on attending the University of Kansas. When he was offered an academic scholarship at Kansas along with the opportunity to make money by selling programs at football games, he "jumped at the chance." He played quarterback on the freshman football team, catcher on the baseball team, and sparingly as a guard on the basketball team. He was a member of the squad that won the national championship under Phog Allen in 1952; one of his "pet peeves" was that, despite playing in the last 47 seconds of the game, the box score did not show that he made an appearance.

Smith was a math major at Kansas but soon decided that he would like to coach one of the sports in which he participated. Allen gave him his first coaching experience in his junior year by instructing him to teach both offense and defense to football players who joined the basketball team after their season ended. Although he was angry at first about this assignment because "the message was I wasn't that important as a player," he later "realized [Allen] was doing me a favor." One of Smith's teammates remarked that "even at that time it was kind of apparent to everybody that he was gonna make a heck of a coach."[51]

After graduating from Kansas, Smith served in the U.S. Air Force in Germany, where he was player-coach on a base team that went 11–1. He also met Bob Spear, a decorated bomber pilot and a former assistant to Ben Carnevale at the Naval Academy. Within a short time, Spear became head coach at the new Air Force Academy in Colorado, and he asked Smith to be his assistant. Coaching at the academy was a difficult job because no player could be taller than 6′4″, the limit for all cadets. Further, the players had many other demanding commitments that left limited time and energy for basketball. Spear and Smith spent long hours devising offensive and defensive strategies that would help overcome their innate disadvantages, and they were remarkably successful. In 1956–57, the academy's first season, the team ended with an 11–10 record, and the following year, it was even better with 17 wins and only 6 losses.

Spear was a good friend of Frank McGuire. When McGuire began searching for a replacement for Buck Freeman, whom Erickson reportedly dismissed for insulting a wealthy booster, Spear highly recommended Smith. McGuire offered him the job as his only assistant at a salary of $7,500, which he claimed would be the highest salary paid to any assistant in college basketball. Smith had some reservations, but when he visited Chapel Hill for the first time in April 1958, "I fell in love at first sight." After Smith signed on, McGuire was much impressed with his dedication, attention to detail, and aptitude for teaching. And he quickly discovered that Smith was a fierce competitor. "I was a good handball player," McGuire once recalled, "and he'd do anything off a couple of walls to get a point."[52]

Smith was an able but not highly visible assistant to McGuire for three years, and when he took over as head coach, he remained an "unknown quantity." Fred Hobson, who played on UNC's freshman team in 1961–62, later commented that those who compared Smith unfavorably with McGuire or remarked on his lack of charisma missed "the steel of the man, the toughness, and the extent to which a first-rate intellect could be applied to basketball strategy." Smith's approach was quite different in important ways from McGuire, who used no offensive plays and depended heavily on Freeman for strategy. Smith was a master of x's and o's. He ran set offensive patterns rather than allowing the "free lance type of offense of past years," and he taught "myriad defenses" that he expected his players to execute. He was a much stricter disciplinarian than McGuire. "Coach McGuire would get mad and call me a Jew bastard, and it rolled off my back," Larry Brown later commented. "But Coach Smith would just say, 'Larry, I think you could have fought over that screen,' and it would hurt me much more." Despite some early grumbling from his players, Smith won their respect and affection. In part, they responded to their recognition that, as Hobson put it, "he was an extremely kind and decent man, a disciplinarian but an eminently fair one." The team members also realized that his methods could be effective, and the most telling sign that he had won them over was that they played hard for him. Despite the burdens they faced, Brown, Don Walsh, and Jim Hudock led them to a record of 7–7 in the conference and 8–9 overall in 1961–62. It was an impressive debut for the rookie coach.[53]

The following season was even better. In January 1962, Aycock and NC State chancellor Caldwell decided to allow their teams to play 19 games during the regular season. North Carolina's prospects were vastly improved by the addition of sophomore Billy Cunningham to the lineup. He was the last great player to arrive from New York via McGuire's underground railroad; Dick Herbert noted before he had played a single varsity game that "some say he is going to be the best player Carolina ever had." Cunningham was an exceptionally gifted offensive threat who soon earned the nickname "Kangaroo Kid" for his leaping ability. He lived up to the lofty expectations by averaging 22.7 points and leading the ACC in rebounding with 16.1 per game. Larry Brown ran the offense and contributed 14.2 points per game. North Carolina finished the season with an overall record of 15–6. It went 10–4 in the conference and lost to Wake in the second round of the tournament, 56–55. Perhaps the most memorable victory came against Kentucky in Lexington early in the season. North Carolina was a decided underdog, and Smith decided that if he got a lead, he would slow the pace of the game by using a spread offense that he had worked on occasionally in practice. Brown ran it to perfection, and UNC won, 68–66. Smith did not invent the spread offense; coaching colleagues, including John McLendon of the North Carolina College for Negroes and other schools, Chuck Noe of the University of South Carolina, and Bob Spear, used variations of it with good results. But Smith later refined it and deployed it regularly, to the disgruntlement of opposing fans. It became famous (or depending on one's perspective, infamous) as the "Four Corners."[54]

After North Carolina's excellent performance in 1962–63, the following season was a disappointment. "I did the worst coaching job of my career," Smith later wrote. Cunningham led the league in scoring and rebounding, but Smith leaned on him too heavily and the team never achieved balance or consistency. It ended with a record of 12–12 overall and 6–8 in the conference (the restrictions on scheduling had been lifted by this time). Early in the following season, the team appeared to be heading toward similar mediocrity and indications of disaffection with the coach were growing. On January 6, 1965, after a crushing defeat at Wake Forest, 107–85, the Tar Heels' record was 6–6. When the team bus arrived at Woollen Gym after the trip from Winston-Salem, coaches and players saw a figure hanging

Billy Cunningham leads the fast break with Duke's Jack Marin (24) chasing, 1965.
(Courtesy The North Carolina State Archives; reprinted by permission of
The News and Observer of Raleigh, North Carolina)

in effigy. There was no doubt that it represented Smith, he later recalled, "because of its long nose." Cunningham bounded off the bus and tore the dummy down. Smith later insisted that he did not "dwell on the episode," but at the time he did not let bygones be bygones. In its next game, North Carolina pulled off an "enormous upset" over Duke, ranked sixth in the country, in Durham. When the bus arrived back in Chapel Hill this time, it was greeted by cheering students who called on Smith to say a few words. Even in the glow of a tremendous victory, he replied: "I can't. There's something tight around my neck that keeps me from speaking." Perhaps inspired by the insult to their coach, UNC rallied in the second half of the season and finished 15–9, 10–4 in the ACC. Cunningham again led the conference in scoring and rebounding and was named Player of the Year.[55]

During the 1964–65 season, North Carolina benefited from the play of Smith's first blue-chip recruit, sophomore Bob Lewis from Washington, D.C. In his first three years as head coach, Smith depended on the talent that McGuire had brought to Chapel Hill, especially Cunningham. He had limited experience in recruiting and, initially, little success. He was not a natural salesman for his program, and, in writer Frank Deford's view, "his distance and diffidence" placed him at a serious disadvantage against "the hail-fellow raconteurs" who approached high school standouts "with grace and aplomb and silver tongues." Smith described his own recruiting style as "honest and sincere," and he and his assistant, Ken Rosemond, emphasized the quality of education available at the University of North Carolina, the beauty of its campus, and the "wonderful college-town atmosphere." Those attributes tended to impress parents more than teenaged prospects, and they did not succeed at first in landing top players. The 6'3" Lewis was a "gazellelike leaper and great scorer inside" who was highly recruited and who originally had no interest in North Carolina. His attitude changed after watching Cunningham play against Notre Dame in a rare national television broadcast. When he made a visit to Chapel Hill, Cunningham showed him around and made a strong case for attending UNC. Lewis "had a great time," found the campus to be "gorgeous," and thought Rosemond was "just a great guy." His parents were particularly taken with Smith's promises that "he would do everything possible to make sure" their son graduated. With those considerations in mind, Lewis enrolled at North Carolina and quickly became a star. During his sophomore year, he averaged 21.0 points and 8.0 rebounds per game.[56]

The decisive recruiting breakthrough for Smith occurred in 1964 when he prevailed over Bubas in a head-to-head battle to sign one of the country's top prospects, Larry Miller. Miller came from Catasauqua, Pennsylvania, a blue-collar community near Allentown, where his father was a Mack truck mechanic. At an early age, he worked out with ankle weights and a weighted vest and became strong enough and skilled enough as an eighth grader to play for the Allentown Jets of the Eastern Basketball League, a refuge for many former college standouts. By the time he reached high school, the 6'4" Miller could leap high enough that his elbows extended above the rim. During his senior year, he averaged more than 30 points and 30 rebounds, including a game in which he scored 65 points, six more than the opposing team. Many schools attempted to recruit him, and he received "a lot of illegal offers." Miller later disclosed that "I could have had summer jobs making more money than my father made in an entire year."

Miller rejected programs that broke the rules, and his final choice came down to Duke or North Carolina. Duke first contacted him when he was a high school freshman, which was unusually early even by its standards, and he was much impressed with Bubas and Waters. But he also liked the North Carolina coaches. Rosemond spent long hours drinking beer with Miller's father without letting on that he detested the taste of beer. Miller

Bob Lewis, surrounded by Duke's Steve Vacendak (left), Jack Marin, and Bob Verga, 1966. (Courtesy The North Carolina State Archives; reprinted by permission of *The News and Observer* of Raleigh, North Carolina)

Larry Miller, 1967.
(*Yackety Yack*, University
of North Carolina)

agonized over his decision before settling on North Carolina for reasons
that even he could not pinpoint. "I just had a feeling that Carolina was
the place for me," he later explained. At a time when UNC was still struggling, he thought he could help "be the start of something." In 1965–66,
the first season that Miller and Lewis played together, North Carolina went
16–11 overall and 8–6 in the conference. Lewis led the ACC in scoring with
an average of 27.4, and Miller contributed 20.9 points and 10.3 rebounds
per game. Smith went to his spread offense against Duke in the tournament semifinals to slow the pace and counter the Blue Devils' speed and
rebounding. Although Duke won the game, 21–20, North Carolina, with
Lewis, Miller, and several talented players moving up from the freshman
team, appeared to be poised for big things.[57]

By April 1966, Smith was proud enough of his accomplishments and
confident enough of his position to seek a five-year contract. He reminded
Erickson that when he had been hired as head coach, Aycock planned to

seek tenured faculty status for coaches and had advised Smith that "a contract was not necessary for security." As long as Aycock had remained chancellor, he had strongly supported Smith even when fans had complained about the team's performance. He had recently left the post, however, without gaining tenure for coaches. Smith told Erickson that North Carolina was the only school he knew of at which football and basketball coaches did not have either tenure or a contract. He suggested that he deserved a long-term contract because he had "recruited good student-athletes to the University and young men of which the University can be proud." Every one of the varsity lettermen who had played for Smith had graduated in four years, and 68 percent of them had earned advanced degrees. Three of his players were elected class presidents, and several others served in leadership positions on campus. Smith also argued that he had fulfilled the objectives Aycock had outlined in 1961 and at the same time built "a creditable won-loss record against the best competition in America." He revealed that he had received inquiries from other schools about his availability. Although he wanted to stay at North Carolina, he advised Erickson that "a refusal of this request would be a disappointment to me and lead me to believe that you and the administration . . . do not share my confidence in the future of the University's basketball program." Smith received a contract, but apparently the university made no public announcement.[58]

End of an Era at NC State

After winning the ACC championship in 1959, NC State suffered a series of setbacks, both on and off the court. The 1959–60 team, for the first time in Case's tenure as coach, ended with a losing record overall (11–15) and in the conference (5–9). It did not have a single player among the top ten in scoring or rebounding in the ACC. The following season, it improved to 16–9 and 8–6 in the conference but lost in the first round of the tournament to South Carolina. Shortly after the season ended, NC State was hit with the shock of the point-shaving scandal, which was a terrible blow to the basketball program and to Case personally. "For a man to whom basketball was his whole life and to whom loyalty meant everything," former State player and future coach Norm Sloan later remarked, "that scandal was just total devastation." In 1961–62, playing under the restrictions laid down by President Friday, the Wolfpack finished third in the conference and went 11–6 overall. Jon Speaks, a junior who had turned down Adolph Rupp to attend State instead of Kentucky, averaged 17.4 points per game and made first-team All-Conference. But the Wolfpack was embarrassed, 67–46, in the first round of the tournament by Clemson.[59]

The next two years, State's fortunes took an even more dramatic downturn. In 1962–63, it went 10–11 overall and 5–9 in the ACC. The disappointment of the season was compounded by tragedy. On May 26, 1963, Speaks was killed in a car accident. He had served as vice president of his senior class and was about to graduate with a "B" average in applied mathematics. He was, said his friend and teammate Les Robinson, a "solid, All-American kid" who "was the kind of kid you would want your son to grow up to be." The following year, State won just 8 games while losing 11, and its 4–10 conference record doomed it to a tie for last place with Virginia. It was apparent during the 1963–64 season that Case's health was failing. He missed several games when he spent time in the hospital, and although the cause of his illness was not disclosed, he was diagnosed with incurable multiple myeloma, a blood cancer.

Case resolved to keep coaching as long as he could, and he was hopeful that his 1964–65 team would return State to the top echelons of the ACC. After coaching the first two games, however, he found that he could not continue. Following a loss at Wake Forest, he summoned assistant coach Press Maravich and freshman coach Charlie Bryant into a shower room where his players could not hear and told them that he felt too poorly to keep coaching. He announced his decision on December 7, 1964. Case's friends and former adversaries expressed their regret and admiration. Bubas commented that "the South and the Atlantic Coast Conference area in particular are deeply indebted to him for bringing them big-time basketball." Frank McGuire, his biggest rival, remarked that Case "added a lot of color and a lot of class to the sport." Within a short time, the ACC agreed on a fitting tribute by naming the recognition of the most valuable player in the conference tournament the Everett N. Case Award.[60]

When Case resigned, Maravich stepped in as head coach. Case had designated Maravich as his heir apparent when he hired him in 1962. He had been greatly impressed with Maravich's coaching abilities when Clemson had blown out State and defeated Duke in the 1962 ACC Tournament. Case realized that he and Maravich shared a trait he valued highly—an obsession with basketball to the exclusion of practically anything else. He persuaded Maravich to leave the head coaching job at Clemson to become his assistant at State, and he was able to offer a salary substantially higher than Maravich received at Clemson. When Maravich told Frank Howard how much Case was willing to pay, Howard made no effort to keep him. The 1962

Jubilant Clemson players carry Press Maravich off the court after upset of Duke in 1962 ACC Tournament. (Courtesy The North Carolina State Archives; reprinted by permission of *The News and Observer* of Raleigh, North Carolina)

tournament was the best moment of Maravich's tenure at Clemson, but in his six years as coach, he had accomplished the remarkable feat of making Clemson basketball competitive. Howard had hired him in 1956 after Vic Bubas, Bones McKinney, and at least one high school coach turned him down. Maravich, at that time coach at Aliquippa High School in western Pennsylvania, accepted the Clemson job for $5,600 a year, which was a reduction in salary. Despite limited talent and resources, little support from his athletic director, and an antiquated field house, Maravich won 24 games against 59 losses in the conference, a considerable improvement over the school's record of 1–36 in the first three years of ACC competition.[61]

Maravich was an able and inspiring coach, and, like Bubas before him, he handled much of the practice and bench coaching as Case's assistant. When he took over in December 1964, he inherited a team that had to make the most of its talent to succeed. It featured 6'6" Larry Lakins, who had enrolled at State College in 1957 and had his playing career interrupted by military service and academic ineligibility. As a 25-year-old under-sized center, he averaged 19 points a game and was named first-team All-

Conference. Lakins was supported by 6'5" forward Pete Coker, who averaged 12.6 points and 10.0 rebounds, and 6'2" guard Tommy Mattocks, who averaged 13.6 points. Sophomore guard Eddie Biedenbach was an excellent ball handler but undisciplined enough that his teammates called him "Wildhorse." The team worked hard for Maravich and learned to play the pressing, running style he introduced with skill and confidence.

NC State finished the regular season with a record of 17–4 and tied for second in the ACC at 10–4. In the tournament, it defeated Virginia and Maryland to earn a matchup against Duke in the finals. NC State took the title by beating the favored Blue Devils, 91–85, behind the torrid shooting of junior Larry Worsley. Worsley was not a starter and had averaged 7.4 points during the season. But to his teammates' surprise and Duke's frustration, he was unstoppable in the tournament finals, hitting on 14 of 19 field-goal attempts and totaling 30 points. Duke tried a matchup zone, a man-to-man, and finally a box-and-one to slow Worsley, all to no avail. He received the first Everett Case Award from Case himself. In a poignant scene after the game ended, State players hoisted Case on their shoulders to cut down the last threads of the net. "You talk about symbolism and emotion," NC State sports information director Frank Weedon once recalled. "There wasn't a dry eye in the place." It was Case's last tournament appearance; he died on April 30, 1966.[62]

Maravich was the overwhelming selection for ACC Coach of the Year in 1965. The following season, without any player who placed among the top ten scorers in the ACC (though Biedenbach, Mattocks, and Coker were close), he guided State to a record of 18–9 overall and 9–5 in the ACC, second to Duke. The Wolfpack fell to Duke in the tournament finals this time, but the outlook for the future looked bright because of the likelihood that Press's son Pete would enroll at NC State. Press had groomed Pete to become a basketball prodigy from a very young age, and Pete had grown into a spectacular offensive player with magical skills and charisma. In two years of high school in Raleigh after the move from Clemson, he set a career scoring record for the state of North Carolina.

Although Pete demurred when asked if he intended to play for his father, there was never any ambivalence on Press's part. But his plans were thwarted by Pete's academic difficulties. Press had not stressed the importance of academic achievement in his drive to develop Pete's basketball talent, and Pete was, at best, an indifferent student. The ACC had recently adopted a rule that in order to receive an athletic scholarship at a conference school, a prospective basketball player had to have a combined score of at least 800 on the Scholastic Aptitude Test (SAT). Pete took the exams several times without making 800. After he graduated from high school, Press sent him to a military school, in part to prepare him for the SAT. But he still failed to meet the standard. In spring 1966, Louisiana State University offered Press its head coaching job along with a substantial raise in salary. More important to Press was that the Southeastern Conference had no academic standard comparable to that of the ACC, and Pete's SAT scores would not be an issue. He dragooned Pete, with whom he had a stormy relationship, into agreeing to attend LSU. On the same day that Case died, NC State basketball suffered another blow when Maravich resigned to accept the job at LSU.[63]

The ACC's Academic Commitment

The ACC had adopted the 800 rule on SAT scores that prevented Pete Maravich from playing at NC State in May 1964. The requirement stated that a high school athlete must achieve a total of 800 on the math and verbal sections of the "college boards," as the SAT was often called, to qualify for an athletic scholarship in football or basketball. One of the principal reasons for the founding of the ACC in 1953 had been to establish a healthy balance between athletic and academic programs after several college presidents concluded that the Southern Conference had failed in this regard. The 800 rule was an extension of the ACC's commitment to academic integrity, and indeed, leadership, among big-time college athletic conferences.

The position of ACC schools on the goal of sponsoring winning teams without compromising academic integrity was in part a result of their unhappy experiences in the Southern Conference. It also reflected their strong ambitions to improve their academic standards and elevate their national stature. After World War II, universities throughout the South in general and in the ACC in particular saw unprecedented opportunities to enhance their reputations by encouraging faculty research, upgrading or creating graduate programs, and attracting better students. This was an uphill battle. Melissa Kean, a historian of higher education in the South, wrote in 2008 that in the late 1940s, "there was no university in the South that could even approach the attainments of any number of schools in the Northeast, the Midwest, and California." An informal national ranking of graduate programs in the arts and sciences in 1957 did not place a single school in the

South on its list of the top 20 institutions. In 1966, the American Council on Education rated the quality of 30 departments at more than 100 universities, and, overall, no Southern school was included among the top 20.[64]

Admission standards for all students at ACC schools were generally low in the 1950s and early 1960s. According to a survey conducted by the University of Maryland in 1958, applicants to the University of North Carolina had to score only 675 out of a maximum of 1,600 on the college boards, and the university reserved the option of rejecting "any student who ranked in the lower half of his graduating class." In 1963, UNC adopted minimum admission requirements of a total of 800 on the SAT and at least 350 on each section. NC State did not reveal its standards for SAT results to the University of Maryland survey, but presumably they were roughly comparable to those of UNC. At Wake Forest, the minimum combined SAT score was 800. South Carolina and Clemson required out-of-state applicants to take the college boards, while in-state students took a specially designed entrance examination. The schools did not reveal the cutoff scores on the tests that disqualified applicants for admission. At Virginia, SAT scores in the College of Arts and Sciences averaged about 1,000. It usually rejected out-of-state students in the lower half of their graduating class. For in-state students, "very valid reasons have to be found for . . . rejection," but in no case did the university accept an applicant in the lower quarter of his high school class. Duke did not disclose its standards, but it ranked with Virginia as the most demanding of ACC schools (in 1965, the average SAT scores of its freshmen were in the 1,300 range). By comparison, Ivy League schools in the late 1950s used a cutoff of about 1,100 on the SAT, which would have made the average score for incoming students substantially higher. The University of Maryland did not discuss its own entrance requirements in the survey it conducted, but an earlier study had shown that graduates of high schools in Maryland and from other states were admitted if they had a "C" average.[65]

No matter what standards they set for their applicants, ACC schools resolved to tighten them as a means of upgrading their academic programs. The ACC's decision to become the first conference in the nation to require minimum SAT scores for prospective football and basketball players was a logical extension of the push among member schools for academic improvement. Conference officials viewed the policy as a way to establish national leadership in promoting a reasonable balance of academic and athletic goals. But they did not arrive at an agreement quickly or easily. For years, Duke pressed for a rule that would limit athletic scholarships to those who graduated in the top three-quarters of their high school class. This proposal had originally failed for a lack of a second in 1953 and received little support at later conference meetings.

Gradually, however, the idea that the conference should decide on a uniform standard for awarding athletic scholarships gained momentum. Despite the strong opposition of some coaches, the conference voted unanimously in May 1960 to adopt a minimum total SAT score of 750 for applicants for financial aid in basketball and football. The 750 score was a compromise; four members favored an 800 minimum but accepted the lower value to win unanimous consent. The 750 standard, as Dick Herbert pointed out, was "not difficult to attain" but would ensure that an "athlete will have to have some scholastic ability to meet it." It was generally consistent with the SAT scores that most of the conference schools required for all of their entering students. Edgar F. Shannon Jr., who had replaced Colgate Darden as president of the University of Virginia in 1959, declared that he was "elated" by the ACC's effort to "raise and equalize the scholastic standards for athletes." NC State athletic director Roy Clogston expressed hope that "neighboring Conferences will see fit to follow our example" and that "the NCAA [will] do this on a national basis."[66]

Within a short time after the ACC approved the 750 requirement, some members began to argue for a higher standard. In November 1961, Charles E. Jordan, faculty chairman of athletics at Duke, told Commissioner Weaver that a minimum score of 900 would be preferable to the existing rule. He reported that scholarship athletes in the ACC were averaging SAT scores of about 850 and suggested that changing to 900 was "unlikely [to] hurt member Institutions and could enhance our standing in national circles." In May 1963, Virginia moved that the standard be raised to 800, but it won the support of only three other schools—Duke, North Carolina, and Wake Forest. A year later, however, the dissenters had changed their position, and the 800 requirement passed by a vote of 7–1 at a conference meeting on May 1, 1964. The only negative vote was cast by Duke, which objected to watering down Virginia's initial proposal for a requirement of 850.[67]

Academics and Athletics at ACC Schools

At the same time that the ACC was considering conference-wide measures to strike a reasonable academic-athletic balance, several member schools were dealing with the same issue as it applied to them individually. North Carolina and NC State addressed the question of the proper role of sports in their institutions under critical conditions as a result of the point-shaving scandal of 1961. President Friday and Chancellors Aycock and Caldwell agreed that the balance had shifted much too far toward an emphasis on winning, and Friday took a series of stern actions to deemphasize basketball and thereby "save athletics." When Dean Smith was appointed as head coach at North Carolina, he assured Friday, "I understand the part that intercollegiate athletics plays in the overall University program. I will do my best to continue with a basketball program of which the University and its many friends may be proud."[68]

The University of Maryland reexamined its position on the role of athletics during the late 1950s after it hired a new president to replace Curley Byrd. As long as Byrd was president, there was little doubt, despite his denials, that his top priority was athletic achievement, especially in football. Byrd resigned from the university to run for governor of Maryland in 1954. During the campaign, his performance as president became an issue, and Byrd cited selected quotations from a recent evaluation of the university by an accreditation board, the Middle States Association of Colleges and Secondary Schools. The report was confidential, but the university's Board of Regents, troubled that Byrd had distorted the study's findings for political purposes, released a frank summary. The entire document was made public in January 1955.

The Middle States Association was highly critical of the University of Maryland on several counts, including the priorities that Byrd assigned to academic and athletic programs. "Physical facilities for intercollegiate athletics are superb," the report observed. "But to allow the expenditure of such large sums of money for the superb athletic plant and, at the same time, permit the existence of such woefully inadequate educational facilities as the University library provides is a policy which does not appear in the best interests of higher education." The evaluation team concluded that "there is unmistakable evidence of overemphasis, imbalance, and . . . disproportionate attention to intercollegiate athletics at the University of Maryland that . . . have already endangered, and unless corrected will impair, the integrity of the University." The Middle States Association was so deeply concerned about what it discovered that it deferred "reaffirmation of accreditation" to the university. It urged that the weaknesses it identified be rectified in order to support the renewal of accreditation when it carried out another review within two years.[69]

The University of Maryland addressed the findings and recommendations of the report to the satisfaction of the Middle States Association and received its "reaffirmation of accreditation" in 1955. Nevertheless, Maryland's new president, Wilson H. Elkins, was keenly aware of the criticisms that had endangered the university's accreditation, including the problem of overemphasis of athletics. He set out to repair the damage that Byrd's practice of giving precedence to athletic needs had inflicted on Maryland's academic reputation. The new president was not opposed to strong athletic programs as long as they did not undermine academic integrity, in part because his own athletic talents had enabled him to attend college. He was an outstanding athlete at the University of Texas, where he was known as "Bull Elkins" and won eight varsity letters in football, basketball, and track. He also made Phi Beta Kappa and was elected president of the student body. He earned his Ph.D. at Oxford University on a Rhodes scholarship. He rose through the ranks of academic administration after he returned to Texas, and before accepting the job at Maryland, had served as president of Texas Western College. Like Byrd, Elkins recognized the value of college athletics for building school spirit and attracting alumni support. Unlike Byrd, he also recognized the value of academic research and scholarship, and he invited the faculty to assume a major role in the governance of the university. In contrast to the charming Byrd, Elkins was aloof and formal; he was greatly respected but not widely loved.[70]

Within a short time after taking over as Maryland's president, Elkins made clear his intention to improve the university's academic reputation and correct the imbalance on the academic-athletic spectrum. He did not mince words when he commented that Maryland suffered from having "a large stadium and a small library." He announced that he planned "to scatter a few books around campus so that the students will know what they are." On a more serious note, he suggested that a university could not "stay on top in football year after year and not impair its educational program." Elkins sought to reorder Maryland's priorities without dismantling its athletic programs or de-emphasizing them to the point that it could not remain competitive in the ACC. He told boosters that although he did not wish to "destroy athletics," he had determined that "certain adjustments may be necessary." One of the adjustments was to provide more scholarship money for the student body as a whole, which reduced the amount of financial assistance available to athletes. A primary goal for Elkins was to overturn the perception that Maryland was a "football factory."[71]

Maryland's basketball program was little affected by the change in administrations. Bud Millikan later remarked that the basketball team did not receive a great deal of financial support when either Byrd or Elkins was president, especially compared to the Big Four. Maryland was competitive with the North Carolina schools for the first few years after the founding of the ACC and won its only championship of Millikan's career in 1958, three years after Elkins arrived. Nevertheless, over time the relative decline in resources for athletics caused Maryland basketball to fall behind its conference rivals, especially on important matters such as the hiring of full-time assistant coaches and recruiting budgets. By the early 1960s, Maryland faced growing difficulties in its efforts to keep up with the leading basketball powers in the ACC.[72]

At about the same time that North Carolina, NC State, and Maryland were dealing with problems that arose from overemphasis on athletics, Harold Tribble, president of Wake Forest, came under fire for the opposite reasons. In 1955, students staged a protest and hung Tribble in effigy for allegedly de-emphasizing sports programs. The immediate cause of the students' demonstration was the resignation of Wake football coach Tom Rogers and athletic director Paddison (Pat) Preston. Students and other supporters of Wake athletics viewed the departure of Rogers and Preston as evidence that the college was scaling back on its support for athletics, and they placed the blame on Tribble. On the night of December 5, 1955, "hundreds of students" marched to his home to voice their opinions. Tribble, dressed in pajamas and an overcoat, stood by the burning dummy and greeted them by saying, "Thank you for coming." He denied that he planned to de-emphasize sports and pointed out that "we are spending more money than ever before on athletics." He expressed his dismay, however, that the budget for the athletic department had run a deficit of $85,000 the previous year and that the shortfall had to be covered by taking money from other programs. The protesters listened with varying degrees of courtesy and then left quickly when some of their number began to call for a panty raid. The questions that the students raised about the relationship between athletic and academic priorities at Wake Forest were not resolved so easily.[73]

Some members of Wake Forest's Board of Trustees shared the views of the protesting students, and shortly before the demonstration, several of them had instigated an investigation of Tribble's performance as president. Although they did not specify their complaints, one of the issues they regarded as most important was the status of athletic programs at the college. Despite his reservations about the value of athletics, Tribble paid close attention to the details of athletic administration and coaching; in November 1955, for example, he sent Preston instructions on such matters as drinking at football games and travel arrangements for the football team. The athletic staff found Tribble's domineering and sometimes prickly style annoying. Partly out of resentment toward the president, Jim Weaver left his position as athletic director to become ACC commissioner, Bill Hensley departed as sports information director to take the same job at NC State, and baseball coach Taylor Sanford, whose team won the national championship in 1955, resigned the following year. There were reports in local papers in 1955 and early 1956 that Tribble wanted to fire Murray Greason as basketball coach, and perhaps Bones McKinney as well, and that Preston had refused to carry out his orders to look for replacements. Tribble had several bitter opponents on the Board of Trustees, and they pushed hard for his dismissal as president. He claimed that the "agitating group seems to be determined to have big-time athletics at any cost." Although Tribble voiced his "strong belief" that they would not prevail, he barely survived a vote on his removal in February 1956.[74]

After Tribble was nearly ousted, he seemed chastened enough that he refrained from interfering in such a heavy-handed way in the conduct of Wake's athletic programs. The success and national prominence the basketball team achieved under Bones McKinney undoubtedly helped to ease the pressures that generated so much criticism and ill will. At a fund-raising event in May 1964, Tribble declared that "athletics are a vital part of our total program here. They are not just an extra." He announced that "we have been through some trying times but we have come through them well and now we are in splendid condition."[75]

A special committee made up of members of the Board of Trustees, the faculty, and alumni conducted a study of athletic programs at Wake Forest in 1964 and presented a more equivocal view. Members of the Board of Trustees were vocally dissatisfied with Wake's football program, which had won only 1 of 20 games in 1962 and 1963. In addition, administrators and faculty were concerned that the athletic department ran a deficit of more than $188,000 in 1962–63. The special committee was formed to study those problems and to evaluate the role of athletics in promoting the "ultimate good of the college as a whole." It found that students, alumni, and the local chamber of commerce favored improving athletic programs, especially in football. The college faculty was more ambivalent. Although it "considered the intercollegiate athletic program more an asset than a liability," it worried about overemphasis on winning, costs, and professionalism. Queried about the point at which overemphasis of sports occurred, most faculty members answered, "when the academic program is weakened" and "when winning becomes more important than academic achievement." The special committee suggested that "until now, the college has kept the so-called evils of intercollegiate athletics well under control," but it cautioned that "there is a tendency for the undesirable elements to multiply as the emphasis on athletics is increased." In its report, completed in August 1964, it recommended that the status and influence of Wake's athletic programs be reviewed again in three or four years.[76]

At the University of Virginia, faculty concerns about overemphasis of sports, expressed clearly in the Gooch report of 1951, remained hypothetical as long as Darden served as president. When Shannon took over, he did not make dramatic changes in the university's approach to athletics. He had little experience with athletic policies and little knowledge of what was required to become competitive in football and basketball in the ACC. Nevertheless, he was more inclined than Darden to take steps to overcome Virginia's status as the doormat of the ACC in the two major sports. In April 1962, Shannon sent a report to the athletic committee of the university's Board of Visitors on "educational philosophy and policy governing athletics at the University." It grew out of discussions surrounding the hiring of a new football coach and athletic director. Shannon advised the Board of Visitors of the conclusions that he had reached, in collaboration with the search committee, on the proper role of athletics at Virginia. He suggested that it was "axiomatic that 'a sense of excellence' should permeate all aspects of the University." He further maintained that athletics were "an important aspect of the university" and that "every legitimate effort to field competitive teams within the Atlantic Coast Conference" should be made. The report outlined general principles and objectives without explaining how they would be carried out, and Virginia still had a long way to go to achieve parity with its rivals in the ACC. Nevertheless, the statement of policy signaled a new direction in Virginia's approach to athletics and represented, at least in concept, a turning point in its efforts to balance academic commitments and athletic objectives.[77]

Unlike the other members of the ACC, Duke, South Carolina, and Clemson did not have pressing reasons to carefully assess academic-athletic relationships at their institutions between the founding of the conference and the mid-1960s. But the dominance of the Big Four and the 800 rule on admissions for scholarship athletes were soon challenged in ways that brought important, permanent changes to the competitive fabric of ACC basketball.

6

THE REVOLT
OF THE ALSO-RANS

On January 7, 1967, *The State*, the leading newspaper in South Carolina, ran a headline that would have been inconceivable in the first few years of ACC basketball: "Gamecocks, Tigers Meet in Vital ACC War." From the founding of the conference in 1953 through 1965, the University of South Carolina and Clemson had consistently ranked among the worst teams in the ACC. Clemson, despite its improvement under Press Maravich, won just 42 of 163 conference games during that period. South Carolina was scarcely better with 46 victories in 164 ACC contests. Only Virginia demonstrated the same level of sustained futility by winning just 39 of 159 conference games between 1953 and 1965.[1]

After Maravich departed for NC State, he was replaced by his assistant, Bobby Roberts. Roberts had played basketball and baseball at Furman University. He compiled a record of 89–20 as a high school coach in South Carolina and joined the staff at Clemson in 1958. His freshman teams won 49 games against 20 losses over four seasons. After taking over as head coach, he built on the foundations that Maravich had established to elevate Clemson beyond mere respectability. Under his guidance, the Tigers achieved their first-ever winning records in the ACC. Roberts had a friendly, easygoing personality, but his coaching style was tough and demanding. He succeeded because he taught his teams to play with discipline and inspired them to play with enthusiasm. More important, he recruited the talent he needed to compete in the ACC. Clemson turned in its best performance since the founding of the ACC in 1965–66. It tied for third with North Carolina in the regular season standings and finished with a record of 15–10 overall, 8–6 in the conference. Before the 1966–67 season began, Clemson players, coaches, and fans hoped to be "in the thick of the wild scramble for the ACC crown."[2]

South Carolina had similar ambitions. It had improved greatly since hiring Frank McGuire as its coach in 1964. Within a short time after McGuire arrived, he adopted the same strategies that had worked so well for him in Chapel Hill. He charmed legislators, administrators, and boosters to gain the resources he needed to win at South Carolina. He brought in Buck Freeman as an assistant coach. He recruited heavily in the New York area, consulted with Harry Gotkin, and soon had the underground railroad rumbling to Columbia. McGuire suffered through his first season with a team that went 6–17. The next year, led by sophomores whom he recruited, the Gamecocks improved to 11–13. By the beginning of the 1966–67 season, South Carolina expected to be "more than respectable," and if McGuire could use top recruit Mike Grosso, whose eligibility was questionable, it seemed possible that the team could compete for the ACC championship.[3]

The Clemson–South Carolina game of January 7, 1967, therefore, matched programs that were moving upward and that harbored increasingly realistic aspirations for greater things. The importance of the contest was magnified by the bitter rivalry between the two state-supported schools, which had usually been played out in football rather than in basketball. The game took place in Columbia, and the outcome proved to be a huge disappointment for South Carolina's fans. Clemson jumped out to an early lead and cruised to an easy 80–68 victory before a sell-out crowd and a television audience. As the home-team fans became increasingly disgruntled, some threw ice, paper cups, peanuts, fruit, coins, and other debris on the floor and screamed abuse at the officials and Clemson players. The crowd's conduct overshadowed Clemson's outstanding performance; one account of the game reported that the Tigers "completely outclassed" their rival.[4]

The rematch was played in Clemson on February 7, 1967. The stakes were even higher than they had been in January. South Carolina had righted itself after the Clemson debacle a month earlier and came into the game with a record of 10–3, 4–1 in the conference. Clemson was 11–6 overall, 3–4 in the ACC. The outcome of the second meeting was the same as the first; Clemson won in a rout, 73–57. McGuire remarked that "it could have been much worse" and hailed Roberts for doing "a wonderful job with his team." But he complained bitterly that Clemson had stationed football players behind his bench and told them to harass him. When the game ended, McGuire remained on the floor to carry on an animated, uncongenial exchange with Clemson athletic director Frank Howard. Howard issued a statement in which he denied that Clemson students had acted improperly and described McGuire's objections as "the typical whinning [sic] of a poor loser."[5]

Although neither Clemson nor South Carolina won the ACC title in 1966–67, both had, by their previous standards, excellent seasons. Clemson placed fourth in the ACC with a record of 9–5, 17–8 overall. Its performance included victories over each member of the Big Four, which it had never done before, in a magical run over a period of eight days. South Carolina was third in the regular season standings with a record of 8–4 and went 16–7 overall. One result of success was unprecedented zealotry on the part of fans at both schools, demonstrated in extremis by the embarrassment of the trash-throwing exhibition in Columbia. Clemson and South Carolina had long been renowned for their inhospitable behavior toward visiting opponents. When their teams improved to a point of parity with conference rivals, the numbers and seemingly the mania of their supporters grew commensurately. As the stakes of games increased, so too did the focus on winning and in some cases the belligerence of principals, as the exchange between McGuire and Howard, neither of whom was bashful about expressing his opinions, indicated. "Time was when basketball in South Carolina excited no one. Teams from Clemson and the University of South Carolina went out and took their regular lickings, and nobody knocked down the doors to see them," observed Evan Bussey, sports editor of the *Charleston News and Courier*, in February 1967. "Now, that's all a part of the dim, dark past." Although Bussey condemned the unruly behavior of fans, he suggested that it went along with reaching a position in which the two "South Carolina teams are no longer door mats for the rest of the ACC."[6] At about the same time, Virginia and Maryland took important strides toward improving their programs. The eventual result was a conference that was more competitive from top to bottom and no longer dominated by the Big Four.

"Major League Status" for Clemson

When Press Maravich resigned as coach at Clemson in August 1962, he told the president of the college, Robert C. Edwards, that "basketball at Clemson has finally achieved . . . major league status." He expressed his appreciation for the patience and support that Edwards had shown in the efforts to improve the basketball program. Edwards, who had become president of the college after the sudden death of Robert F. Poole in 1958, was a strong patron of Clemson athletics; they were his "great joy." He was a particularly ardent football fan who was an admirer of Frank Howard and a former president of the Clemson athletic booster organization. Edwards was so avid that he sometimes led the football team's charge from the locker room to the playing field dressed in a jacket and tie and wearing cleats. Some faculty members thought that his highly visible cheerleading gave the false impression that he placed undue emphasis on football and other sports at the expense of academic achievement.[7]

Edwards was dedicated to upgrading Clemson's academic programs and reputation. He was an extraordinarily loyal alumnus who once declared, "I love Clemson University more than life itself." He entered Clemson at age 15 on an academic scholarship and graduated with a degree in textile engineering in 1933. He built a successful career as a textile industry executive before accepting an offer to become Clemson's vice president for development in 1956, a move that reduced his salary by about 75 percent. His performance was so impressive that the college's Board of Trustees appointed him as president despite his lack of an advanced degree and limited academic experience (he later was awarded honorary doctorates). Edwards was an outgoing man of decisive action, restless energy, and, as a corollary, limited patience. During his 20-year tenure as president, he presided over Clemson's transition from a military school to a civilian institution, the arrival of women in large numbers, notable improvements in academic quality, the dramatic growth in the size of the college and its transformation to a university, and the admission of black students.[8]

At a time when racial issues were extremely sensitive and unsettled in South Carolina's educational institutions, Edwards demonstrated in a memorable way his personal commitment to combating discrimination at Clemson. And appropriately, he did it at the football stadium. Clemson admitted its first black student, Harvey Gantt, in January 1963 without incident. But some Clemson supporters who did not object to integrating the college's classrooms were less receptive to opening the football field to black players. Blacks were not allowed inside the stadium, known as "Death Valley," as spectators or in any other capacity. The issue came to a head in November 1963 when the University of Maryland arrived with a squad that included the first black football player in the ACC, Darryl Hill, a halfback, wide receiver, punt returner, and backup kicker. The day of the Clemson game, Hill was told that he would be kicking extra points, and he went out on the field before his teammates to practice. He was greeted by a barrage of racial insults from the crowd. Frank Howard made clear his disgust at having a black player on the grounds of Death Valley by standing close to Hill for several minutes and glaring at him without saying a word.

As Hill was warming up under less than agreeable conditions, a student manager came out to tell him that there was a problem with his mother and a ticket taker at the gate. He did not know that his mother, Palestine Hill, had taken a train from her home in Washington, D.C., to attend the game by herself after her husband found that he had to work. Hill left the field, located his mother, and argued at length with the authorities at the entrance about honoring her ticket. His efforts were futile, and he started to return to the locker room to change clothes and accompany his mother back to Washington. At that point, Edwards and his wife, Louise, suddenly appeared, either because someone had told them about the confrontation or by coincidence. Edwards immediately defused the situation in a spontaneous act of grace and decency. He invited Palestine Hill to watch the game as his guest in the president's box. From that vantage point, she had the pleasure of watching her son set a Maryland record by catching 10 passes. She got along very well with her hosts, despite Darryl's performance against their team, at least in part because she was a high school teacher with a Ph.D. President and Mrs. Edwards asked her to spend the night at their home and drove her to the train station the next morning.[9]

Clemson fans had much to cheer about during Bobby Roberts's first five seasons as head basketball coach. In 1962–63, the Tigers placed fourth in the ACC and finished with an overall record of 12–13, their best since the founding of the conference. They improved to third in the ACC standings the next year with an 8–6 record and enjoyed their first winning season in league history with 13 wins, 12 losses. After a losing season in 1964–65, Clemson climbed to new heights with the 1965–66 and 1966–67 teams that won 32 games and commanded the respect of the ACC.

The turnaround in Clemson's basketball fortunes was spearheaded by four brothers who played consecutively and sometimes concurrently on every team between 1960 and 1970—Tommy, Donnie, Randy, and Richie

Mahaffey. They grew up in LaGrange, Georgia, and knew about Clemson because their father had played baseball at the college. Although the oldest of the brothers, Tommy, felt no pressure at home to attend Clemson, he accepted a scholarship offer, in no small part because he wanted to play in the ACC. He led Clemson in rebounding during his sophomore and junior seasons, but as a senior, his brother Donnie, a sophomore who had been high school Player of the Year in Georgia, surpassed him by a margin of one-tenth of a rebound per game. Tommy and Donnie played together on the 1961–62 team that made the finals of the ACC Tournament, the high point for Clemson in conference competition to that time. As a senior, Donnie Mahaffey experienced another milestone as a member of the first Clemson team to compile a winning record since the formation of the ACC, and he led the squad in rebounding.

Randy Mahaffey began his storied career the following season. He rejected overtures from, among others, Adolph Rupp, to sign with Clemson because "it just made sense." He was a 6'7" left-handed forward who enhanced his shooting and rebounding abilities by being smart, rugged, and tenacious. When Pat Conroy played for The Citadel against Clemson, he found that Randy Mahaffey had "all the grace and speed of impalas and lions combined nicely with the strength of water buffalo." Randy exceeded his older brothers' considerable achievements. "Randy's motor was tuned up a notch or two higher," Donnie later remarked. "He could do things we couldn't." He averaged 16.0 points and 9.7 rebounds during his career and made first-team All-ACC as a senior. He also was president of his junior class and a Dean's List student in a premedical program. Richie played with Randy as a sophomore in 1966–67 and averaged 10.2 points and 7.8 rebounds. The next year he improved to 16.6 points and 11.5 rebounds. After fighting a serious injury, Richie ended the Mahaffey saga at Clemson with career averages of 13.6 points and 9.4 rebounds.[10]

Players who were not members of the Mahaffey family also made important contributions to Clemson's improvement in the early and mid-1960s. Maravich and Roberts benefited from the skills of outstanding scorers Choppy Patterson, Jim Brennan, Garry Helms, and Jim Sutherland. Patterson averaged 16.4 points as a sophomore in 1959–60 and 19.0 as a junior to lead his team before an injury in a car accident reduced his effectiveness during his final season. He was the first Clemson player to be selected to the All-ACC first team (in 1960). Brennan led Clemson in scoring for three consecutive years and made second-team All-Conference as a junior in

Bobby Roberts and his starting five, 1965. Left to right: Hank Channell,
Garry Helms, Jim Sutherland, Buddy Benedict, and Randy Mahaffey.
(Courtesy The North Carolina State Archives; reprinted by permission
of *The News and Observer* of Raleigh, North Carolina)

1963 and a senior in 1964. Helms was the top scorer with a 19.2 average and
a 51.2 field-goal percentage on the 1965–66 team that went 15–10. Sutherland was an "uncannily graceful" 6′5″ guard who averaged 18.8 points per
game the following season and was named second-team All-Conference.
He starred, along with Randy Mahaffey, on the team that produced Clemson's best record ever. Like Mahaffey, Sutherland was a superb student in a
premed curriculum. He had been a close friend of Pete Maravich when he
grew up in the town of Clemson and had benefited from the coaching that
both boys received from Press Maravich. He later remembered sneaking
into Clemson's basketball arena, Fike Field House, with Pete to play against
each other and practice the drills they learned from Press. "If you could
pick anything you wanted to do, any place you wanted to be, that was it,"
Sutherland later remarked. "It was heaven."[11]

Teams that competed against Clemson in Fike Field House described
it in less lyrical terms. Visiting players and coaches called it, among

other things, a "hell-hole," a "snakepit," and a "house of crazies." Bones McKinney once remarked that there "wasn't any place I dreaded playing more than at Fike Field House . . . That place was so-o-o dark that the referees had to come in wearing coal miners' helmets." Conroy recalled from his visits with The Citadel team that "a game at Clemson was as hallucinatory and disquieting an encounter as a basketball player could experience." The arena seated about 4,500, and the front rows of the stands were very close to the court. The fans were boisterous, no matter whether their team was winning or losing. When Conroy first played at Fike as a sophomore, he learned firsthand about the indelicate customs of Clemson's supporters. As he stood on the sideline to make an inbound pass, "two of them pinched my butt hard and two more put cigarettes out on the back of my legs." When he protested, the referee "simply shrugged his shoulders." By the time the game ended, Conroy had suffered five cigarette burns, and "Clemson fans had depilated a third of the hair from the back of my legs."[12]

As Clemson grew larger in the 1960s, it became apparent that Fike Field House was not adequate for seating basketball fans or for a variety of other student activities. The university broke ground for a modern arena in 1966, and Littlejohn Coliseum, named for a high-level administrator at Clemson in the early twentieth century, opened in November 1968. By that time, Clemson basketball had declined precipitously. In 1967–68, the year after Clemson's best season ever, the team went 4–20 overall and 3–11 in the conference. The following season was equally disappointing with only 6 wins in 25 games and a 2–12 record in the conference. The only bright spot was that Butch Zatezalo, a 5'11" guard, led the ACC in scoring both seasons. But Roberts lacked the depth of talent to compete in the conference, and he was unable to sign top-notch recruits. Clemson fans soon lost patience, and reports surfaced as early as February 1969 that Roberts would be replaced by Davidson College coach Lefty Driesell. It was not only Clemson's won-lost records that troubled Clemson supporters but also the lack of promise shown by the freshman teams. To make matters even more galling, Frank McGuire's South Carolina teams were among the leaders in the ACC. Roberts's backers expressed hope that the opening of the new arena would help significantly with recruiting, and Edwards confided that he was "terribly distressed" by the rumors that Roberts would be fired. Nevertheless, in the middle of a third consecutive disastrous season in 1969–70 (7–19 overall, 2–12 in the conference), Roberts, who had led Clemson to its greatest success as a member of the ACC, resigned under pressure.[13]

McGuire at South Carolina

Like Clemson, the University of South Carolina in the early 1960s had a weak basketball tradition and a strong desire to elevate its program. In 1961–62, under the coaching of Bob Stevens, the Gamecocks finished with their second-best overall record (15–12) and best conference record (7–7) since the founding of the ACC. Art Whisnant, a 6'5" center, scored 21.0 points per game and joined Grady Wallace as the only South Carolina players to make first-team All-Conference. After the season, Stevens accepted a job at the University of Oklahoma. In an effort to build on his achievements, South Carolina hired Chuck Noe, a 5'7", 120-pound dynamo who had played at Virginia during the late 1940s and proven his coaching abilities in stints at Virginia Military Institute and Virginia Tech. Noe was well known for his ambition and emotion. "He had his goals set high. He wanted to be up there with Adolph Rupp," one colleague remarked. "Even when he was a player at Virginia he was high strung and emotionally involved with every play." In his first season as coach, South Carolina finished with a record of 9–15 overall, 4–10 in the ACC.[14]

Noe's eagerness to establish a winning program at South Carolina and his combustible personality sometimes led to antics that crossed the lines of propriety. In December 1963, highly ranked Duke visited South Carolina for a game at University Field House. The arena, like Clemson's Fike Field House, was small, antiquated, and often populated with rowdy fans. In an atmosphere "bulging with emotion," a crowd of about 3,500 watched Duke struggle to a 3-point halftime lead. Before the second half began, Noe told the public address announcer to make an appeal to the fans: "Coach Noe says the team needs your support the second half, so let's give it to him." Noe also instructed the leader of the school band, which sat directly behind the Duke bench, to play loudly when Coach Bubas was talking to his players during time-outs. The trombone player kept moving his slide past Jay Buckley's head, which Buckley, not a volatile sort, found so annoying that he grabbed the instrument and threw it on the floor.

The conditions were so objectionable that Bubas received permission from the referees to huddle with his team at the center of the court instead of on the sidelines. Even this action did not shield him from the South Carolina cheerleaders who surrounded the Duke team and "conducted a foot stomping war dance." Eventually, Jeff Mullins and Hack Tison led Duke to a harrowing victory, 77–70. South Carolina's president, Thomas F. Jones, offered an apology to his counterpart at Duke, Douglas M. Knight, "for the several incidents of unsportsmanlike conduct on the part of some of our students." Knight replied that Duke also occasionally encountered problems of "overenthusiasm" with its own fans. Despite the friendly exchange between the two presidents, Eddie Cameron proposed to South Carolina athletic director Marvin Bass that the best way to overcome the "spirit of antagonism" on display in Columbia was to move future games to a neutral site.[15]

Less than a month after the Duke game, Noe's coaching career at South Carolina ended abruptly. Citing "nervous exhaustion," he resigned on January 12, 1964, and entered a hospital for treatment. He was replaced in midseason by his assistant, Dwane Morrison, a former star player at South Carolina. Morrison, who took over when the team had a 6–6 record, did a commendable job under trying circumstances. South Carolina finished fourth in the regular season conference standings with 7 wins and 7 defeats; overall it was 10–14. Ronnie Collins, a 6'3" guard, averaged 23.7 points per game, third in the conference behind Billy Cunningham and Mullins, and made first-team All-ACC. Morrison hoped to be appointed head coach but never received serious consideration. Even before the season ended, South Carolina had made arrangements to hire Frank McGuire.[16]

After resigning at North Carolina, McGuire had guided the Philadelphia Warriors to the NBA playoffs, where they lost in game seven of the division finals to the Boston Celtics on a shot at the buzzer. Among the highlights of the season was a game against the New York Knicks in Hershey, Pennsylvania, in which Wilt Chamberlain set an all-time record by scoring 100 points. After the season ended, the team was sold to a group of owners who moved the franchise to San Francisco. McGuire decided that he did not want to relocate to the West Coast and took a job with a public relations firm in New York. But he was restless away from coaching. In early 1964, Jeff Hunt, a Columbia businessman and strong supporter of South Carolina athletics, accidentally encountered McGuire at a restaurant in Ashville, North Carolina. He suggested casually that McGuire should become coach of the Gamecocks and was surprised that he did not receive a prompt rejection. McGuire merely said, "Well, you've already got a basketball coach." When Hunt informed him that South Carolina had an interim coach whom it planned to replace, McGuire indicated that he would be interested if he would not be taking "someone else's job."

Hunt informed Sol Blatt Jr., chairman of the athletic committee of the University of South Carolina's Board of Trustees, of McGuire's potential interest. The coach wanted to learn more about the job and about the school from Blatt and President Jones, but only if it were done in a way that did not attract the attention of local reporters. Therefore, they immediately made a trip to New York to recruit McGuire. Blatt exercised a great deal of influence over the policies of the university not only because of his position on the Board of Trustees but also because his father, Sol Blatt Sr., was the Speaker of the South Carolina House of Representatives and arguably the most powerful politician in the state. McGuire insisted that he would accept the coaching job only if the university built a modern field house; he vividly recalled his disappointment that the University of North Carolina had failed to act promptly to replace Woollen Gym. The Blatts were well positioned to give credible assurances on a new arena, and as a result, McGuire agreed to become South Carolina's new head coach. His appointment was announced several weeks later on March 12, 1964.[17]

A short time after he took over at South Carolina, McGuire almost backed out in a disagreement with the president of the university. When Dwane Morrison found out that he would not be offered the head coaching job, he sought to stay on as an assistant to McGuire. Jones supported Morrison's bid and made his position clear to McGuire. McGuire had nothing against Morrison but refused to be forced into hiring an assistant not of his own choosing. Rather than yielding to Jones's pressure, he left Columbia and returned to New York. When Sol Blatt Sr. learned what had happened, he instructed Jones to travel to New York and bring McGuire back. He told Jones that "he could get a new president easier than he could get another Frank McGuire." After Jones drove to New York and assured McGuire that he could hire anyone he wished, the coach returned to Columbia and resumed his efforts to upgrade South Carolina's basketball program.[18]

Taking a long trip for the purpose of groveling to McGuire could not have been a happy experience for the man who had become president at South Carolina in 1962. Like his counterparts at other ACC schools and throughout the South, Jones was committed to improving the academic quality and reputation of the university he headed. His goal was to "provide an opportunity for the optimum intellectual development of every young man or woman of our State who can profit from higher education." He faced a difficult task. The university, even after the progress made during the 1950s, remained underfunded compared to other southern institutions. Faculty salaries were low, and in 1959, more than half of the faculty members did not have doctorates. Jones was a native southerner who had graduated from Mississippi State College. He had gone on to earn a Ph.D. in electrical engineering at the Massachusetts Institute of Technology and later taught there. In 1958, he left MIT to become dean of the school of electrical engineering at Purdue University. With his southern background, his academic accomplishments, and his reputation as an innovator in educational methods, he was an attractive choice to lead the University of South Carolina. Jones was known for his energy and optimism in tackling tough assignments, which were also important assets in striving to achieve his ambitions as president.

Jones was a supporter of athletics, which, he said, provided "the individual in the student body an opportunity to identify with the university." In contrast to Robert Edwards at Clemson, however, he was not a devout follower or highly visible fan of South Carolina teams. He commented shortly before arriving in Columbia: "I am always thrilled by the enthusiasm displayed by individuals at football games and would very much like to see some of this tremendous enthusiasm transferred to the classroom." He later remarked that "athletics are good, but they're not worth a night's conversation." Jones, despite the limits of his appreciation for the value of sports, recognized their importance to the university and to winning support for his academic objectives. He was also keenly aware, as his trip to New York to placate McGuire demonstrated, that his own control of athletic programs at South Carolina was circumscribed by the power and priorities of Sol Blatt Sr. and the state legislature, Sol Blatt Jr. and the Board of Trustees, and strong-minded coaches.[19]

McGuire's arrival at South Carolina generated unprecedented excitement among its long-suffering fans. He brought star power, charm, and high expectations. He brought the credibility of a coach who had competed successfully in the ACC and won a national championship. He soon brought the players who could raise the level of South Carolina basketball, including Frank Standard and Jack Thompson from Brooklyn and Skip Harlicka from New Jersey. And he brought controversy. A bitter dispute over the signing of Mike Grosso, an outstanding prospect from New Jersey, pitted McGuire against Jim Weaver and Eddie Cameron, whom he viewed as sinister adversaries, and eventually against other ACC officials and the NCAA.

The Grosso Controversy

Mike Grosso was an exceptionally gifted 6'8" player who led his high school team to the New Jersey state championship in 1965 and was heavily recruited by college coaches. Vic Bubas described him as "one of the great,

great prospects in the country," and added that "some say he is as good as Lew Alcindor," who enrolled at UCLA that year and later changed his name to Kareem Abdul-Jabbar. Grosso initially accepted an offer of a full scholarship from the University of Miami, but just before he announced his decision at a high school banquet, McGuire convinced him to attend South Carolina instead. He was McGuire's prize recruit; the coach once compared Grosso's importance to his program with that of Billy Cunningham to North Carolina and Art Heyman to Duke.[20]

Grosso's choice of South Carolina raised questions within the ACC because he did not meet the requirement, adopted in May 1964, that football and basketball players had to score at least 800 on the college boards to qualify for an athletic scholarship. Nor did he make the 750 he needed to qualify for admission at South Carolina, which, according to the school's rules, was necessary because he ranked in the lower quarter of his high school class. Grosso took the SAT three times when it was administered nationally by the Educational Testing Service (ETS). He took it twice more in "institutionally administered" tests at the University of South Carolina. The second time he scored 789, high enough to be admitted to the university but not to receive a basketball scholarship. And the ETS did not recognize the results of the second test taken at South Carolina because it permitted only one "institutionally administered" exam. Nevertheless, Grosso was able to enroll at South Carolina.[21]

Although Grosso was not eligible for an athletic scholarship, McGuire took advantage of a loophole in the ACC's rules. The conference did not prohibit a student who fell short of the 800 standard from playing football or basketball as long as he was not awarded a scholarship. Therefore, McGuire insisted that Grosso could play basketball at South Carolina because his family was providing the money for his expenses. Grosso came from a family of modest means who could not afford the costs of college, but two of his uncles, who owned a bar and grill, agreed to pay his bills. Under those conditions, Commissioner Weaver had no choice but to declare Grosso eligible to play at South Carolina. But he was not happy about it. He confided to Cameron that he had "not closed the door" on investigating the circumstances surrounding Grosso's enrollment. He and others wondered, for example, why the player elected to pay his own way at South Carolina when other schools had offered him a free ride. The conference soon took action to close the loophole in the 800 requirement by stipulating that a player had to attain that score to participate, not just to receive a scholarship. This action did not apply retroactively to Grosso.[22]

In December 1965, Eddie Cameron announced that Duke would refuse to play against South Carolina when Grosso moved up to the varsity the following season. This decision reflected in part Cameron's ill will toward McGuire, whom he described privately as a "phony." To a much greater extent, however, it was a consequence of Cameron's conviction, which was shared by at least some of his conference colleagues, that Grosso's participation in ACC competition would be a major affront to the academic standards that Duke and other member schools strongly favored. "My feeling in this whole matter is that the spirit of the rules is just as important as the letter of the rules and we all agreed a number of years ago to have some sort of a floor on entrance requirements," Cameron told Clemson president Edwards. "This was a mutual agreement and now it is being avoided by trickery." Duke's objections to Grosso's enrollment were serious enough to risk forfeiting two games by declining to schedule South Carolina in 1966–67.[23]

While Duke's position fueled the growing controversy, the ACC and the NCAA quietly investigated possible infractions not only in the recruiting of Mike Grosso but also in South Carolina's football program. On June 4, 1966, Weaver reported to President Jones that "it seems that the University of South Carolina has been in violation of certain Atlantic Coast Conference and NCAA regulations." He asked for more information on the possibility that football players had "received illegal aid." Jones replied that he was "deeply concerned" about the "clear evidence of irresponsible management" and that he had already taken corrective action. The burden of responding to the inquiries of the ACC and the NCAA and of implementing the "great improvement" that Jones demanded fell to South Carolina's new athletic director, Paul Dietzel. Dietzel was a highly regarded football coach who had won a national championship at Louisiana State University in 1958. Dietzel was hired in hopes of developing a winning tradition in football at the university. "When I took the job at South Carolina," he later wrote, "I realized that the football program had become an embarrassment to the university, its alumni, and the team's fans."[24]

One of Dietzel's first duties as athletic director was to respond to the allegations of the ACC that his predecessor, Marvin Bass, had committed "gross malpractices." Weaver found evidence of a number of violations, the most serious of which was that three football players had received scholarships without scoring 800 on the SAT. Dietzel confirmed that the charges were true and pledged that he would introduce new procedures to prevent a recurrence. Weaver commended Dietzel for his cooperation but decided that the university must be sanctioned for its "flagrant disregard" of conference regulations. He ruled that the three players who were given illegal assistance could not participate in any future ACC games. He also required that South Carolina forfeit all the games in which those team members had played. Dietzel immediately announced that he would follow the commissioner's dictates in order "to remain a member in good standing of the Atlantic Coast Conference."[25]

The problems in South Carolina's football program kept the question of Mike Grosso's eligibility in the spotlight. University officials had expected the punishment that Weaver imposed on the football team. But they were surprised that the commissioner also ruled that any South Carolina athlete "whose eligibility is questioned" had to be held out of competition "until it is established to the complete satisfaction of the Conference that there has been no violation." This provision obviously applied to Grosso, and it was greeted by protests that Weaver was presuming Grosso's guilt until he could prove his innocence. Herman Helms, executive sports editor of *The State*, argued that "Weaver contradicted a legal system accepted and practiced throughout the free world." Contrary to the complaints of Helms and other critics, however, Weaver's action was not an arbitrary judgment that was prejudiced against South Carolina. The commissioner and Arthur J. Bergstrom, assistant executive director of the NCAA, had been conducting interviews with Grosso and his parents, his uncles, and authorities at his high school for several months. Their findings suggested to Weaver that South Carolina had committed violations in Grosso's recruiting and enrollment. Further, he was well aware of the likelihood, if not the certainty, that the NCAA would slap penalties on the university after it completed its investigation.[26]

South Carolina appealed Weaver's decision on Grosso's eligibility to the ACC's three-member executive committee, which had overruled the commissioner on "numerous occasions." In this case, however, "it found no basis for modifying the action taken by Commissioner Weaver" during a meeting in Raleigh. McGuire, who attended with other South Carolina officials, was so angry that, according to a report in *Sports Illustrated*, he "had to be restrained by Dr. Jones." McGuire commented bitterly that the conference's position showed that "they are not after Grosso, they are after me." A short time later, he made widely reported remarks that were even more inflammatory. He "stole the show" at a press gathering with ACC basketball coaches by calling unnamed conference officials "skunks" who "have forced me into the gutter with them." He repeated his sentiments at a civic function in Charlotte by asserting that the questions about Grosso were "a spite vendetta in which two athletic directors are trying to stop me." He added: "I have never gotten into the gutter with the skunks before in my life, but this time I have."[27]

McGuire's statements elicited sharp criticism. Morris Siegel, a columnist for the *Washington Evening Star*, suggested that "McGuire's epithet smells up the ACC" and called for a "public reprimand" of his "ugly manner of dissent." More ominously for South Carolina, authorities at other ACC schools were greatly offended. NC State chancellor John Caldwell told Jones that he needed to do "some repair work" in an upcoming meeting of conference presidents, faculty athletic chairmen, and athletic directors. "I can't believe that anything short of an institutional apology can meet the situation adequately," he observed, "and even that may leave much to be overcome." Even before McGuire sounded off, Clemson's Edwards told Maryland athletic director William Cobey that he thought it "incredible that a member institution would be unwilling to comply with both the letter and the spirit of the constitution and the bylaws" of the ACC.[28]

Jones found himself in an extraordinarily awkward situation. On the one hand, some South Carolina alumni were circulating a petition that called for the university to withdraw from the ACC. Jones made his opposition clear by declaring publicly that the "right and proper thing is to work out any and all problems within the conference." On the other hand, administrators of conference schools were incensed by South Carolina's violations of the 800 rule, which it had already admitted in the cases of the three football players, and by McGuire's insults. Jones, in turn, was annoyed with McGuire. When he and perhaps others tried to write a statement claiming that McGuire was misquoted on calling ACC officials "skunks," he eventually gave up by noting on a much-edited draft, "Forget it."[29]

On December 9, 1966, at the meeting of the presidents, faculty athletic chairmen, and athletic directors at ACC schools, Jones offered a profuse apology. "Certain statements made by Mr. McGuire in recent speeches," he said, "have been embarrassing both to the University and to the conference." He reported that "Coach McGuire has been reprimanded" and that "such unbefitting behavior will not occur again." Jones elaborated on his position after the meeting ended. He described McGuire as "a great basketball coach" and "a personal friend," but faulted him for going "past the bounds of propriety in certain public statements" in a way that "threatened the integrity of the university and the conference." Jones's statements were welcomed by ACC officials and accomplished his goal of reducing tensions.

Herman Helms praised Jones for "protecting the welfare of the university and its athletic program at the risk of a loss of personal popularity." He suggested that the president "prevented a conceivable destruction of the intercollegiate athletic program at USC."[30]

During the same meeting at which Jones apologized for McGuire's behavior, the conference decided that members could choose to cancel their basketball games with South Carolina in 1966–67 without suffering forfeits. The only school to take advantage of this policy was Duke. Cameron announced that Duke made this decision because of "the unfortunate series of events connected with the determination of the eligibility of a University of South Carolina basketball player." He defended Duke's action by informing a critic that it "was based on the fact that there was an unhealthy atmosphere between the two institutions created by some uncomplimentary statements that have been made." Duke president Douglas Knight was more blunt. He described McGuire as "libelous in his statements and totally unscrupulous in his practices." Duke authorities strongly, and truthfully, denied allegations that they had instigated the Grosso affair by reporting South Carolina to the ACC and the NCAA for potential rules violations.[31]

While South Carolina was addressing the issues that the Grosso controversy raised within the ACC, it was waiting with foreboding for the results of the NCAA's investigation. The hammer fell on January 8, 1967. The NCAA placed the South Carolina football and basketball teams on probation for two years because of financial and academic infractions. The teams were prohibited from participating in postseason tournaments or bowl games and from appearing on NCAA-sanctioned television broadcasts. The NCAA's penalties were based in part on the illegal financial assistance that South Carolina had provided to football players and on the use of funds that were not controlled by the university for making payments to players who did not qualify for aid.

The NCAA supported the ACC's position on Mike Grosso's eligibility. It found that he had been admitted by means "contrary to the regular published entrance requirements of the institution." It pointed out that he had not met the school's standards until he scored a 789 on a second "institutionally administered" test that was not recognized by the Educational Testing Service. Further, the NCAA determined that Grosso's college expenses were paid by "a corporation upon which the student-athlete was neither naturally or legally dependent." The corporation in question was run by Grosso's uncles, and they refused to provide information on financial arrangements. Finally, the NCAA cited an illegal tryout in which Grosso and three others participated while still in high school. It named Harry Gotkin as the "representative of the University of South Carolina's athletic interests" who "arranged for and conducted a basketball game" in which the four players "were provided the opportunity to display their talents."[32]

The NCAA's punishment of South Carolina was harsh, but Jones regarded it as "light compared to what it might have been." Dietzel had talked with members of the Committee on Infractions and NCAA staff members shortly after the organization announced its findings, and he learned that unless the university "took firm and unequivocal action" to prevent further violations, it *would be suspended* from membership in the organization (emphasis in original). NCAA representatives advised him in confidence that the university must gain control over the "outside pressures" that exercised undue influence "in the running of our own athletic department." They expressed doubt that McGuire would "adhere to the proper structures within the University and forgo working with outside influences." With Dietzel's report in mind, Jones sent stern instructions to McGuire. He told him that "all public comments must contain no derogatory statements about athletic and administration personnel in this and other institutions." He directed McGuire to follow the "letter and spirit" of ACC and NCAA regulations and to avoid any "questionable connection" with "professional recruiters." He made clear that he would permit no deviation from those requirements and that McGuire's "complete cooperation" was "imperative."[33]

The outcome of the investigation of Mike Grosso's eligibility provoked sharp criticism of the University of South Carolina and of McGuire, even among those who had previously sided with him. Herman Helms, who had been highly critical of Weaver, commented that the NCAA acted "with objectivity and without prejudice." Its conclusions, he wrote, were "more embarrassing and more damaging to the university" than any previous events "in the long and turbulent athletic history at the University of South Carolina." The *Charleston News and Courier* suggested that "the discovery that a coach dealt under the table with a basketball player . . . brought the University more bad publicity in a few weeks than a legion of public relations men can make good in a year." It lamented that the episode "has hurt the reputation of the state as a whole."[34]

The NCAA's ruling ended Mike Grosso's career at South Carolina. He had proven his ability when he played on the freshman team and averaged 22.7 points and 26 rebounds. But he never appeared in a varsity game with

South Carolina. The conference allowed him to practice with the team, and he injured his knee so badly in a scrimmage as a sophomore that he would probably have been unable to play even if eligible. With McGuire's help, Grosso received a scholarship to play at the University of Louisville, where he averaged 16.2 points and 14.2 rebounds over two seasons. McGuire made no public comments about the NCAA's decision. But in February 1967, he told Gene Warren, a reporter with the *Greensboro Daily News*, that he was "very unhappy." He insisted that with Grosso, South Carolina could have won the ACC and "had a good shot at the national title." Warren concluded that the coach would never get over the loss of Grosso and warned his ACC rivals: "Frank McGuire is a bitter man and has a long memory."[35]

In the wake of the NCAA's ruling, South Carolina officials sought to make reforms that would avoid further problems and to mend fences. Jones had taken the first step to restore friendly relations with his ACC colleagues by apologizing for McGuire's name-calling at the conference meeting in December 1966. Dietzel reached out to Eddie Cameron, whom McGuire regarded as his chief nemesis. Dietzel told Cameron that "I am doing my darndest to bury any resentments from the past" and confided that "I have been embarrassed by some of the things that have been said." He offered to drive to Durham to "apologize personally" to Duke's athletic council. But the peace offerings were not enough to heal the mutual animosity between South Carolina and other conference schools that the battle over Grosso's eligibility produced. The lingering ill will from the controversy laid the foundations for South Carolina's departure from the ACC just a few years later. It is no small irony that the university decided to withdraw from the conference in 1970 not because of McGuire's complaints but because of Dietzel's objections to the 800 rule.[36]

Virginia's Quest for Respectability

The University of Virginia had no problems with the 800 rule, but it had great problems with fielding competitive football and basketball teams in the ACC. Its athletic programs suffered from insufficient funding, inadequate facilities, inflexible academic requirements, and little alumni support or fan interest. In early 1958, football coach Ben Martin, upon his resignation to take a job at the Air Force Academy, told President Darden of his "deep concern over the future prospect of a sound athletic program at the University." He said that he had "presented a rather modest program" that would "give us at least the opportunity to be successful while still preserving all the traditions and high standards of the University." But he realized that "chances for acceptance of the program, which involved receipt of additional funds, were very slim." After Martin's departure, Virginia's football team tied an NCAA record by losing 28 games in a row between 1958 and the end of the 1960 season.[37]

The basketball program was caught in a similar morass. Billy McCann, who took over as coach in 1957, was highly regarded as an individual and well respected as a coach. He was one the leading candidates for the Duke job in 1959 when Cameron hired Bubas. But he faced daunting obstacles to success at Virginia. The most glaring was his inability to hire a full-time assistant. The *Raleigh News and Observer* pointed out in 1957: "A sign of Virginia's lack of big-time basketball backing is the assistant coach. Other teams have student managers but Virginia has the only student coach." Gene Corrigan went to Virginia in 1958 to coach lacrosse and soccer and also taught three classes of physical education. He led the lacrosse team to the league championship in 1962, Virginia's first ACC title in any sport. Along with his other responsibilities, he served as coach of the freshman basketball team. At one point he said to Gus Tebell, Virginia's athletic director: "We're not going to get anywhere in basketball unless Billy gets somebody full-time because he needs to recruit year-round." Tebell answered: "Well, I don't have any money to do anything."[38]

McCann's teams performed creditably during his first two seasons as coach. The 1957–58 squad posted an overall record of 10–13, 6–8 in the conference. The following season, Virginia went 11–14 overall, 6–8 in the ACC. Then the bottom dropped out. During the next four seasons, the Cavaliers won just 8 games in the ACC against 48 losses and had overall records of 6–18, 3–23, 5–18, and 5–20. Virginia had some outstanding players who received conference recognition despite the records of their teams. Herb Busch, a 6'7" center was second in the ACC in scoring and third in rebounding in 1958 and made first-team All-Conference. Paul Adkins, a high-scoring 6'0" guard made second-team All-Conference in 1959 and 1960. Tony Laquintano, a 5'11" guard who averaged 19.8 and 20.4 points in his third- and fourth-year seasons, matched Adkins's achievement. Gene Engel, a 6'6" forward, placed fourth in the conference in scoring in 1963, behind Art Heyman, Billy Cunningham, and Jeff Mullins, and was named second-team All-ACC. Hunter "Chip" Conner, Virginia high school Player of the Year in 1960, was once described by the *Charlotte News* as "the splendid Chip Conner." He was a quick, slashing 6'3" guard who was arguably Virginia's best player since Buzz Wilkinson. He averaged 17.0 points for his career and was elected to the All-ACC first team in 1964, the year after McCann resigned as coach. Despite the skills of some of its players and an occasional upset over one of the conference powers, Virginia was not competitive in the ACC, and its prospects for improvement were not promising.[39]

Gradually, however, university officials decided that the embarrassment of losing big and often was not an honorable condition. Edgar F. Shannon Jr., who replaced Darden as president in 1959, was an unlikely source of support for improving Virginia's athletic stature, but he began the slow and unsteady process of making the football and basketball programs respectable. When Darden resigned, there was no heir apparent waiting to become president, and the selection committee made a surprise choice in Shannon. He was a renowned scholar on the poetry of Alfred, Lord Tennyson, and he had just been promoted to full professor in the English department. Shannon had little administrative experience other than what he had gained as a U.S. Navy officer during World War II. His service in the navy, however, was more memorable for his participation in the fierce island campaigns of the Pacific War; on one occasion he spent several perilous hours in ocean waters after his ship was sunk. When Shannon was elected president of the university, he was just 40 years old. His distinguished appearance and dignified manner gave him the aura of a university president whom central casting might have designated for the role. Shannon's top priority was to improve the academic reputation of the university, which he hoped to accomplish by hiring eminent professors for selected departments and by tightening admissions standards.[40]

The problems that faced Virginia's coaches were not among Shannon's major concerns, but he found that he had to address athletic issues. In February 1961, he assured one correspondent that the university was "making no academic concessions to athletes," and he suggested that the proper approach was to make games "interesting for intelligent young men to play in a sportsmanlike manner." Shannon had come to the presidency from the College of Arts and Sciences, where support had been strongest for the recommendations in the 1951 "Gooch report" that the university abolish athletic scholarships and guard against overemphasis on sports. His position on athletic questions tended to be informed by those concerns and by his deference to faculty sensibilities. In January 1962, Billy McCann, Gene Corrigan, football coach Bill Elias, and two of their colleagues requested that Shannon relax a rule on eligibility that required athletes to attain a grade point average of 2.0 the semester before they participated in intercollegiate sports. The coaches argued that as long as an athlete was eligible to remain in school, his average the previous semester was immaterial. They also pointed out that most schools had adopted the more lenient practice they recommended, including Duke, North Carolina, Army, and Navy. Shannon was not persuaded. He consulted with B. F. D. Runk, dean of the university, who expressed "doubts that there would be any prospect of obtaining a vote of the faculty to change the regulation" and thought "that it would be unwise . . . to make any move that would appear to be lessening the academic requirements for participation in athletics."[41]

Nevertheless, Shannon endorsed the conclusions of a special committee he appointed that urged that Virginia's athletics be "encouraged and supported." In April 1962, he reported to the Athletic Committee of the Board of Visitors that it was "axiomatic that 'a sense of excellence' should permeate all aspects of the University," including athletics, and that the university would "make every legitimate effort to field competitive teams" in the ACC. After reaching that policy position, Shannon did not issue directives to carry it out and left the determination of how to achieve it to others. He was acutely aware of the "unfavorable financial picture" for Virginia athletics. In 1960–61, for example, the athletic department ran a deficit of about $47,000. Its income depended heavily on gate receipts, which were small because attendance at football and basketball games was generally abysmal. Therefore, Shannon's commitment to striving for excellence in the university's athletic programs did not produce immediate results. But there were some improvements. In 1962, McCann was authorized to hire a full-time assistant, and the arrival of Gene Mehaffey in that post made Virginia the last school in the ACC to support two basketball coaches.[42]

Another hopeful development for Virginia's basketball program was the construction of a new arena. Memorial Gymnasium was built in 1923 with money provided by alumni, and by the mid-1950s, it was flaunting its age. An internal report on the Virginia athletic department called it "antiquated and inadequate" in 1957. The gym had a floor that was dark and "full of wrinkles and bulges from moisture leaks," the wiring was "badly worn and dangerously loaded," the locker rooms were "very crowded and poorly designed," and the space was too small to accommodate the needs of intercollegiate sports and intramurals. The cost of a new field house was estimated at $2.5 million, and in 1959, the university's Alumni Association undertook a campaign to raise $500,000 in hopes that this would encourage the General Assembly to pay the remainder. The campaign committee assured prospective donors that Thomas Jefferson would have supported the project as a means of training leaders. "It must have been Mr. Jefferson's intention," a pamphlet sent to alumni affirmed, "that the facilities needed to build leaders would be provided to keep pace with progress." The alumni came through, the legislature appropriated funds, and in November 1965, University Hall was officially dedicated with pride and a sense of wonder over a playing floor without bumps and locker rooms with ample capacity. The arena, which in the end cost about $4 million, seated 9,500 for convocations, 2,900 for concerts, and 8,500 for basketball.[43]

By the time that University Hall opened, Virginia had a new head basketball coach. On February 4, 1963, in the middle of his sixth season at Virginia, Billy McCann suddenly resigned. He did not give his reasons for quitting except to say that it was "an accumulation of things." Athletic Director Steve Sebo, a former football coach at the University of Pennsylvania who had replaced Tebell, commented, "We didn't know that was coming. We hadn't made advance plans." In April 1963, Sebo hired 35-year-old Bill Gibson, the coach at Mansfield State College in Pennsylvania, a school with about 800 students. Mansfield State played in a league of former teachers' colleges that was highly competitive at a level considerably below the ACC. It was not a power in the conference until Gibson took over as coach in 1956. In seven years his teams compiled a record of 102–37, and in his last three seasons they went 57–3. "He knows what to do to win," Sebo said of Gibson. "We have ourselves a good man, a strong and able coach in every respect." He reported that under McCann, the university had gradually increased the number of basketball scholarships to 14, though it had never used all of them, and therefore Gibson would have what he needed to win in the ACC.[44]

Gibson brought energy, toughness, and above all, optimism, to the Virginia basketball program. He grew up in the gritty steel mill town of Donora in western Pennsylvania and was the first member of his family to attend college. He played basketball on good teams at Penn State in the early 1950s and then coached high school for four years before moving to Mansfield State. His achievements along the way from Donora to Mansfield had instilled confidence that he could overcome adverse conditions. "I just think he had incomparable self-confidence," Chip Conner, whom Gibson hired as his assistant in 1967, later commented. "He really thought no matter the obstacle, no matter the lack of resources . . . by God, he was good enough to do it." Gibson's confidence in his ability to succeed, in turn, made him a tremendous salesman for his program. Gibson was outgoing, charming, and funny. When he told recruits that he would build a winning

Bill Gibson (right) and Chip Conner, 1971. (Courtesy The North Carolina State Archives; reprinted by permission of *The News and Observer* of Raleigh, North Carolina)

program at Virginia, he said it with such conviction that he seemed eminently credible. Within a short time after arriving in Charlottesville, he also set out to increase fan "interest in and support for the basketball program" by encouraging the formation of the Virginia Basketball Club. The club had "78 active members" and was "constantly growing" less than a year after Gibson became coach.

The downside of Gibson's strong belief that he could succeed at Virginia was his impatience with those whom he viewed as obstacles to fulfilling his objectives. In those cases, his toughness took on an abrasive edge. He leaned on admissions officers to rule favorably on prospects whose applications would not necessarily be accepted. He complained to his bosses, Sebo and later Gene Corrigan, about the continuing shortage of recruiting funds compared to what his ACC rivals received, and to their ire, aired his frustrations to members of the basketball club, neighbors, and other outsiders. Gibson also stirred the resentment of players at times by punishing them in a manner that was counterproductive. In the first game at University Hall on December 4, 1965, Virginia's opponent was a powerful Kentucky team that played in the NCAA finals the following March. The Cavaliers were talented but young, and they lost in a rout, 99–73. Gibson compounded the humiliation by holding a practice immediately after the game, which the players regarded as pointless and demeaning.[45]

Despite the attributes that Gibson brought to the job at Virginia, he did not accomplish his goal of producing a winning team for several years. He recruited some outstanding players, but the results of his efforts were a disappointment to him and to Virginia fans. His first two teams finished with records of 8–16 and 7–18. This was not surprising, but hopes were high for the 1965–66 team. It included high-scoring junior Jim Connelly and a group of sophomores who had led the freshman team to a 14–1 record the previous season. The team's loss to Kentucky in the inaugural game at University Hall turned out to be a harbinger of a season in which the Cavaliers compiled a record of 7–15, 4–10 in the ACC. The pattern held during the next two seasons with records of 9–17 and 9–16. Some individual players performed admirably. Connelly scored 20.0 points per game and made second-team All-Conference in 1966–67. Mike Katos averaged 18.5 points and 8.9 rebounds the next year and received the same honor. Gibson's losing record as an ACC coach did not prevent him from earning the esteem of his peers. In May 1966, he was a leading candidate to replace Press Maravich at NC State before he removed himself from consideration. But Virginia was a long way from respectability, and dissatisfaction was growing.[46]

Gibson remained confident that he could establish a winning tradition. "It's tough, discouraging, but you can't lose confidence," he remarked in early 1967. "Virginia has been after a winner a long time. I don't know how long it will take, but I promise I'm going to do it." He hoped that greater resources and some relief on entrance requirements would enable him to succeed. In accordance with Shannon's wishes, the university had tightened admissions standards during the 1960s. As the postwar baby boomers came of college age, Virginia received more applications than ever and became much more selective. In 1963, it generally expected applicants to be in the upper half of their high school class and to score at least 500 on one part of the SAT and 450 on the other. By 1967, this had been revised to 500 on both parts of the college boards. The College of Arts and Sciences also had a foreign language requirement for admission. Sebo told Shannon that Virginia was "at the top of our Conference with regard to academic requirements, class standing and achievement scores for entering student-athletes." He also affirmed that Duke, North Carolina, and other schools admitted athletes "at the bottom of their standards." They did not "drop below their entrance requirements," but they did "go to the limit." Sebo sought some relaxation, or at least some flexibility, in Virginia's admission standards along the same lines. But Marvin B. Perry Jr., who served as dean of admissions until 1967, was notoriously intractable. He was effectively implementing Shannon's goal of raising admissions standards, and the president was not inclined to overrule him to support the athletic department.[47]

In April 1967, Sebo requested his coaches to list their recommendations for changes that would make it possible "to win the Conference championship at least one out of eight years." Gibson responded that the university's admission standards, including the foreign language requirement, "must soon level off and be more flexible." He also cited his need for an enlarged recruiting budget and a second full-time assistant coach to strengthen recruiting. "I believe you can be as strong athletically here as you can academically," he once commented. But the effort to strike the proper balance still seemed to Virginia's coaches and athletic administrators to favor the academic side of the scale so heavily that it made winning a championship even once in eight years a tall order.[48]

Boot the Hoot

During his first six years as coach, Gibson contended that he had not produced a winning season because he lacked the depth of talent to play on an even keel with the strongest teams of the ACC. Some of his players, however, believed that Virginia's struggles were at least as much a result of inferior coaching as a shortage of talent. Although they liked Gibson personally, they concluded that his coaching experience at Mansfield State had not prepared him for the ACC. He was not good at drawing up plays, making adjustments, or taking advantage of the skills of the players he recruited. This caused disillusionment that culminated in March 1969, when two Virginia players suggested publicly that Virginia's losing records were attributable to Gibson's failures. The result was a bitter and highly publicized controversy over a campaign to "Boot the Hoot." Gibson was sometimes referred to as "Hoot" after the famed star of old-time western movies, "Hoot" Gibson.[49]

Before the 1968–69 season, Virginia had the ingredients of a team that could rank among the best in the ACC. It had size, speed, experience, and offensive firepower. Early in the season it beat good Duke and South Carolina teams. But a series of injuries wrecked a season that seemed to hold great promise. Chip Case, the best all-around player and the squad's leader, tore knee cartilage in the second game. John Gidding, the team's top scorer and rebounder at the time, injured his knee seriously enough to reduce his effectiveness. Other players suffered from illness and academic difficulties.

The team ended the season on a gloomy note by losing its last five games, including a 99–86 defeat by Duke in the first round of the ACC Tournament. This marked the tenth consecutive time that Virginia had failed to advance to the second round of the tournament. After an exceptionally hopeful beginning, the Cavaliers finished with a record of 10–15, 5–9 in the conference.[50]

Following the loss to Duke in the tournament on March 6, 1969, two players, juniors Tony Kinn and John English, attended a party for reporters and vented complaints about Gibson's coaching style and competence. They suggested that several team members planned to petition the university to fire their coach. The entire team, however, did not support the effort to oust Gibson. Three players, including co-captains Case and Norm Carmichael, declined to sign a petition and criticized their teammates for making their disaffection public. A few days later, the entire team agreed on a statement in which they apologized "for the manner in which the situation has been handled." Nevertheless, they made clear that they had "a number of justifiable grievances which were catalytic to the premature exposure of certain team members' feelings."[51]

The "player revolt" was a big story in the Virginia community from the time that Kinn and English disclosed their views, and it took on greater prominence and acrimony after the university's student newspaper, the *Cavalier Daily*, ran a series of articles that harshly condemned Gibson. Sports columnist Ted McKean attacked Gibson for mishandling the players he brought to Virginia and submitted that the failure to win was not a result of a shortage of talent. He named several outstanding recruits who, he claimed, had left school because of their disenchantment with the coach. The only way to improve Virginia's basketball program, McKean argued, was to apply "enough pressure . . . to Bill Gibson to produce his resignation."[52]

The dissatisfaction that the players aired in general terms and the articles in the *Cavalier Daily* elicited sharp criticism. Chauncey Durden of the *Richmond Times-Dispatch* commented that the "Cavalier malcontents lacked judgment and manners." Bill Brill of the *Roanoke Times* argued that the protesting players had forced Sebo to support Gibson because he could not yield to "out and out insubordination." Brill also quoted an ACC coach who disagreed with the players who questioned Gibson's coaching ability. "Is Gibson a bad coach?" he growled. "He had the sixth best talent in the league. He finished sixth." A group of 106 Virginia athletes, mostly football and lacrosse players, signed a petition that strongly backed Gibson. They called the actions of the dissenting basketball team members "irrational, irresponsible and detrimental . . . to the image of the University." They also denounced the authors of anti-Gibson articles in the *Cavalier Daily*, including McKean, as "biased" and "incompetent."[53]

Amid the tension that the controversy created, Sebo and members of the university's faculty athletic committee met in closed session with members of the basketball team for more than five hours. The following evening, the same group had another long discussion with players and separately with Gibson. The specific grievances the players cited were not made public, though Chip Case, acting as a spokesman for the team, announced that the players did not and would not ask for Gibson's dismissal. The players cited two fundamental complaints during the meetings that hardly seemed to justify a revolt. One was that Gibson had fixed the outcome of their election of a team captain, which turned out to be a misunderstanding. The other was that Gibson had not kept promises he had made to nonscholarship team members to give them more playing time and award them scholarships. It was clear during the meetings that, whatever the merits of the arguments, communication between the coach and his players was badly impaired. It was also clear that the protests could not be shrugged off as petty whining by a handful of disgruntled players. After weighing the information he collected, Sebo issued a far-from-rousing vote of confidence in Gibson. "We have had frank and open discussions with members of the basketball team and Coach Gibson. There have unquestionably been misunderstandings on both sides," he declared. "We have come to the conclusion, however, that it is in the best interests of the University and its overall athletic program for Mr. Gibson to remain as basketball coach." L. Starling Reid, faculty chairman of athletics, told colleagues that he thought the players and Gibson shared responsibility for the discontent and depicted it as "a very messy situation."[54]

The controversy over his coaching record, and even more over his coaching ability, was an exceedingly painful episode for Gibson. But there were two promising developments that boosted his spirits and sustained his hopes for the future. During the heat of the "Boot the Hoot" campaign, four highly regarded members of the freshman basketball team—Frank DeWitt, Scott McCandlish, Chip Miller, and Tim Rash—made their views known in a letter to the *Cavalier Daily*. "Having been recruited by Coach Gibson and having practiced with the varsity this past season," they wrote, "we know Mr. Gibson, the man, and Mr. Gibson, the coach. We respect him on and off the court. We came here to play basketball for Virginia and we are still looking forward to playing basketball here at Virginia—under Coach Gibson." At about the same time, Virginia announced the signing of an All-State player from Pennsylvania, Barry Parkhill. In what proved to be an understatement of monumental proportions, Gibson said of Parkhill, "He has all the tools to be a good one."[55]

Maryland on a Slide

From the time that the ACC was founded until the latter half of the 1960s, the only team outside of the Big Four that competed successfully in the conference was Maryland. It was alone among conference members not located in the state of North Carolina to win an ACC title between 1953 and 1971. Even after the graduation of Gene Shue, who led the 1953–54 squad to a 23–7 record, Bud Millikan's teams performed well in the ACC. During the next three seasons, they finished with records of 17–7 (10–4 in the conference), 14–10 (7–7), and 16–10 (9–5). Bob Kessler, a 6'4" forward who handled the ball like a guard, averaged 20.3 points as a junior in 1954–55 and 20.4 points the following season. He made second-team All-ACC both years.[56]

By the beginning of the 1957–58 season, Millikan had corrected the most glaring weakness in his earlier lineups by adding a skilled center. Al Bunge, who stood 6'8", was a stalwart defender and an aggressive rebounder despite chronic problems with ulcerative colitis. Another outstanding sophomore was 6'6" Charlie McNeil, who was an excellent jump shooter. Bunge and McNeil joined a team that was talented, experienced, and, by the standards of college basketball, old. Three players—guards John Nacincik and Tom Young and backup center Perry Moore—were military veterans. They brought a level of maturity, steadiness, and tolerance of Millikan's incessant criticism that was invaluable for team chemistry. Millikan, in turn, had enough confidence in his team to allow it depart from his controlled offensive patterns and to run more than his previous teams. As a result, the 1957–58 Terrapins set a school record by averaging more than 69 points per game. They provided an early preview of their potential when they defeated top-ranked Kentucky, 71–62, in a game at Cole Field House.

Maryland finished the regular season in fourth place in the ACC with a conference record of 9–5; overall they were 17–6. Four ACC teams were nationally ranked going into the tournament in 1958; Duke was 6th, North Carolina 13th, NC State 14th, and Maryland 17th. The Terrapins had the toughest draw, but they defeated fifth-seeded Virginia in a close game and

Duke in overtime to reach the finals against North Carolina, the defending national champions. The Tar Heels jumped out to a 13-point advantage and led at halftime, 34–27. In the second half, Maryland shot 60.8 percent from the field, scored 59 points, and won the game handily, 86–74. McNeil scored 21 points, forward Nick Davis had 16, and Bunge contributed 13 points and 12 rebounds. In keeping with a tournament tradition of producing unlikely heroes, Bill Murphy, who averaged 2.7 points during the season, scored 19 in the championship game. Three days later, Maryland defeated Boston College in the first round of the NCAA Tournament, 86–63, and then lost a tight game to Temple in the eastern regionals. It ended the season with a record of 22–7 and a ranking of 6th in the nation.[57]

Maryland's ACC championship was the culmination of eight consecutive winning seasons that Millikan produced after taking over a moribund program in 1950. Ironically, he won the title after he compromised his preference for a slow offensive tempo. He did so because he had a mature and talented team, but he did not adopt a faster pace as a permanent fixture. Millikan remained wedded to what he called the "science" of disciplined offense. "I'm not saying that every team should play our deliberate style of basketball," he declared in 1952, "but I think there should be some science to the playmaking, not just wild shooting." Millikan emphasized the importance of ball control and shot selection and objected to "needless running up and down the court." By teaching his teams to play possession offense and hardnosed defense, he kept Maryland competitive in the ACC even when its Big Four rivals had more talent and institutional support.[58]

Millikan was a stern and demanding taskmaster. He made certain that his players went to class and graduated. Tom Young later remarked that no player wanted to be summoned for a meeting in Millikan's office, especially those whose academic performance was deficient. Millikan drilled his teams on skills, strategy, and discipline. On occasion, he drove home his points with a physical reminder. In a game against Kentucky in Lexington in December 1958, Maryland had a three-point lead with just a few seconds remaining. During a time-out, Millikan told his players not to commit a foul under any circumstances and emphasized his instructions by slapping each player hard in the face. Apparently, he should have slapped Al Bunge a little harder. When a Kentucky player drove to the basket, Bunge, according to one witness, "put him in the third row" of seats. The Kentucky player sank a shot as he was fouled and made the free throw. Kentucky won the game in overtime, and Bunge later joked that his foul might have been the "most memorable moment" of his career.[59]

When Maryland won the ACC Tournament in 1958, Dick Herbert raised a troubling prospect for Big Four fans. His view was summarized in a headline that read: "Terps' Reign May Last for Spell." But the reign did not last. In 1958–59, Maryland suffered its first losing season in Millikan's tenure as coach, finishing with a record of 10–13. McNeil led the team in scoring with an average of 14.8 points and was named second-team All-ACC. The Terrapins rebounded the following year with a record of 15–8, and Bunge became the first Maryland player since Gene Shue to make first-team All-Conference. After a 14–12 campaign in 1960–61, Maryland's performance declined sharply. In the three seasons between fall 1961 and spring 1964, its records were 8–17, 8–13, and 9–17. The only ACC school that won fewer games during that period was Virginia.[60]

Maryland's woes were attributable in part to Millikan's inability to attract top talent. He was not a great recruiter even when his teams were winning. Millikan was further hampered by a relatively small recruiting budget and the lack of a full-time assistant. In 1961, when he was finally able to hire an assistant, he brought in Frank Fellows, who had played for him in the early 1950s and was the coach at a local high school. Fellows was an able and personable recruiter, but he also had to teach a full schedule of classes in the off-season. This limited the time he could spend on contacting and visiting promising players. When Fellows talked to prospects, he emphasized Maryland's proximity to Washington, its membership in the ACC, and above all, the opportunity to play at Cole Field House, still one of the premier basketball arenas in the country. For all its splendor, however, it seldom provided Maryland with a home-court advantage. In 1963, Millikan estimated that Cole had been filled only four or five times since it opened in 1955. Often the crowds were so small and quiet that it seemed like a neutral court, especially in comparison to the clamorous and partisan atmosphere that prevailed at other ACC arenas.[61]

Suddenly, after fans became increasingly disgruntled and students hung Millikan in effigy, Maryland made its best showing since 1958. The 1964–65 team finished 18–8 and 10–4 in the conference, good for a second place tie with NC State and North Carolina in the regular season standings. It was led by junior Gary Ward, who averaged 18.0 points and 10.4 rebounds, and three talented sophomores, Jay McMillen, Joe Harrington, and Gary Williams. Fellows's recruiting ability was instrumental in landing McMillen and Harrington. McMillen was a high school star in Mansfield, Pennsylvania, and he chose Maryland over other schools because he was impressed with Cole Field House and wanted to play in the ACC. A contributing fac-

Bud Millikan instructs his players, 1965. To his right is assistant coach
Frank Fellows. (Courtesy The North Carolina State Archives; reprinted by
permission of *The News and Observer* of Raleigh, North Carolina)

tor in his decision was that his mother liked Fellows, in contrast to some of
the other coaches she met.

Harrington was a heavily recruited standout from Phippsburg, Maine,
who was inclined to accept a scholarship at the University of Cincinnati,
especially after he met Oscar Robertson. But he and his parents were also
favorably impressed with Millikan and Fellows. Further, Harrington's high
school basketball coach had gone to Maryland as an assistant football
coach, which gave him a Maine connection in College Park. Williams was
not a highly coveted prospect out of Collingswood, New Jersey, and he
signed with Maryland after his preferred choice, St. Josephs, failed to recruit him. Williams did not know that Jack Ramsey, the St. Josephs' coach,
waited for high school coaches to contact him about players rather than

actively pursuing them. As sophomores, McMillen averaged 19.7 points to lead the team and 7.3 rebounds, and Harrington added 10.6 points and 6.2 rebounds. Williams was not a scorer, but he was a tough and dependable playmaker.[62]

With its top seven players returning from a team that had gone 18–8, hopes soared for Maryland's prospects in the 1965–66 season. In December 1965, *Sports Illustrated* ranked the Terrapins 15th in the nation in its preseason forecast. It concluded that "Coach Bud Millikan's team looks like the best ever at College Park" and suggested that Maryland might be good enough to play in the NCAA championship rounds the following March, which would be held at Cole Field House. The team got off to a strong start, and it seemed to vindicate the preseason predictions when it defeated the University of Houston, led by Elvin Hayes, and the University of Dayton, led by Donnie May, to win the Sugar Bowl Tournament over the Christmas holidays.

Then, inexplicably, the team fell apart. It was trounced by North Carolina, suffered a shocking defeat by Virginia, and lost five conference games in a row. An acutely disappointing season ended with a record of 14–11, a fifth-place finish in the conference, and elimination in the first round of the ACC Tournament. One reason was that Harrington severely injured his knee. Gary Williams was convinced that a more important cause of the slump was that his teammates lost their focus. Several joined fraternities and seemed more interested in activities other than basketball. Jay McMillen agreed that "we had a bunch of screw-ups" who "could have done better." The next year, a Maryland team that was undersized and outmanned again began the season well and collapsed at the end. It wound up with a record of 11–14.[63]

Maryland's record during the 1965–66 and 1966–67 seasons increased the pressure to replace Millikan. In January 1966, a group of alumni, without signing their names, told President Elkins that Millikan should be dismissed because "his record is poor considering the material he has." They threatened to "cut off our aid and advise other alumni to do likewise." Elkins responded by sending the letter to Athletic Director William Cobey with a sarcastic notation: "These are *brave* people." Despite his disdain for anonymous grumbling, Elkins was increasingly attentive to the problems in Maryland's football and basketball programs. During his first few years as president, his primary concern was to redress Curley Byrd's legacy of overemphasis on athletics and to improve Maryland's academic stature. By the early 1960s, he had made significant headway. One indica-

Joe Harrington goes high for Maryland as teammate Gary Williams watches, 1965. NC State's Tommy Mattocks (10) ducks and Pete Coker (54) observes. (Courtesy The North Carolina State Archives; reprinted by permission of *The News and Observer* of Raleigh, North Carolina)

tion of tighter admission standards was that in 1961, the university, for the first time in its history, rejected the applications of some in-state students. Another sign of Maryland's improving academic reputation was that Phi Beta Kappa awarded the university a chapter in 1964, which it had refused to do during Byrd's presidency.[64]

As Maryland's progress on the academic front gained recognition, Elkins placed greater emphasis on improving its performance in football and basketball. "I learned a lesson—that is, you can't go half-way and be successful. You have to try to compete and do it totally, or you should get out," he later remarked. "You should operate within the academic framework of the University, but when you are within the rules you cannot go half-way towards having an athletic program. It just won't work." Maryland took a big step to "do it totally" in 1966 when it hired Lou Saban, a highly successful professional coach, as its head football coach. In March 1967, it made another move in the same direction by, according to most accounts, forcing Millikan to resign. The circumstances surrounding Millikan's departure were, and remain, somewhat murky. Years later, he insisted that he had decided on his own to leave coaching. Other well-informed observers were certain that his only options were to resign or be fired. Although Cobey was directly responsible for hiring and firing coaches, in the case of Millikan, he would not have acted without Elkins's knowledge and consent. Asking Millikan to resign was consistent with Elkins's desire for improvement in the basketball program.[65]

Whatever the extent to which Millikan's departure was voluntary, he left Maryland as the most successful basketball coach in the school's history. In 17 seasons he won 243 games while losing 182. During the first years of the ACC, he made Maryland consistently competitive and claimed the championship in 1958. But, except for one excellent season in 1964–65, Maryland slipped from the top rungs of the conference during the 1960s. Millikan's downfall was in large part a result of his failure to recruit the talent he needed to keep up with his ACC rivals. Jim Kehoe, who succeeded Cobey as Maryland's athletic director, later commented that Millikan "was one of the outstanding coaches in America" and "got an incredible amount out of the material he had." But, Kehoe added, "he couldn't recruit." Millikan's shortcomings as a recruiter were a consequence, at least in part, of his steadfast commitment to a deliberate offensive style. When Jeff Mullins was being recruited, he visited Maryland and was much impressed with the school, the facilities, and the coaches. He asked Millikan about his preference for a slow offensive tempo, and the coach replied that he would run when he had the players to do it effectively. Mullins thought the team already had the ability to use a fast-breaking style, and because of his doubts that Millikan would change his approach, he scratched Maryland off his list.[66]

Millikan's own players were frustrated by the controlled offense that he imposed. Jay McMillen later commented the "our style of offense was just atrocious for modern-day play." He thought that if Millikan "had just let us run, we would have maximized our potential." Billy Jones, who played during Millikan's last two seasons, believed that the coach failed to take full advantage of the skills of his players or to adjust his offense to match his talent. Rather than capitalizing on the speed and quickness he had available to beat opponents down the court, he allowed teams that were bigger and slower to set up their half-court defense. Millikan excelled in teaching his teams to play stellar defense, and that was the key to the success he achieved. But he fell behind the times with his devotion to the "science" of disciplined offense, and the game, increasingly characterized by what he called "needless running up and down the court," passed him by.[67]

When Millikan resigned, Maryland immediately announced that he would be replaced by Frank Fellows. In six seasons as Millikan's assistant, Fellows had coached freshman teams to 70 wins against 21 losses, including a 12–1 record in 1966–67. He disclosed that he would follow Millikan's example by emphasizing strong defense and, depending on the skills of his players, perhaps run more on offense. Fellows had the benefit of an outstanding staff; both of his assistant coaches went on to become successful head coaches at other schools. Tom Young was the full-time assistant, and Tom Davis, a graduate student in the Department of Education, was a part-time assistant. What Fellows did not have was outstanding talent. Maryland lacked size at center, and without a good rebounder, he resorted to a ball-control offense. This was a source of concern to President Elkins. Early in Fellows's first season, Elkins asked the two full-time coaches to come to his office the day after a low-scoring game. He told them that he regarded the outcome of games as less important than the manner in which they were played, and he urged the coaches to find ways to increase scoring and generate excitement. He also asked about ways in which Maryland could improve its recruiting. Despite Fellows's best efforts, his teams did not fare well. In 1967–68 Maryland went 8–16 and placed sixth in the conference with a 4–10 record. The following season was worse. The Terrapins finished with an overall record of 8–18 and a conference record of 2–12 to tie with Clemson for last place. In early 1969, Kehoe replaced Cobey as athletic director, and one of his first actions was to fire Fellows. He concluded, regretfully, that the basketball program was unlikely to improve without a new coach who would make dramatic changes.[68]

Crowd Control

From the time the ACC was founded, crowd behavior was a chronic headache for university administrators. They recognized the great, if immeasurable, value of enthusiastic fan support for a basketball team, but they also realized that abusive conduct damaged the reputation of their schools. They periodically issued apologies to their opponents and admonitions to their students and fans, usually with little effect. Although the arenas at South Carolina and Clemson were the consensus picks as the worst places to play in the ACC, they did not lack for competition. In March 1957, Dick Herbert reported that the Atlantic Coast Conference Sportswriters Association planned to award a trophy for the school that showed the "best sportsmanship," but he added that "it is difficult to find a worthy candidate for the honor." Fellow writer Smith Barrier suggested that the award would end up with "an eight-way tie . . . for last place."[69]

In February 1961, ACC commissioner Weaver denounced the "small segment" of "juvenile delinquents" at conference schools who mocked visiting teams with "nauseating boos and jeers." Although his indictment applied to all ACC members, he made his comments after the fight at Duke Indoor Stadium that resulted in the suspension of Art Heyman, Larry Brown, and Don Walsh. Blue Devil fans were notorious for taunting opponents; Frank Weedon, sports information director at NC State, once referred to Duke's arena as a "cesspool." In one game that North Carolina's Pete Brennan played in Durham, he was preparing to shoot a free throw when he heard somebody in the crowd yell an insult about his mother. The fan kept shouting snide comments about her by name for several minutes. Brennan managed to avoid reacting visibly, but he was angry that a Duke supporter would stoop to making offensive remarks about his mother as a way of provoking him. He was also amazed that the fan had somehow learned the name of his mother, who was Irish, had an unusual first name, lived in New York, and was certainly not known to most ACC followers.[70]

In December 1965, *Sports Illustrated* lamented the conduct of fans at basketball arenas around the country. "There was a time when every college area had one particular gym that visiting teams referred to as 'the snake pit,'" it commented. "Today, nearly every court is a snake pit for visiting teams." The magazine used Duke as an example of "fairly typical" misbehavior by college basketball crowds. It reported that in a recent game against UCLA in Durham, Duke fans "screamed in chorus: 'UCLA, go to hell!'" They "whistled shrilly" when Bruin players shot free throws. And during the pregame introductions, they chanted, "Who's he?" as each UCLA starter was announced. Duke president Knight and Eddie Cameron claimed that *Sports Illustrated* had exaggerated the misdeeds of the home crowd to make its point. Nevertheless, in response to the "severe criticism" that Duke had suffered, Cameron issued an appeal to Blue Devils fans to back their team in an "enthusiastic and energetic *BUT FAIR*" manner.[71]

Duke was not alone in stirring criticism for the antics of its fans. Virginia's Memorial Gym was infamous for drawing raucous crowds that were known to throw cups, scorecards, and garbage onto the court. In 1965, a veteran referee described how Virginia fans had delighted in harassing North Carolina's Billy Cunningham. "They grabbed him on the sidelines, shoved him, spit on him," he disclosed. "I told Cunningham I'd throw anybody out I could catch, but how are you going to call them in the stands? There's enough happening on the floor." Crowds at other ACC schools could be equally obnoxious. Through the years, there were reports of fans littering the court with paper at North Carolina, spitting on visiting players at NC State, dumping popcorn boxes, soft drinks, and ice on opponents at Wake Forest, and throwing rubber balls on to the court at Maryland. Such misbehavior was an embarrassment to presidents, athletic directors, coaches, players, students and alumni, and it was, at least in the worst cases, the work of a few overzealous and addle-brained individuals. It was an unwanted byproduct of the intensity of the rivalries that made ACC basketball so colorful and unique. NC State's Norm Sloan once remarked that the "biggest difference in basketball in North Carolina or the ACC—as opposed to the Big Ten or the SEC [Southeastern Conference], where the play, the caliber of the players is the same—is the maniacal interest of the fans."[72]

Although opposing players were the primary targets of "maniacal" ACC partisans, referees were also frequently the victims of their wrath. The officials expected crowds to object vocally to their calls, but one of the best and most popular ACC referees, Charley Eckman, commented in 1967 that fans' behavior was "getting worse" and was "almost unbelievable." He did not "mind the booing and all that" because it was "part of the game, part of the color and atmosphere." He was appalled, however, that unruly spectators threw anything within their reach to vent their fury. ACC competition, he said, was "like World War IV."[73]

In addition to abuse from fans, referees could count on coaches to provide contentious and frequently profane critiques of their performance in any game. Bones McKinney once accidentally kicked his loafer out to center court in the middle of a game, and when he went out to retrieve it, he was assessed a technical foul. He then said "something a little uncomplimentary" to the referee, who responded, "I thought you were a preacher." McKinney retorted, "Yea, and I thought you were a referee!" Bill Gibson became so angry at the calls in a Virginia game that he walked up to one of the officials, handed him his sports jacket, and commented, "You've taken everything else away from me, you might as well take this as well." His sarcasm earned him an immediate ejection. Bobby Roberts complained bitterly that Big Four teams always seemed to get the "close calls" after Clemson lost to NC State by one point in the first round of the 1963 ACC Tournament. "What can you expect when an official gets chewed out for 39 minutes and 40 seconds by the other bench?" he said. "It eats me up to see us get a jobbing when we come into the Big Four."[74]

Although it was difficult for referees to influence the behavior of crowds, they had ways of tempering the conduct of coaches, particularly the threat of calling a technical foul, or in extreme cases, tossing the offender from the game. In addition, the ACC took action, with mixed results at best, to try to reduce the harassment of referees by coaches. Weaver's attempt to ban coaches from leaving the bench to protest calls in 1960 produced much hilarity when McKinney put on a seat belt, but it did not solve the problem. In 1969, the conference again decided to limit the movement of coaches by instructing referees to allow them "to move about only in that area immediately in front of the bench." The only exception was that a coach could walk to the scorer's table to ask for information, but only if it were done in an "orderly" fashion. This was not a new rule, but the conference placed new emphasis on it because coaches were increasingly seen "standing in front of the opposition's bench." The coaches did not react favorably. At a meeting in November 1970, they agreed that "because we are human beings it is impossible to sit on a bench throughout an entire basketball game." They argued that referees were enforcing the measure too strictly and requested that it be administered "through common sense and understanding." Referee Steve Honzo, described by the *Raleigh News and Observer* in 1971 as "one of the top four college basketball officials in the nation," commented that he would not penalize a coach who jumped off the bench "on a tremendous offensive play, or something like that." He made clear, however, that coaches who stood for the purpose of "baiting an official . . . should be slapped with a technical."[75]

Despite the frequency and intensity of disputes over calls in the heat of competition, coaches and officials concurred on the need to maintain order and generally recognized the difficulties of each other's jobs. This helped to promote civility, or at least mutual tolerance. Officials tended to over-look coaches' tantrums as long as the protests did not cross an ill-defined line of acceptability. Some referees won the respect, and even the affection, of coaches and fans for their ability, showmanship, and humor. Lou Bello, whose manner of making calls was consistent with his last name, was a fan favorite for his entertaining style. He would joke with players on the court, twirl a basketball on one finger while talking to reporters at the press table, and sit down on the lap of a cheerleader while a game was in progress. Honzo called Bello the "Clown Prince" who was "one whale of an official."[76]

Bello's prominence and popularity among ACC referees were exceeded only by Charley Eckman. Eckman was so revered by Duke fans, a tough audience, that on at least one occasion they gave him a standing ovation when he appeared on the floor to officiate. He won the esteem of coaches for his fairness, competence, and firm control of games. Eckman was born in Baltimore and began refereeing games in the city at age 16 to earn money to help his widowed mother. He gained enough of a reputation that he was hired to call games in the Basketball Association of America, a forerunner of the National Basketball Association, and he moved on to the NBA when it was formed in 1949. The owner of the Fort Wayne Pistons, Fred Zollner, was so impressed with Eckman that he hired him as the team's coach. Eck-man justified the surprising decision by leading the Pistons to the NBA's Western Division championship in 1954–55 and winning the NBA's Coach of the Year award. Nevertheless, even after another division title, he was fired by Zollner in the middle of his fourth season as coach. He returned to the Baltimore area and soon began to officiate college games in the ACC and elsewhere.[77]

Eckman commanded respect for his skill and feel for the game and charmed spectators with his humor. In one game, North Carolina went into a stall late in a tie game. Eckman asked Larry Brown, who was holding the ball, when the team planned to shoot and was told "with about ten sec-onds left." Eckman walked over to the sidelines, picked up a chair, carried it out to half-court, and sat down. "Hell, if you ain't going to play," he ex-plained, "I ain't going to officiate." Eckman had a special affinity for college players. He talked to them during games, praised their good plays, and wanted them to do well. He once officiated a Maryland game in which Gary Williams had not scored as time was running out and the outcome was as-

Charley Eckman, 1967. (Courtesy The North Carolina State Archives; reprinted by permission of *The News and Observer* of Raleigh, North Carolina)

sured. During a pause in the action, Eckman stood next to Williams and said in a low voice: "I'm going to get you to the line." A short time later, he called a touch foul on the player who was defending Williams. When Williams went to the line, Eckman handed him the ball and said: "OK, now, don't blow it." Eckman retired from refereeing in 1967 in part because of a variety of physical ailments and in part because he believed that fan behavior was getting out of hand. The conduct of "kids on the campuses" of ACC schools and other colleges, he remarked, "has been so bad that I'm inclined to believe games should be played on neutral courts."[78]

Efforts to arrest the trend toward worsening crowd conduct that distressed Eckman and others met with little success. Student newspapers denounced offenders and appealed for civility. South Carolina's *Gamecock*, for example, rebuked the "few retarded imbeciles" who hurled cups at referees in 1965, and Wake's *Old Gold and Black* complained about "bush league fans" who "acted like spoiled brats" by throwing ice and cups at the South Carolina team in 1971. Coaches also tried to reduce the unruly antics of their fans without losing the benefit of their vocal support. Bill Gibson told Virginia students in 1971 that although he greatly appreciated their "enthusiasm and encouragement," he did not want them "over-reacting to officials' calls by throwing items on the floor and by yelling off-color cheers." University administrators expressed regret at the misdeeds of their fans and took steps to improve comportment and security. But it was difficult, as Duke president Terry Sanford pointed out in 1971, "to contain the behavior of all spectators (especially those who are not University-related)."[79]

The behavior of ACC fans had never been exemplary, but the regression that many observers noticed in the late 1960s and early 1970s could be attributed to two critical factors. One was the effort of non–Big Four teams to become more competitive with their rivals in North Carolina. Once they achieved or at least aspired to greater success on the court, the stakes of the games increased and fan conduct seemed to take a turn for the worse. Evan Bussey of the *Charleston News and Courier* had commented in 1967 that ugly crowd behavior was a by-product of the improvement of Clemson and South Carolina, and the same thing occurred at Maryland and Virginia with greater frequency and volume when their teams began winning in the early 1970s. A perhaps more important reason for increasingly inappropriate crowd conduct was the cultural trends that prevailed throughout the United States. College basketball, like other public activities, suffered the effects of the disrespect of many young people for established customs and institutions, the coarsening of expressions of disagreement, and the tolerance of crude language. Robert Fachet, a columnist for the *Washington Post*, condemned both Maryland and Virginia fans in 1972 for their promiscuous use of the term "bullshit" to voice their disapproval of referees' calls. "Bull—may be a relatively common word these days," he wrote after a Maryland game, "but somehow even acknowledgement of the goals of Women's Lib doesn't prevent us from being turned off by the sight of young women standing and waving their right arms while screaming 'Bull—' as loudly as possible." Maryland athletic director Jim Kehoe lamented that there was little he could do about offensive fans because "there exists a philosophy now that people can say anything they want, behave any way they want, do anything they want, and it's okay."[80]

The revolt of the also-rans in the ACC after the mid-1960s had not turned into a revolution by 1970. The only non–Big Four team that ranked among the leaders in the conference by that time was South Carolina. Frank McGuire, even after the departure of Mike Grosso, attracted top talent to Columbia and made the Gamecocks a formidable opponent for ACC rivals. Clemson, Virginia, and Maryland endured hardships, losses, and unhappy players and fans during the later 1960s. But each took important steps toward improvement and soon became a force to be reckoned with in ACC play. The result was a conference that was more balanced, more competitive, and at least for the new arrivals in the top of the standings, much more fun.

7

THE INTEGRATION
OF ACC BASKETBALL

On December 1, 1965, twelve years after the first ACC basketball game, another milestone event took place. Billy Jones, a 6'1" guard from Towson, Maryland, became the league's first black varsity basketball player by appearing briefly for the University of Maryland in a road game against Penn State. Three days later, when Jones came off the bench and scored two points in a rout of Wake Forest at Cole Field House, he became the first black player to participate in a varsity game between two conference schools. In retrospect, Jones's pioneering performances were critical steps toward shattering the racial barriers that had prevailed in ACC basketball since the founding of the league. At the time, however, the Washington and Baltimore newspapers that covered Maryland athletics and the university's student paper, *The Diamondback*, gave Jones's signal contribution to ACC basketball history almost no attention. The only mention of his appearance was in the account of the Wake game in the *Baltimore Sun*, and it merely noted in passing that he was the "first Negro to play basketball in the A.C.C."[1]

The exclusion of black players from ACC basketball teams before 1965 reflected the customs and attitudes of ACC schools, where racial integration had occurred gradually and grudgingly, though peacefully. With the exception of a single applicant admitted to the University of Maryland under threat of a court order in 1951, no conference member accepted black students as undergraduates until after the U.S. Supreme Court's 1954 ruling in *Brown vs. the Board of Education of Topeka, Kansas*, which struck down the "separate but equal" approach to education that was standard practice in the South and some parts of the North. Maryland, Virginia, North Carolina, and NC State began to accept black undergraduates in small numbers in the mid-1950s; Duke, Wake Forest, Clemson, and South Carolina followed suit in the early 1960s. Most ACC schools did not recruit black basketball players for several years after they desegregated, despite the growing concern of coaches that they were missing out on a rich pool of talent. There were, in addition, a series of other racial issues surrounding athletic events in the ACC, including segregated seating in arenas and housing arrangements for visiting teams that had black players on their rosters. In all cases, administrators sought to resolve those problems in a way that would meet legal requirements without frontally challenging racial norms in the South or causing racial incidents. Eventually, this delicate balancing act became an anachronism, but the integration of ACC basketball did not happen quickly or easily.

Race Matters in College Basketball

Before World War II, few blacks played on the basketball teams of predominately white colleges and universities. Most who played basketball attended black colleges that had their own leagues and tournaments. Many teams at black schools favored a style of play that featured fast breaks, quick ball movement, and jump shooting. This required that coaches place a great deal of trust in their players to improvise and make spontaneous decisions. John McLendon, who studied with James Naismith at the University of Kansas during the 1930s, used the fast-break style with great success after he became coach at the North Carolina College for Negroes in Durham in 1940. McLendon did not play at Kansas, which prohibited blacks from participating in intercollegiate sports. But Naismith recognized his abilities and tried to ameliorate some of the worst discriminatory practices that McLendon faced as the first black student in physical education at the university. McLendon graduated from Kansas in 1936.

When McLendon began coaching at North Carolina College, the center jump after every basket had been eliminated only three years earlier. Drawing on what he learned at Kansas and on his own ideas, he stressed conditioning to build up the strength of his players, a running offensive attack, and relentless defensive pressure to wear down and demoralize the competition. "Contrary to its reputation," he once wrote, "the fast break is not an 'aimless,' 'helter skelter,' 'run and shoot,' 'fire horse' game. . . . It is a planned attack with multiple applications; it is a designed offense which can be utilized in one or more of its several phases each time a team gains possession of the ball." McLendon's teams were so good and so entertaining that other coaches at black schools adopted his approach. His achievements did not receive much notice outside of the black college basketball circuit for many years, and some prominent white coaches, including Everett Case, effectively deployed their own running games. But McLendon's innovations were instrumental in introducing and promoting by example a style of play that came to be called, in a misleading generalization, "Negro basketball."[2]

After World War II, as college basketball became more popular, blacks in growing numbers played for the teams of predominantly white schools. The numbers were still not large, but as Charles H. Martin, the leading scholar of the integration of college sports, has written, "by the mid-1950s most college teams outside the South had achieved a token level of integration." The change came about slowly. In the late 1940s, three major conferences, the Big Ten, the Big Six (later the Big Eight), and the Missouri Valley, observed unwritten "gentlemen's agreements" by which they pledged not to recruit blacks for at least some of their teams. In the Big Ten, the prohibition applied to basketball, swimming, and wrestling. Gradually, the northern and midwestern conferences dropped such policies, either by a vote or, in the case of the Big Ten, by the decision of a university president, Indiana's Herman B. Wells, to challenge the existing arrangements.[3]

The growing presence of black players on teams from outside the South raised troubling issues for schools that remained segregated. The first question, in terms of both timing and potential consequence, was whether to compete against integrated opponents. Through the mid-1940s, this was not a problem. Northern schools commonly yielded to the demands of southern rivals by keeping their own black players out of the lineups in football and basketball games, even at home. In December 1945, for example, Long Island University's Clair Bee refrained from using his two black players in a matchup against the University of Tennessee in New York. A year later, Tennessee, after making a trip to Pennsylvania, declined to play against

Duquesne University unless Chuck Cooper, the Dukes' leading scorer, remained on the bench. Duquesne attempted to compromise by promising to insert Cooper only if the score was close late in the contest, but Tennessee refused. As a result, Duquesne called off the game even after its fans had arrived at the gymnasium.[4]

After World War II, northern schools generally became more reluctant to surrender to the racial conventions of southern opponents, and the practice of withholding their black players from competition eventually ended. As far back as the 1930s, some southern schools, including future members of the ACC, occasionally relaxed racial barriers in the interests of playing against intersectional opponents. Maryland prohibited a black quarterback from Syracuse University, Wilmeth Sidat-Singh, from playing in a game in Baltimore in 1937 but consented to his participation in a rematch the following year in Syracuse. Duke visited Syracuse the same season and made no effort to prevent Sidat-Singh from playing. North Carolina competed against New York University and its black halfback, Ed Williams, for three consecutive seasons, 1936–38, in games played in New York. In 1947, Harvard brought a black player, Chester Pierce, to a football game against Virginia in Charlottesville. Although some fans greeted Pierce with racial insults, the Virginia players treated him with respect, and most of the crowd cheered him. Black basketball players made their first appearances in Reynolds Coliseum in 1952, and after the founding of the ACC, its members regularly competed against integrated teams in tournaments and nonleague contests. Nevertheless, these were small and uncertain steps that fell short of recruiting blacks to play for conference schools.[5]

While the ACC remained a conference for white athletes only, black basketball players in other leagues achieved growing prominence. In 1947, Don Barksdale of UCLA became the second African American and the first since 1931 to be named to an All-American team. By 1958, five of the six players who gained consensus All-American recognition were black: Wilt Chamberlain, Oscar Robertson, Elgin Baylor of Seattle University, Bob Boozer of Kansas State, and Guy Rodgers of Temple (the only white member of the squad was Don Hennon of the University of Pittsburgh). Black stars not only shined individually but also led their teams to national acclaim. During the 1954–55 and 1955–56 seasons, Phil Woolpert, coach of the University of San Francisco (USF), took an unprecedented step in major college basketball by using three black starters—Bill Russell, K. C. Jones, and Hal Perry. Their teams set an NCAA record by winning 55 games in a row on the way to capturing two national championships.[6]

The increasingly visible role of black players in college basketball did not resolve long-standing racial tensions. Indeed, it often made racial issues more conspicuous. In at least some cases, coaches at predominantly white schools limited the number of black players they would recruit. Under pressure from President Wells, Indiana's Branch McCracken reluctantly broke the "gentlemen's agreement" on black players in Big Ten basketball by agreeing to give Bill Garrett, chosen as the state's best high school player in 1947, a fair chance to make the university's team. Garrett took advantage of the opportunity by excelling at Indiana; he was selected for the All-Conference first team and the UPI and *Sporting News* All-American squads in 1951. Nevertheless, McCracken told a high school coach two years later that he offered scholarships to only a "quota of Negroes." When the University of Kansas recruited Wilt Chamberlain in 1955, it showed no interest in two of his black high school teammates who Chamberlain believed "could easily have made the team at Kansas." Instead, it signed a white teammate whom he regarded as a "nice guy" but less talented.[7]

Fans expressed similar reservations about overpopulating college teams with black players. Phil Woolpert incited hate mail for using a majority of blacks in his lineup; one USF alumnus complained that the contingent of African American players was "scarcely representative of the school." Such criticism was mild compared to the vitriol that some crowds directed at black players from opposing teams. During a Christmas tournament in Oklahoma City in 1955, fans threw coins at USF players as they practiced and jeered them with racial insults. In 1957, Kansas was matched up against Southern Methodist University in the NCAA's Midwest Regional Tournament in Dallas. "Their crowd was brutal," one Kansas player commented. "We were spat upon, pelted with debris, and subjected to the vilest racial epithets imaginable." Integrated teams also had to deal with hotels and restaurants that denied service to black players. When Indiana traveled to St. Louis in 1948, the Chase Hotel eased its racial prohibitions and allowed Bill Garrett to stay with his teammates. But it also insisted that he not eat in the hotel's dining room. Conditions were even worse when Kansas made its appearance in the NCAA regionals in Dallas. The hotel designated for use by participating teams refused to provide accommodations to blacks, and the Kansas squad moved to less convenient and less agreeable quarters 15 miles away.[8]

Even when northern and western schools recruited black players who led them to high national rankings, teams representing southern colleges and universities remained rigidly segregated. After the Supreme Court handed down the *Brown* decision in 1954, the South redoubled its efforts to resist racial integration in education and other long-segregated activities, including sports. As racial tensions increased and racial barriers hardened, states in the Deep South enacted new restrictions to prevent teams from white schools from competing against opponents with black players and vice versa. Louisiana led the way in this regard by passing a law in 1956 that prohibited black and white athletes from playing against one another in "games, sports, or contests." Other southern states adopted similar policies. The governor of Georgia, Marvin Griffin, explained the rationale for those actions: "There is no more difference in compromising the integrity of race on the playing field than in doing so in the classroom," he declared. "One break in the dike and the relentless seas will rush in and destroy us."

The fear of blurring racial divisions that prompted bans on competition between black and white athletes imposed severe penalties on affected teams, fans, and businesses. Sugar Bowl officials, political leaders, and business interests in New Orleans opposed Louisiana's law because they worried that it would hamper their efforts to draw top-ranked teams, national attention, and sell-out crowds for the New Year's Day bowl game and events connected with it. They urged Governor Earl Long to veto the measure, but he signed it into law. As a result, three northern schools immediately dropped out of the Sugar Bowl basketball tournament. For several years, only segregated southern teams played in the Sugar Bowl football game and basketball tournament, and both events suffered the consequences of diminished visibility and prestige.[9]

On several occasions, the prohibition of interracial competition cost college basketball teams a trip to the NCAA tournament. Mississippi State University earned the SEC championship in 1959, 1961, and 1962, and each time, in accordance with an unwritten state law that forbade competing against integrated opponents, declined its invitation to the NCAA Tournament. In 1963, after winning the conference again, Mississippi State president Dean W. Colvard announced that the school would participate in the NCAAs. His decision won support from students, faculty, alumni, fans, and most assuredly from the players. But it still required an elaborate subterfuge and perhaps the collusion of a local sheriff to avoid an injunction that would have prevented the team from leaving the state. In the regional tournament, Mississippi State lost to Loyola University of Chicago, which started four black players and eventually claimed the national championship. A short time later, the Board of Trustees of Institutions of Higher Learning in Mississippi voted to end the ban on integrated competition.

Its members seemed willing to risk the dangers of the "relentless seas" that Georgia's governor had warned about just a few years earlier.[10]

The Integration of ACC Schools

Racial restrictions at ACC schools were not as strict or as sweeping as those in the Deep South. None of the states in which ACC members were located imposed a prohibition on athletic competition between races. Teams with black players were invited to appear in the Dixie Classic. No ACC school turned down an invitation to the NCAA tournament out of fear that it might have to play an integrated opponent. Nevertheless, ACC schools faithfully observed traditional southern customs on race, and they integrated undergraduate programs only when forced to do so by court rulings. They took even longer to integrate their basketball programs. The position of ACC colleges and universities on racial issues reflected, in varying degrees, their political and cultural environment and the views of their governing bodies and administrators.

The University of Maryland was the northernmost conference school and eventually became the first ACC member to recruit black players in both football and basketball. But its stance on integrating its undergraduate student body before *Brown* was consistent with that of the other ACC schools. During his long tenure as Maryland's president, Curley Byrd was firmly committed to preventing black students from attending the university. He was alarmed when the school's efforts to remain segregated were compromised by court decisions. This initially occurred in 1935 after the university rejected Donald G. Murray's application to attend its School of Law in Baltimore because of his race. Murray challenged the university's policy of racial exclusion in court, and when he won his case, he became the first African American to enroll in the law school since it banned the admission of black students in 1890. Byrd worried that this case would set a dangerous precedent for the university's other programs. "Confidentially and personally," he wrote to the dean of the law school, "if negro students are allowed to enter College Park, it will come pretty close to ruining us."[11]

To stave off the threat that he perceived, Byrd campaigned vigorously for funding to improve the state's black institutions of higher learning. He wished to provide programs that were comparable to those at the College Park campus in order to fulfill "separate but equal" legal requirements. In that way, he hoped to maintain segregated campuses in the event of lawsuits that made claims for integrating College Park. His strategy did not succeed. In 1949, in a development of full-circle irony, Donald Murray represented six black students who applied to and were rejected by various undergraduate, graduate, and professional schools at Maryland. The university lost in court once again, and as result, black students enrolled in graduate and undergraduate programs at College Park. Hiram T. Whittle became Maryland's first black undergraduate in 1951 with a major in engineering. But others did not follow his path until after the *Brown* decision. A short time after the Supreme Court's ruling, the University of Maryland's Board of Regents voted to allow the admission of qualified black students who were state residents "to the undergraduate schools at all branches of the university." Wilson Elkins, who took over as Maryland's president in 1954, carried out the regents' mandate on race and, in contrast to Byrd, welcomed black students to the university's undergraduate and postgraduate programs. But he did not adopt what he later called "an aggressive policy that attempted to admit a large number of minorities, almost regardless of admission requirements." By the mid-1960s, less than 300 black students out of a total enrollment of 28,000 attended Maryland's undergraduate and graduate schools in College Park.[12]

Maryland was the first ACC school to respond to the *Brown* decision by removing restrictions to the admission of black undergraduates. The Consolidated University of North Carolina also integrated its undergraduate schools after *Brown*, though not voluntarily. As a result of court decisions, a few black students were allowed to enter the law school and medical school at Chapel Hill and graduate programs at NC State in the early 1950s. Members of the Board of Trustees protested the desegregation of professional and graduate schools, and some even lobbied to shut down the law school rather than permit black students to enroll. President Gordon Gray did not support integration of the university's postgraduate schools, but he saw no acceptable alternative. The *Brown* decision was another unwelcome blow to the opponents of integration. Gray commented in December 1954 that although he viewed intercollegiate athletics as his "biggest problem," the Supreme Court's ruling seemed likely to create new difficulties that were almost as trying. The following year, three black high school seniors sought admission as undergraduates to Chapel Hill, and after they were turned down on the basis of their race, they sued. The university contended that *Brown* did not apply to colleges and that it had no obligation to admit black students to its undergraduate programs. A federal district court promptly rejected those arguments, and the Supreme Court upheld its decision. The three students integrated UNC–Chapel Hill in 1955, and two black undergraduates entered State College the following year. But the number of black students at Chapel Hill and NC State remained small for many years.[13]

The University of Virginia was even slower to integrate its undergraduate student body beyond token levels than the University of Maryland or the Consolidated University of North Carolina. Neither the Board of Visitors nor President Darden was receptive to admitting blacks to the university. When Gregory Swanson applied to take courses at the Virginia School of Law in 1950, the board voted to reject him in the face of advice from the state attorney general that this position could not stand up in court. Swanson sued successfully, and his challenge to racial exclusion at Virginia enabled a limited number of black students to enroll in graduate and professional programs. Darden strongly believed that segregated schools were the best approach to educating blacks and whites. "I feel certain," he wrote in 1952, "that both White and Colored have more to gain by separated schools than by mixed ones." He recognized that the "facilities offered the Negroes were . . . terribly inferior." But he insisted that progress would be made on racial issues, "even though the process is painful and slow," over the span of a generation or so. Darden regarded the *Brown* decision as "unbelievably reckless." Nevertheless, in the wake of the ruling, the University of Virginia admitted three students as its first black undergraduates in 1955. Like the outcome of the end of segregation at Maryland, North Carolina, and NC State, only a few black students attended Virginia in the 1950s and 1960s. In 1968, there were 17 black undergraduates among a student body of about 5,100 enrolled at the university.[14]

The other ACC schools did not desegregate for some time after the *Brown* decision. At Duke, President Edens was a cautious supporter of integration, but his halting steps to enable black students to enroll met with unyielding opposition from the Board of Trustees. Edens was keenly aware that continuing to deny admission to black applicants would severely damage his goal of elevating the university's national stature. In 1956, he urged the Board of Trustees to reconsider Duke's position on accepting black students, but it steadfastly refused even to study the issue. Finally, as pressure to desegregate from students and faculty increased, J. Deryl Hart, who served as Duke's acting president after Edens departed, and other top-level administrators convinced the board of the need to integrate. They argued forcefully that the failure to admit blacks "has created barriers to the fullest development of Duke University and has resulted in a decline in its prestige." On that basis, the board voted in March 1961 to open Duke's professional and graduate schools to qualified black students. In June 1962, it agreed to extend this policy to the university's undergraduate programs. Like other ACC schools, Duke's black enrollment remained small during the 1960s. In 1969, there were 85 black undergraduates in a student body of about 4,300.[15]

The patterns were similar at Wake Forest, the other private, religiously affiliated school in the ACC. In 1955, the North Carolina Baptist Convention passed a resolution that declared that Baptist colleges should open their doors "to qualified applicants regardless of race." But Wake's Board of Trustees spurned that advice. Some students and faculty also demonstrated reluctance to support the admission of black students. One faculty member wrote in 1955 that the "time [for integration] is certainly not ripe now, and I fervently hope that it never will be." A student governing body considering a resolution that called for an end to racial exclusion voted it down, 15–5, in 1957. Gradually, however, the opposition to integrating Wake Forest softened. In 1960, ten Wake students joined with students from Winston-Salem Teachers College in a sit-in to integrate the lunch counter at a local Woolworth's store. This action came a week after the same kind of protest began in nearby Greensboro. The Wake demonstrators, who were arrested and found guilty of trespassing, were viewed as heroes by their fellow students. On April 27, 1962, as the pressure mounted, the Board of Trustees voted, 17–9, to allow the admission of qualified undergraduates "regardless of race." An editorial in the *Old Gold and Black* hailed the trustees for "lifting the College from the mire of outmoded tradition and prejudice." The first 2 black undergraduates enrolled at Wake in September 1962. But only a limited number of black students followed them in the following few years. In 1966, Wake had just 4 black students; by 1970 the number had risen to 21 in a study body of about 2,500.[16]

The University of South Carolina and Clemson were the last two ACC members to desegregate. In terms of both geography and racial attitudes, the state of South Carolina was closer to the Deep South than to its ACC neighbors. An article in the *Saturday Evening Post* in 1963 described South Carolina as "emotionally, the deepest Deep South state of them all." In the early 1960s, state officials and university administrators worried that efforts to integrate its two leading institutions of higher learning would produce acute tension, rioting, and violence. They had observed with foreboding the stormy protests against the enrollment of black students at the flagship universities of the other three states that refused to accept integration: the University of Georgia, the University of Alabama, and the University of Mississippi.

In South Carolina, matters came to a head first at Clemson. When Harvey Gantt, a native of Charleston, applied for admission to Clemson's school of architecture in 1962, he was turned down, officially on procedural technicalities. But a federal court determined that the application was rejected on the basis of race, and in January 1963, it ordered that Gantt be admitted to the college immediately. Clemson president Edwards was personally committed to integration, and his attitudes on race were clear in his hospitality to Palestine Hill at the Clemson-Maryland football game later in the year. He reached out to members of the Board of Trustees, influential businessmen, and political leaders for their support in achieving peaceful integration at Clemson. Some of those whom he contacted were strong opponents of admitting blacks to white schools in South Carolina, but he convinced them of the need for orderly compliance with the court ruling. Governor Ernest F. "Fritz" Hollings took the same position on the primacy of "a government of laws rather than a government of men." When Gantt arrived to enroll at Clemson on January 28, 1963, about 160 newspaper, magazine, radio, and television reporters and a large security force were present to monitor his movements. He registered for classes without arousing protests while a group of about 200 students poked fun at the media throng that waited in vain for an uproar.[17]

Although Gantt registered without incident, he worried about what would happen when he ate a meal on campus for the first time. He remembered that when James Meredith had integrated the University of Mississippi, students had pounded on tables and given him a "really rough" reception in the dining hall. When Gantt went to dinner on his first day, he was greeted by the cooks, servers, and other workers, all of whom were black. It was an inspiring and illuminating experience. "I was going to be taken care of," he later observed. "They gave me the biggest portion of meat. They gave me the best desserts." More importantly, Gantt realized that "now they could see that their children, their uncles and their nieces, their nephews, their cousins could be in that [food] line, too." After watching the dining hall staff's "collective chest swell with pride," he said, "for the first time it really hit me what this meant."[18]

At the University of South Carolina, President Jones used the same strategy that worked well for Edwards. In July 1963, a federal judge ordered the university to end its policy of racial exclusion, and three black students made plans to enroll for the semester beginning two months later. Jones laid the foundations for their arrival by taking steps to limit media coverage and by appointing a faculty committee to prepare the university for "I-Day"

(Integration Day). The committee made arrangements for a massive show of force by law enforcement officials. The Board of Trustees, which was hardly pleased with the court's action, contributed to the campaign for peaceful integration by announcing its commitment to the "preservation of the dignity of the orderly process of education at the University of South Carolina." On September 11, 1963, the black students enrolled without incident. The University of South Carolina became the "last flagship southern state university to desegregate," and it did so without triggering angry demonstrations. Following the pattern of other ACC schools, black enrollment remained small throughout the 1960s at Clemson and South Carolina. In 1969, Clemson had about 75 black students, and in 1970, about 279 black students attended South Carolina out of an undergraduate and graduate population of about 15,000.[19]

The end of segregation at ACC schools did not mean that individual black students avoided isolation, loneliness, hostility, and taunts. But their courage and determination led to the end of exclusionary racial policies at ACC schools and eventually in ACC athletic programs.

Integration in the Arena

As ACC schools gradually integrated their student bodies, they also slowly abandoned other vestiges of segregation, including those that applied to athletic programs. One common practice in the early years of the conference was racial segregation in the seating of crowds at games. Clemson took an uncomplicated approach to this issue by prohibiting black fans from entering its football stadium. Other schools were somewhat less categorical in their restrictions but still set aside separate sections for blacks and whites. This created problems, for example, after the University of North Carolina allowed black students to enroll in its law school in 1951 and issued football tickets to them in end zone seats reserved for African American spectators. Chancellor Robert House explained that the stadium was "not an educational facility" and drew a careful distinction "between educational services to Negro students and social equalization." House relented by making seats available in the previously all-white student section of the stands only under the threat of a lawsuit. As late as 1960, Chancellor William Aycock had to decide that general admission tickets in one section of the stadium would not be designated for blacks only.[20]

The same kind of questions arose over seating during the Dixie Classic. One section of Reynolds Coliseum was reserved for black fans during the tournament. If black spectators did not purchase all the tickets in this section, seats were sold to white fans. In response to complaints about the de facto integration of the "Negro section," NC State chancellor Carey Bostian apologized but suggested that there was no way to avoid "a very small amount of non-segregated seating." State College faced an equally delicate problem of housing arrangements for integrated teams that competed in the Dixie Classic. Since teams with black players could not stay at segregated hotels in downtown Raleigh, the college provided considerably less opulent lodging near campus.[21]

The participation of black athletes in ACC competition began in a limited way shortly after integration first occurred at conference schools. Two NC State freshmen, Irwin R. Holmes Jr. and Manuel Crockett, became the first black athletes to appear in an ACC intercollegiate contest when they ran in a freshman indoor track meet at Chapel Hill in February 1957. Holmes was also an outstanding tennis player who joined the State College team and served as its captain during his senior year. His presence aroused some controversy within the conference; South Carolina and Clemson announced that he could not play in matches on their campuses because their tennis courts were available only to whites. NC State was unwilling to compete without Holmes, and eventually, the problem was resolved when South Carolina and Clemson consented to hold the matches in Raleigh. During the early 1960s, a few black athletes integrated other ACC sports by participating in soccer, lacrosse, wrestling, swimming, and outdoor track.[22]

Despite the breach of racial barriers in minor sports with low visibility, ACC schools delayed in recruiting blacks to play football and basketball, by far the most prominent and most popular sports. This was a de facto rather than a de jure condition; once conference schools integrated, there was no formal institutional prohibition against using black athletes in any sport. There were, however, institutional, social, and cultural deterrents. Leaders at ACC schools were relieved that integration was accomplished without causing ugly protests or stirring racial tensions. They were also aware that racial strife that would bring unwanted attention, bad publicity, and bitter ill will remained an ominous possibility. Therefore, they were wary of moving too fast on racial issues. Placing black athletes wearing school colors in highly visible and highly vulnerable positions on the football field or basketball court seemed to run the risk of getting too far ahead of public, and especially alumni, acceptance. Administrators had ample bases for such concerns. When Wake Forest, for example, announced that it would "actively recruit" black athletes in all sports in early 1963, one alumnus told

President Tribble that he felt "quite a degree of disgust" that Wake would "scout for 'nigger' football players." Another suggested that a "bi-racial athletic program is not possible without social integration," and, therefore, that "Wake Forest College . . . will be strengthened with no athletic program at all rather than an integrated one." As late as December 1969, an anonymous correspondent sent Maryland president Elkins a drawing of a monkey scoring a basket and complained that under coach Lefty Driesell, the animal would be "a good candidate for Univ [*sic*] of Maryland basketball."[23]

The presidents of ACC schools faced little pressure to integrate their football and basketball teams during the late 1950s and early 1960s. They carried out their legal obligations when they removed racial restrictions on admitting students to all of their academic programs. The major impetus to recruit black athletes came from at least some coaches. In 1957, for example, Everett Case pushed for approval to go after Walt Bellamy, an exceptionally promising player from New Bern, North Carolina. Chancellor Bostian's response, then and later, was consistently along the lines of, "I don't believe we're quite ready." The pressures to integrate ACC football and basketball increased, however, as the civil rights movement gathered national momentum, support, and attention. A Duke student reported in 1964 that he was "embarrassed" by his school's failure to take a position of leadership in recruiting black athletes with strong academic ability. In his view, the university "was losing out on the talented Negro student-athlete" and should "take the initiative" to attract black students who were not "sought with the sole intention of improving Duke athletics."[24]

Eventually, the embarrassment and the competitive disadvantages of not integrating ACC football and basketball programs took precedence over the risks of using black players. Leading private universities in the South, including Duke, integrated their student bodies when they concluded that the price of segregation, assessed through the damage it caused in their campaigns to build national stature, was too high. In a similar manner, ACC schools gradually recognized that the cost of failing to recruit black athletes in football and basketball was excessive. Coaches watched with regret as high school basketball stars such as Bellamy, Lou Hudson, and Happy Hairston left their homes in North Carolina to play in the Big Ten and other northern conferences. When Bill Tate, Wake's football coach, was asked by dubious boosters about plans to recruit blacks, he replied: "Yes, we're going to recruit them, and if the rest of the teams don't, we'll have a real good time." ACC schools reached the same conclusion at different times and under different circumstances, apparently without a great deal of internal deliberation. In the cases of the University of North Carolina and NC State, William Friday, the president of the Consolidated University, later commented that a command decision was not necessary to recruit black players in the major sports. It was obvious by the mid-1960s, he said, that "the time had come."[25]

The time had come first at the University of Maryland. In May 1962, Dick Herbert reported that Maryland was likely to "have Negro players on its football and basketball teams within two years" and that this "could create some major problems" for the conference. Later in the year, Lee Corso, an assistant football coach at Maryland, persuaded Darryl Hill, who had decided to transfer from the Naval Academy, to become the ACC's first black football player. At about the same time, Bud Millikan, whose program was struggling, also began to recruit blacks. Before the 1964–65 season, it appeared that his first black player would be Chris Richmond, who attended high school in Washington, D.C., and graduated from Citrus Junior College in California. But Richmond failed to make the team.[26]

By that time, Millikan had signed two talented black players who were members of Maryland's freshman team, Billy Jones and Julius "Pete" Johnson. Jones led his Towson High School team to a state championship his junior year and the finals of the state tournament the following season. He wanted to attend Maryland, in part because he enjoyed playing at Cole Field House during the state championship games. He was aware that he would be the first black player in the ACC when he accepted Millikan's offer of a scholarship, but he did not think much about it. Jones had attended a high school that was mostly white, and the likelihood that he would face hostile crowds as the ACC's first black basketball player did not register with him. "I was really naïve," he later remarked. "I honestly thought the other schools were going to do the same thing." His mother, whose husband was killed in an accident shortly after Billy was born, was much more concerned. She grilled Millikan at length before concluding that Maryland was the right school for her son. For his part, Millikan consulted with the Towson high school coach to satisfy himself that Jones could handle the pressure of integrating ACC basketball. Jones regarded his scholarship as the path to a college education, and Millikan saw it as a fitting reward for a "very deserving young man who could play basketball."[27]

In May 1964, about a month after Jones accepted a grant at Maryland, Millikan signed a second black player. Pete Johnson had averaged 23 points a game for Fairmount Heights High School in Maryland, just outside Wash-

Billy Jones. (*Terrapin*, Special Collections, University of Maryland Libraries)

ington, D.C., and led it to the state championship (in a different division than Jones's Towson team). Jones and Johnson roomed together on campus and demonstrated their ability when they played together on Maryland's freshman team. Johnson led the squad in scoring with a 20.6 average and Jones was second with a 17.3 average. "Billy was a good athlete playing basketball," Gary Williams, who became a teammate on the Maryland varsity, later observed. "Pete was more of a pure basketball player." The plan to have them debut at the same time as the ACC's first black basketball players went awry, however, when Johnson encountered academic difficulties and sat out a year to catch up.[28]

As a result, Jones integrated ACC varsity basketball alone in December 1965. He was the target of racial slurs when Maryland played on the road, especially at Virginia, Clemson, and South Carolina. In one especially memorable incident in Columbia, he chased a loose ball that wound up at the feet of a Gamecock supporter. Chomping on a cigar and affecting the appearance of a Southern gentleman, the spectator spat out one word with breathtaking venom when Jones looked up: "Nigger!" Jones had heard the word before, but he never forgot the depth of contempt and malice that the man packed into a single utterance. The offensive actions of some fans were at least partly counterbalanced when Jones made his first appearance in the ACC tournament in Raleigh in 1966. As he entered the game, the crowd gave him a round of applause. "I really think the fans appreciated basketball," he said later. "I think it was acknowledging the fact that this young black kid had survived the season." Jones played sparingly as a sophomore, but during his junior year he started and averaged 11.6 points. As a senior and team captain, he averaged 10.2 points. Johnson joined the varsity in 1966 and was a starter throughout his career. In 1967–68, he led the team with an average of 15.0 points, and for his career he scored 13.2 points per game. But Maryland placed in the lower half of the ACC standings during those years, and the pioneering achievements of Jones and Johnson were sometimes underappreciated or overlooked.[29]

Wake Forest followed closely behind Maryland in deciding to recruit black football and basketball players. It failed to sign a black prospect in basketball for several years but not for lack of effort. Bones McKinney, who had drafted one of the NBA's first African American players, Earl Lloyd, when he coached the Washington Capitols in 1950, welcomed the opportunity to improve his roster by recruiting black talent at Wake Forest. During the 1964–65 season, he called Billy Packer for assistance. Packer had graduated and was working in the insurance business, but he was willing to help. McKinney wanted him to talk to Herm Gilliam, a player at an all-black high school in Winston-Salem. After Packer saw Gilliam play and learned that he was a good student, he convinced him to attend Wake. Despite outstanding high school grades, however, Gilliam fell just short of the 800 score on the college boards that the ACC required. With regret, Packer arranged for him to attend Purdue University, where he was an All-Conference performer in the Big Ten.[30]

Contrary to some allegations, the 800 rule was not designed to exclude blacks from playing in the ACC. The conference approved the standard in May 1964, just as a few member schools were beginning to recruit blacks aggressively. But the timing was coincidental. There is no evidence to suggest that the rule was intended to discriminate against black athletes; it was the culmination of a decade of advocacy by some ACC schools for setting a minimum academic standard for football and basketball prospects. The league adopted the original SAT requirement of 750 in 1960, well before the recruitment of black football and basketball players became a prominent issue. The conference's academic standard and the decisions of individual schools to recruit blacks in major sports were separate matters that happened to merge, or collide, inadvertently.

Shortly after the disappointment of delivering Herm Gilliam to another league, Packer joined Wake's coaching staff and, in September 1965, McKinney resigned. As an assistant for Jack Murdock and then for Jack McCloskey, Packer continued to seek talented black players who could meet the ACC's academic requirements. His search led him to New York City, where he made valuable contacts and roamed the streets of Harlem to watch players with dazzling skills compete in summer league games. He was responsible for the signing of Wake's first black player, Norwood Todmann, in spring 1966. Todmann was an accomplished student as well as an unusually promising offensive player. A willowy 6'3" guard with an effective post-up game against shorter defenders, he averaged 13.3 points per game during his sophomore season at Wake and 11.0 points as a junior. As a senior, however, his playing time diminished significantly because of his defensive liabilities and because he played the same position as Charlie Davis, one of Wake Forest's all-time greats. Ironically, Todmann was instrumental in persuading Davis, who was a year younger and grew up in the same Harlem projects, to sign with Wake.[31]

The Recruiting of Charles Scott

In spring 1966, at the same time that Wake signed Todmann, Dean Smith scored a major triumph for North Carolina by landing Charles Scott, an exceptionally gifted player who came from the same New York neighborhood as Todmann and Davis. Scott was a legend on the New York playgrounds by the age of 14 or so. He was a tall (at that time, 6'3") guard who handled the ball well, passed to open teammates, and used a variety of shots to score against tough competition. Scott's family had little money, and when he was offered a scholarship to attend high school at the Laurinburg Institute in Laurinburg, North Carolina, he readily accepted. Laurinburg was a well regarded private preparatory school for black students. Frank McDuffie Jr., who was the headmaster, basketball coach, and band director at the school, later commented that when Scott arrived, he "hadn't had a real meal in two months." At first, he showed no interest in academics or other activities outside of basketball. But he thrived at Laurinburg. Scott graduated as the valedictorian of his class, performed well on the SAT, and electrified college coaches with his talent.[32]

The first coach to take a strong interest in Scott was Lefty Driesell of Davidson College. Scott had attended Driesell's summer basketball camp, and Driesell was the first coach to recruit him and to offer him a scholarship. Scott "took a great liking to Lefty," and he verbally committed to playing for Davidson. It appeared that Driesell had taken another important step in making Davidson, a small college with an excellent academic reputation but no big-time basketball tradition, into a national power.[33]

By the time that Driesell recruited Scott, he had earned recognition as one of the best and most colorful young college coaches in America. He was raised in Norfolk, Virginia, and led his high school basketball team to a state championship. He went to college at Duke and spent his career as a reserve on Hal Bradley's first teams; during his senior year, 1953–54, he appeared in 23 games and averaged 5.0 points. After graduating from Duke, he returned to the Norfolk area and earned a masters degree at William and Mary. He taught school, coached basketball, and for a time also sold encyclopedias to supplement his salary. He quickly proved his ability as a coach. In three years at Newport News High School, his teams captured a state title and compiled a 57-game winning streak. Driesell's record soon attracted attention in the college ranks. He was contacted by Duke's Eddie Cameron, who asked if he would be interested in a coaching job at Davidson, which was coming off twelve consecutive losing seasons. The school's president, David Grier Martin, admitted that the basketball team was "a doormat" and suggested that it "didn't belong in the Southern Conference." Driesell accepted Davidson's offer in 1960 at age 28. He received a decidedly modest salary of $6,000 per year and an even more modest recruiting budget of $500 per year. When Driesell brashly announced that he planned to make Davidson into a big winner, the reaction was, at best, profound skepticism.[34]

To the shock of the Davidson community and the college basketball world, Dreisell made good on his promises. He won his first game in an upset over an excellent Wake Forest team and finished the season with a surprisingly respectable record of 9–14. He searched far and wide for prospects who could meet Davidson's academic standards and help fulfill his pledge to build a winning basketball program. He usually drove a battered Chevy station wagon the college owned, and with a severely limited recruiting budget, often slept on a mat in the back of the car. Driesell's first important recruit was Terry Holland, a high school star in Clinton, North Carolina. Holland wanted to attend Wake Forest because he had close friends who were going there and his high school coach, Jack Murdock, had taken a job as an assistant to Bones McKinney. Driesell, however, insisted that Davidson was the place for him. Holland was dubious, but his mother was more sympathetic. On the night of Holland's senior prom, Driesell pulled up in front of his house in a fancy, two-tone, Ford Fairlane. He flipped the keys to Holland, who was delighted to drive his date, Ann Johnson, to the prom in luxury. Driesell then spent the evening with Holland's mother, enumerating the virtues of Davidson College. Although Holland continued to harbor reservations, his mother settled the issue by forging his signature on Davidson's letter of intent. Holland went to Davidson, scored in double figures in all three years of varsity play, and led the nation with a field-goal percentage of .631 in 1964.[35]

Holland was soon joined by other top recruits, and Driesell transformed the Davidson basketball program. In his second season as coach, the team went 14–11. This was followed by records of 20–7 in 1962–63, and 22–4 in 1963–64, good for a ranking of tenth in the final national polls. In its basketball preview before the 1964–65 season, *Sports Illustrated* named Davidson the number one team in the nation. It noted that the college had for decades produced "a species called the Davidson Gentlemen—hand-polished Southerners of good manners and great learning." Now, it added, "the last place one would expect to find the best basketball team in the country" had the "fastest, fairest, band of educated ruffians around."[36]

The band of ruffians included, among other outstanding players, Fred Hetzel, who became a consensus All-American in 1965, and Dick Snyder, another future All-American. Driesell's ability as a recruiter soon became legendary. His persistence and salesmanship were enhanced by his charisma and quick wit. When he made a recruiting visit to Hetzel's home, he was caught by surprise when the family's pet snake began to crawl down his arm. Hetzel's mother remarked that one coach in the same predicament had commented that "where he came from, they stomp on snakes." Driesell opted for a different approach by replying, "I love snakes." His response helped convince Mrs. Hetzel that Davidson was the right place for her son.[37]

A prominent feature of Driesell's recruiting pitch was his pose as an unlettered rube. This demeanor was in part natural and in part a put-on, and no one could be sure of where the dividing line was. It enabled him to charm recruits and their families, reporters, and others he wanted to impress. Along with his easygoing, country-bumpkin persona, Driesell demonstrated a fierce competitive drive that was most apparent in his eruptions during games. He was, Louis Chestnut of the *Charleston News and Courier* wrote, "a foot-stomping, shouting coach with a violent temper." Driesell's antics were a matter of concern to the Davidson administration and faculty, which did not regard them as consistent with the image the college wanted to project. "It was terrible public relations," stated President Martin, who instructed Driesell with mixed success to improve his bench behavior. The coach's inelegant use of grammar was also out of line with Davidson's status as a center of "great learning." This was a source of amusement to what *Sports Illustrated* called his "far more erudite" players. But he had a ready response to titters about his language infractions: "I may be dumb, but I am not stupid."[38]

At times, Driesell would have benefited from literal dumbness. He displayed a frequently exercised sensitivity to slights or to what he regarded as insufficient acclaim. Mel Derrick, a columnist for the *Charlotte Observer*, which covered Davidson as a home team, revealed that Driesell would "harass the newspapers. He'd call up and yell about getting a two-column headline instead of a three-column headline." Driesell overindulged his tendency to shoot from the hip without considering possible consequences; he later commented that "I was always opening my mouth, saying controversial things, getting into trouble." In 1964, after losing for the third consecutive time to Duke in Durham, he blasted Vic Bubas for refusing to play Davidson at its home court. "If he doesn't come to my place next year, he's yellow," Driesell intoned. He apologized two days later, but not before offending Duke's coach, administrators, and fans. Driesell did not make similar charges against Dean Smith in public, but he resented North Carolina's refusal to schedule Davidson. He was further angered by what he viewed as Smith's lame excuse, which was that if the Tar Heels competed against Davidson they would be forced to play other nonconference schools located in North Carolina.[39]

Despite Driesell's impressive achievements in his first five years at Davidson, he was far from satisfied. He was particularly disappointed that after excellent regular season records and high national rankings, his teams lost in upsets in the Southern Conference Tournament in 1963, 1964, and 1965. Therefore, they did not win conference championships or appear in the NCAA Tournament. Driesell was delighted that Charles Scott verbally committed to attending Davidson in 1965, and he had good reason to hope that Scott's arrival would help take his teams to even greater heights.[40]

Although Scott assured Driesell that he planned to attend Davidson, he also made trips with Laurinburg headmaster McDuffie to other schools. This was not a matter of great concern to Driesell because Scott told him that he "wanted to sign a letter of intent as the earliest time possible" with Davidson. He did not appear to waver even after an embarrassing incident in the town of Davidson. As Driesell and Terry Holland, who was then Davidson's assistant coach, were having dinner at a small restaurant called the Coffee Cup, Scott, McDuffie, and McDuffie's wife, Sammie, unexpectedly walked in. Dreisell and Holland immediately invited Scott and the McDuffies to join them at their table. This offer caused a scene when the waitress, who owned the restaurant along with her husband, told Scott and the McDuffies that they could not share a table with the coaches but had to sit on the "colored side." Driesell and Holland protested furiously to no avail, and eventually everyone stalked out.[41]

Long after the Coffee Cup incident, Scott continued to reaffirm his commitment to Davidson. But his resolve weakened after he made a visit to Chapel Hill. After Dean Smith first heard of Scott's exceptional basketball and academic abilities in January 1966, he worked hard to convince him that he should sign with North Carolina. Smith was scrupulous about not recruiting players who had made a firm commitment to another program, but he knew that Scott was still visiting schools. Further, McDuffie told him that Scott was "open to recruitment." Both Scott and McDuffie seemed attracted to the idea of Scott's becoming the first black basketball player at "the state's oldest university."[42]

Smith had been looking for a player with both the athletic talent and academic credentials to integrate North Carolina basketball for some time. The search reflected not only Smith's coaching priorities but also his personal convictions. When he first moved to North Carolina, he was "shocked" by prevailing racial customs such as separate water fountains. His opposition to such practices made him receptive to an appeal from the minister of his church, Robert Seymour, to help integrate a popular restaurant in Chapel Hill, the Pines. The Pines was frequented by the North Carolina basketball team, and Seymour asked Smith to accompany him and a black student there for dinner. Smith agreed, and the three men were served "without incident." Although Smith later played down the importance of this gesture, his willingness to dine with a black student at a previously segregated restaurant was an act of conscience that clearly demonstrated his views on racial issues. Smith at that time was an assistant coach who was not a prominent figure even in Chapel Hill, and his position could have generated controversy and ill will. After becoming head coach, he was receptive to signing black players, but not aggressive about it. "If I had been truly courageous," he later wrote, "I would have gone to every black high school gym in the state looking for players." In 1964, Smith brought in a black player named William Cooper with little fanfare. Cooper played for the freshman team, and Smith planned to "invite him to walk on the varsity" the following year. In that event, Cooper would have been the first black member of the North Carolina varsity in the same season that Billy Jones integrated ACC basketball. But Cooper was a serious student who decided to drop basketball to keep up with his studies.[43]

In 1966, therefore, Smith was still seeking academically qualified black players, and Charles Scott fit the bill admirably. When Scott visited Chapel Hill in March 1966, he found much to like. He appreciated Smith's courtesy in asking what name he wanted to be called. He replied that he preferred "Charles" to "Charlie." Scott was struck by Smith's invitation to attend church with him. "I hadn't been to church with any of the other coaches," he later remarked. "I had seen Lefty seven or eight times. I never went to church with him." Scott got along well with the players who would be his teammates. They raved about the university and the basketball program and took him to a party on campus. Scott went off on his own for a couple of hours to see how he would be treated in Chapel Hill when he was not accompanied by coaches who were well known in the community. He was favorably impressed with the way he was received and concluded that Chapel Hill provided "much more cosmopolitan" surroundings than Davidson. With those considerations in mind, Scott ultimately decided to sign with North Carolina.[44]

Scott called Driesell's home to tell him of his decision, but the coach was in Houston. After learning the bad news from his wife, he immediately phoned Scott to request a meeting with him the next day. Driesell and Holland flew to Laurinburg on May 3, 1966, in a private plane. After arriving, Driesell and Holland saw Dean Smith, who extended his hand. Driesell looked down at Smith's hand and shook his head to indicate that he was not ready to concede defeat. But he found that the trip was in vain because Scott had already signed with North Carolina.[45]

Charles Scott, 1968. (*Yackety Yack*, University of North Carolina)

The announcement that Scott would become the first black athlete to receive a scholarship at the University of North Carolina was a major topic in newspapers that covered the ACC. Mel Derrick commented in the *Charlotte Observer* that it "was another big feather in Smith's recruiting cap" and "heartbreak for Lefty Driesell." Smith suggested that Scott would be an integral part of the student body at UNC and "not just a gladiator." Scott's performance at North Carolina fully met the high expectations that his signing triggered. He averaged 22.1 points and 7.1 rebounds during his career. He made the All-Conference first team in all three of his varsity seasons and the AP and UPI All-American second teams as a junior and a senior. As a sophomore and junior, Scott's scoring, rebounding, passing, and defensive skills were instrumental in producing ACC championships and Final Four appearances in the NCAA Tournament. In 1969, after he hit a long jumper at the buzzer in the NCAA regional finals to defeat a superb

Davidson team, Lefty Driesell had another bitterly unforgettable reason to lament Scott's decision to enroll at North Carolina.[46]

The Rocky Road to Color Blindness

Other ACC schools integrated their basketball teams in the latter half of the 1960s with considerably less drama than occurred in the recruiting of Charles Scott. The second ACC school to include a black player on its varsity roster was Duke. C. B. Claiborne joined the Blue Devil squad in 1966, a year after Billy Jones at Maryland and a year before Norwood Todmann at Wake Forest and Scott at North Carolina. He attended Duke on an academic scholarship and played basketball as a walk-on. He was an occasional starter who averaged 6.3 points as a senior. At one point in his career, he was unable to attend Duke's basketball banquet because it was held at a segregated country club. NC State's first black basketball player also began his career as a freshman walk-on. Al Heartley showed enough talent to make the freshman squad in 1967 and then earned a scholarship as a sophomore. A rugged defensive specialist and a heady playmaker, he became a starter as a junior and was named team captain as a senior. Clemson and South Carolina signed their first black basketball players in 1969. Both Craig Mobley of Clemson and Casey Manning of South Carolina were outstanding students and high school stars, but neither enjoyed much quality time on the court in college. The last ACC school to integrate its basketball program was Virginia. In the late 1960s, the university substantially stepped up its efforts to increase black enrollment, which was meager even by the standards of the ACC. One reason it had difficulty attracting black athletes was the dearth of African Americans in its student body. Al Drummond became Virginia's first black basketball player when he signed in 1970. He had a solid career as a defensive standout who "could cause stuff to happen."[47]

By 1971, when Drummond made his varsity debut at Virginia, every ACC school had integrated its basketball program, though the number of blacks in the league remained small. The arrival of black players did not signal an end to jaundiced racial attitudes or virulent racial taunting. The consensus was that the most abusive fans were found at Clemson, South Carolina, and Virginia. In Columbia, for example, a fan followed Charles Scott as he left the court and called him a "big, black baboon." Clemson supporters threw chocolate candy bars at Charlie Davis. In 1971, members of the Maryland freshman team were astonished by the racial hostility of the crowd during a matchup in Charlottesville. Years later, Len Elmore, who played in the game, vividly recalled the epithets the fans shouted, and George Raveling, who coached the Maryland freshmen, commented that it "was the worst language and racial taunts I've ever heard in my life." The other conference schools were hardly innocent of racial abuses. The misbehavior of ACC fans was in part an extension of a time-honored tradition of ill-mannered treatment of opposing teams and in part an extension of racial attitudes that were deeply seated in southern culture.[48]

The racial derision that black players suffered was not simply a matter of obnoxious Neanderthals caught up in the emotions of a basketball game. Even Charles Scott, for all his contributions to North Carolina's success in the late 1960s, was the subject of racial insults from Tar Heel partisans. In 1969, after Scott sank the game-winning shot to beat Davidson in the NCAA regionals, some students thought he should be selected as the "King" of campus. One fan regarded that as insufficient recognition, and bellowed, "Charlie for God." A short time later, when Scott had a bad game as Purdue routed North Carolina, the student who had urged his deification remarked, "It just proves 'niggers' choke in the clutch." The same year, Scott complained of racial motivations when he lost the vote for ACC Player of the Year to South Carolina's John Roche. Roche had a splendid season and was a deserving recipient, but Scott's case was strengthened by the fact that five writers left him off their ballots completely.[49]

Objections to and doubts about the increasingly visible role of black players in major college sports were presented in forums far beyond basketball arenas and, perhaps, Player of the Year voting. Reservations were clearly expressed, for example, during at least one meeting of the Commissioners of College Athletic Conferences. In 1968, ACC commissioner Jim Weaver reported that at a recent gathering, "we had quite a discussion on the problem of the black athlete." He revealed that some of his colleagues worried "that the time may come when a team having several black athletes will perhaps experience an embarrassing situation." Among the concerns were that black players might refuse to participate in a game just as it was ready to start. Further, supporters in the stands might "make an attempt to keep the game from being played." Weaver expressed his own view that the ACC "might run into difficulty should we have a team composed of several black student-athletes." He did not "know what the answer" was, but he was convinced it was "a problem, growing all the time."[50]

The misgivings among conference commissioners indicated how far blacks still had to go to gain full acceptance in college sports. Nevertheless, the pioneering black basketball players in the ACC, despite the indignities they endured, made a permanent contribution to racial tolerance. At least in the arenas in which they competed and perhaps far beyond, they promoted the gradual growth of color blindness among fans who regarded winning games as far more urgent than observing racial dogma. Once Billy Jones entered his first game, there was no turning back.

The ACC in the Postwar South

In the three decades after the end of World War II, the South underwent profound economic, educational, cultural, and social changes. In 1938, the federal government announced that the South was "the nation's number one economic problem." In the postwar era, the region achieved remarkable economic progress and, by any standard, greatly improved standards of living. The South went from a largely agricultural economy with a heavily rural population to a growing industrial base with an increasingly urban population. During the 1930s, more than half of the region's people lived in rural areas and about 20 percent lived in cities. By 1960, 15 percent of the population remained on farms while 44 percent of the population lived in urban areas. In the span of a generation, millions of southerners left their farms, often involuntarily, and migrated to cities in the South and in other sections of the country. Industry boomed, wages increased, and military bases proliferated in southern states, all of which fueled the trends toward industrialization, urbanization, and unprecedented prosperity.[51]

Growing economic resources and increasing need for an educated work force encouraged much-needed improvements in education. In 1945, the general condition of elementary and secondary schools in the South was glaringly deficient. Although some white public schools in urban areas received adequate funding, southern states were notoriously parsimonious in their expenditures for education. One study conducted in the 1950s showed that out of every 100 students who began first grade in southern states, only about 10 graduated from high school. Educational achievement was further retarded by racial strife. The most extreme case was Prince Edward County, Virginia, which shut its public schools in 1959 rather than opening them to black students. They remained closed until 1964. Despite such setbacks, southern states, in varying degrees, took effective steps to combat educational shortcomings in the postwar era. They provided increased resources for school buildings, teachers, supplies, and other prerequisites of educational reform. By the 1960s, historian Thomas D. Clark concluded, the South had "made phenomenal educational progress." Along with raising the quality of their secondary schools, Southern states also took important steps to upgrade their universities by supporting new programs, faculty research, enlarged enrollment, and more demanding admission standards.[52]

The changes in the South's economy, distribution of population, and educational priorities after World War II inevitably brought about major social and cultural shifts. The most obvious transformation occurred in the area of race relations. Despite the strong and often violent resistance of those who opposed integration and fought it by every means available, racial accommodation gradually gained traction. This was not an easy process, but the outcome dramatically reoriented southern society. Southern culture changed in other important ways. As racial divisions softened, some hoped and others feared that the South would surrender its sectional identity. They reasoned that this could happen because the South's self-image and its status as a unique section of the country were based so heavily on strict segregation and all the customs and attitudes that went with it. In this regard, some commentators argued that the South should aspire to becoming more like the rest of the nation. Many southerners, however, did not view emulating the North as a worthy goal. They had long resented the North for its cultural arrogance, economic dominance, and self-righteousness on racial issues. They wanted to identify and accentuate those aspects of society that made the South different. Ironically, sectional distinctions during the 1950s were highlighted by traditions that survived the collapse of the rural South. Even as southern cities expanded, the culture of the South was shaped by customs and tastes that migrants from rural areas brought with them. Two primary examples were music and stock car racing, which became staples of southern life long after the countryside that spawned them was decimated. "Ultimately, even people who had no memory of rural life or less savory lowdown habits," historian Pete Daniel has written, "embraced racing, country music, and the accompanying scene, as if their respectable jobs created a need for such spectacles."[53]

The Atlantic Coast Conference was in some ways a product and in some respects a reflection of the momentous changes that occurred in the postwar South. The primary reasons for the ACC's success in basketball were the caliber of competition and the bitter rivalries between schools. Nevertheless, the league's academic principles, fan appeal, and financial well-being were influenced by the educational, economic, and cultural environment in which it operated. The ACC was founded in 1953 in significant part because of the determination of several members to establish better control of their athletic programs and to promote academic integrity. During the 1950s and 1960s, the presidents and top administrators of every conference member made the improvement of academic programs, standards, and performance an urgent priority. This was the motivation behind the requirement on minimum college board scores for signing football and basketball players. The ACC was the first league in the country to impose such a rule, and it was consistent with the objective of improving the academic stature of colleges and universities that prevailed not only in the conference but throughout the postwar South. As coaches at NC State, Wake Forest, and other schools discovered, the 800 rule that the ACC adopted had a serious impact on the outcome of their recruiting efforts.

In a similar manner, the recruiting of black basketball players was affected in important ways by the policies of the governing boards and administrators of ACC schools. For competitive reasons, coaches tended to be progressives on favoring the integration of their teams. Making headway on easing racial barriers in ACC basketball, as in conference universities and the South as a whole, was, at best, sluggish and incremental. But gradually, it did take place.

The growing prosperity of the South in the postwar era provided benefits for ACC basketball. The economic boom of the postwar era did not arrive quickly in all sections of North Carolina. Nevertheless, as Pamela Grundy has suggested, the national recognition of the excellence of ACC basketball "stood as a symbol of the state's promise."[54] As industry replaced agriculture as the foundation of the South's economy, much of the population of the ACC region enjoyed higher pay and more leisure time. Just as some southerners opened their wallets to attend stock car races, others helped to fill arenas for basketball games. They also bought television sets on which they could watch ACC basketball.

One strong indication of the increasing wealth of southern states and greater emphasis on higher education after World War II was the rapid growth of state universities. From around the time that the ACC was established through 1968, undergraduate enrollment at Clemson went from about 3,000 to 5,800, at Maryland from about 15,000 to 25,000, at NC State from about 4,000 to 9,600, at UNC from about 5,000 to 9,800, at South Carolina from about 3,000 to 12,500, and at Virginia from about 3,600 to 5,100. The numbers were imprecise but the trend was clear. And every state university in the ACC expected its enrollment to climb further in the near future. The growth in size was accompanied by the building of modern field houses for basketball and other activities at several ACC schools. Duke and NC State had opened their arenas before the ACC was established, and Maryland's Cole Field House was under construction at that time. Wake Forest played in a new municipal facility after it moved to Winston-Salem. Clemson, South Carolina, and Virginia built new arenas in the 1960s. North Carolina, long after Frank McGuire left, finally replaced Woollen Gym. For years, the state legislature had balked at allocating money for an up-to-date field house. In the early 1960s, it imposed a moratorium on spending for new buildings at all state colleges, but it made funds available to expand or improve standing structures. Therefore, UNC built three sides of a new arena that were joined with one wall of Woollen Gym. It seated 8,800 and was named for Billy Carmichael. The first game was played at Carmichael Auditorium in December 1965, and its construction strengthened Dean Smith's hand when he talked to prospects about attending North Carolina.[55]

Once the new and larger arenas opened, the increased discretionary spending in the population of the South helped to pack them with fans. The key to attracting big crowds to ACC games, of course, was to build winning teams. NC State generally sold out Reynolds Coliseum when it consistently fielded championship teams, but when the program slumped in the early 1960s, so did attendance. Even winning titles did not guarantee sellouts. Duke did not fill its arena for most of its games until the 1963–64 season, and Wake Forest faced the same problem at Memorial Coliseum in Winston-Salem. The programs that struggled seldom drew capacity crowds. But as the league became more competitive from top to bottom, growing legions of fans turned out to cheer for their schools and to rain abuse on opponents. Sellouts of arenas that featured successful ACC teams eventually became the rule rather than the exception. The same pattern applied for the ACC Tournament. The tournament was always a popular attraction, but it did not sell out completely until 1965. A correlation between, on the one hand, jammed arenas and hard-to-find tournament tickets and, on the other hand, the growing prosperity of the postwar South seems axiomatic.[56]

A final way in which ACC basketball reflected developments and attitudes of the postwar South was that it proved to be an effective means for at least some southerners to thumb their collective noses at the North. The ill will toward other sections of the country that was exacerbated by the battles over civil rights fed southerners' inclination to assert the superiority, or at least the legitimacy, of their way of life. This was an element in the joyous celebration that followed North Carolina's national championship in 1957. For the same reason, ACC supporters took pride in the national acclaim that the conference received for the high quality of its basketball programs. The goal of demonstrating the South's virtue vis-à-vis other sections perhaps led to increased pressure to triumph over all intersectional adversaries by winning more national championships.

8

"COLLEGE BASKETBALL'S STRONGEST LEAGUE"

As the 1969–70 basketball season approached, the University of Virginia Cavaliers appeared in danger of descending from disarray into full-fledged chaos. The previous spring, coach Bill Gibson had survived a disappointing record and the "Boot the Hoot" campaign, but only with a tepid endorsement from Athletic Director Steve Sebo. The prospects for the new season were hardly promising. The top four scorers and top three rebounders from the 1968–69 squad, which had finished with a 10–15 record, were gone. The players who moved up from the freshman team (which was often called the "first-year team" at Virginia) provided some cause for optimism. They had won 15 games against only 2 losses. But the Virginia squad was young and unproven as the new season began, and expectations for its performance were low. ACC writers picked the Cavaliers for last place in the conference. Gibson hoped they could finish "as high as sixth."[1]

In addition to the trials of an inexperienced team, Gibson had to deal with off-court annoyances as the season got underway. Some students arranged for the production of "Boot the Hoot" buttons and planned to pass them out to disgruntled fans. After an appeal from Sebo, they halted distribution at least until the team played its first game. But the campaign to force Gibson out appeared ready to resume. Gibson suffered another blow when the university administration turned down his request to authorize seven basketball scholarships for the coming year. This was a part of his effort to reach parity with his ACC rivals; Virginia at that time allowed him five grants-in-aid per year. William A. Hobbs, director of the Office of Development and Public Affairs, told him that school officials "are in full agreement with your desire to have the University be highly competitive in basketball." But, he added, "there is a problem of financing each and every project no matter how worthy it may be." Gibson still remained upbeat about the long-term prospects for Virginia basketball. Just before the 1969–70 season began, he commented, "We're still playing catch-up basketball at Virginia, but we're getting there."[2]

The performance of the 1969–70 team finally gave some credibility to Gibson's insistence that Virginia could compete in the ACC. Although it did not break the string of 15 consecutive losing seasons between 1954–55 and 1968–69, it far exceeded expectations. After the painful "Boot the Hoot" episode of the previous spring, Gibson did not change his approach to coaching in obvious ways. He did not believe that his methods required major modifications. In the first meeting with his team in fall 1969, he handed the players a list of new rules of conduct, which they regarded as pointless and, in some regards, comical. But perhaps as a result of his greater experience in coaching in the ACC, the comments his players made during their so-called revolt, or a combination of both, he did a better job of handling his team and getting the most from his talent. He definitely tried to improve communications with his players and to clarify their individual roles on the team. Players from Gibson's teams before and after the "Boot the Hoot" affair had sharply contrasting views of his coaching ability.

Virginia's 1969–70 squad benefited from the return of Chip Case, who came back from knee injuries that had forced him to the sidelines the previous two seasons. It also gained offensive and rebounding power from the great improvement of forward Bill Gerry, who had learned from Case and assistant coach Chip Conner to use his strength to go hard to the basket. Gerry became, in Case's description, "unstoppable," and led the team in scoring. The second-year players on the squad—Tom Bagby, Frank DeWitt, Scott McCandlish, Chip Miller, and Tim Rash—contributed generous measures of skill and camaraderie that assisted in building the intangible asset of team chemistry. Conner later suggested that their decision to come to Gibson's defense at the height of the "Boot the Hoot" controversy created a bond that helped their performance on the court. McCandlish, a 6'10" center who averaged 13.5 points and 9.6 rebounds in his first varsity season, was the quiet leader of the second-year players. As a group, Conner recalled, they "were down to earth, completely honest, completely humble, completely unselfish." Although they did not take themselves too seriously, they were "intense competitors."[3]

Early in the 1969–70 season, the Virginia team showed signs that the pre-season predictions had underestimated its potential. After a 1–5 start, the Cavaliers pulled off a surprise by defeating the University of Richmond and the College of William and Mary to win a tournament in which five schools from the state of Virginia competed. The "Big Five" victory was an important confidence-booster for the players and coaches. Virginia struggled through much of the ACC season and placed seventh in the standings, but it concluded with six wins in its last eleven games. In the final regular season contest, it stunned Duke with a 61–57 upset before 3,350 gleeful fans at University Hall. The outcome of the next game was even more shocking. In the first round of the 1970 ACC Tournament, Virginia edged second-seeded North Carolina, 95–93, overcoming a 41-point offensive show by Charles Scott. It was Virginia's first tournament victory since 1959. In the semifinals, the Cavaliers narrowly lost to NC State, the eventual champion, 67–66. The team's 10–15 record was exactly the same as that of the previous season, but players, coaches, and fans believed that the strong finish boded well for the future. After the win over North Carolina, Gibson commented: "This has been a long time coming. I can't say enough about our kids. They were all great. It has been a pleasure to work with them." Despite a losing record, the team earned the support of a growing body of Virginia fans, and the "Boot the Hoot" buttons remained in storage.[4]

The 1969–70 campaign proved to be a prelude for the success that Virginia achieved the following season, when it broke its skein of losing records, ranked in the top twenty nationally for a time, and packed University Hall with raucous fans. Although Chip Case had graduated, the other four starters returned, and they were joined by guard Barry Parkhill, who had averaged 27 points per game for the freshman team. Parkhill had been Virginia's star recruit two years earlier, though Gibson signed him with reservations. As a high school player in State College, Pennsylvania, he made the All-State team, but he was not regarded as a top college prospect. Wake Forest was the only other ACC school to express interest in him, and Parkhill's home town university, Penn State, did not value his poten-

Chip Case clutches towel while watching tense action between Virginia and North Carolina in the 1970 ACC Tournament. (Courtesy The North Carolina State Archives; reprinted by permission of *The News and Observer* of Raleigh, North Carolina)

tial enough to recruit him. He came to Virginia's attention when he played at Gibson's summer basketball camp in Gettysburg, Pennsylvania, before his senior year in high school. Gibson was out of the country at the time, but Chip Conner watched as Parkhill "lit it up" in competition with other campers and then with much more accomplished counselors. Parkhill, who knew little about the University of Virginia, was pleased when Conner suggested that his skills might qualify him for a scholarship. On a weekend visit to Charlottesville in fall 1968, he was so impressed with the school, the players, and the coaches that he immediately decided that he wanted to attend Virginia. Gibson, however, was dubious about signing a player whom he had not seen in action and who was not viewed as a first-tier prospect. He agreed to do so only after Conner convinced him that Parkhill's ability was worthy of a scholarship. Conner began to worry after Gibson accepted his evaluation. "Barry was not rated high," he later commented. "He was a 6′4″ inside player for a small high school."[5]

In his first season of varsity play, Parkhill quickly vindicated Conner's judgment. Virginia began the season by winning its first six games, includ-

Barry Parkhill, 1972. (*Corks and Curls*, Special Collections, University of Virginia Library)

ing a comeback victory over ninth-ranked Duke before a rollicking sell-out crowd at University Hall. While Gibson praised the contributions of all his players, he pointed to Parkhill as "the one who makes the team go" and could "make things happen." Not only was the second-year guard an effective scorer, but he also ran the offense, found teammates for open shots, and took on "more responsibilities than any single player." He was an intense competitor who, his teammate Jim Hobgood later remarked, "had a burning desire to be the best." Parkhill wanted the ball in his hands in a close game. A. J. Carr, a writer for the *Raleigh News and Observer*, commented in 1971 that he seemed "to have the poise of a prince and the guts of a prizefighter." Parkhill's scoring and playmaking talent, commitment to winning, and leadership were vital to Virginia's dramatic and unexpected improvement. ACC writers had picked the Cavaliers to finish in seventh place in the conference in preseason forecasts.[6]

After opening the season with six wins, the first time since 1914–15 that Virginia had started so well, the team dropped two games. It quickly returned to early form with a winning streak that inspired the nickname of the "Amazin' Cavaliers." In January 1971, Virginia delighted its supporters and astonished its opponents by defeating three ACC rivals and a good Georgia Tech team in consecutive outings. The most surprising and most important victory came against South Carolina on January 11. The Gamecocks were ranked sixth in the nation after an overtime loss to Maryland two days earlier. Virginia used a well-executed slow-down offense and won the game when Parkhill hit a 12-foot jump shot with seven seconds to go in the game. A short time later, Virginia made its first appearance ever in college basketball's top 20 with a ranking of 19th. It rose to 15th in the national polls but then faltered in the last few weeks of the season. It ended with a record of 15–11, its best by far since the 1953–54 squad had gone 16–11. Parkhill, who averaged 15.9 points, and Gerry, who averaged 14.8 points and 9.3 rebounds, were named to the All-Conference second team. "I don't have super players," Gibson was fond of saying. "I just have super kids."[7]

Along with winning games, the Amazin' Cavaliers also attracted an unprecedented number of fans. For the first time since it had opened in 1965, University Hall was consistently filled with loud, partisan crowds. During the 1969–70 season, the average attendance at Virginia's home games was about 4,000; during the 1970–71 season, it increased to 7,500. The fans provided boisterous encouragement to their team. After the big victory over Duke early in the season, Gibson thanked Virginia fans for the "fact that we couldn't introduce the players for three or four minutes while the crowd stood and yelled." He pointed out that his teams had played on the road against opponents with vocal fans for years. "Now we know what it is like," he said, "and boy do we love it!" In contrast to the "Boot the Hoot" campaign of less than two years earlier, Virginia students began chanting "Hoot, Hoot, Hoot," when Gibson walked into the arena before each game. Fans also hung a banner announcing their affection for "Hooter's Heroes," a takeoff on a popular television show called *Hogan's Heroes*. In addition, the basketball club raised money to buy a new Mercury and presented it to Gibson before the final home game. After the season ended, Gibson suggested that "our program has turned the corner." This time, his optimistic assessment rang true. It seemed apparent that Virginia basketball had finally arrived as a serious competitor in the ACC.[8]

A Balanced League

For more than a decade after the ACC was founded, coaches of Big Four teams did not worry a great deal about losing to the conference schools located outside North Carolina. They could usually count on winning both regular-season games against Virginia, South Carolina, and Clemson, and they hoped for at least a split with Maryland. They regarded a record of 7–1 against the weakest conference teams as a likely outcome and focused their attention on beating their Big Four rivals. This pattern broke down in the late 1960s as the non–Big Four teams strengthened their programs and the league became much more evenly balanced.

ACC coaches and other observers had predicted for years that the conference was on the verge of becoming competitive from top to bottom and that the have-nots were ready to rise. Dick Herbert told his readers in the Raleigh area in 1956 that Big Four dominance of the ACC was "a source of some resentment at the other schools" and that they were showing signs of improvement. This development, he wrote, was "a good thing for basketball in our league." Herbert's advisory proved to be premature, but others made similar predictions with the same results. Dean Smith suggested in 1962 that the ACC was "stronger all the way through," and Everett Case agreed with him that the conference was "better balanced than ever." Bones McKinney, who was out of coaching at the time, reported in January 1967 that "this is the first year I can truthfully say I really believe the top team can be beaten by the bottom one." At about the same time, Louis Chestnut, executive sports editor of the *Charleston News and Courier*, argued that the "ACC, as a unit, just might be the nation's best balanced league."[9]

The claims about the ACC's balance were finally realized in the early 1970s. In an article in *Sports Illustrated* in March 1970, Curry Kirkpatrick called the ACC "college basketball's strongest league." He pointed out that the traditional excellence of the conference was no longer limited to the Big Four schools. Kirkpatrick cited the sharp improvement of South Carolina under Frank McGuire and Maryland since hiring Lefty Driesell. Within a short time he could have added Clemson and Virginia to make his case for the balance of the league and the ability of the former also-rans to challenge the Big Four. Other leagues had great teams at the top, but by the early 1970s, none compared with the ACC in the level of talent and the keenness of competition throughout the entire conference. Kirkpatrick commented that coaches "from other parts of the country, envious of the conference's large recruiting budgets, resent the stature and reputation of the league." He suggested that assets other than recruiting expenditures explained the ACC's rank as the nation's best conference: "warm climates, majestic arenas, high academic standards, miniskirted dixiecups and a young prospect's awareness that, in an area where football is misery, basketball is far and away No. 1 in tradition, enthusiasm, and respect." *Basketball Weekly* magazine supported Kirkpatrick's position on the superiority of ACC basketball by ranking it as the top conference in 10 of 11 seasons between 1966 and 1976.[10]

North Carolina's Rise to Dominance

Despite the greater balance in the ACC and the improvement of the non–Big Four schools, during the late 1960s, the dominant team in the conference was North Carolina. Following a record of 16–11 and a one-point loss to Duke in the ACC Tournament in 1966, the Tar Heels had a lineup in 1966–67 led by senior Bob Lewis and junior Larry Miller, described by the Associated Press as the "top one-two punch in the conference." They were joined by three outstanding sophomore starters. Rusty Clark, a 6′10″ center from Fayetteville, North Carolina, provided size. Bill Bunting, a 6′8″ forward from New Bern, North Carolina, provided exceptional quickness in the front court. Dick Grubar, a 6′3″ guard from Schenectady, New York, was a post player in high school. Dean Smith was impressed with his passing ability and his "basketball savvy," and thought he would make a good point guard. Before the season began, North Carolina was regarded as a threat to topple defending champion Duke, though Smith cautioned that the ACC was not a "sophomore league."[11]

Despite its youth, North Carolina started well and never looked back. Miller was the team's leading scorer with an average of 21.9 points, and Lewis, who had reduced his own scoring opportunities by moving to a guard position, added 18.5 points per game. North Carolina rolled though the regular conference season with a record of 12–2 and entered the tournament ranked third in the country. It captured the ACC title for the first time since 1957 by defeating Duke in the finals, 82–73. Miller made 13 of 14 field-goal attempts and scored 32 points while Lewis chipped in with 26 points. The Tar Heels won the NCAA eastern regionals with victories over Princeton and Boston College. They suffered a decisive upset, 76–62, in their national semifinal matchup with the University of Dayton, perhaps because they were looking ahead to a championship game against UCLA. Nevertheless, North Carolina finished with a 26–6 record, a league championship, national rankings of third in the UPI poll and fourth in the AP poll, and reason to hope that the next season could turn out even better.[12]

Lewis was the only starter to graduate, and he was replaced in the lineup in 1967–68 by Charles Scott. North Carolina edged Duke to claim the regular season title with a record of 12–2, and it captured the tournament championship with a rout of NC State. Larry Miller scored 22.4 points per game and was named ACC Player of the Year; Scott and Clark, who set a UNC record by collecting 30 rebounds in a game against Maryland, made first- and second-team All-Conference respectively. After winning the ACC Tournament, Smith told reporters that the Tar Heels had achieved their "first major goal," and that now they sought another—the national championship. They crushed unbeaten and third-ranked St. Bonaventure in the first round of the eastern regional tournament, and then downed Lefty Driesell's Davidson squad, 70–66, to advance to the Final Four. In the NCAA Tournament's final rounds, North Carolina handily defeated Ohio State to face defending champion UCLA for the national title. Smith elected to open the game with his four-corner offense, which helped to keep the Tar Heels close. But Lew Alcindor led the Bruins in scoring bursts that put the game out of reach. The final score was 78–55; Alcindor scored 34 points and grabbed 16 rebounds. Smith commented that "UCLA has to be the best basketball team ever assembled."[13]

Even without Miller, North Carolina fielded another powerhouse in 1968–69. Scott scored 22.2 points per game, and Bunting (18.0), Clark (14.4), and Grubar (13.0) averaged in double figures. After the Tar Heels defeated highly ranked Kentucky early in the season, Curry Kirkpatrick suggested that Scott was not only the "first black man to play varsity basketball for his school" but also "black or white, most likely the best." He led his team to a 12–2 record and first place in the regular season standings, then scored 40 points (28 of them in the second half) to overcome Duke's serious bid for an upset in the tournament finals. North Carolina became the first school to win both the regular season and ACC Tournament championships in three consecutive years. It then became the first team to take three straight eastern regional championships in the NCAA Tournament by beating Duquesne, 79–78, and Davidson, 87–85, on Scott's jump shot at the buzzer. In the national semifinals, North Carolina's season ended abruptly with a shockingly one-sided loss to Purdue, 92–65. Rick Mount put up 36 points for the Boilermakers, and Herm Gilliam, whom Wake Forest had hoped to sign, did an effective job of slowing Scott. It was a disappointing finish to another splendid season for the Tar Heels.[14]

By the end of the 1968–69 season, North Carolina was clearly the team to beat in the ACC. Dean Smith recruited excellent players and taught them to perform with a rare combination of intelligence, discipline, and team-work. Even as he and his highly respected assistants, John Lotz and Bill

Coach Dean Smith flanked by assistant coaches John Lotz (on his right) and
Bill Guthridge, 1969. To Guthridge's left is Bill Bunting. (Photo by Hugh Morton,
North Carolina Collection, University of North Carolina Library at Chapel Hill)

Guthridge, took the Tar Heels to appearances in the Final Four, they recruited prospects who kept the pipeline full of outstanding players. Waiting
in the wings after the 1968–69 season were a number of talented freshmen
and newly signed high school stars, including Dennis Wuycik, George Karl,
and Bill Chamberlain. In 1969–70, North Carolina had, by its standards, a
disappointing season. Scott led the league in scoring with an average of 27.1,
but the team's record was 18–9. It was upset by Virginia in the first round of
the ACC Tournament and then lost in the first round of the NIT to Manhattan College. North Carolina bounced back in 1970–71. It won the regular season championship before falling to South Carolina in the ACC Tournament final. The Tar Heels won the NIT and achieved a national ranking
of 13th in both the AP and UPI polls. After a subpar season and the failure
to sign highly sought recruits in 1970, Smith suggested, the 1970–71 team
"really sustained the Carolina program" because it demonstrated unselfish
play, hustle, and unity of purpose. "We had more than a winning team," he
wrote. "We had a winning program."[15]

Smith, like Frank McGuire before him, believed that his players should travel first-class and dress smartly. "It was my hope that our appearance would bespeak achievement without shouting it," he later commented. Smith was ever solicitous about promoting and guarding a positive public image of his teams and the university they represented. In May 1969, he protested angrily when a local newspaper, the *Chapel Hill Weekly*, published information that the UNC basketball team had been reprimanded by the NCAA. The NCAA cited North Carolina because three players, without the knowledge of the coaches, had taken a prospect to a party in Greensboro ("a community considerably removed from Chapel Hill") during a recruiting visit in 1966. The reprimand was a minor disciplinary action that carried no penalty, but Smith feared that the article would hurt his program. He argued that since the NCAA had not specified which UNC sport had been guilty of the infraction, the newspaper should not have done so either. He complained that the story appeared in the "middle of recruiting season" and "could hurt our recruiting." Smith was particularly offended that the paper's publisher, Orville Campbell, had suggested privately to him that his position was "selfish" and not in the best interests of the university. "I have always held to the fact that the University is much bigger than the Athletic Department or any segment of it," he wrote. "This is now my University and I am doing everything within my power to represent it with dignity and respect."[16]

North Carolina fans returned the favor. The success of the basketball team commanded rapt attention, generated financial support, and produced intense excitement. Carmichael Auditorium was sold out for every game. Students flocked to the arena to watch practices and cheered the team as it went through its drills. Students and fans at other ACC schools, by contrast, were demonstrably less pleased with North Carolina's rise to dominance. They could empathize with the sentiments that Lefty Driesell aired before Davidson's game in the NCAA's eastern regional finals in 1969: "I'd rather die than lose to North Carolina again." The growing resentment was in large part a predictable result of North Carolina's unprecedented ascendancy. It was also fueled by the perception that the Tar Heels looked down on their opponents with poorly concealed smugness. North Carolina's collective approach to the business of winning basketball games was the subject of gentle ribbing in *Sports Illustrated* in January 1968. When the team traveled to Portland, Oregon, for a holiday tournament, Joe Jares wrote, it arrived "like a big-business task force—confident, intelligent, well-dressed, and organized right down to a synchronized post-dinner burp." Fans of other ACC schools tended to place North Carolina's style in a most

unflattering light and to view its confidence and sense of purpose as insuf-
ferable arrogance. Intense dislike of conference rivals, especially successful
ones, was a well-established tradition in the ACC, but it reached new levels
of animosity after UNC's streak of championship runs.[17]

Duke in the Middle

As North Carolina rose to the top of the ACC, and, as a corollary, incited
the ill will of its conference rivals, Duke, the ACC's standard-setter for most
of the 1960s, descended toward the middle of the pack. The decline began
in Vic Bubas's final year as coach in 1968–69 and continued when Bucky
Waters replaced him. Duke remained highly competitive in the conference,
but it took a step down from the lofty status it had attained when it went to
the NCAA's Final Four three times in four years between 1963 and 1966. At
the same time, as a consequence of the university's growing financial difficulties, a faculty committee recommended that Duke de-emphasize its athletic programs and drop its membership in the Atlantic Coast Conference.

After Duke's trip to the Final Four in 1966, it had a disappointing season,
at least by its standards under Bubas, in 1966–67. The team went 18–9 overall and 9–3 in the conference for a second-place finish in the regular season
standings. It lost to North Carolina in the tournament finals, a game that
in retrospect represented a changing of the guard. The ACC had reversed
its policy on postseason appearances to allow one of its teams that failed
to make the NCAA Tournament to play in the NIT, and Duke became the
first to take advantage of the opportunity. But its visit to the NIT was brief;
it fell in the first round to a Southern Illinois team led by Walt Frazier,
72–63. Duke ended the season ranked 19th in the nation, its lowest position ever under Bubas. The next year, Duke came back strong to compile a
22–6 record and to finish second behind North Carolina in the regular season. Senior Mike Lewis led the team in scoring with a 21.7 average and the
league in rebounding with a 14.4 average. In one of the most bizarre games
in ACC tournament history, the Blue Devils lost to NC State in the second
round by the score of 12–10. They once again went to the NIT, where they
made the second round before losing to St. Peter's College, 100–71.[18]

In 1968–69, Duke slumped to a record of 15–13 in what turned out to be
Bubas's last season. After 18 years of unflagging devotion to the demands
of coaching in the ACC, Bubas burned out. He deliberated over resigning
for a long time before deciding that he wanted to do something else. "I just
got tired of doing the same things over and over," he later explained. "I'd

run out of challenges and I was going stale. I needed something new and something with a little more substance." Duke's young team struggled for much of the 1968–69 season, but it provided Bubas with an enormously satisfying win in his last home game by upsetting North Carolina, 87–81. At age 42, Bubas left coaching with a record of 213 victories and 67 losses and a winning percentage of .761. He was even better in the ACC, where he had a record of 106–32 and a winning percentage of .768. He was especially proud that 29 of the 33 players he signed to play at Duke earned their degrees. After his coaching career ended, he became vice president for community relations at Duke.[19]

The choice of Bubas's successor came down to two exceptionally strong candidates, Lefty Driesell and Bucky Waters. Driesell was a Duke graduate and had built an excellent program in the unlikely setting of Davidson College. But the image of an untutored bumpkin that he cultivated and his sometimes impolitic statements, such as calling Bubas "yellow" in 1964, undermined his chances of landing the Duke job. After Waters was hired, Duke president Douglas Knight told a faculty member who had supported Driesell: "We picked the man who can add true stature, not only to the University's athletic program but to the University at large."[20]

Waters had appeared "to have the inside track" on the Duke job after Bubas resigned. He had served as an assistant to Bubas for six seasons before accepting the head coaching position at the University of West Virginia in 1965 at age 29. In his first three seasons, his teams went 57–27, won the Southern Conference in 1967, and appeared in the NIT in 1968. Waters was named Southern Conference Coach of the Year in 1967. His 1968–69 squad suffered from injuries and finished at 13–13. But West Virginia was building a new 15,000 seat arena, the freshman team was talented, and Waters had good reason to stay. On March 12, 1969, he wired Knight to tell him that he wished to remove his name from consideration for the Duke job. He then went to inform James B. Harlow, president of the university, that he planned to remain in Morgantown. As he sat in Harlow's office, the phone rang, to Harlow's annoyance. It turned out that the caller was Douglas Knight, who asked to speak to Waters. Harlow left his office, and Knight made a pitch for Duke that Waters found irresistible. He later explained that his heart told him to accept the Duke job and his head told him to stay at West Virginia. In the end, Waters sided with his heart. His decision received a warm greeting in Durham. Bubas commented: "Bucky is an excellent teacher, an astute handler of young men, an excellent tactician, a top-notch organizer, and a great recruiter."[21]

Despite Waters's impressive record and the accolades he received when he arrived at Duke, his tenure as the Blue Devils' head coach was marked by discord and disappointment. He inherited a promising group of players, led by 6'10" center Randy Denton, forward Rick Katherman, and guard Dick DeVenzio. Denton made the All-Conference squad in 1971 after averaging 20.4 points and 12.8 rebounds. Waters's teams went 17–9 in 1970–71 and 20–10 in 1971–72 and participated in the NIT each time. But they lost in the first round of the ACC Tournament in both of Waters's first two seasons. Denton was puzzled by Duke's early exits. "Obviously, we weren't ready to play," he later commented. "But that's hindsight. We had good practices, we thought we were ready, and we took the floor expecting to win. Then, nothing happened."[22]

As Duke fell short of its own expectations and its previous standards, students and other fans began to grumble. The complaints grew louder and more passionate the following year, when the Blue Devils finished with a record of 14–12 and tied for fourth in the regular season standings. The major highlight of the season occurred in January 1972, when Duke Indoor Stadium was renamed in honor of Eddie Cameron, who had announced his retirement. Otherwise, the season provided few occasions to celebrate and the pressure on Waters escalated. In December 1971, a group calling itself "Concerned Students for Duke Basketball" began a "Fire Bucky" campaign on campus. The growing discontent was fueled by the loss of several top players who elected to leave school. Their reasons varied, including academic difficulties, lack of playing time, and aversion to Waters's strict rules and demanding style. Some players made their grievances public, which created a great deal of ill will within the team. The 1972–73 squad stumbled to a 12–14 record, Duke's first losing season since 1939. The problems were compounded when the NCAA placed Duke on probation for one year in 1972 for a recruiting violation by an overzealous or uninformed alumnus. The clamor to dismiss Waters intensified. Waters pressed Carl James, who had replaced Cameron, for a vote of confidence, though without success, and then worked out an agreement with President Terry Sanford. Waters announced his resignation in September 1973 to become assistant to William Anlyan, Duke's vice president for health affairs, where, among other things, he would raise money for the Duke Medical Center.[23]

At the same time that Duke struggled to maintain its position on the top rungs of ACC basketball, a committee formed by the university's Academic Council, an influential faculty body, recommended that Duke withdraw from the conference. During the mid- and late 1960s, Duke faced serious financial problems. Although President Knight sharply denied that he was dealing with a "financial crisis," the university ran deficits every year from 1964 through 1968. In 1967, the shortfall exceeded $800,000, and in 1968, it was nearly $500,000. Duke had a reputation as a wealthy school because of the income it received from the Duke Endowment, but as expenses grew, the funds the endowment provided could not keep up with the university's commitments. Despite James Buchanan Duke's generosity in 1924, the endowment of the university he created ranked only 29th among colleges in the United States in 1968. In that context, the Academic Council appointed an "ad hoc committee on Duke athletics" to investigate the costs of Duke's athletic program and to make judgments about "the worth of the program."[24]

The role of athletics at Duke had taken on considerable urgency because, after years of generating more revenue than they consumed, the cost of sports programs had recently exceeded receipts. This raised the question of whether the value of athletics justified the expense. The ad hoc committee pointed out that "several positive values have been ascribed to the presence of an intercollegiate athletic program at a university." The attributes included attracting students and faculty, encouraging financial support from alumni and others, providing visibility to the university, building a sense of community, and offering "interesting and wholesome entertainment." The committee found, however, that athletic programs had a limited effect on the decision of students to attend Duke and very little effect on hiring faculty members. Further, the success of Duke's teams played "no significant part in inducing individuals to support the University, or in the magnitude of their support."

The ad hoc committee suggested that the key issue was whether the other advantages of athletic programs were a fair trade-off for their costs. It concluded that the benefits could be achieved without remaining in the ACC and contended that Duke's membership in the conference was a drain on financial resources. The problem was that "academic standards and programs at Duke University differ significantly from those of a majority of Conference members." The committee argued that the "differences have recently intensified and Duke finds it increasingly difficult to recruit athletes in the face of so-called competition." Therefore, it seemed that Duke could compete only by lowering its academic standards. The alternative that the committee recommended was to "leave the Atlantic Coast Conference and seek competition with educational institutions whose standards, programs, and interests are compatible with our own."[25]

The ad hoc committee submitted its report to the Academic Council in November 1969, and it quickly generated, according to Duke's director of alumni affairs, "national publicity [and] excited editorial comment on numerous sports pages." Eddie Cameron took issue with the contentions of the ad hoc committee and complained that they had "done considerable harm to the intercollegiate athletic program of our University." He argued that withdrawing from the ACC and finding more compatible opponents would be "very difficult" at best. Further, he pointed out that the ACC had provided national leadership in requiring that college board scores for scholarship athletes meet a certain minimum. The ad hoc committee's recommendation on quitting the ACC received much attention and underscored the ever-present tensions between academic and athletic priorities. But the practical effect of the report was limited to proposals of lesser consequence, such as expanding intramural programs. When former North Carolina governor Terry Sanford took over as Duke's president in 1970, he concluded that although "athletics must not be allowed to invoke inordinate attention, *or to detract from Duke's educational program*," he viewed intercollegiate sports as "an inherent part of this University" (emphasis in original). He also announced that he had decided after "careful thought" that the "best athletic affiliation for this institution at this time is the Atlantic Coast Conference." He hoped to ease the financial burden of competing in the ACC by increasing contributions from alumni and other Duke supporters. Sanford's position ended the discussion of Duke's withdrawal from the ACC.[26]

McGuire's Return to the Top

While Duke was sliding from the top of the ACC basketball standings, the former also-rans in the conference were passing it on the way up. The first of the non–Big Four programs to reach the upper echelons during the 1960s and early 1970s was South Carolina. Frank McGuire built excellent teams despite the loss of Mike Grosso and the two-year probation that the NCAA imposed in January 1967. His 1967–68 squad tied for third in the regular season standings with a record of 15–7, including two highly satisfying wins over Duke. Despite concerns about ugly incidents when Duke visited Columbia after it had refused to play against the Gamecocks the previous year, South Carolina fans behaved well and their team won a thriller. South Carolina also defeated North Carolina, then ranked third in the country, in Chapel Hill. Three Gamecock players were selected for the

All-Conference teams. Skip Harlicka, who averaged 21.8 points, made the first team, and Gary Gregor (17.9 points and 12.2 rebounds per game) and Frank Standard (16.2 points and 10.4 rebounds) made the second team.[27]

The success of McGuire's South Carolina teams in 1966–67 and 1967–68 did not produce comparable results in recruiting. McGuire failed to land blue-chip high school players during and immediately after the Grosso affair, and when the NCAA imposed its penalties, the university forced him to sever his ties with Harry Gotkin. The most important player he signed in 1966 was a New Yorker named Bobby Cremins, who was not a heavily recruited prospect. But when McGuire saw him play, he was "impressed with his hustle and determination." Cremins "was all over the floor, diving after loose balls, and really scrapping." McGuire offered him a scholarship on the spot. It was, he later commented, "one of the best moves I ever made. . . . Bobby had so much heart and determination that it rubbed off on the other players."[28]

Cremins not only provided leadership to McGuire's teams but also played a key role in recruiting two players who were instrumental in South Carolina's rise to the top of the ACC. One of Cremins's close friends in New York was Tom Owens, a 6'10" star who was highly sought by college coaches. Owens, in turn, wanted to play in college with his teammate, John Roche, a slender 6'3" guard with superb ball-handling, playmaking, and defensive skills. The two players, after agreeing to attend the same school, narrowed their choices to Duke and South Carolina. As Roche later explained, Duke did not seem a comfortable fit for them. "The students were generally different from kids we grew up with," he said, "from a more affluent base, a more national base, a more sophisticated base." He and Owens were also uncertain that Bubas fully appreciated their talent. They found South Carolina more to their liking, and McGuire's freewheeling offensive style was especially appealing. When they committed to South Carolina, Cremins remembered that he and assistant coach Donnie Walsh "whooped" and "danced" in jubilation. "And sure enough," he added, "those two kids put South Carolina basketball on the map."[29]

Roche's exceptional talent was critical to South Carolina's appearance on the map. Even as a sophomore, he had become, in Cremins's words, "the man." He had a singular ability to run the offense and dictate the tempo of a game, and consequently, he had the ball in his hands up to 75 percent of the time his team had possession. "Roche is the best I've ever seen at controlling a game," McGuire commented. He was capable of gliding through defenders to the basket, using his height to post up and score, or feeding the

John Roche guarded by Steve Previs and George Karl (22), 1971.
(Courtesy The North Carolina State Archives; reprinted by permission of
The News and Observer of Raleigh, North Carolina)

ball to open teammates. He was also an excellent outside shooter with great range and a "picture perfect" delivery. Roche's brilliance as a player and as a floor leader once inspired Tates Locke, who became Clemson's coach in 1970, to suggest that he should be named not only the ACC's Player of the Year but also its Coach of the Year.[30]

On November 30, 1968, South Carolina played its first game at the new Carolina Coliseum, which cost $9 million to build, seated 12,400, and was known as "the house that McGuire built." In a starting lineup that featured Cremins and four sophomores, Roche and Owens made their varsity debuts. The other sophomores were Bill Walsh, a guard with a good outside shot who was an excellent complement to Roche, and John Ribock, a rugged 6'8" Georgian who quickly earned a reputation as a no-holds-barred, no-punches-pulled enforcer. Even one of his own teammates called Ribock "insane." The Gamecocks won the inaugural game in the new coliseum over Auburn University when Roche hit a last-second jumper. They posted a record of 21–7 in 1968–69 and placed second to North Carolina in the ACC's regular season standings with an 11–3 record. South Carolina lost in the second round of the ACC Tournament in an upset to Duke. It received an invitation to the NIT, where it defeated Southern Illinois and then was trounced, 59–45, by an Army team coached by future legend Bobby Knight. The Gamecocks ended the year with a national ranking of 13th in the AP poll, and Roche was named ACC Player of the Year.[31]

The success of the Gamecocks caused an epidemic of basketball fever in South Carolina. Large crowds cheered the team when it landed at the Columbia airport after road games. Roche's image graced billboards throughout the city. And every game, Ron Morris later wrote, "was the biggest event in the state." The euphoria reached new heights as the 1969–70 season approached. With its entire starting lineup returning, South Carolina was rated the number one team in the nation by *Sports Illustrated* and many other magazines. The team was strengthened by the addition of Tom Riker, a 6'10" sophomore center who had been "one of the most sought-after players in the nation" as a high school senior. South Carolina lost its number one ranking early in the season after a narrow defeat by Tennessee, but it rolled through its conference schedule with a record of 14–0. Roche was selected as ACC Player of the Year for the second consecutive year. But the ACC Tournament once again led to heartbreak. In the semifinal contest against Wake Forest, Roche suffered a severely sprained ankle after stepping on the foot of another player. He gamely played in the finals against NC State, but the injury sharply reduced his effectiveness. NC State won the championship game in double overtime, 42–39. McGuire, who had always detested the ACC Tournament, complained bitterly about his misfortune. "I thought it was a bad way of determining the champion when I came into this league, and I still think so," he said.[32]

The pain of losing the championship was compounded when many fans in the Charlotte Coliseum hooted at the Gamecock players as they left the floor. By that time, South Carolina had earned the enmity of its conference rivals to the point that it was even more despised than North Carolina, a considerable achievement. Whereas opposing fans disliked the Tar Heels because of their arrogance, real or perceived, they loathed the Gamecocks for their indisputably real belligerence. The South Carolina team reflected McGuire's unabashed antagonism toward conference rivals, which the Grosso controversy had magnified. Roche and his teammates played with a chip on their collective shoulder that other teams delighted in removing if they could. The mutual antipathy was especially prominent during the 1970–71 season. South Carolina players committed indefensible and unbecoming acts of hostility. Roche, for example, kicked North Carolina's George Karl in the stomach after a skirmish for a loose ball, and he was assessed a technical foul for kicking Duke's Dick DeVenzio after being called for a charging foul. Ribock, whom Curry Kirkpatrick described as the ACC's "reigning butcher," slugged Maryland coach Lefty Driesell in the fight that broke out when Maryland played in Columbia in December 1970. Fans of rival teams repaid in kind. At Chapel Hill, a UNC fan walked behind the South Carolina bench and stuck a wad of gum in Tom Owens's hair. At Virginia, McGuire had to be restrained from attacking a writer for a local newspaper who screamed insults at him the entire game. At Wake Forest, cheerleaders fired up the crowd by flushing a dummy wearing Roche's number down a mock toilet during player introductions.[33]

Although Roche later admitted that the unrelenting hostility he encountered made him surly and diminished his love of the game, at the time he seemed to thrive on it. "I love it," he told Kirkpatrick for a cover story in *Sports Illustrated*. "The people must be maniacs, but they just make me play harder." South Carolina's 1970–71 team was talented, experienced, and determined to erase the disappointing finishes of the previous two seasons. Kevin Joyce, an exceptionally promising sophomore guard, replaced the departed Cremins, and the other four starters returned. The South Carolina squad was not as dominant as that of the previous year, and it suffered memorable upsets at the hands of Maryland and Virginia in January 1971. Nevertheless, it finished second in the regular season with a record of 10–4, one game behind North Carolina. In the tournament, South Carolina defeated Maryland and NC State to meet North Carolina in the finals. In a nail-biting game, the Tar Heels led 51–50 with six seconds remaining. North Carolina's 6'10" Lee Dedmon lined up for a jump ball with the 6'3" Joyce. Somehow, Joyce controlled the tip, the ball went to Owens under the basket, and he laid it in. South Carolina won its first and only ACC championship.[34]

Even in victory, the Gamecocks showed their contempt for their adversaries. As they left the court, several players flashed obscene gestures at the crowd, most of which had cheered for North Carolina. When Dean Smith walked up to Roche and offered his congratulations, Roche dismissed him with an exceedingly crude epithet. "South Carolina spent the early part of this season proving to the world that it was a poor loser," Bill Millsaps, who covered the ACC for the *Richmond Times-Dispatch*, commented after the tournament final. "The Gamecocks showed they could also win with a similar lack of grace." In the first round of the NCAA eastern regionals, held in Greensboro, South Carolina was routed by the University of

Pennsylvania, ranked third in the nation, by the score of 79–64.The crowd, presumably made up of many ACC fans, strongly and vocally supported Penn. The Gamecocks also fell in the consolation game against Fordham University, 100–90. The loss to Fordham was South Carolina's last game as a member of the ACC.[35]

"The UCLA of the East Coast"

Like the University of South Carolina, the University of Maryland's basketball fortunes improved dramatically after the arrival of a new coach. When athletic director Jim Kehoe fired Frank Fellows at the end of the 1968–69 season, he seriously considered only two candidates: Morgan Wootten and Lefty Driesell. Wootten, the coach at nearby DeMatha High School, had graduated from Maryland and ranked among the finest coaches in the country at any level. Kehoe tended to favor Driesell, in part because he had just hired a high school coach for the Maryland football team and was hesitant to do the same in basketball. But his main consideration was Driesell's remarkable performance in building a national power at Davidson. Kehoe was keenly aware that Driesell might not accept an offer from Maryland, especially since he had a strong nucleus of players returning at Davidson and was also a leading candidate to replace Bubas at Duke. Wootten was not certain that he wanted to leave DeMatha, but decided he "would take the job if Lefty turned it down."[36]

After Duke elected to hire Bucky Waters, Driesell faced a tough choice between two enviable options. The salary and benefits that Davidson and Maryland offered were comparable. On March 16, 1969, he announced on his weekly television program in Charlotte that he had decided to accept the Maryland job. "I didn't reach a decision until 4 this morning," he said tearfully. "Five minutes before that I was still going to stay at Davidson." Driesell elected to move to Maryland in part because of his desire to coach in the ACC. "I consider it the strongest conference in the country for basketball," he explained. "I always felt that I could have won a national championship at Davidson and I think now I can do it at Maryland." He seemed impressed by the arguments of Maryland partisans that his chances of achieving his goal were greater in College Park. Driesell also believed that recruiting would be easier at Maryland, partly because admission standards were not as rigorous as those at Davidson and partly because he would be in the middle of an area that was rich in basketball talent.[37]

Driesell arrived at Maryland with a flourish. The day that he was going to be introduced as the new coach, he had breakfast with former Terrapin players Jay McMillen and Joe Harrington, along with Jack Heise, a financial supporter and devoted fan of Maryland athletics. McMillen commented that "Maryland would be a great place for Lefty" and spontaneously suggested that he could make it "like the UCLA of the East." Driesell elaborated on that thought when he spoke to a crowded press conference on March 19, 1969. "I feel that Maryland has the potential to become the UCLA of the East Coast," he declared, "or I wouldn't be here." He made clear his belief that he could "win the national championship" at Maryland and do it "more than one year." Driesell charmed the audience with his "folksy humor." When one reporter asked, presumably in the context of running a basketball program, if he was "austere," Driesell replied: "I don't even know what that word means. Let's get back to some country talk."[38]

Driesell did not need to look up the meaning of "austere" because Kehoe told the press conference that Maryland was "embarking on a new era in basketball" in which the program would be "top drawer, all the way and nothing less." President Elkins added his support by affirming that "we want to excel in basketball." The contrast between the resources extended to Driesell and those provided to his predecessors was most apparent in the size of their staffs. After many years without a full-time assistant, Bud Millikan was able to hire Frank Fellows, who still had to teach classes in the off-season. When Fellows took over, he had one full-time assistant, Tom Young, and a part-time assistant, Tom Davis.

By the time that his first season at Maryland began, Driesell had hired three full-time assistants. At his March 19 press conference, he introduced George Raveling, who was the first black assistant coach in the ACC. Raveling had played and then served as an assistant at Villanova, where he had gained a reputation as an outstanding recruiter. A persistent and persuasive salesman, he gave up a lucrative job with the makers of Converse sneakers to sign on at Maryland. "I wouldn't have done that," he said, "if I didn't have a lot of confidence in Coach Driesell." Driesell arranged to bring Terry Holland, his assistant at Davidson, with him, but the plans fell through when Davidson promoted Holland to head coach in summer 1969. Davidson turned to Holland after its first selection, North Carolina alumnus Larry Brown, changed his mind about accepting the post. Along with Raveling, Driesell hired Jim Maloney, formerly head coach at Niagara University, and Joe Harrington as assistants. Harrington was close to the family of his former teammate, Jay McMillen, and Driesell was already eyeing Jay's younger brother Tom as a top prospect.[39]

Driesell and Raveling hit the recruiting trail immediately after deciding to take on the challenge of coaching at Maryland. Within three days after Driesell announced his decision, they had contacted 80 prospects. They were especially hopeful of signing top players from the local area. "I don't see," Driesell remarked, "why we can't get the three or four best boys in Washington." One poorly conceived part of the effort to land players who fit that category soon caused embarrassment to the university and commanded the attention of the NCAA. On March 31, 1969, a full-page advertisement appeared in the *Washington Post* under the heading, "We Want You." It featured photographs of four of the leading prospects in the Washington area—James Brown (who later achieved fame as a football broadcaster), Jim O'Brien, Floyd Lewis, and Dave Freitag. The ad told the players that Maryland wanted them because they could "successfully meet the matchless academic and athletic challenges presented at the University." It also suggested that they could "bring exciting basketball back to the Baltimore-Washington area" and "help bring the NCAA Championship to its rightful place . . . the Nation's Capital."[40]

The advertisement was Raveling's idea and was sponsored by the M Club, an organization of former Maryland athletes, and the Terrapin Club, the chief booster and fund-raising group. It is unclear whether Driesell knew about the poster before it was published, but it was soon unmistakably clear that Elkins was greatly displeased with it. He summoned Kehoe to his office to tell him that that he thought the advertisement was "in bad taste and brought discredit both to the University and the sport." Elkins instructed Kehoe to "reprimand the athletic staff members who had had any part in the advertisement." The NCAA conducted an investigation and concluded that the poster "placed intercollegiate athletics, NCAA member institutions, and the association itself in a poor light." It issued a formal reprimand of the university but did not impose penalties for the infraction. The punishment might have been stiffer if the NCAA had determined that the university was directly involved in preparing and paying for the advertisement. Jack Heise had written a personal check to cover the costs, and this might have shielded the university from harsher sanctions. The ad proved to be of limited effectiveness; Jim O'Brien was the only player pictured to enroll at Maryland.[41]

When the 1969–70 season got underway, Maryland's performance showed substantial improvement under Driesell's guidance. The team finished the season with a record of 13–13 with four of the same starters who had gone 8–18 the previous year. Driesell used the coaching techniques that had worked so well for him at Davidson. He drove himself and his assistant coaches relentlessly. He regularly put in 14–16 hour days recruiting, promoting his program, and drilling his team, and he expected his staff to do the same. "I would never do that again, go to a school as low as Maryland was," Driesell later remarked. "Life is too short." He ran carefully planned practices and prepared meticulously for games. He had his assistants splice film strips as a means of figuring out ways to beat an opponent. He had his team practice plays from five different locations on the court that could be run when time was running out in a game.[42]

Driesell was notoriously tough and demanding with his players. "There was a whole new pressure in practice," Will Hetzel, a second-team All-ACC player on the 1969–70 squad and brother of former Davidson star Fred Hetzel, later commented. "George Raveling and Lefty were terrors." A player who made a mistake during practice would be sharply reminded that Maryland would never win a national championship if such lapses were not corrected. Driesell berated his players in practice and for as long as "a full hour" after losses, which stirred wonder at the ferocity of his temper and sometimes resentment. When he coached at Davidson, his team once voted against accepting an invitation to the NIT, at least in part because of fatigue with Driesell's carping. "Coaching is not a popularity contest," Driesell said in response to questions about his players' complaints. "But I think my players know I'll go to war for them if I think they're getting a raw deal in life."[43]

In contrast to the mixed emotions among his players, Driesell quickly won idolatrous support from many Maryland fans. One of his top priorities was to create an atmosphere at Cole Field House that would give his teams an advantage, which was rarely the case when Millikan and Fellows were coaching. The permanent stands in the arena were far removed from the court, and Driesell wanted to place folding chairs on the floor, which was customary for NCAA games played at Cole. Kehoe was told that this could not be done during the regular season because gym classes lasted until 3:00 in the afternoon, too late to set up chairs. Driesell then asked Kehoe if he could have his folding chairs by showing that they could be in place by 5:00 in the afternoon after classes ended. Kehoe agreed, and Driesell enlisted coaches, students, and anyone else he could find to move chairs. The job was finished by 4:30, and Kehoe kept his part of the bargain.

Driesell generated excitement that attracted fans to cheer his teams and watch his antics. Early in his first season, he emerged from the locker room as the pep band played "Hail to the Chief" and flashed a "V" sign at the

Lefty Driesell, 1970. (*Terrapin*, Special Collections, University of Maryland Libraries)

crowd. "When the fans think you're going to get beat you have to come up with something," he said. The gesture became a ritual that never failed to bring a roar from the crowd. After his teams improved, Driesell stopped using the "V" sign because he no longer viewed it as necessary to fire up the fans. Another tradition began at Maryland in the wake of a 40-foot desperation shot that Hetzel hit to defeat Duke in 1970. The pep band, to the delight of home fans and the immense irritation of opponents, played the spiritual "Amen" after a victory and sometimes before the game ended. In Driesell's first season, Maryland led the ACC in attendance. Cole Field House was still the largest arena in the conference, and it no longer seemed like a neutral court to visiting teams.[44]

Driesell's second season showed only a slight improvement. The team finished with a record of 14–12, and its 5–9 conference record was the same as the previous year. But there were memorable moments during the season, especially the 31–30 overtime victory over South Carolina before a delirious home crowd. And the future looked bright. The two leading scorers were sophomores who had been members of Driesell's first recruiting class. Jim O'Brien averaged 16.3 points and 7.8 rebounds while guard Howard White averaged 15.6 points. Even better, the freshman team went undefeated and was regarded as the best in the country. It included four prized recruits who seemed to make Driesell's quest for a national championship a realistic goal. They were Mark Cartwright, a 7-footer from Illinois, 6'9" center Len Elmore and guard Jap Trimble from Power Memorial High School in New York, and Tom McMillen, whom *Sports Illustrated* described as the "focus of one of the most intense, bitter recruiting hassles in history." Despite their youth, the magazine named the Terrapins the fifth-best team in the country in its preseason rankings in 1971.[45]

The Recruiting Circus

The excellence of the talent that Driesell brought to Maryland in his first two years highlighted the importance of recruiting in the success of ACC teams. It was axiomatic, of course, that winning programs depended on landing top high school players year after year, and conference rivals often engaged in hard-fought, head-to-head recruiting battles. In the history of the ACC, the outcome of the recruiting wars had proven to be decisive several times in rearranging the power structure of the league. This occurred when Lennie Rosenbluth went to North Carolina instead of NC State, when Art Heyman wound up at Duke instead of North Carolina, when Len Chappell chose Wake Forest over other ACC schools, and when Larry Miller picked North Carolina over Duke. Tom McMillen's arrival at Maryland raised hopes among Terrapin fans of a similar shift in power.

As a conference, the ACC had traditionally been successful in attracting great players, both within and outside its geographical region. This was partly a tribute to the caliber of the competition in the conference and the brilliance of its coaches. It was also doubtlessly a result of the considerations that Curry Kirkpatrick listed in ranking the ACC as the nation's best league in 1970: enthusiastic fan support, strong academic programs, warm weather, modern arenas, and "miniskirted dixiecups." Another critical element in the ACC's appeal to scholastic standouts was television. Even after the great success of Castleman D. Chesley's broadcasts of North Carolina's path to the national championship in 1957, conference officials remained concerned about the effects of televising games on attendance. Chesley, with the support of the Pilot Life Insurance Company, began showing an ACC "Game of the Week" during the 1957–58 season, but televising even a limited number of games continued to encounter opposition. During the 1959–60 season, television broadcasts of both ACC football and basketball were suspended because of drops in attendance. Nevertheless, Chesley persisted and eventually expanded his coverage. In 1964, he persuaded the ACC to allow him to broadcast the championship game of the ACC Tournament. In 1971, he added a few weekday evening games to the Saturday "Game of the Week," and the number of broadcasts rose from 9 in 1964 to 17. The areas that received ACC games also grew to include not only the regions in which conference schools were located but also other sections of the East.[46]

The impact of the ACC broadcasts was huge. Gene Corrigan, who worked for the conference in the 1960s and then became Virginia's athletic director, later commented that Chesley was "the guy who made our conference." The reason, he explained, was that television coverage of college basketball was still rare in the 1960s, and the chance to appear on the ACC "Game of the Week" was a key drawing card for top players. For example, Duke's Steve Vacendak, a native of Scranton, Pennsylvania, declared: "I came to Duke because of TV basketball." When Len Elmore was growing up in New York, he knew about the ACC because local stations sometimes carried the "Game of the Week," and he enjoyed watching fellow New Yorker Charles Scott. Elmore, whose defensive, shot-blocking, and rebounding skills drew comparisons to Bill Russell, eventually chose Maryland because he very much liked Driesell and Raveling and because he was impressed with the school's academic programs and abundance of attractive coeds. But he viewed the prospect of playing in the ACC as another important benefit.[47]

The widening audience for ACC telecasts was consistent with the continuing growth in the popularity of college basketball throughout the nation. Attendance at college games increased from about 15 million in 1964 to more than 25 million in 1972. The NCAA championship game was shown on network television for the first time in 1962, but only as a delayed broadcast on ABC's *Wide World of Sports*. In 1968, NBC carried the semifinals and the finals live for the first time. By that time, the NCAA Tournament had taken major strides toward drawing an enormous national audience and acquiring the status of an iconic event.[48]

The growing popularity of college basketball was soon accompanied by

Len Elmore and, in the background, Tom McMillen.
(Special Collections, University of Maryland Libraries)

growing concerns about excesses and abuses in recruiting. The increasing pressure to win games, capture titles, and earn an invitation to the NCAA Tournament made successful recruiting more essential than ever. It was, some college administrators suggested, a "Roman circus." The drive to gain glory and to satisfy fans was nothing new, of course, but by the early 1970s, it was further energized by financial imperatives. Despite rising attendance at games and revenue from television, college athletic programs faced severe financial problems. About 90 percent of them operated in the red, largely because the costs of salaries, scholarships, travel, recruiting, and other items went up much faster than income. This, in turn, intensified the pressure on coaches to recruit players who could fill stadiums and arenas, attract television coverage, and lead teams to bowl games in football and postseason tournaments in basketball. "The pressure to win is a hell of a lot more than just hiring or firing a coach," commented Don Canham, athletic director at the University of Michigan. "It's keeping your whole program going. Recruiting . . . is a necessary evil."

Many coaches and administrators agreed that recruiting pressures and practices were lamentable and getting worse. In 1973, the American Council on Education sponsored a preliminary study on the possibility of updating the famous report on college sports that the Carnegie Foundation for the Advancement of Teaching had published in 1929. The Carnegie Foundation had strongly criticized colleges and universities for offering "subsidies" to athletes. In 1956, the NCAA had finally resolved the bitterly debated issue of subsidies by authorizing its members to grant scholarships to athletes without regard to need. George Hanford, executive vice president of the College Entrance Examination Board, who led a task force that conducted the preliminary investigation for the American Council on Education, concluded that "there's a moral problem in college athletics." Among the recruiting abuses he cited as examples were altering high school transcripts, finding substitutes to take entrance examinations, failing to honor promises for financial assistance, and providing relatives with jobs. Hanford and his colleagues did not focus on cash inducements to prospects, but others suggested that this was another part of recruiting incentives delivered by some schools or their boosters.[49]

The recruiting process, even when carried out according to the rules, was demeaning for coaches and stressful for prospects. The legendary Boston Celtics guard Bob Cousy commented after stepping down as coach at Boston College, "You recruit a kid by licking his boots." James Brown, one of the players targeted in Maryland's "We Want You" advertisement, played at DeMatha High School for Morgan Wootten, who did not tolerate any recruiting transgressions by coaches. Nevertheless, the demands on Brown's time were so great during his senior year that he collapsed during a game from exhaustion. Richard "Digger" Phelps, coach at the University of Notre Dame, blamed the existing system for the strain it imposed on players and their families. "I've seen families change. From the time you start recruiting them in the fall, they think it's fun," he remarked. "By the last week in April, they can't talk to each other. That's how confused they are. That's how uptight they are. I think we've created a monster."[50]

The Recruiting of Tom McMillen

Tom McMillen experienced the monster in extremis. Although the three ACC schools that were finalists in competing for his talent ran clean programs, the burden of making a choice between them was a "sad, painful episode" for him and his family. "I emerged on the verge of a nervous breakdown," he later wrote. His mother called the recruiting marathon "a miserable, miserable time in my life."[51]

McMillen, who grew up in the small college town of Mansfield, Pennsylvania, had caught the attention of college coaches at an early age. When he was 14 and stood 6'4", he attended Dean Smith's basketball camp. The coaches were so impressed with his ability that they sent him to play with the 17-year-old campers, and he still excelled. After he led his high school team to a state championship as a junior, college coaches began to "run amok" in their efforts to recruit him. In February 1970, McMillen's senior year, *Sports Illustrated* ran a cover story in which it called him "the best high school player in America." It cited the array of skills that dazzled coaches, including effective inside moves, great range and shooting touch, and deft ball-handling. McMillen was often compared with Lew Alcindor and Bill Bradley. In the view of college recruiters, *Sports Illustrated* reported, "he may help the school he chooses to the same dominance of college basketball that UCLA enjoyed during Alcindor's varsity years." Like Bradley, McMillen was an outstanding student who wanted to attend a college that offered strong academic programs. At Mansfield High School, he was a straight-A student, president of the student council, first-trombonist in the band, and regional winner of an oratorical contest. "In Tom, you have a rare athlete," George Raveling commented. "He'd be a credit to a school's program even if he never played a minute on the court."[52]

McMillen's parents were familiar with the demands and inconveniences of the recruiting process from their experiences with Tom's brother Jay, who was seven years older. They placed strict limitations on coach's contacts with Tom and encouraged him to narrow the list of schools he might choose to attend. While coaches waited anxiously (though some tried to skirt the family's rules by claiming to be passing through remote Mansfield by happenstance), McMillen averaged 47.7 points and 22 rebounds per game during his senior year. In early April 1970, as the signing date for letters-of-intent grew near, he reduced his list to three ACC schools— Maryland, Virginia, and North Carolina. He invited Driesell, Gibson, and Smith to make one last visit and promised that he would make his decision by April 15.[53]

Each of the final contenders had advantages that their coaches hoped would be decisive. Although Gibson still had not posted a winning record, his 1969–70 team had finished the season with a strong showing in the ACC Tournament and provided reason to believe that Virginia had turned the corner. Gibson thought that McMillen could be the piece he needed to climb to the upper reaches of the ACC. His chances were greatly strengthened by his long-time friendship with the McMillen family, whom he knew well from his coaching tenure at Mansfield State College. Driesell had some strong advantages as well. Jay McMillen had not found his experiences as a player at Maryland altogether satisfactory, but he was convinced that Driesell's arrival would transform the Terrapins into big winners. Further, assistant coach Joe Harrington was a close friend of Jay and regarded as "practically a member of the family." He had spent an entire summer with the McMillens when he was an undergraduate. Shortly after Driesell accepted the job at Maryland in 1969, he offered Harrington a job on his staff and told him that his primary assignment was to recruit McMillen. Driesell's quick wit was also a major asset. McMillen carefully researched the academic quality of the schools on his short list, and on one occasion he told Driesell about his concern that the library at Maryland had many fewer books than those at Virginia and North Carolina. Driesell promptly responded that once McMillen "finished reading every book in Maryland's library," he would personally find him any other book that he wanted.[54]

Dean Smith had a different set of points in his favor. In contrast to Virginia and Maryland, his program was well established and carried what McMillen later called the "Tar Heel mystique." North Carolina had been the first school to show serious interest in him and he both liked and admired Smith and his assistant coaches. After listening to the coaches of his top three choices make their pitches, McMillen went off by himself for two days. He made careful comparisons of what each school had to offer, academically and athletically, and finally made his decision. On April 14, he called Smith and asked: "Coach Smith, how will I look in Carolina blue?" Smith was delighted and got "visibly excited." The results of his recruiting efforts to that time had been disappointing, and he was not sure he would sign any top-tier prospects. McMillen's decision suddenly turned his recruiting campaign into a colossal success. With McMillen's concurrence, he immediately arranged to put out an announcement.[55]

At that juncture, the story of McMillen's recruiting turned into what he later called a "painful episode." He and Smith had agreed to hold a press conference in Mansfield, but the plans changed after McMillen's high school coach, Rich Miller, called Smith to tell him that McMillen's parents strongly disapproved of Tom's decision. McMillen later wrote that he "had greatly underestimated my parents' opposition to Dean and North Carolina." Neither of his parents would sign the letter of intent, which would make it invalid. Margaret McMillen was a strong-willed woman who called herself the "drill sergeant" of the household and suspected that she had acquired "the reputation of an old ogre" with coaches. She wanted her son to attend Virginia because she had a high opinion of Gibson. She had been offended by some of Smith's actions. The most serious affront was that he had urged her son to call Tom Burleson, a heavily recruited prospect from western North Carolina, to discuss playing together at UNC. Margaret McMillen insisted that Tom should not make such a call because it would inappropriately make him a recruiter for North Carolina. When Tom placed the call anyway, she was incensed. She was not placated by Smith's attempt to "downplay the situation."

McMillen's father, James, who strongly favored Maryland, was equally indignant about Tom's decision. He wanted his son to sign with Maryland in part because it would be much easier to attend games in College Park than in Charlottesville or Chapel Hill and in part because he liked Driesell, whom he described as a "man's man." The elder McMillen was a dentist who had always taken great pride in the athletic achievements of Jay and Tom but who also pushed them very hard. He incessantly demanded perfection and criticized his sons harshly when they fell short of impossible standards. Dr. McMillen left no doubt about his unhappiness with Tom's choice of colleges. At about the same time, Jay, who had not pressed Tom to attend Maryland, began to talk up the advantages of his alma mater. In the conditions that followed his selection of North Carolina, Tom found Jay's advocacy of Maryland annoying. His choice of schools, rather than ending the pressure of the recruiting process, produced unanticipated and highly unwelcome family strife.[56]

In light of his family's reaction, McMillen carefully reassessed his decision. After a few weeks, he reached the same conclusion. On June 23, 1970, he told an elated Smith that he still wished to attend North Carolina and that he was prepared to sign a letter of intent even without his parents' consent. Both Smith and McMillen were aware that the letter would not be binding without the signature of a parent, but Tom hoped that it would "diminish the zeal of recruiters from other schools and the hostility of my family." Smith also suggested that announcing McMillen's plans to enroll at North Carolina "might take some of the heat off Tommy." As a smiling Smith looked on at a restaurant in Elmira, New York, about 20 miles from Mansfield, McMillen signed what was purported to be a letter of intent and was in fact a napkin.[57]

The staged signing ceremony backfired. Rather than reducing the heat, it created new tensions. McMillen's parents were furious. "This is nasty, dirty business," James McMillen said. "We are grief stricken." His wife told the press that "we absolutely will not sign the grant, now or ever." She did not blame her son for what had happened because "he's been brainwashed," but she complained bitterly that a "coach can't step in and take over parental duties." A few days later, after newspapers across the country ran stories about conflicts within the McMillen family, Dr. McMillen announced that news reports had "grossly misinterpreted and exaggerated our reaction to Tom's decision." He said that family members were "perfectly content" with Tom's choice of colleges. But McMillen's parents did not sign a letter of intent, and Smith, trying to smooth over the ill will that the Elmira "signing" had created, did not ask them to do so. Tom remained committed to North Carolina, but deferred further action to seal his enrollment while he played with the U.S. Olympic Development Team in Europe.[58]

Getting away from the divisions and "hypertense" situation at home allowed McMillen to clear his mind and rethink his decision. He realized that he "would probably be happy at any of the three schools" on his list. "They're all members of the Atlantic Coast Conference," he explained, "and offer about the same combination of basketball, academics, and social life." Although he still leaned toward North Carolina, a series of considerations began to push him toward Maryland. When he returned from Europe, he learned that his father was "very sick." This made him feel "enormously guilty over the stress under which we had all been living." It also reminded him that playing at North Carolina would cause hardship for his father, who "had never missed a single one of my games." Further, McMillen had just been appointed as the youngest member ever of the President's Council on Physical Fitness and Sports, a position he took very seriously, and attending Maryland would allow him to participate actively in the organization's work. Finally, and most importantly, by the end of the summer, he could evaluate the recruiting classes of the three schools. North Carolina had not signed Burleson, who opted for NC State, and Virginia "was even thinner in freshman talent." Maryland, on the other hand, "had hit the jackpot." McMillen was especially impressed that Elmore would be a teammate at Maryland. With Elmore at center, McMillen would be able to play forward, which he regarded as his best position.[59]

McMillen was still mulling over those variables only a few hours before he had to register for the fall semester. North Carolina thought he was coming to Chapel Hill. Bill Gibson had arranged for a private plane to fly McMillen from Mansfield to Charlottesville if needed. Jay McMillen was at home and ready to drive his brother to College Park. When Tom packed his bags for college, he still was not certain where he was going. After staying up for most of the night talking to his father and brother, McMillen ended the drama the next morning by loading his bags in Jay's car and heading to College Park. He later reflected on the recruiting ordeal. "I'm just glad it can only happen to you once," he observed. "And now that it's over, I want to put it all behind me and never, never think about it again."[60]

"A New Personality" at College Park

After McMillen and Elmore (until he injured a knee) led their freshman team to a record of 16–0, the expectations for Maryland's performance when they joined the varsity for the 1971–72 season were extraordinarily high. The chief cheerleader was their coach, who made no secret of his ambitions. "They were told they would win a national championship when they were recruited," he said, "That's their aim." It was soon clear that talk of a national title was premature for a team that was young and unproven in ACC competition. After two easy victories to open the season, the Terrapins suffered a rude introduction to conference play when they were trounced at Virginia, 78–57. As they continued to struggle in defeating weak opponents, Curry Kirkpatrick suggested that they were plagued with "the dread overpromotion pox, the dread press-release measles, and the dread bighead mumps."[61]

Maryland gradually began to jell and took a 12–2 record into a showdown with North Carolina at Chapel Hill. Dean Smith pleaded with UNC students to treat McMillen, who had been reviled by Tar Heel fans after his decision to attend Maryland, in a civil manner. North Carolina fans responded by giving McMillen a standing ovation when he was introduced. Then they cheered their team to a 92–72 victory. The Terrapins rebounded to finish the regular season with a record of 21–4, including a heart-stopping overtime win over North Carolina at Cole Field House. In the ACC Tournament, they defeated Clemson and Virginia but fell to North Carolina in the title game. It was the first time since 1958 that Maryland had reached the tournament finals. The team happily accepted an invitation to the NIT, and it swept four games to capture the championship. "This is the greatest game I've ever had," Driesell remarked after the win in the finals, "because it's the first national championship I've ever had." He still set his sights on the other national championship, but by any standard, Maryland's young team turned in a splendid performance.[62]

In his first three years at Maryland, Driesell elevated a struggling program into a national power. He won games, brought in top recruits, challenged the powers of the ACC, packed Cole Field House, and created unprecedented excitement over basketball at the university. "Dreisell has given College Park a new personality," Bill Tanton, sports editor of the *Baltimore Evening Sun*, wrote. "He has brought [the campus] to life in a way that no one else has ever done. . . . I didn't see how any one man could transform lackadaisical Maryland into the UCLA of the East . . . But now I can see how Lefty Driesell can do it." Driesell accomplished what he was hired to do, and the prospects for even greater achievements looked exceedingly favorable.[63]

What Driesell did not do was to project an image that enhanced the reputation of the University of Maryland as an academic institution. This was not a part of his job, of course, but the actions and statements of a nationally prominent coach inevitably influenced how the entire university was viewed from the outside. Although Driesell took genuine interest in the academic performance of his players, his public posture as an unschooled country boy was hardly consistent with the university's efforts to upgrade its academic standards and standing. This was a sensitive issue at Maryland because Elkins had made great strides in overcoming the academic deficiencies that had existed under President Byrd. But the university's reputation still suffered from the legacy of Byrd's misplaced priorities. Driesell's program seemed to some to be a throwback. After the "We Want You" advertisement appeared in 1969, the *Charlotte Observer* editorialized that it suggested a return to an era "that nearly destroyed Maryland as an institution of higher learning." Driesell gave credence to such perceptions by claiming not to know the meaning of words such as "austere" and "potential." This was presumably an act on his part—he had degrees from two prestigious institutions—but others appeared to find it convincing. Duke students paraded around Cameron Indoor Stadium with a cari-

Tom McMillen soars to basket as North Carolina's Bill Chamberlain (31), Robert McAdoo (35), and Dennis Wuycik (44) watch, 1972. (Courtesy The North Carolina State Archives; reprinted by permission of *The News and Observer* of Raleigh, North Carolina)

cature that showed Driesell's high forehead painted to look like a car's fuel gauge with the needle on empty. North Carolina fans taunted their rivals at Duke by saying that there had to be something wrong with a school that taught law to Richard Nixon and English to Lefty Driesell.[64]

Driesell was proud of the fact that the players he recruited in his first two years at Maryland had average SAT scores that exceeded 1,000, even before McMillen arrived. They were outstanding representatives of the improving quality of the university, academically as well as the athletically. Bill Millsaps later remarked, only partly in jest, that Maryland might have had the "smartest teams in the history of ACC basketball" during the Elmore-McMillen era. There would be a great deal of competition for such an award, but the point that the first players Driesell recruited brought great credit to the university was clear. This was a substantial and perhaps a pivotal contribution to what was a huge, amorphous, and impersonal institution. Although Maryland had many strong academic programs, its students did not generally demonstrate the same pride in and affection for their university that was commonly found at some other ACC schools. Undergraduates at North Carolina, Duke, and Virginia, for example, had a high opinion of the virtues of their institutions and did not hesitate to make their views known. Maryland's basketball teams of the early 1970s provided a sense of pride and community to a school that was often short of both. And this was a key element of the "new personality at College Park" that eventually extended far beyond the basketball court.[65]

NC State on the Move

Along with South Carolina and Maryland, North Carolina State emerged as a leading challenger to North Carolina's dominance in the early 1970s. When Press Maravich resigned as State's coach on April 30, 1966, the search for his successor quickly came down to three candidates, Virginia's Bill Gibson and two NC State alumni who had played for Everett Case: Mel Thompson, head coach at The Citadel, and Norm Sloan, head coach at the University of Florida. Soon after Gibson removed himself from consideration, athletic director Roy Clogston offered the job to Sloan. The appointment was announced on May 7, 1966. "It's something I've always dreamed about," Sloan commented.[66]

Sloan grew up in Indiana and was a part of the first recruiting class that Case brought to NC State in 1946. After a high school teacher who knew Case recommended him, he paid his own bus fare to Raleigh to visit the

State College campus. Case offered him a scholarship without even seeing him "bounce a ball." After three years on Case's powerful teams, he became dissatisfied with his playing time. He was a backup guard behind Vic Bubas, and, convinced that he should be starting, told Case that he was better than Bubas. Case immediately ended the conversation by saying, "No, you're not." Partly because of his limited playing time and partly because he was told that his best chance to land a coaching job after graduation was to gain experience in both basketball and football, Sloan quit the basketball team. He played football for two years, participated in track, and became the last athlete at NC State to earn a letter in three sports. Despite leaving the basketball team, he greatly admired Case. "Coach Case was one of the most exciting experiences of my life," he recalled many years later. "He made [basketball] so exciting and so meaningful, there wasn't anything mundane about any game or any practice."[67]

Sloan graduated from State College in 1951 and found a job as the head basketball coach and an assistant football coach at Presbyterian College in Clinton, South Carolina. He also coached golf, which he had played "three or four times," and served as an assistant track coach. In four seasons, his basketball teams won 69 games and lost 36. He moved on to Memphis State as a basketball assistant for one year, and then accepted the head coaching position at The Citadel in 1956. In four years at a military school where recruiting was always difficult, he achieved a record of 57–38 and was named Southern Conference Coach of the Year. His success at The Citadel led to an offer from the University of Florida, where he took over a team that had gone 6–16 in 1959–60. Sloan proved his ability once again by turning around a floundering program. In his first season at Florida, he was selected as Southeastern Conference Coach of the Year after guiding his team to a record of 15–11. In six years, he won 85 games while losing 63, including Florida's best-ever record of 18–7 in 1964–65.[68]

Sloan arrived at NC State with a reputation as an excellent coach. He worked his players and assistants hard but won their loyalty. "Norm was misunderstood by a lot of people who didn't really know him," his longtime assistant Sam Esposito once commented. "He was a great guy to work for." Sloan also had a fiery temperament. He earned the nickname of "Stormin' Norman," which he hated but admitted he deserved. "I'm an intense person and I guess it shows," he said. During a game at Maryland in 1967, he became "as upset as I have ever been in a basketball game" over what he regarded as missed calls by officials in a close contest. When he questioned the fortitude of one of the referees, George Conley, he was assessed a technical foul. He objected and received another technical. Again he protested in a less than discreet manner. At that point, Conley ended the game with 1:15 left on the clock and Maryland leading by five points. NC State chancellor Caldwell agreed that Conley was "wrong in stopping the game" but reminded Sloan that "it behooves you . . . to restrain yourself appropriately and avoid incurring technicals." Sloan's short temper could make him "brutal" in criticizing his players when they made mistakes. He would sometimes schedule a practice at 4:00 A.M. to punish his team for a bad game. But he got over his anger quickly.[69]

Most of Sloan's players learned to live with his outbursts and to appreciate his coaching prowess, and he was steadfastly supportive of them. His loyalty was evident on one occasion in the early 1970s when he accidentally ran into Bill Gibson at a golf club near Gastonia, North Carolina. The two coaches got into a loud, animated argument over who was the best center in the ACC, State's Tom Burleson or Maryland's Len Elmore. Neither Sloan nor Gibson would give any ground, and the tenacity of their debate astonished other patrons at the club. It finally ended only after Sloan's wife, Joan, prevailed on his golfing partner, Charlie Bryant, to intervene. Sloan's friend, Marquette University coach Al McGuire, remarked that "you always knew where you stood with him . . . You could look at him and know by his face whether he was in your corner or an opponent." Although Sloan's flashes of temper were short in duration, he held lingering grudges toward some administrators and rival coaches. McGuire suggested that "he spent too much time envying Dean Smith, when he could have taken notes on how to be a smoothie."[70]

Sloan began his tenure at his alma mater with a severe shortage of talent. Seven of the top eight scorers on the previous year's squad had graduated. The only one who returned was Eddie Biedenbach, who had led the team with a 16.2 average. But he injured his back and missed the entire season. The prospects for the future were dimmed when several recruits bailed out after Maravich resigned. Sloan asked Charlie Bryant, whom he retained as assistant coach, if there were any good high school players available to sign. Bryant mentioned a "skinny kid," Vann Williford, who had not been highly recruited but who had led his team to the North Carolina state championship. Without any offers from big-time schools, he had decided to attend Pfeiffer College in North Carolina. He had always dreamed of playing for NC State and was delighted to change his plans and accept a scholarship from Sloan. The lightly regarded Williford worked hard to develop his skills and eventually became a two-time, first-team All-Conference performer.

During his freshman season of 1966–67, Sloan's varsity sank to the bottom of the ACC with a record of 7–19 overall, 2–12 in the conference.[71]

The following season, Biedenbach returned and made All-Conference first team. The much-improved Wolfpack tied for third in the regular season standings at 9–5 and went 16–10 overall. This set the stage for the tournament game that ranks among the most bizarre in ACC history. In the semifinals, State met a Duke team that was ranked sixth in the country and had won their matchups during the season by large margins. Blue Devil center Mike Lewis had dominated both games, and Sloan decided to limit his effectiveness by drawing him away from the basket. He ordered his undersized center, Bill Kretzer, to stand at midcourt and hold the ball. To Sloan's surprise, Bubas, afraid that State's superior quickness would prevail, told Lewis to stay under the basket. The game ground to a halt, and Duke led at half, 4–2. The second half was equally uneventful, and the crowd became increasingly disgruntled. At one point, Joan Sloan sent her son down to the bench to tell his father, "Mama wants to know what's going on." What went on at the end was that NC State won the game, 12–10, on a last-second put-back of a missed shot. "It was pure coaching genius, even though we never planned on holding the ball," Williford later commented. "In the end, Norm completely outcoached [Bubas], because he knew how stubborn Bubas was." Newspapers derided the game as "The Refrigerator Bowl" and "The Great Ice Show," but NC State supporters were ecstatic, and Sloan was unapologetic. "I'm hired to try to win," he told reporters. State, which Sloan later acknowledged "had no business being in the final," lost to North Carolina, 87–50.[72]

In 1968–69, Williford led the Wolfpack to a record of 15–10 and a tie for third place in the ACC regular season standings. The following season, it improved to 19–6 during the regular season, for a second-place tie with North Carolina, as Williford averaged 23.7 points and 10 rebounds. In the tournament, State defeated Maryland and edged Virginia to reach the finals against South Carolina. Once again, Sloan used a slow-down strategy as a means of neutralizing South Carolina's huge height advantage. With Roche hobbled by an ankle injury, State pulled off a 42–39 upset in double overtime. Despite a loss in the first round of the NCAA Tournament, the season produced Sloan's first ACC championship and recognition as conference Coach of the Year. The team finished with national rankings of 10th in the AP poll and 12th in the UPI poll. Shortly after the season ended, hopes for even greater glory soared when Tom Burleson announced that he would attend NC State.[73]

Norm Sloan, seated next to his players, 1969. To his left are assistant coaches Charlie Bryant and Sam Esposito. (Courtesy The North Carolina State Archives; reprinted by permission of *The News and Observer* of Raleigh, North Carolina)

Burleson grew up on a farm in the mountains of western North Carolina in a family of modest means. At Avery County High School in Newland, which had a population of 550, he led his teams to a record of 112–10 in four years. His talent and his size attracted the attention of more than 300 colleges, including North Carolina, Duke, and NC State. When he was a 6′8″ eighth grader, he traveled to Raleigh on a 4-H Club trip with his uncle, Ben Ware, who was a graduate of NC State and the only member of his family to attend college. After touring the school of agriculture, Ware decided they should drop by the basketball office. When they entered Bryant's office, Ware asked whether State would be interested in recruiting his nephew. Bryant took the visitors into Sloan's office, and the coaches quickly agreed that they would indeed be interested. Esposito later described the scene: "Burleson walked in and he had to bend down to keep from hitting his head coming in the door. We almost had a heart attack."[74]

Although State faced stiff competition in recruiting Burleson, it had many assets in its favor. Ware wanted his nephew to sign with State. Burleson's parents were greatly taken with both Sloan and his wife. Burleson planned to major in agriculture and was impressed with State's program. And, despite his success as a high school player, he was not certain that he was good enough to play for North Carolina or Duke. In November 1969, Burleson's father, Loren, called Sloan to tell him that Tom had decided on State. But he insisted that Sloan not make an announcement because some of Tom's teachers were North Carolina fans, and he worked at Grandfather Mountain, a resort owned by Hugh Morton, a friend of Dean Smith and a staunch Tar Heel supporter. Sloan kept up appearances by faithfully attending Burleson's games. When Burleson announced his decision in spring 1970, an angry Smith lashed out at Sloan for the deception. "They didn't tell anybody. Maybe Norm wanted me to spend my time recruiting [Burleson] instead of anybody else," Smith complained. "I spent a lot of time going to the mountains to show interest." Sloan replied that he had "only followed the wishes of the Burleson family" and that he would "have loved to announce that Tommy was going to sign with us" because it "would have helped our recruiting."[75]

Burleson was, Sloan later wrote, "the biggest recruiting success we ever had." He was thin and at times looked gawky, but he was an excellent athlete who had more than his 7'4" height to contribute to his team. He was remarkably agile, with soft hands, a deft touch, and a devastating hook shot. He was also, Sloan approvingly noted, a "fierce competitor." Burleson worked hard to gain strength and to improve his skills, and the results were apparent when he played for the freshman team in 1970–71. He averaged 26.1 points and 15.4 rebounds for a squad that went 14–2. In his first season on the varsity, he placed second in the ACC in scoring with an average of 21.3 points and led the conference in rebounding with a 14.0 average. NC State had an overall record of 16–10 and tied for fourth in the regular season standings. After the season ended, Burleson's accomplishments and his reputation were severely marred when he acquired a key to campus pinball machines and stole money from them. By the time he was caught, he had taken a total of $117. Burleson was mortified and offered an apology for the "embarrassment" he had caused the university and its supporters. He later explained that the impact of his actions did not fully register until he went to court and saw the two children of the man who owned the machines. "The kids looked up to me. In fact, they even asked me for my autograph," he said. "For the first time, I realized that [it] wasn't just quarters I had taken, but food right out of the kids' mouths." Burleson's misconduct, he said, gave him "extra determination" to provide State fans with a "good team" the following season. He would have plenty of help to achieve that

Tom Burleson shoots over the entire Duke team, 1972. In the first row behind
the basket, North Carolina's John Lotz, Virginia's Bill Gibson and Chip Conner,
and Maryland's Joe Harrington and George Raveling watch with interest.
(Courtesy The North Carolina State Archives; reprinted by permission of
The News and Observer of Raleigh, North Carolina)

goal, especially with the arrival of an extraordinarily gifted player, David
Thompson.[76]

Thompson's skills had made him a legend in North Carolina even as a
player at Crest High School in Shelby. Eddie Biedenbach, who joined the
NC State staff after Bryant resigned, told Sloan after watching Thompson
play for the first time, "This is the best guy I have ever seen." Thompson
was particularly well known for his sensational leaping ability, but he was
also an exceptional scorer, rebounder, and defensive player. He was highly
sought by many colleges, and for a time North Carolina appeared to have
the inside track. Thompson admired Smith and had grown up watching
Charles Scott on television. He began to rethink his choice of schools after
Biedenbach asked, "Do you want to go to North Carolina and follow in the
footsteps of Charlie Scott or do you want to go to North Carolina State and
forge your own identity?" Thompson found the question "so profound" that
he reexamined his options in a whole new light.[77]

Thompson was the youngest of eleven children in a hardworking but poor family who lived in a cinder-block house on an unpaved road. As speculation about his choice of schools grew, he had trouble making up his mind. Finally, he decided on NC State, in part because he would have the opportunity to make his "own mark" and in part because with Burleson enrolled at State, he "knew that Coach Sloan was building something special in Raleigh." Sloan, of course, was elated, but within a short time, he was facing accusations of breaking NCAA rules to recruit Thompson. Both the ACC and the NCAA launched thorough investigations of the allegations. ACC commissioner Robert C. James, who had taken the job when Jim Weaver died suddenly on July 11, 1970, concluded that NC State had not offered illegal inducements or excessive aid to Thompson and his family. He found no evidence to support charges that university supporters had paid to have the road to the Thompson home paved. James faulted Sloan and his staff for other "acts of poor judgment" that occurred after Thompson signed his letter of intent. They included allowing Thompson to stay in a dormitory room with friends from his hometown during Sloan's basketball camp in June 1971, and holding pickup games on campus in which Thompson and Biedenbach participated (which qualified as a "tryout"). In December 1971, James issued a formal reprimand of Sloan and Biedenbach that carried no penalties. Chancellor Caldwell responded that he viewed James's "investigation as thorough and fair" and his "findings valid."[78]

The NCAA's investigation supported James's conclusions but resulted in a much harsher punishment. It uncovered no convincing evidence that Sloan, his staff, or boosters had made illicit offers in order to lure Thompson to NC State. Like James, the NCAA cited several violations of existing rules after Thompson made his decision. In the mind of the NCAA, the violations merited stern discipline. On October 24, 1972, it announced that it had placed NC State on probation for one year, which meant that the Wolfpack could not participate in the NCAA Tournament in 1973. Caldwell, who had taken strong action after the point-shaving scandal in 1961 and who had ordered changes to correct the problems that James reported, found the NCAA's sanctions unjustified. He commented that "we remain convinced that the University in no respect violated the Association's rules knowingly or willfully or in fact," though he admitted that Sloan had failed to exercise "hard-nosed vigilance" on procedural technicalities. Sloan was outraged that a series of "administrative mistakes" consigned NC State to the same category as "notorious cheaters . . . who gained an advantage by violating recruiting rules." Despite the blow from the NCAA, it was clear that Sloan had built a powerful team at NC State that now had an additional incentive to excel.[79]

Signs of Improvement at Wake Forest and Clemson

When Bones McKinney resigned as Wake Forest's coach in September 1965, Jack Murdock was named "acting head coach" for the season that was soon to begin. The college's administrators, including Athletic Director Gene Hooks, agreed that the basketball program, "which had been retrogressing badly," would be carefully reviewed at the end of the season. During the 1965–66 campaign, Wake slumped to an overall record of 8–18 and tied Virginia for last in the conference under Murdock. This convinced Hooks and his colleagues to look for another coach whose teams had "done well academically as well as in basketball." After conducting its search, Wake hired "one of the nation's outstanding young mentors," Jack McCloskey, head coach at the University of Pennsylvania. As a student at Penn, McCloskey had played football, basketball, and baseball. He was good enough in baseball to be signed to a professional contract by the Philadelphia Athletics and to play in the minor leagues for four years. At the same time, he played professional basketball in the Eastern League, where he made the All-Star team five times and was named Most Valuable Player twice. He began his coaching career at the high school level and went to Penn as assistant basketball coach and head baseball coach in 1954. He became head basketball coach two years later, and in ten years, his Penn teams won 146 games and lost 105. His 1965–66 squad won the Ivy League championship but did not participate in the NCAA Tournament because of a dispute between the Ivy League and the NCAA over grade requirements for athletes.[80]

McCloskey took the Wake Forest job in part because of his frustration that the Ivy League had denied his team a trip to the NCAA Tournament. He brought an outstanding record, deep knowledge of the game, and exceptional toughness. "Jack McCloskey was a tough, excellent basketball man, a real student of the game," Billy Packer recalled. "He was very tough physically himself and was very demanding as far as toughness was concerned." If sufficiently agitated, McCloskey displayed what he called his "'County Cork' temper." When a Wake fan complained in a provocative manner after a loss to Duke in 1970, for example, he responded bluntly that "you know nothing about personnel and basketball."[81]

McCloskey and his two assistants, Packer and former NBA star Neil

Jack McCloskey and Charlie Davis, 1970. (Courtesy The North Carolina State Archives; reprinted by permission of *The News and Observer* of Raleigh, North Carolina)

Johnston, set out to restore Wake basketball to its former eminence. After two years of turmoil in the basketball program, they lacked the talent they needed, with the exception of first-team All-ACC selection Paul Long, to achieve their goal promptly. McCloskey's first two teams at Wake finished 9–18 in 1966–67, and 5–21 in 1967–68, which placed them in a tie for last place in the conference. The following year, Charlie Davis joined the varsity, and Wake improved dramatically. Davis used the skills that had made him a legend on the New York playgrounds to reach the same status at Wake Forest. He was 6′1″ and weighed only about 145 pounds, but his slender frame did not prevent him from scoring from all over the court, frequently against double-teaming defenses. During his three-year career, he averaged 24.9 points by hitting jumpers from long range or driving to the basket. He made 46.0 percent of his field-goal attempts and 87.3 percent of his free throws, and in 1971, he became the first African American to be named ACC Player of the Year. Davis led Wake Forest back to respectability with records of 18–9, 14–13, and 16–10.[82]

Wake's Board of Trustees and administration were pleased with the progress under McCloskey. In June 1969, the trustees voted to increase his salary to $16,000, which was $2,000 higher than his contract stipulated. James Ralph Scales, who had replaced Harold Tribble as president, advised

McCloskey that the raise reflected "unanimous agreement that it is a valid and appropriate investment toward the future of basketball at Wake Forest." The following year, the university extended his contract for five years, because, Scales told him, "we are delighted with your work." School officials and fans were considerably less delighted after the team slumped to 8–18 in 1971–72, the year after Davis departed. When McCloskey resigned in 1972 to become head coach of the NBA's Portland Trailblazers, Athletic Director Hooks suggested that "it was a blessing that he was offered another job" because "he was under a lot of pressure and criticism from our people." The major complaint was that McCloskey had failed to recruit top players except Davis. Wake hired Carl Tacy, head coach at Marshall University, and Hooks reported that "in only five weeks" he had recruited "potentially the best talent since the freshman team of Len Chappell."[83]

Like Wake Forest when it hired McCloskey and again when it hired Tacy, Clemson University hoped that a new coach would reverse its sagging basketball fortunes. In the middle of a third consecutive wretched season, Bobby Roberts resigned under pressure in February 1970. Clemson supporters were particularly troubled that their program had struggled at the same time that archrival South Carolina had taken off. President Edwards declared that "we have no intention of playing second fiddle athletically or otherwise to any other member institution in the Atlantic Coast Conference" and that "we are determined to be Number 1." On March 18, 1970, Clemson signed the coach it hoped would carry out its objective in basketball, 33-year-old Taylor O. "Tates" Locke. Locke had proven his coaching ability at the U.S. Military Academy, where his teams placed third in the NIT in 1964 and again in 1965. He then moved on to Miami University in Ohio. He took his team to the NCAA Tournament in 1969 and was named Mid-American Conference Coach of the Year. The following season, Miami went to the NIT. Locke came to Clemson with a reputation as a "stern, iron-fisted automaton" who instilled tight discipline and insisted that his teams play hardnosed defense. Locke was, *Sports Illustrated* once reported, "as high-strung, aggressive, and gung-ho over college coaching as anyone has ever seen."[84]

Locke had no illusions about the difficulty of winning in the ACC when he took over at Clemson. He set a goal of "moving up" in the conference in three years and reaching "full stature" in five years. "Right now," he said, "we're five years behind the rest of the league." Shortly after arriving at Clemson, Locke concluded that he could not win in the ACC without cheating. He desperately needed a point guard, and the player he wanted,

Bo Hawkins, did not have the grades at his junior college to qualify for admission to Clemson. With the collaboration of a Clemson official in the registrar's office and an academic adviser, Locke overcame this obstacle by altering Hawkins's transcript. "Sneaking Bo Hawkins into Clemson was the worst thing I had ever allowed myself to be party to in my years of college coaching," Locke later wrote. "Within two years, it would seem to be minor compared to the stunts we pulled." The "stunts" included providing players or their families with cars and cash as incentives for signing with Clemson, paid for by well-heeled alumni. Locke knew that those practices were flagrant violations of NCAA rules. "I did it," he said, "because I just got tired of getting my ass beat in the ACC."[85]

Locke's illegal activities enabled him to make Clemson competitive in the ACC. The records of his teams gradually improved from 9–17 in his first season to 17–11 and a trip to the NIT in 1974–75. His tenure at Clemson ended abruptly when he was forced to resign in 1975 as a result of the NCAA's investigation of his transgressions. The NCAA placed Clemson on probation for three years for "serious violations spanning several years" that included "significant benefits and inducements to prospective and enrolled student-athletes." The most outrageous of a long list of violations was Locke's offer to buy a house for the mother of Moses Malone, an extraordinarily talented and heavily recruited 6'11" prospect who decided in 1974 to go directly into professional basketball rather than playing in college.[86]

Virginia's "Delightful" Season

The surprising success of the "Amazin' Cavaliers" in 1970–71, who produced Virginia's first winning season in 17 years, was a prelude to greater glory. With four starters returning, Gibson's team had experience, rapport, and confidence. Picked to finish in fifth place in the ACC by the league's coaches, Virginia used improved defensive pressure and explosive offensive displays to show that it was far superior to preseason predictions. It opened the season with 12 straight victories, including a first-time ever win at Duke Indoor Stadium, a triumph over Wake Forest on the road for the first time since 1959, and a rout of highly ranked Maryland before a full-throated home crowd. Virginia was ranked eighth in the nation when it met number three, North Carolina, at University Hall in what Gibson said "could well be the biggest regular season game Virginia has ever played." After a narrow loss to the Tar Heels, Virginia won its next six games to earn a record of 18–1 and a national ranking of sixth in the AP poll. The leader in the Cavaliers' best performance since joining the ACC, once again, was Barry Parkhill. "He is expected to make the crucial shot, throw the key pass, break the press, set up the offense," the *Washington Post* reported. Gibson explained that "Barry turns the key and then the other guys have to keep the engine from misfiring." The Virginia players were proud of their teamwork, effort, and solidarity. "This is a really close team," commented forward Frank DeWitt. "We know we won't overwhelm teams with talent."[87]

After its excellent start, Virginia lost steam at the end of the regular season. It dropped four of its last seven games, including defeats on the road at league-leading North Carolina and greatly improved Maryland. Still, the season was an unprecedented success for the Cavaliers. In the middle of the 12-game winning streak, Gibson declared, "I've never enjoyed a season more. This is delightful." Virginia ended the regular season with a record of 20–5. It tied Maryland for second place in the conference standings, one game behind North Carolina. It went 8–4 in the conference to post its first winning record ever in ACC competition. It was ranked number 20 in the nation in the final AP poll, the first time that Virginia finished a season in the top 20. Gibson was named ACC Coach of the Year, and Parkhill, who led the league with a scoring average of 21.6, was selected as ACC Player of the Year. No Virginia coach or player had previously received those honors. In addition, Parkhill made five first-team All-American squads and received second-team recognition from AP and UPI.[88]

The bulk of the credit for Virginia's remarkable turnaround went to its once-beleaguered coach. Gibson received accolades for making good use of his talent, adjusting his strategies as appropriate, and winning the confidence of his players. Those attributes had not been prevalent in his first few years at Virginia, and the change, apparently in part as a result of the "Boot the Hoot" campaign, was enormously beneficial to his program. Some observers also gave indirect credit to administrators at the University of Virginia for increasing the financial resources that Gibson required to compete in the ACC. Bill Cate of the *Roanoke Times* reported in December 1971 that Gibson's recruiting budget in his first seven years at Virginia had not exceeded $4,000 per year while coaches at North Carolina, Duke, and South Carolina received $20,000 per year or more in the late 1960s. Gibson's recruiting budget had tripled over three years, and Athletic Director Gene Corrigan admitted that it "still isn't where it should be." But he vowed to "be competitive" with ACC rivals in recruiting expenditures. Shortly after taking over as athletic director in January 1971, Corrigan told the Virginia Student Aid Foundation, which raised money for athletic scholarships, that its performance was inadequate to support winning athletic programs at the university. He pointed out that the foundation owed the university $120,000 in funds advanced for scholarships. When he urged the foundation to "raise $250,000," the response he received was, "You're crazy." But the foundation stepped up its fund-raising activities and set a goal of $300,000 for 1972. The success of the basketball team was critical to its efforts.[89]

After placing second in the regular season standings in 1972, Virginia entered the ACC Tournament with legitimate hopes of winning the championship. It defeated Wake Forest in the first round to earn a second-round meeting with Maryland. The teams had split their games during the regular season, and Maryland won the rubber match in a close contest, 62–57. Virginia's disappointment was soothed by an invitation to the NIT, its first postseason appearance since 1941. In a sign of how far Virginia basketball had progressed in a three-year period, the team took its opponent, Lafayette College, too lightly. Lafayette won the game, 72–71, on a foul shot with three seconds left on the clock, bringing an outstanding season to an abrupt finish. "It was a tough way to end it," Scott McCandlish said of his final game as a Cavalier.[90]

Despite the early departure from the NIT, Virginia hit another high note in 1972 when it signed a heavily recruited prospect from Pennsylvania, Wally Walker. Walker was an All-State player who averaged 31.7 points and 18.8 rebounds per game in his senior year in high school. Virginia was the first ACC school to offer him a scholarship, but he made no commitments and kept an open mind as he weighed his options in spring 1972. His final decision came down to Virginia or North Carolina, and it was an exceedingly difficult call. After a great deal of agonizing, Walker settled on Virginia, in part because it was closer to his home, in part because he hoped to contribute to building a program of sustained excellence, and in part because he was much taken with the prospect of playing with Barry Parkhill. After he announced his choice, Gibson commented, "The signing of Walker measures how far our program has come. We have gambled on the super players hoping to get one and we got him." Walker's decision was also a milestone for Gibson's program because it was the first time that Virginia had gone head-to-head with North Carolina for a top-tier player and won the battle.[91]

"The Greatest Basketball Show in the Country"

As the ACC became increasingly competitive from top to bottom, the conference tournament became an increasingly popular attraction. Eddie Cameron, a strong supporter of the tournament since the founding of the ACC, commented in 1972, "To our area, it hits with as much or more impact than the World Series or Super Bowl." He suggested that the tournament "is what brought us . . . to the level of excellence we now enjoy" because it was "the reason teams keep improving." Although the tournament was always a big draw, after 1965, the first year it sold out completely, tickets became progressively more difficult and expensive to obtain. The *Raleigh News and Observer* reported during the 1965 tournament that tickets were so scarce that scalpers were aggressively and conspicuously peddling their wares. By 1969, scalpers were commanding $100 for a book of tickets that had a face value of $20.[92]

As the availability of tournament seats dwindled, ACC schools faced the delicate problem of meeting the demands of their own students for tickets. The allocation that each conference member received was routinely snapped up by alumni and other boosters who made contributions in part to gain access to the tournament. This practice was an important means of raising money for the athletic programs of individual schools. But it generally shut out students. A. Kenneth Pye, chancellor at Duke, made his concerns about this issue clear to Cameron in 1971: "I fully appreciate that we need to have tickets available to provide to our alumni who contribute to [Duke's] program," he wrote. But he regarded the "criticism of our students" over their inability to attend games as a "matter of considerable importance." Pye suggested holding the tournament over two consecutive weekends, with each game "ticketed separately," or scheduling first-round games at the home arenas of conference schools. Such arrangements, he argued, would provide students with greater opportunities to attend tournament games. The ACC considered those and other ideas in 1972, but the athletic directors of conference members "voted unanimously to make no change in the Tournament format." At that time, NC State and Virginia were the only ACC schools to reserve even a small number of tickets for their students.[93]

ACC coaches expressed reservations about the tournament format for quite different reasons. Many continued to view it as an inappropriate way to decide the league championship. Bubas, whose teams were eliminated in upset losses in the ACC Tournament in 1962, 1965, and most memorably 1968, echoed the term Bud Millikan once used by calling it a "farce" in 1969. His ACC coaching colleagues, especially those who regularly placed at the top of the standings, generally agreed with him that "this tournament method of choosing an ACC representative to the NCAA is crazy." At least some of those who traditionally occupied less exalted stations in the conference hierarchy tended to see greater virtue in the tournament format. After Virginia stunned North Carolina in the first round in 1970, Gibson was asked if he approved of the tournament as the means of selecting a champion. "Is the Pope a Catholic?" he replied. "This is the greatest basketball show in the country."[94]

Despite complaints that the ACC's method of determining its champion prevented deserving teams from advancing to the NCAAs, the tournament titlist was usually the team with the best conference record during the regular season. In 19 seasons between 1954 and 1972, the top-seeded team won the tournament 12 times. The tournament featured many close calls, exciting finishes, and memorable upsets. But the lowest-seeded teams to capture the title, NC State in 1954, Maryland in 1958, and Duke in 1960, all seeded fourth, had very talented rosters and were worthy representatives of the conference in the NCAA Tournament. Although the top-seeded teams had fared well in the ACC Tournament, it was always a harrowing experience for their coaches, players, and fans. "Everything rested on those three days in March," Dean Smith later wrote. "The ACC was such a deep conference that you had to beat three excellent teams to win the tournament. Also, if you were favored, you often had the fans of all seven other schools cheering against you."[95]

Another complaint about the ACC Tournament was more valid than objections that it enabled inferior teams to win the crown. A lament that was aired with growing frequency was that the rigors of the tournament led to disappointing performances by conference representatives in the NCAAs. The tournament created psychological and physical barriers that were difficult to measure but impossible to dismiss. The rivalries of the ACC were so intense that the first priority was to win the conference title. Coaches and players tended to view playing well in the NCAA Tournament and winning a national championship as desirable but considerably less important objectives. Many testified that after claiming a conference title, they found it difficult to apply the same level of energy, commitment, and focus to the quest for the NCAA championship. When North Carolina captured the conference title in 1957, Lennie Rosenbluth commented that "everything is anti-climatic after winning the ACC tournament," and Pete Brennan remarked that "we've got the cake, now we'll go after the icing." Their team got the icing as well, but other ACC champions settled for the cake. "We went to the Final Four my last two years," Larry Miller recalled, "but back then, the ACC tournament was king. The NCAA tournament was almost a letdown." South Carolina players had the same attitude when they captured the ACC title in 1971. "To a man," they regarded the NCAA tournament as "a letdown" that "meant little" to them. Coaches agreed on the primacy of prevailing in the ACC. Bubas said that "the way our conference has [the tournament] set up, and as long as it remains that way, we're going to play it as the most important." Smith affirmed after the 1969 tournament that winning the ACC championship was the most rewarding achievement "because these are the people you have to live with." Added to the burden of mental preparation for the NCAAs was the physical toll of the ACC Tournament. Playing three pressure-packed games in three days was a stumbling block that few other teams in the NCAA Tournament had to overcome.[96]

After North Carolina won the national championship in 1957, the ACC had a mixed record in the NCAA Tournament. Between 1958 and 1971, the ACC champion went to the NCAA's Final Four seven times—Wake Forest in 1962, Duke in 1963, 1964, and 1966, and North Carolina in 1967, 1968, and 1969. This was an impressive achievement, but its luster was dimmed by the fact that those teams lost most of their games in either the NCAA semifinals or finals by large margins. The only close contest in the Final Four appearances by ACC schools during the 1960s was Duke's loss to Kentucky in the 1966 semifinals, 83–79. Otherwise, the performances of ACC teams in games that knocked them out of contention for a national championship fell far short of their own standards. Wake lost by 16 to Ohio State in 1962, Duke by 18 to Loyola in 1963, Duke by 15 to UCLA in 1964, North Carolina by 14 to Dayton in 1966, North Carolina by 23 to UCLA in 1967, and North Carolina by 27 to Purdue in 1969. After the drubbing by Purdue, Smith commented, "I am embarrassed not only for the University of North Carolina, but for all of basketball in the East. . . . We certainly didn't show that we are an outstanding team." Although the ACC representatives lost to excellent teams, their habit of losing in blowouts was a source of perplexity and acute disappointment.[97]

The outcome of the ACC's 1971–72 season followed established patterns. North Carolina won the regular season and was ranked second in the country. After the disappointment of losing recruiting battles for Tom Burleson and Tom McMillen in 1970, Smith had made an exception to his rule of not bringing in players who transferred from other four-year schools or from two-year colleges. He signed the immensely skilled Robert McAdoo, who had grown up in Greensboro and starred at Vincennes Junior College in Indiana. McAdoo was a "natural fit" on a highly talented team and averaged 19.5 points and 10.1 rebounds as the starting center. He made first-team All-ACC along with fellow Tar Heel Dennis Wuycik. Two other members of the squad, George Karl and Bill Chamberlain, were selected for the second team. Virginia and Maryland, which tied for second in the regular season standings, had advanced from the depths of the league just three years earlier. They met in the tournament semifinals, and Maryland, despite Parkhill's 24 points, won a game that went down to the wire, 62–57. In the finals, Maryland started slowly and trailed at halftime, 41–29. The Terrapins rallied in the second half but fell short, and North Carolina earned the championship with a 73–64 victory.[98]

The Tar Heels began the NCAA Tournament with two strong showings. In the first round of the eastern regionals, they thrashed South Carolina, which was playing its first season as an independent after leaving the ACC. North Carolina then dominated Penn, ranked third in the nation, to reach the NCAA's final rounds for the fourth time in six seasons. Smith went to great lengths to encourage his players to focus on their opponent in the semifinals, Florida State University, rather than looking ahead to a matchup with UCLA in the title game. His efforts did not pay off. Florida State ran out to a 23-point lead before McAdoo and Wuycik led a feverish rally. But Florida State held on to win, 79–75. North Carolina suffered what Curry Kirkpatrick called its "traditional NCAA collapse." The ACC, which the same writer had described as "college basketball's strongest league" in 1970, failed once again to support its claim to that distinction by winning a national championship. "Critics of ACC basketball — their criticism is brought on by ACC coaches' boast that their conference in the strongest college roundball league — are quick to put down the South Atlantic's brand of basketball," Chauncey Durden, sports editor of the *Richmond Times-Dispatch*, wrote in March 1972. "Those critics rest their case on the failure of ACC champions to fare better in the NCAA playoffs." After the late 1960s, this was a matter of growing sensitivity to the league's coaches, players, and fans. As the NCAA Tournament gained increasing visibility and popularity, the pressure on the ACC to prove its superiority on the national stage increased.[99]

9

THE 800 RULE
& THE DEPARTURE OF
SOUTH CAROLINA

The Atlantic Coast Conference was founded in 1953 in significant part to establish academic integrity and enforce academic standards among its members. One eventual result of those goals was that the ACC decided in 1964 that football and basketball prospects had to score at least 800 on the SAT to qualify for an athletic scholarship. In 1966, it extended this policy to athletes who participated, with or without financial aid, in any intercollegiate sport. During the late 1960s, the 800 rule generated what the *Raleigh News and Observer* called the "biggest, most controversial, technicality-filled issue in recent league history." The controversy divided the ACC and threatened to cause its dissolution. After much turmoil, the conference decided to keep the 800 requirement even at the cost of losing one of its charter members, and, consequently, the University of South Carolina withdrew in 1971. Within a short time, the 800 rule, after triggering a major uproar and much ill will, was struck down by a federal court.[1]

The 800 rule was a culmination of the ACC's commitment to promoting academic integrity by setting uniform admission standards for athletes. When it agreed on its original minimum SAT score of 750 in 1960, it was the first conference in the country to adopt such a requirement. Even after other leagues approved similar rules, the ACC's 800 standard stood alone as the most rigorous among major college conferences. The rule prevented some basketball prodigies, including Pete Maravich, Mike Grosso, and Herm Gilliam, from playing at ACC schools. But in general, conference members met the requirement with room to spare. In 1962, when the 750 rule still applied, freshman basketball players had average SAT scores that ranged from a low of 883 at South Carolina to a high of 1,135 at Duke. By 1966, the average scores for freshman basketball players at most conference schools had improved. They ranged from a low of 948 at Wake Forest to a high of 1,207 at North Carolina.[2]

The NCAA's 1.6 Rule

After the NCAA decided in 1956 to authorize its members to provide athletic scholarships regardless of need, it adopted the term "student-athlete" for those who received financial assistance. The term was a "mandated substitute" for commonly used expressions such as "player" that the NCAA imposed. By the early 1960s, the organization was becoming increasingly concerned that too many schools placed a higher value on their student-athletes' achievements in sports than on their qualifications for and performances in the classroom. In October 1963, the NCAA appointed a committee to investigate whether it was possible to develop a way "to determine the academic potential of students" and to set a national standard "for awarding financial aid to student athletes." The committee reported in July 1964 that it was possible "to predict first year college grade point averages" on the basis of high school class rank and scores on the SAT or the American College Testing Program (ACT). At its annual meeting in January 1965, the NCAA passed a rule that members would be barred from participation in any NCAA-sponsored event, including bowl games, the national basketball championship, and television appearances, unless they limited athletic scholarships to incoming students who met a minimum academic standard. The standard was a projected college grade point average of 1.6 on a 4.0 system, which was the equivalent of a C-minus. The NCAA also required that athletes maintain a grade point average of at least 1.6 as college students to keep their scholarships and participate in intercollegiate sports. The new rules became effective on January 1, 1966.[3]

The NCAA's member institutions strongly supported the 1.6 rule. "The solid majority of colleges believe this rule in the long run will do as much as any rule the NCAA has ever passed to improve intercollegiate athletics," NCAA executive director Walter Byers commented in 1966. "It is based on the premise that if a college wishes to compete with its sister institutions for national championship honors, it should be willing to certify what its academic procedures and requirements are, confirm them to other members and agree upon a minimum level of academic attainment for athletes." Nevertheless, the 1.6 requirement produced a "stormy controversy." The leading opponents were not schools with low academic standards, though some of them objected, but members of the Ivy League. Ivy League administrators complained that the 1.6 minimum enabled the NCAA to interfere in the internal academic affairs of its members and to make decisions about a student's "stage of development" in an "overly mechanistic and unsound" way. The Ivy League's refusal to go along with the rule prevented its conference basketball champion, the University of Pennsylvania, from participating in the NCAA Tournament in 1966. The Ivy League's position won little sympathy. Clemson president Robert Edwards found it "completely incongruous that the Princetons and the Harvards are putting themselves in bed with the Arkansas' and the Alabamas of the athletic world." Dan Jenkins wrote in *Sports Illustrated* that "when the welfare of the entire collegiate community is considered, the Ivies, despite scattered good points and splendid intentions, are dead wrong."[4]

The 1.6 rule soon set off a sharp debate within the ACC over the continuing need for its own 800 requirement for prospective athletes. Initially, the conference agreed to conform with the NCAA rule and also retained the 800 standard for participation in intercollegiate athletics. This gave it the highest minimum academic requirements of any conference in the nation. The controversy that arose between schools that wanted to abandon the 800 rule and those who favored keeping it centered on the ability of ACC teams to compete with other conferences in football. The ACC's record of failure against nonconference football opponents was a source of distress for schools that held the 800 rule at least partly responsible. In 1969, for example, the ACC ranked last in the nation in victories against teams outside the conference, and since its founding, it had compiled a record against Southeastern Conference rivals of 19 wins and 105 losses.

"ACC football," Bill Cate wrote in the *Roanoke Times*, "is one of the worst frauds ever perpetrated on the southern sporting public."[5]

The academic standards of the Southeastern Conference were lower than those of the ACC; it required SAT scores of 760 for athletic prospects. South Carolina athletic director and football coach Paul Dietzel insisted that the 40-point difference made a significant impact on his program. He claimed that the ACC's standard caused him to scratch five or six potential recruits from his list every year. "Those athletes wind up going to an outside school, usually in the SEC," he said, "and come back to help beat us in a couple of years." Dietzel pushed aggressively for the ACC to eliminate the 800 requirement and simply use the NCAA's 1.6 rule as the academic minimum for recruiting athletes. He received strong support from his counterpart at Clemson, Frank Howard. Howard was not an admirer of Dietzel, whom he once called "Primrose Paul," a vague term that clearly was not intended as a compliment, in a note to Eddie Cameron. But he agreed that the ACC should revise admission requirements for athletes. "I think it is very foolish for us to have the highest academic standards in the country," he told the other conference athletic directors and football coaches. "We are now the laughingstock of the United States."[6]

The presidents of Clemson and South Carolina endorsed the positions of their athletic directors, in part because they wanted to improve their football programs and in part because they worried that the U.S. Department of Health, Education, and Welfare (HEW) would find that the 800 rule violated federal laws by discriminating against black athletes. HEW was investigating the athletic programs of many southern colleges to look for evidence of racial discrimination, and the 800 requirement caught its attention. Robert Edwards readily and regretfully admitted that the rule made it extremely difficult for black athletes to participate in sports at Clemson. He revealed that in 1965, 93.4 percent of the black high school seniors in the state of South Carolina who took the SAT scored less than 800. South Carolina president Thomas Jones went a step further. He called the 800 standard a "racist regulation." He suggested that the key issue in deciding on retaining the 800 rule "was not the success or failure of any athletic program but the morality of the conference." The irony of the accusation of racism from the president of a university that had long resisted the admission of black students in a state that had long deprived black high schools of adequate resources was not lost on some observers. "If Dr. Jones is sincere in his statement, then South Carolina and its university have achieved remarkable strides in the area of social conscience in the past five or six years," commented Bill Ballenger of the *Charlotte News.* "South Carolina standing alone and independent as a forerunner in the field of equal rights would be [a] remarkable image."[7]

The Secession of South Carolina

Clemson and South Carolina's campaign to eliminate the 800 rule received the support of Maryland and NC State. The other ACC schools opposed the change, and Duke and Virginia were especially adamant. They viewed the attempt to discard the conference standard as a step in the wrong direction by diluting the ACC's long-standing commitment to academic integrity. For Duke, this was a pressing issue because of the faculty report to the Academic Council that recommended withdrawal from the ACC. Further, the conference schools that required SAT scores much higher than 800 for admission were concerned that using the less-demanding NCAA rule would widen the gap on academic standards within the conference. This would make it harder for them to compete with their league rivals with lower entrance requirements, especially in football. Chris Cramer, the sports editor of the *Daily Progress* in Charlottesville, suggested in November 1969 that "Virginia, Duke and Wake Forest are schools that we don't believe could survive in the ACC if Dietzel's proposals were to be adopted." What appeared to be at stake in the debate over the 800 standard, therefore, was the survival of the conference.[8]

Matters came to a head in spring 1970 when reports circulated that South Carolina was seriously considering withdrawing from the conference if the 800 rule was not eliminated. At a conference meeting in April 1970, Dietzel's proposal to abolish the 800 requirement was defeated by a vote of 4–4, two short of what he needed. Instead, the ACC's faculty athletic chairmen requested that the institutional heads of the eight ACC schools review the issue and make recommendations. NC State chancellor John Caldwell agreed to chair the study. In light of the ACC's decision to investigate its options, South Carolina's Board of Trustees, "after prolonged and careful consideration," decided "to take no action at this time" on leaving the conference. The status of the 800 rule and the position of the University of South Carolina, therefore, depended on the findings and judgments of the ACC's presidents and chancellors.[9]

In an effort to find a consensus, Caldwell asked each of his colleagues to provide information on the admissions policies at his school and to comment on the advisability of retaining, eliminating, or revising the 800 rule.

The replies confirmed a continuing split of 4–4, with Duke, North Carolina, Virginia, and Wake Forest opposed. The schools that supported removing the 800 requirement believed that the NCAA's 1.6 standard was acceptable. Those that objected argued that taking this step would lower academic standards and allow the admission of athletes who had little chance to succeed academically. Some, but not all, schools on each side favored a compromise that would permit admission of a few "hardship" cases of students who met the NCAA standard but not the ACC's requirement. This was regarded as a means of recruiting more black athletes. When written responses did not achieve a consensus of views, Caldwell organized a meeting of ACC presidents, held on October 21, 1970. The presidents and their representatives discussed the questions surrounding the 800 rule frankly and at times acrimoniously. Not surprisingly, they failed to reach an agreement. They concluded that they lacked sufficient information to make an informed judgment. As a result, they made arrangements with Jay Davis, director of the Southeastern Office of the Educational Testing Service, to conduct a detailed study of the admission practices of each ACC school. He would seek to determine the possible effects of dropping the 800 rule and to come up with a "predicted table" for the college grades of athletic prospects.[10]

South Carolina grew increasingly impatient with the ACC's failure to scrap the 800 requirement. Dietzel told President Jones in September 1970 that his recruiting efforts were greatly hampered by having "the same rules to contend with." He revealed that he was especially anxious to sign ten "blue chip" in-state prospects whom he viewed as instrumental for building his program. Of those ten, only two of the five white players and none of the five black players could qualify for admission under the existing standards. "It's going to be very difficult to explain to people around here," Dietzel lamented, "[that] of all the fine black athletes playing in our newly integrated high schools, we cannot find one of them who can attend his state university." The NCAA expressed support for South Carolina's position. Walter Byers told Jones that the ACC was the only conference with requirements that exceeded the NCAA's 1.6 rule and that the "NCAA Council is strongly opposed to and strongly recommends against the use of minimum cutoff scores . . . in the administration of prediction formulae." On October 23, 1970, the University of South Carolina's Board of Trustees forced the issue. Describing the 800 rule as "educationally unsound and athletically unwise," it authorized Gamecock coaches to recruit on the basis of the NCAA's standard. It pledged that the university would continue to "work diligently" within the ACC to change the 800 requirement, but its action was a direct and uncompromising challenge to the conference.[11]

South Carolina's defiance of the conference stepped up the pressure on its in-state rival, Clemson, which shared Dietzel's view of the 800 rule but was much less inclined to abandon the ACC. Edwards hinted that if the conference refused to change its admission requirements, his school might decide to leave. He emphasized that he wanted to remain, but he insisted that "Clemson cannot live under the regulations of the Atlantic Coast Conference." In an atmosphere of growing tension, the presidents and chancellors of ACC members reconvened on December 9, 1970, to consider their options. The report prepared by Jay Davis of the Educational Testing Service appeared to clarify some issues. He found that the high school record of a prospective student at an ACC school was the "most critical indicator" in predicting academic performance in college. Standardized test scores were helpful in "reducing the error in prediction." Davis also argued that the most important means of protecting academic standards was not through admissions policies but through the grading practices of faculty members.[12]

Caldwell pleaded with his colleagues to "find some ground on which we can agree that will hold us together with our academic colors flying high." Eventually, they arrived at an uneasy compromise. The institutional heads voted 5–3 to recommend to the faculty athletic representatives, who exercised the ACC's rulemaking authority, that the conference retain both the 800 rule and the 1.6 standard for prospective athletes. But they added flexibility to the requirement by allowing the admission of high school students who scored between 700 and 799 on the SAT if they had a predicted college grade point average of 1.75 according to the NCAA's formula. The day after the presidents and chancellors adjourned, the conference held what the Associated Press called its "most momentous meeting since the conference was organized." The faculty representatives voted to adopt the compromise proposal by a margin of 6–2. The two dissenting votes were cast by South Carolina and Clemson.[13]

The trustees at South Carolina promptly rebuffed the ACC's attempt to compromise by reaffirming their decision to recruit on the basis of the NCAA's 1.6 standard. By that time, officials at other conference schools had tired of Dietzel's campaign to abolish the 800 rule and were inclined to let South Carolina leave the conference rather than yield to its demands. John Caldwell, who had worked hard to find a compromise solution that would keep the conference intact, concluded shortly after the presidents' meeting that "if we can't hold all the members . . . on the basis of agreed upon standards, then let the dissident members go." He disclosed that he was "less concerned about the negative effect of such action on the Conference than I was some weeks ago." Further efforts to find a compromise solution that would offer a reasonable balance between test scores and class rank failed to bridge the gap between the competing positions. South Carolina's trustees settled the issue on March 29, 1971, by announcing that the university would resign from the ACC, effective August 15, 1971. They expressed their hope that "this separation will be of a temporary nature."[14]

South Carolina's withdrawal from the ACC was greeted with pro forma expressions of regret from officials at other conference schools but no signs of deep sorrow. Although some Gamecock fans had rallied in favor of abandoning the ACC for years, the action of the university's trustees was not universally acclaimed in the state of South Carolina. "The worrisome thing is that big-name coaches and the fever of big-time athletics seem to have gained too much influence over the members of the board," *The State* commented in an editorial. "Athletic excellence must be secondary to academic excellence at any university worthy of the name." For quite different reasons, Frank McGuire, despite his feuds with conference officials and coaches and his objections to the tournament, was, at best, ambivalent about leaving the ACC. He and Dietzel often disagreed, and he had resented the athletic director's failure to offer him strong support during the Grosso controversy. The ill will between them was on display during at least one conference reception at which they argued in a loud and animated manner over quitting the ACC. With his long experience in the conference, McGuire recognized the competitive and financial advantages of the intense rivalries between excellent programs. "Dietzel's trying to sabotage a good basketball program, but he won't," McGuire declared. "We'll still get good opponents and make the championship tournament."[15]

The End of the 800 Rule

When South Carolina decided to secede from the ACC, some reporters and administrators at conference schools expected Clemson to follow. But Edwards was more cognizant of the benefits of remaining in the ACC than were Jones and the trustees at South Carolina. He emphasized that "Clemson University has enjoyed its affiliation with the other member institutions of the ACC" and had "no intention of withdrawing from the Conference." He continued to press for changes in the ACC's academic requirements. Edwards was "extremely optimistic" that the conference would find a fair solution or that the NCAA would change its rules in a way that would "serve to eliminate the issues on which we have spent so much time fruitlessly within the Conference."[16]

The disagreement over the 800 rule finally ended not as a result of ACC or NCAA action but as a result of a federal court decision. In December 1971, two Clemson students, Joey Edward Beach and James Marion Vickery, filed suit in a federal district court against Clemson and the ACC. They contended that the 800 rule deprived them of their constitutional rights under the 14th Amendment because the requirement applied only to athletes. Neither Beach, who wanted to become a member of the swimming team, nor Vickery, who wished to play football, had been recruited to participate in intercollegiate athletics. Both had SAT scores of less than 800, and they argued that their plans were thwarted by the ACC's academic standards. Beach and Vickery, both of whom were white, were joined in the suit by two football players who were black. Noah Henry Allen and Willie Anderson had been recruited and signed letters of intent before their failure to score 800 made them ineligible for full-ride scholarships (though Anderson received a two-year grant-in-aid in accordance with NCAA rules). The addition of Allen and Anderson turned the original claim into a class-action suit.[17]

On August 7, 1972, U.S. District Judge Robert Hemphill handed down a decision that the 800 requirement was "arbitrary and capricious" because it set a standard for athletes that did not apply to other students. "The score of 800 is arbitrary," he declared, "and the effect it has on the plaintiffs and their class is condemned by the equal protection clause of the 14th amendment." Hemphill found that since ACC schools did "not refer to this 800 score for entrance," it was "not based on valid reasoning." Therefore, he ruled that the conference had no legal grounds on which to enforce its standard. There was speculation that the case "was brought in collusion with Clemson," and Edwards immediately released a statement that expressed no disappointment about losing in court. "We are pleased," he announced, "that this ruling has removed the confusion and misunderstanding which has surrounded the eligibility question." The ACC seriously considered appealing Hemphill's decision, but it eventually concluded that this would not produce a favorable outcome. On August 18, 1972, the ACC "bowed to the inevitable" by voting to drop the 800 rule and to adopt the NCAA's 1.6 requirement. After years of controversy and the loss of one charter member, the ACC abandoned its effort to stand on a higher plane than the other conferences in the country by imposing a more demanding academic standard.[18]

The ACC's decision drew a mixed response. The *Greensboro Daily News* admitted that the 800 rule did not guarantee "academic excellence at ACC schools." But it suggested that the rule had "important symbolic value" by showing that the "ACC, alone among NCAA conferences, was not setting the lowest acceptable academic standards for its athletic programs." It regretted that with the rule eliminated, "the ACC is down there in the basement with everyone else." By contrast, Bill Ballenger of the *Charlotte News* argued, "All the 800 rule accomplished in its many years of running was to foster bad relations, pitiful football, and great hypocrisy." ACC football coaches were delighted to escape the burden the requirement placed on their recruiting efforts. Their basketball counterparts, who had not openly opposed the rule, were also pleased. Dean Smith had complained even before the court ruling that the ACC's standard discriminated against black athletes. "The S.A.T. is aimed at the white middle class. . . . The boards are a joke," he said when he recruited Walter Davis, a superb swingman who planned to attend prep school because his test scores did not qualify him for admission to the University of North Carolina or participation in ACC basketball. Lefty Driesell commented after the court decision: "It was a good rule to abolish. It's not fair to let a boy into school and then tell him he can't participate in athletics." He promptly signed a gifted guard from Philadelphia, Maurice Howard, who, *Sports Illustrated* reported, "almost surely could not have been admitted to college under the old regulation."[19]

The Academic Imperative

The ACC was founded in 1953 as a result of the coincidence of interests among, on the one hand, administrators who wished to protect academic integrity and raise academic standards, and, on the other hand, those who wished to improve opportunities for their football teams to play in bowl games. By the late 1960s, those motivations had diverged to a point that they produced sometimes heated controversy and conflict. The schools that wished to maintain higher academic requirements than other conferences clashed with those who viewed the ACC's academic standards as a direct cause of futility in football. In both cases, basketball coaches were interested observers but not prominent participants. Nevertheless, the commitment to academic integrity and the decision to impose minimum academic requirements were important elements in the evolution of ACC basketball.

ACC members proved that it was possible to build powerful programs even with academic standards that were higher than those of the NCAA and other collegiate conferences. They also demonstrated that it was possible for schools with rigorous admission standards to compete in the conference and in the NCAA Tournament against opponents that were less academically demanding.

But it was not easy. Each ACC school had to decide how to balance academic and athletic objectives in two fundamental areas—allocating resources and establishing academic standards. The discrepancy in resources that different institutions provided their athletic programs was sometimes large. At one extreme, Maryland's Curley Byrd found the money he needed to build a football stadium and a field house before he supplied adequate funding for the university library. At the other extreme, the University of Virginia gave very limited support to its sports programs for more than a decade after the founding of the ACC, and as a result, it served as the doormat of the conference in both football and basketball. The other ACC members fell somewhere between those extremes. The question of how to strike a reasonable balance was a constant challenge for university officials on matters that included hiring coaches, building arenas, and recruiting players.

The same kind of issue arose over academic standards. Administrators had to make decisions about the extent to which, if at all, they would compromise academic principles in order to promote athletic success. The 800 rule eased this problem by setting a minimum standard, but it remained a difficult call for schools that expected applicants to have much higher scores on the SAT. This was the case with Duke and Virginia in the early years of the conference, and as academic standards improved during the 1960s, it became a growing concern for others as well. Each ACC school made its own determination on where to draw the line for admitting athletes. The 800 rule was helpful in preventing glaring discrepancies among conference members, and Frank McGuire's attempt to subvert the requirement in the Mike Grosso affair received no support from the rest of the ACC. The NCAA's 1.6 predictive standard was not drastically less stringent than the 800 rule, but at least some ACC schools were reluctant to abandon a policy that set them apart from other leagues across the country. The debate over keeping the 800 rule ended only when it was judged to violate the 14th Amendment.

The ACC's controversy over the 800 standard highlighted the central issue surrounding college athletic programs—the proper role of sports in academic institutions. Presidents, chancellors, and other top officials at ACC schools during the first twenty years of the conference uniformly affirmed the importance of athletics as a worthy part of university life. Sports programs provided benefits that were difficult to measure but also difficult to achieve by any other means. They were critical to building attributes such as a sense of community and pride among students, alumni, other fans, and in the cases of many universities, entire states. But those advantages did not come cheaply. The costs of athletic programs were substantial and increasing, and by the late 1960s, many schools were losing money in their efforts to become or remain competitive. This was enough of a problem at Duke that a faculty committee recommended leaving the ACC. In addition, college administrators, to their dismay, had to devote considerable time and attention to various issues that arose in attempting to maintain a healthy and defensible balance between athletic programs and academic objectives. The commitment became even more onerous when ACC schools faced crises such as the point-shaving scandal and the Grosso controversy or were subjects of NCAA investigations and sanctions. It was little wonder that John Caldwell told Thomas Jones during the height of the Grosso dispute, "Too bad, isn't it, that we institutional heads have to spend so much time on an activity which is not central to the purposes of the institution."[20]

ACC presidents and chancellors were keenly aware that vigilance over and control of their athletic programs were essential, either directly or through their subordinates. A failure to exercise careful supervision could too easily lead to penalties that embarrassed the school and set back both its academic and athletic aspirations. During the first two decades after the ACC was formed, every conference school except Virginia and Wake Forest was guilty of infractions in its basketball program that led to NCAA probation or reprimands. NC State led the way by incurring probation on three separate occasions, and McGuire pulled off a rare feat by taking actions that resulted in NCAA sanctions at two different schools. In his memoirs, Dean Smith pointed out that athletic programs were often the "front porch" of a university. The main part of the house carried out the fundamental purpose of a college or university by educating its students.[21] But the front porch was the most visible feature, and football and basketball coaches were usually better known than the president of the school for whom they worked and the professors who taught students and performed groundbreaking research. Therefore, coaches and players carried a heavy burden. Their competitive success as well as their conduct, charisma, fluency, and wit had a major impact on the public image of their schools. If the front porch appeared defective, outsiders were more likely to view the rest of the house as similarly flawed.

Coaches of college teams had an obligation to recognize that they were a part of an institution that had goals that extended far beyond success on the court or the playing field. Although they were hired to win games, they also worked for a college or university that had a primary function of education. Therefore, they assumed the responsibility for doing all they could to make certain that their players made satisfactory academic progress and for respecting the primacy of the educational mission of their institutions. Teams in professional sports are created with the sole purpose of winning games and championships, but college athletic programs, much as they are encouraged to win, exist in institutions with quite different priorities.

College coaches should be judged not only on the basis of their won-lost records but also on the basis of whether their players went to class, made at least passing grades, and received degrees. Smith and Bubas were exemplary in ensuring that nearly all of their players graduated, but they were not exceptional. Basketball players at ACC schools between 1953 and 1972 had to meet minimum academic requirements and, although statistics on graduation rates apparently were not compiled, most earned their degrees. It was not unusual during that period for players who did not perform adequately in the classroom to be declared ineligible. The generally admirable academic record was, in various measures at different schools, a tribute to the philosophies of school administrators and commitments of the players themselves as well as to the demands of coaches. It was also in part a result of the 800 rule, which, despite its imperfections and its low threshold, provided a reasonably effective means of judging the academic potential of prospective athletes. But without the support of coaches for academic principles and their stern enforcement of academic requirements, the athletic-academic balance sheet in ACC basketball surely would have been less commendable.

College coaches should also be judged on whether the front porch they constructed was a credit to the less visible sections of the entire house. Coaches work under enormous, relentless, and highly conspicuous pressure. For that reason, they should be forgiven all but the most outrageous acts of misconduct or indiscretion in the heat of a game. They should be held strictly accountable, however, for breaking well-established rules of the NCAA or the conference in a way that harms the school they represent. In the first two decades after the ACC was founded, the most egregious violations were committed by Everett Case, Frank McGuire, and Tates Locke.

Case's recruiting practices on two separate occasions landed NC State on NCAA probation for a total of five years during the mid- and late 1950s. Whatever the facts in the Jackie Moreland case, both Consolidated University president William Friday and State College chancellor Carey Bostian regarded Case's actions and the NCAA's penalties as a serious blow to efforts to improve the academic reputation of NC State. Case was too entrenched and too popular to dismiss without unambiguous evidence of his infractions, but his cavalier treatment of existing rules was a disservice of major proportions to the institution that paid his salary.

McGuire's transgressions that led the NCAA to place the University of North Carolina on probation were considerably less serious than those of his chief rival, but Chancellor William Aycock still viewed them as an embarrassment to the school. As a result, he forced McGuire to seek other coaching jobs. When McGuire later went to South Carolina, he caused a major rift within the conference and considerable discomfort to the school's administration by disregarding the 800 rule to enroll Mike Grosso. President Jones was in too weak of a position to fire McGuire, but he offered profuse apologies to the ACC for the coach's behavior and later dictated strict rules of conduct to him. Locke's misdeeds after arriving at Clemson were the worst in the history of the ACC to that time, though they did not become confirmed public knowledge until the NCAA completed its investigation and placed the university on probation for three years in 1975. The brilliance of all three coaches and their accomplishments on the court must be balanced against the damage that their illegal activities caused to the front porch of their universities and the remainder of the structure attached to it. The best college coaches win games without undermining the purposes or the stature of their schools as institutions of higher learning. For the most part, successful ACC basketball coaches between 1953 and 1972 met that standard.

The Way Forward

After the secession of South Carolina in 1971, the ACC carried on with seven members for several years. South Carolina officials considered applying for readmission after Dietzel departed in 1974. As attendance at Gamecock basketball games declined, McGuire complained that "we don't have the [fan] interest like the ACC anymore." He suggested in 1977 that "South Carolina should be in the ACC" from "the standpoint of geography, interest, everything." But proposals that South Carolina return to the ACC did not advance beyond the talking stage, and it was far from clear that the conference would have responded favorably if the university had decided to submit a formal application. In April 1978, the ACC resolved the issue of expansion by voting unanimously to admit Georgia Tech as the eighth member of the conference. Georgia Tech was an attractive addition because its location in Atlanta would substantially increase the ACC's fan base and television market. Further, it was a strong academic institution with a rich football tradition and a reputable basketball program. Its association with the ACC appeared to be mutually advantageous. "It is one of those very natural things," Commissioner Bob James commented. "I think it will be a very compatible conference with eight doggone fine educational institutions."[22]

The ACC remained an eight-member league until it admitted Florida State in September 1990. This occurred at a time when college football was in a state of flux as conferences realigned and independents sought leagues to join. Florida State had a powerful football team that had finished among the top five teams in the country since 1987, and ACC schools were convinced that it would greatly strengthen the conference's prestige and competitive position in football. It also opened important television markets to the ACC; expanding into Florida provided access to a population that was twice the size of any state in which a conference school was located. The ACC expanded again by adding Virginia Tech and Miami in 2004 and Boston College in 2005. As with Florida State, the motivation was largely to improve the conference's stature in football. The twelve-member league was divided into two divisions, which meant that there would no longer be home-and-home basketball games with every team in the ACC. The conference tried to preserve traditional rivalries in the divisional setup, but the matchups that were most intense and most critical to the regular-season standings varied from year to year. And generally, contests between longtime members and newer teams did not arouse the same level of passion that had long been a prominent feature of ACC basketball. Fans grumbled that conference basketball had suffered an undeserved penalty in an effort to upgrade football. One example of the sometimes awkward status of the new members came in the designation of "ACC Legends," in which one player or coach from each school was given special recognition during the ACC Tournament. John Feinstein, a keen observer of conference basketball history and tradition, found it "silly" to select "ACC Legends" from schools that had only recently joined the league.[23]

The expansion of the conference reduced the frequency of meetings between longtime adversaries and, in that way, diluted the intensity of ACC basketball rivalries that had prevailed for decades. The growth of the conference did not, however, change the ACC's commitment to one of the fundamental principles that had led to its founding in 1953—academic excellence. When the ACC was established, none of its members ranked among the best schools in the country. By the early twenty-first century, and in some cases much earlier, the seven charter members who were still in the ACC had dramatically improved their academic programs and national reputations. In 2010, for example, the *U.S. News and World Report* ratings of top public national universities placed Virginia in a tie for second, North Carolina fifth, Maryland tied for 18th, Clemson tied for 22nd, and NC State tied for 39th. Among all national universities, Duke ranked 10th, Virginia tied for 24th, Wake Forest and North Carolina tied for 28th, Maryland tied for 53rd, Clemson tied for 61st, and NC State tied for 88th. The newer members of the conference also received good grades. Among public national universities, Georgia Tech placed 7th, Virginia Tech 29th, and Florida State 48th. Boston College earned a ranking of 34th and Miami tied for 50th among national universities. The academic progress that colleges and universities in the South in general and the ACC in particular made in the second half of the twentieth century was a source of justifiable pride. It increased the importance of avoiding misconduct or rules violations in athletic programs that could undermine hard-won gains.[24]

The innate tensions between academic and athletic objectives that had commanded so much attention during the first twenty years of the ACC continued to generate discussion and occasional anguish in subsequent years. In the early 1960s, the ACC set a precedent by adopting academic standards for admitting athletes and later by enforcing a rule that exceeded the requirements of the NCAA. But when the 800 rule failed to survive the court ruling of 1972, the ACC was placed on the same academic plane as all other members of the NCAA. That plane took a serious dip when the NCAA voted in 1973 to abolish the 1.6 rule. "Losing the 1.600 rule was one of the most painful experiences in the 22 years I had then served as [NCAA] executive director," Walter Byers later wrote. "It was a terrible day for college athletics. Supposedly responsible educators had voted for sports expediency." The 1.6 requirement was replaced by a weak stipulation that prospective athletes had to have a 2.0 high school grade point average without consideration of courses taken or standardized test scores. In 1983, the NCAA passed a somewhat stronger measure, Proposition 48, that would become effective in 1986. It required a high school grade point average of 2.0 and a

700 combined score on the SAT or 15 on the ACT to be eligible to compete as a freshman. Those qualifications fell far short of the jettisoned 1.6 rule.[25]

The weakening of academic requirements for athletes led to abuses that almost certainly would not have occurred under the tighter standards that the ACC and the NCAA had once imposed. In ACC basketball, the most grievous violations of academic integrity took place at the University of Maryland and at NC State during the 1980s. Revelations about the poor academic qualifications and records of Maryland basketball players followed the death of ACC Player of the Year Len Bias from an overdose of cocaine in June 1986. Lefty Driesell had taken great pride in the academic achievements of his players at Davidson and in his early years at Maryland, but his interest in classroom performance had declined in the face of pressure to win. A number of investigative reports on Maryland basketball after Bias's death showed that the average SAT scores for Driesell's teams between 1980 and 1986 was 670. This was about 100 points lower than the average for football players at Maryland and far below the average SAT score of about 1,000 for all students at the university. Driesell had lobbied hard for the admission of players who failed to meet normal standards; in one year he succeeded in awarding scholarships to two players who had SAT scores of 510 and 610. Accordingly, the graduation rates of his players decreased to a point that alarmed John Slaughter, the chancellor of the College Park campus. Slaughter was also deeply disturbed by the introductory courses that players often took throughout their college careers, a practice that he called "abominable." The abundance of stories in the local and national news media about the academic deficiencies of Driesell's players was a serious embarrassment to the University of Maryland. Eventually, Slaughter forced Driesell to resign over the academic shortcomings of his program (and not, as was sometimes charged, to make the coach a scapegoat for Bias's death).[26]

The same pattern of compromising academic standards to improve basketball fortunes occurred at NC State under Coach Jim Valvano. This became an issue that received national attention after Peter Golenbock, who had published best-selling books on the New York Yankees and other sports topics, made serious allegations about the State basketball program in a book titled *Personal Fouls: The Broken Promises and Shattered Dreams of Big-Money Basketball at Jim Valvano's North Carolina State* (1989). He made a series of sensational but poorly documented charges of payments to players, cover-ups of drug use, and altering of grades. In response, the University of North Carolina system (an expansion of the former Consolidated

University) and the NCAA undertook investigations. Neither inquiry supported Golenbock's most lurid accusations, but both found evidence of wrongdoing. The NCAA placed NC State on probation for two years for relatively minor infractions, including the sale of sneakers and game tickets by players. The report of the university system confirmed that "the academic processes and standards of North Carolina State University have been misused in a number of instances to benefit some individual basketball players." It criticized Valvano for recruiting players whose grades and test scores provided no indication of ability to handle college course work, for failing to monitor the academic performance of his players, and for steering team members into courses intended to assure their eligibility rather than to offer a "coherent program of study."[27]

The most flagrant example of "misuse" of academic protocol was the enrollment of Chris Washburn at NC State in 1984. Washburn was an exceptionally talented 6'11" center who scored a combined total of 470 on his college boards. He later recalled that NC State coaches told him, before he took the SAT, that his scores were of no consequence. "When they told me it didn't matter what score I was getting," he said, "I went in for about 22 minutes" and "just marked down" answers more or less randomly. Valvano pushed to allow Washburn's admission and Chancellor Bruce R. Poulton approved it. Other players arrived at NC State with obvious academic deficiencies, managed to stay eligible by taking easy courses, and made little progress toward a degree. After the findings of the investigation conducted by the university system were announced, Poulton resigned as chancellor at NC State. Valvano acknowledged that he had not effectively kept tabs on the academic performance of his players. He was a learned individual with a genuine appreciation for the importance of education, and he insisted that, if given the chance, athletes would take advantage of the opportunity to earn a college degree. Nevertheless, Valvano could not have been blind to the small likelihood that some of the players he recruited would turn into even marginally capable students. As much as he valued education, he also was an intense competitor who valued superior talent that would help him win games and championships. Under his regime, academic integrity took a backseat to athletic aspirations. As a result, he lost his job and the academic reputation of North Carolina State University took a beating.[28]

The goal of fostering and maintaining academic integrity in athletic programs, even as it became more difficult to achieve after the demise of the 800 rule, was one of the two primary legacies of the first two decades of the history of the ACC. The other great legacy of the formative years of the conference was top-to-bottom excellence in basketball. In this regard, the ACC built on the traditions that developed between 1953 and 1972 by demonstrating sustained balance and brilliance both in league competition and on the national stage. The ACC's drought in winning a national championship, a source of growing concern among at least some coaches, players, and fans, ended in 1974 when NC State captured the title. The Wolfpack, led by David Thompson, Tom Burleson, and Monte Towe, a 5'7" guard with magical ball-handling skills, edged defending champion UCLA in double overtime in the semifinals and then defeated Marquette in the finals.

NC State would never have had the opportunity to win the NCAA title if it had not beaten Maryland in the ACC Tournament. The 1974 tournament championship game between two powerful and closely matched rivals is widely regarded as the finest conference game ever played and is arguably the finest college basketball game ever played. State came into the tournament ranked number one in the country with a record of 23–1. Maryland was 21–4 and ranked fourth in the nation. This was Lefty Driesell's greatest Maryland team; it featured seniors Tom McMillen and Len Elmore and sophomore backcourt aces John Lucas and Mo Howard. The pressure on both teams was enormous. Only the winner would go to the NCAA Tournament, and it was the last chance at a national championship for McMillen, Elmore, and Burleson. Both teams performed magnificently. Maryland shot 61 percent for the game and all five starters scored in double figures. State shot 55 percent; Burleson played the best game of his career, with 38 points and 13 rebounds. Maryland jumped out to a 25–12 lead, but after State rallied, the game turned into a series of runs for each team that kept 15,451 fans at Greensboro Coliseum and a regional television audience in a state of tense and incredulous excitement. The score was tied at 97 at the end of regulation, and as fatigue and foul trouble took their toll on Maryland, State won in overtime, 103–100. It was a bitter defeat for the Terrapins, who were, by any standard, one of the top three or four teams in the nation but could not advance to the NCAA Tournament. An achingly disappointed Driesell made his way to the State locker room to congratulate the ACC champions and to wish them well in the NCAAs.[29]

The Maryland–NC State game pointed out the unfairness, or at least the competitive disadvantages, of limiting each conference to one representative in the NCAA Tournament. Driesell had expressed his view on the subject just before the loss to State. "It makes me sick," he declared. "I see who is getting bids to this NCAA Tournament and I know that we and Carolina and State are better than most of those teams. But only one of us is going. It's not fair." In August 1974, the NCAA's executive committee tacitly agreed with him by approving the expansion of the tournament from 25 to 32 teams and allowing two schools from a single conference to participate. It eventually enlarged to 65 teams with no limit on the bids awarded to each conference. The growth in the size of the NCAA Tournament took some of the edge and much of the pressure off the ACC Tournament, which still determined the league champion but no longer decided which team moved on to compete for the national title. In contrast to the 1950s and 1960s, players, coaches, and fans no longer regarded winning the ACC championship as their primary objective and the NCAA Tournament as mere icing on the cake. Television broadcasts of tournament games, especially after the expansion of the conference in 2004 and 2005, often showed wide swaths of empty seats.[30]

In the years between 1975 and 2010, the ACC took full advantage of the increased opportunities to play in the NCAA Tournament. The expanded format was well suited to the across-the-board quality and balance in ACC basketball. Conference schools won ten national titles in that period, and no other league came close to that number. North Carolina and Duke each won four NCAA championships and NC State and Maryland each claimed one. In five of those cases, the team that won the national title did not win the ACC Tournament (North Carolina in 1993, 2005, and 2009, Duke in 1991, and Maryland in 2002). In addition to the ten national championships won after 1975, six different ACC schools made a total of 20 appearances in the NCAA Final Four (which was now officially a capitalized term). The balance in ACC basketball was evident throughout the period after 1975. In 1977–78, for example, every team finished with a winning record for the first time in conference history. In 1979–80, six ACC teams won at least 20 games and all went to either the NCAA Tournament or the NIT. In 1984–85, every team had a winning record for the second time and received a bid for postseason play. The ACC routinely placed six or more teams in the field for the NCAA Tournament after it expanded to 64 teams in 1985 (the 65th team was added in 2001).[31]

The ACC was created in 1953 in large measure for the purpose of establishing an appropriate balance between academic and athletic programs. It sought to maintain academic integrity even as it participated fully in bigtime athletics. The founding ideal was impossible to carry out flawlessly, and ACC schools suffered on several occasions from embarrassments and penalties that arose from overemphasis on winning and underemphasis on academic requirements. Nevertheless, the ACC's commitment to promoting both academic and athletic objectives produced a generally favorable record. William Friday, who served as president of the University of North Carolina system for 30 years between 1956 and 1986, commented as the 50th anniversary of the conference approached: "If you're going to do it, if you're going to be in big-time sports, the ACC does it about as well as you can expect anybody to do it."[32] The impact of forming a new conference on the basketball programs of prospective members was not an important consideration in 1953. Over the next twenty years, however, the ACC developed into a balanced and intensely competitive league that was best known for its excellence in basketball. Its success was a tribute to the administrators who made it possible, the coaches who made it happen, the players who made it memorable, and the fans who made it matter. The foundations of ACC basketball preeminence were fixed firmly in place during the formative years of the conference between 1953 and 1972.

NOTES

Prologue

1. *The State*, December 2, December 3, 1953; *Washington Post*, December 3, 1953; *Raleigh News and Observer*, December 3, 1953.

2. *The State*, December 3, 1953; *Evening Star*, December 3, 1953; *Washington Post*, December 3, 1953; *Baltimore Sun*, December 3, 1953.

3. *Evening Star*, December 17, 1970; *Washington Post*, December 17, 1970; George Conley to Norvall [Neve], December 17, 1970, Box 22 (Men's Basketball, MD-SC 1971), Records of Athletics—Media Relations, University Archives, University of Maryland, College Park.

4. *Evening Star*, December 17, December 18, 1970; *Washington Post*, December 17, December 18, 1970; *Diamondback*, December 17, 1970; Coach Driesell to Jim Kehoe, January 29, 1971, Box 22, Records of Athletics—Media Relations, University of Maryland Archives; Jack Zane, interview with author, Silver Spring, Md., February 9, 2007.

5. Thomas F. Jones to Wilson H. Elkins, December 17, 1970, Elkins to Jones, December 18, 1970, Box 440 (Basketball—S.C., Univ. of, Dec 16/70 & Jan 9/71), Wilson H. Elkins Presidential Records, University of Maryland Archives.

6. Undated note attached to T. Eston Marchant to Norvall Neve, January 4, 1971, Box 1 (Board of Trustees—Secretary, 1971), Records of the Office of the Provost—William H. Patterson, University of South Carolina Press Release, January 5, 1971, Box 6 (Associations and Boards: Atlantic Coast Conference, Misc.), Records of the Office of the President—Thomas F. Jones, 1970–71, University Archives, University of South Carolina, Columbia; Jim Kehoe to Wilson H. Elkins, December 28, 1970, Box 22, Records of Athletics—Media Relations, University of Maryland Archives.

7. *Diamondback*, January 8, 1971; *Evening Star*, January 9, 1971; *Washington Post*, January 9, 1971.

8. Curry Kirkpatrick, "The Toughest Kid on Anybody's Block," *Sports Illustrated*, January 4, 1971, pp. 21–22; *Diamondback*, January 8, January 11, 1971; *Evening Star*, January 9, 1971; *The State*, March 9, 2003. The description of the atmosphere at Cole Field House also draws on my own memories from attending the game.

9. *The State*, January 10, 1971; *Sunday Star*, January 10, 1971; *Washington Post*, January 10, 1971; *Evening Star*, January 11, 1971; *Diamondback*, January 11, 1971; Joe Harrington, interview with author, Leesburg, Va., March 20, 2007.

10. *Diamondback*, January 11, 1971; *Columbia Record*, January 13, 1971; *Charleston News and Courier*, January 17, 1971; Harold Peterson, "The Week," *Sports Illustrated*, January 18, 1971, pp. 57–58; Paul Dietzel to Jim Kehoe, January 11, 1971, clipping of Associated Press story, "Obscene Signs Draw Protest," n.d., Box 22, Records of Athletics—

Media Relations, University of Maryland Archives; Report by Joe Petty, WIS-Television, Columbia, S.C., January 13, 1971, Box 4 (Athletic Affairs: Basketball), Thomas F. Jones Records, 1970–71, University of South Carolina Archives.

11. Norvall Neve, handwritten note to Jim [Kehoe], n.d., Kehoe to Neve, January 18, 1971, Kehoe to S. H. Morrow, January 22, 1971, Box 22, Records of Athletics—Media Relations, University of Maryland Archives.

12. Curry Kirkpatrick, "One More War to Go," *Sports Illustrated*, March 2, 1970, p. 12.

13. *Duke Chronicle*, February 13, 1953; George H. Callcott, *The University of Maryland at College Park: A History* (Baltimore: Noble House, 2005), 107–9.

Chapter 1

1. John E. Hocutt, oral history interview, August 6, 1976, Oral History Collection, Special Collections, College of William and Mary, Williamsburg, Va.; Susan H. Godson et al., *The College of William and Mary: A History* (Williamsburg, Va.: Society of Alumni of the College of William and Mary, 1993), 768–72; John Sayle Watterson, *College Football: History—Spectacle—Controversy* (Baltimore: Johns Hopkins University Press, 2000), 219–23; Ronald A. Smith, "The William and Mary Athletic Scandal of 1951: Governance and the Battle for Academic and Athletic Integrity," *Journal of Sport History* 34 (Fall 2007): 353–73.

2. John E. Hocutt to Members of NASPA [National Association of Student Personnel Administrators], September 27, 1951, Box 12 (Southern Conference), Papers of Geary Eppley, University Archives, University of Maryland, College Park; *Richmond News Leader*, September 20, 1951; *Richmond Times-Dispatch*, September 20, September 21, 1951; *New York Times*, September 20, 1951; *New York Herald Tribune*, September 22, 1951.

3. Jack Falla, *NCAA: The Voice of College Sports—A Diamond Anniversary History, 1906–1981* (Mission, Kans.: National Collegiate Athletic Association, 1981), 1–47; Watterson, *College Football*, 9–129.

4. Howard J. Savage, Harold W. Bentley, John T. McGovern, and Dean F. Smiley, *American College Athletics* (New York: Carnegie Foundation for the Advancement of Teaching, 1929), vi, xv, xxi, 119, 224–65; John R. Thelin, *Games Colleges Play: Scandal and Reform in Intercollegiate Athletics* (Baltimore: Johns Hopkins University Press, 1994), 13–46; Richard O. Davies, *Sports in American Life: A History* (Malden, Mass.: Blackwell Publishing, 2007), 161–75; Watterson, *College Football*, 143–76.

5. Richard Stone, "The Graham Plan of 1935: An Aborted Crusade to De-Emphasize College Athletics," *North Carolina Historical Review* 64 (July 1987): 274–93; Pamela Grundy, *Learning to Win: Sports, Education, and Social Change in Twentieth-Century North Carolina* (Chapel Hill: University of North Carolina Press, 2001), 107–18; Watterson, *College Football*, 184–86.

6. Falla, *NCAA*, 130–31; Watterson, *College Football*, 197.

7. Thelin, *Games Colleges Play*, 101–2; Watterson, *College Football*, 209–12.

8. Murray Sperber, *Onward to Victory: The Crises That Shaped College Sports* (New York: Henry Holt, 1998), 233–42; Walter Byers, *Unsportsmanlike Conduct: Exploiting College Athletes* (Ann Arbor: University of Michigan Press, 1995), 53–55, 67; Watterson, *College Football*, 212–16.

9. "Report of the Athletic Committee of the Academic Faculty of the University of Virginia," October 10, 1951, RG 2/1/2.591, President's Papers, Box 2 (Athletics—1952), University Archives, University of Virginia, Charlottesville; Virginius Dabney, *Mr. Jefferson's University: A History* (Charlottesville: University Press of Virginia, 1981), 196–200; *Evening Star*, November 30, 1949; Stone, "Graham Plan of 1935," 280; Savage et al., *American College Athletics*, 242; Watterson, *College Football*, 214–15.

10. Guy Friddell, *Colgate Darden: Conversations with Guy Friddell* (Charlottesville: University Press of Virginia, 1978), 137; *Washington Post*, December 6, December 25, 1949, January 8, 1950; Watterson, *College Football*, 214.

11. H. C. Byrd to Clarence P. Houston, January 3, 1948, Box 65 (Athletics Miscellaneous, 1949), H. C. Byrd Presidential Records, University of Maryland Archives; George H. Callcott, *A History of the University of Maryland* (Baltimore: Maryland Historical Society, 1966), 243–44, 295, 314–23; George H. Callcott, interview with author, University Park, Md., November 30, 2006.

12. H. C. Byrd to Clarence P. Houston, December 14, 1948, Box 65, Byrd Presidential Records, University of Maryland Archives; *Washington Post*, January 15, 1950; Watterson, *College Football*, 216–17; Sperber, *Onward to Victory*, 237–40.

13. *Washington Post*, January 13, January 14, 1950; Watterson, *College Football*, 217–18; Sperber, *Onward to Victory*, 240–42; Byers, *Unsportsmanlike Conduct*, 54–55.

14. Byers, *Unsportsmanlike Conduct*, 67–73; Falla, *NCAA*, 149.

15. Neil D. Isaacs, *All the Moves: A History of College Basketball*, rev. ed. (New York: Harper and Row, 1984), 19–22; Michael Mandelbaum, *The Meaning of Sports: Why Americans Watch Baseball, Football, and Basketball and What They See When They Do* (New York: Public Affairs, 2004), 216–19; Davies, *Sports in American Life*, 96–97, 105–6; Grundy, *Learning to Win*, 40–68.

16. Isaacs, *All the Moves*, 61–63; Mandelbaum, *Meaning of Sports*, 217–19; Davies, *Sports in American Life*, 107, 157.

17. Frank Fitzpatrick, *And the Walls Came Tumbling Down: The Basketball Game That Changed American Sports* (New York: Simon and Schuster, 1999; reprint, Lincoln: University of Nebraska Press, 2000), 98; Isaacs, *All the Moves*, 26, 113–15; Mandelbaum, *Meaning of Sports*, 220–21.

18. Isaacs, *All the Moves*, 35, 56–59, 128–29; Davies, *Sports in American Life*, 157, 253; Falla, *NCAA*, 186, 283; *New York Times*, March 28, 1939.

19. *Raleigh News and Observer*, February 25, 1951; Charley Rosen, *Scandals of '51: How the Gamblers Almost Killed College Basketball* (New York: Seven Stories Press, 1978), 21; Stanley Cohen, *The Game They Played* (New York: Carroll and Graf, 1977), 25–27; Davies, *Sports in American Life*, 155–57; Isaacs, *All the Moves*, 76–80.

20. Rosen, *Scandals of '51*, 12–18, 93; Cohen, *Game They Played*, 215–17; Sperber, *Onward to Victory*, 305–6.

21. Clair Bee, "I Know Why They Sold Out to the Gamblers," *Saturday Evening Post*, February 2, 1952, p. 26; "L.I.U.'s Buzzer," *Time*, January 15, 1951, pp. 36–37; Rosen, *Scandals of '51*, 18–22; Sperber, *Onward to Victory*, 316–23; Randy Roberts and James Olson, *Winning Is the Only Thing: Sports in America since 1945* (Baltimore: Johns Hopkins University Press, 1989), 73–74.

22. "Young Businessmen," *Newsweek*, January 29, 1951, pp. 80–82; Albert J. Figone,

"Gambling and College Basketball: The Scandal of 1951," *Journal of Sport History* 16 (Spring 1989): 44–61; Rosen, *Scandals of '51*, 1–7.

23. "Who's Clean?," *Newsweek*, March 5, 1951, pp. 81–82; Richard O. Davies and Richard G. Abram, *Betting the Line: Sports Wagering in American Life* (Columbus: Ohio State University Press, 2001), 51–58; Rosen, *Scandals of '51*, 26–30; Cohen, *Game They Played*, 57–60; Figone, "Gambling and College Basketball," 44–51.

24. Rosen, *Scandals of '51*, 29–30; Davies and Abram, *Betting the Line*, 56–60; Cohen, *Game They Played*, 60–67; Alexander Wolff and Michael Atchison, "Utah: The First Cinderella," *Sports Illustrated*, March 22, 2010, pp. 71–78; Figone, "Gambling and College Basketball," 47–51.

25. Rosen, *Scandals of '51*, 118–28; Cohen, *Game They Played*,90–114; Figone, "Gambling and College Basketball," 52–53; Sperber, *Onward to Victory*, 311–25.

26. *New York Times*, November 20, 1951; Rosen, *Scandals of '51*, 59–60, 141–43, 195, 210–13; Cohen, *Game They Played*, 76, 157; Sperber, *Onward to Victory*, 306–21; Bee, "I Know Why They Sold Out," 26–27.

27. *New York Times*, February 21, May 1, 1951.

28. Cohen, *Game They Played*, 105, 107, 172–91; Rosen, *Scandals of '51*, 129, 146–90; Sperber, *Onward to Victory*, 327–43.

29. *New York Times*, November 20, December 8, 1951, April 30, 1952; Figone, "Gambling and College Basketball," 58–60.

30. *New York Times*, August 8, August 9, August 10, 1951; Sperber, *Onward to Victory*, 344–57.

31. "The Big Money," *Time*, March 5, 1951, p. 45; "Let's Not Duck the Real Issue in Sports Mess," *Saturday Evening Post*, March 24, 1951, p. 10; *New York Times*, March 18, 1951.

32. *New York Times*, March 18, August 10, 1951; Bee, "I Know Why They Sold Out," 27.

33. Byers, *Unsportsmanlike Conduct*, 57–61.

Chapter 2

1. *Roanoke Times*, November 28, 1951.

2. Gordon Gray to Clarence P. Houston, January 6, 1951, Subgroup 2, Series 2, Subseries 3, Box 10 (NCAA: General), "Statement Made to Herb O'Keef re Athletic Situation," December 2, 1951, Subgroup 2, Series 2, Subseries 3, Box 10 (General, 1951), Records of the Office of the President: Gordon Gray Files, University Archives, University of North Carolina, Chapel Hill; James L. Godfrey, "William Brantley Aycock: University Administrator, 1957–1964," *North Carolina Law Review* 64 (January 1986): 215–18; Philip M. Stern, *The Oppenheimer Case: Security on Trial* (New York: Harper and Row, 1969), 258–59; William D. Snider, *Light on the Hill: A History of the University of North Carolina at Chapel Hill* (Chapel Hill: University of North Carolina Press, 1992), 238–39; William A. Link, *William Friday: Power, Purpose, and American Higher Education* (Chapel Hill: University of North Carolina Press, 1995), 73–75.

3. Gordon Gray to Joe R. Fletcher, December 7, 1954, Subgroup 2, Series 2, Subseries 3, Box 10 (General, 1954–55), Gray Files, University of North Carolina Archives; Link, *William Friday*, 24–25, 98–99.

4. Alwyn Featherston, *Tobacco Road: Duke, Carolina, N.C. State, Wake Forest and the History of the Most Intense Backyard Rivalries in Sports* (Guilford, Conn.: Lyons Press, 2006), 4–17; Adam Powell, *University of North Carolina Basketball* (Charleston, S.C.: Arcadia Publishing, 2005), 9–37; Richard Stone, "The Graham Plan of 1935: An Aborted Crusade to De-Emphasize College Athletics," *North Carolina Historical Review* 64 (July 1987): 274–93; Snider, *Light on the Hill*, 3–4, 24–237.

5. Roy B. Clogston to James H. Weaver, November 15, 1958, Box 1 (Atlantic Coast Conference), Collection UA 15.007 (Department of Athletics Subject Files), University Archives, Special Collections Research Center, North Carolina State University, Raleigh; Alice Elizabeth Reagan, *North Carolina State University: A Narrative History* (Raleigh: North Carolina State University Foundation and North Carolina State University Alumni Association, 1987), 18–26, 45–81, 93–96, 160; Furman Bisher, "Each Game He Dies," *Collier's*, January 31, 1948, pp. 22–23, 48; Link, *William Friday*, 24–25; Snider, *Light on the Hill*, 215–18.

6. Bill Beezley, *The Wolfpack: Intercollegiate Athletics at North Carolina State University* (Raleigh: North Carolina State University, 1976), 117–34, 239, 334–36, 339–41.

7. A. Hollis Edens to Gordon Gray, February 15, 1951, Minutes of the Meeting of Presidents, Faculty Chairmen, and Athletic Directors of the Southern Conference Members, March 3, 1951, Box 68 (Southern Conference), A. Hollis Edens Records, University Archives, Duke University, Durham, N.C.; H. C. Byrd to Gordon Gray, June 4, 1951, Minutes of the Meeting of Presidents, Faculty Chairmen, and Athletic Directors of the Southern Conference Members, September 28, 1951, Box 109 (Southern Conference), H. C. Byrd Presidential Records, University Archives, University of Maryland, College Park; Lee W. Milford, "Annual Athletic Report, 1951–1952," Box 2 (Athletic Council), Records of the Athletic Council, Special Collections, Clemson University, Clemson, S.C.

8. Minutes of the Meeting of the Presidents, September 28, 1951, Byrd Presidential Records, University of Maryland Archives; *Durham Sun*, September 28, 1951; *Winston-Salem Journal*, October 1, 1951.

9. Gordon Gray to E. A. Darr, January 15, 1951, "Statement Made to Herb O'Keef," December 2, 1951, Subgroup 2, Series 2, Subseries 3, Box 10 (General, 1951), Gray Files, University of North Carolina Archives; "Suggested Joint Statement by Southern Conference Presidents," n.d., Box 68 (Southern Conference), Edens Records, Duke University Archives; Harold W. Tribble to H. C. Byrd, February 5, 1952, John L. Plyler to Byrd, February 18, 1952, Box 109 (Southern Conference Presidents, 1952, Ltrs. re. Bowl Games), Byrd Presidential Records, University of Maryland Archives.

10. Wright Bryan, *Clemson: An Informal History of the University, 1889–1979* (Columbia, S.C.: R. L. Bryan Co., 1979), 1–193; Henry H. Lesesne, *A History of the University of South Carolina, 1940–2000* (Columbia: University of South Carolina Press, 2001), 1–10.

11. Sam Blackman, Bob Bradley, and Chuck Kriese, *Clemson: Where the Tigers Play* (Champaign, Ill.: Sports Publishing, 2001), 237–41, 245–48; Bryan, *Clemson*, 71–78, 206–11.

12. R. F. Poole to Wilbur C. Johns, February 12, 1952, Box 2 (Athletic Council, 1952), Athletic Council Records, Special Collections, Clemson University; *Anderson Independent*, January 31, 1958; Bryan, *Clemson*, 122–25.

13. H. C. Byrd to Herbert O'Keef, November 3, 1951, Box 240 (Athletics, Misc., 1951), Byrd Presidential Records, University of Maryland Archives; *Washington Post*, November 12, 1951.

14. George H. Callcott, *A History of the University of Maryland* (Baltimore: Maryland Historical Society, 1966), 313–45; David S. Brown, *Richard Hofstadter: An Intellectual Biography* (Chicago: University of Chicago Press, 2006), 37–41; Bob Considine, "Curley Byrd Catches the Worm," *Saturday Evening Post*, June 28, 1941, p. 14; "The Coach," *Time*, August 3, 1959, p. 52; George H. Callcott, interview with author, University Park, Md., November 30, 2006.

15. Tim Cohane, "How Maryland Became a Football Power," *Look*, November 2, 1954, pp. 50–58; Paul W. Bryant and John Underwood, *Bear: The Hard Life and Good Times of Alabama's Coach Bryant* (Boston: Little, Brown, and Co., 1974), 85–90; Callcott, *History of the University of Maryland*, 354.

16. H. C. Byrd to J. Mears, December 14, 1951, Box 240 (Athletics, Misc., 1951), Byrd Presidential Records, University of Maryland Archives; *Washington Post*, November 12, 1951; *Diamondback*, November 18, 1953, January 19, 1954; "The Losers Are Winners," *Newsweek*, November 24, 1958, pp. 68–70; *New York Times*, February 18, 1989; Kent Baker, *Red, White, and Amen: Maryland Basketball* (Huntsville, Ala.: Strode Publishers, 1979), 85–86; Callcott, *History of the University of Maryland*, 354–57.

17. Minutes, Annual Meeting, Southern Conference, December 14–15, 1951, Box 13 (Southern Conference Annual Meeting, 1951), Geary Eppley Papers, University of Maryland Archives.

18. H. C. Byrd to Gordon Gray, June 4, 1951, Box 109 (Southern Conference, 1951), Byrd to Bernie Moore, December 20, 1951, Box 240 (Athletics, Misc., 1951), Byrd to Robert B. House, May 5, 1952, Box 109 (Southern Conference Presidents), Byrd Presidential Records, University of Maryland Archives.

19. Lee W. Milford to A. C. Mann, December 19, 1951, Box 2 (Athletic Council, 1951), Athletic Council Records, Clemson University; R. F. Poole to H. C. Byrd, January 30, 1952, Box 109 (Southern Conference Presidents, 1952, Ltrs. re. Bowl Games), Poole to Byrd, May 9, 1952, Box 109 (Southern Conference Presidents), Byrd Presidential Records, University of Maryland Archives.

20. *Durham Morning Herald*, May 9, 1953; Bruce A. Corrie, *The Atlantic Coast Conference, 1953–1978* (Durham, N.C.: Carolina Academic Press, 1978), 42–43; John Roth, *The Encyclopedia of Duke Basketball* (Durham, N.C.: Duke University Press, 2006), 124–26; Barry Jacobs, *Golden Glory: The First 50 Years of the ACC* (Greensboro, N.C.: Mann Media, 2002), 22–23; Bill Brill, *Duke Basketball: 100 Seasons, A Legacy of Achievement* (Champaign, Ill.: Sports Publishing, 2004), 35.

21. Norman M. Smith to H. C. Byrd, January 28, 1952, Box 109 (Southern Conference Presidents, 1952, Ltrs. re. Bowl Games), Donald Russell to Byrd, November 10, 1952, Box 109 (Southern Conference—Letters to Presidents re. Bowl Games), Byrd Presidential Records, University of Maryland Archives; Lesesne, *History of the University of South Carolina*, 78–80.

22. Lesesne, *History of the University of South Carolina*, 1–65.

23. Ibid., 65–67, 115–16; Donald Russell to Gordon Gray, June 15, 1954, Box 1 (Associations: Atlantic Coast Conference), Records of the Office of the President: Donald S.

Russell, 1953–54, University Archives, University of South Carolina, Columbia; "Football Record Book," "Men's Basketball Record Book," www.soconsports.com (accessed October 8, 2008).

24. Featherston, *Tobacco Road*, 1–12; Bynum Shaw, *The History of Wake Forest College: Volume 4, 1943–1967* (Winston-Salem, N.C.: Wake Forest University, 1988), 49; Robert F. Durden, *The Launching of Duke University, 1924–1949* (Durham: Duke University Press, 1993), 465; Harry Henson, ed., *World Almanac and Book of Facts, 1950* (New York: New York World-Telegram, 1950), 550; Reagan, *North Carolina State University*, 126.

25. Gordon Gray to J. G. Stipe, January 22, 1952, Subgroup 2, Series 2, Subseries 3, Box 10 (General, 1952), Gray Files, University of North Carolina Archives; "Suggested Joint Statement by Southern Conference Presidents," Edens Records, Duke University Archives; Edwin G. Wilson, interview with author, Winston-Salem, N.C., September 22, 2008.

26. Gordon Gray to H. L. Riddle, September 12, 1952, Subgroup 1, Series 1, Subseries 2, Box 2 (Athletics Relationships, 1952–53), Gray to Kemp D. Battle, October 21, 1952, Subgroup 2, Series 2, Subseries 3, Box 10 (General, 1952), Gray Files, William C. Friday oral history, November 28, 1990, Item L-146, Southern Oral History Program, University of North Carolina Archives; Minutes of the Meeting of the Presidents of Southern Conference Institutions, March 8, 1952, Box 68 (Southern Conference), Edens Records, Duke University Archives; William C. Friday, interview with author, Chapel Hill, N.C., August 15, 2006.

27. Robert F. Durden, *The Dukes of Durham, 1865–1929* (Durham: Duke University Press, 1987), 199–260; Durden, *Launching of Duke University*, 67–168, 492–501; "Tobacco and Erudition," *Time*, October 24, 1949, p. 49.

28. A. Hollis Edens to Colgate W. Darden Jr., October 4, 1956, RG 2/1/2.634, President's Papers, Box 3 (Athletics), University Archives, University of Virginia, Charlottesville; Durden, *Launching of Duke University*, 236–44; Roth, *Encyclopedia of Duke Basketball*, 124–29; *New York Times*, March 18, 1951; "Football Record Book," "Men's Basketball Record Book," www.soconsports.com (accessed October 8, 2008).

29. Thomas K. Hearn III, *Wake Forest University* (Charleston, S.C.: Arcadia Publishing, 2003), 7–8, 111; Shaw, *The History of Wake Forest College*, 1–3; Wake Forest College Birthplace Society, "History," www.wakeforestbirthplace.org (accessed October 7, 2008).

30. *Raleigh News and Observer*, October 25, October 26, October 28, 1954; Harold W. Tribble to Gordon Gray, c. November 5, 1954, Box 17, File 1058 (UNC–Chapel Hill Controversy), Records of the President's Office: Harold W. Tribble, University Archives, Wake Forest University, Winston-Salem, N.C.; Shaw, *The History of Wake Forest College*, 25–106; Wilson interview.

31. Harold W. Tribble to Bryan Haislip, February 12, 1953, Box 15, File 900 (Athletics, Criticism, 1950–1964), Tribble Records, Wake Forest University Archives; Hearn, *Wake Forest University*, 85–90; Shaw, *History of Wake Forest College*, 56–59, 77–78, 325–34.

32. Gordon Gray to Chancellor Harrelson and Chancellor House, November 10, 1952, Subgroup 2, Series 2, Subseries 3, Box 10 (Southern Conference, General), Gray Files, University of North Carolina Archives; Gray to H. C. Byrd, Box 109 (Southern

Conference.—Letters to Presidents re. Bowl Games, 1952), Byrd Presidential Records, University of Maryland Archives; E. M. Cameron to Hollis Edens, May 15, 1953, Box 53 (Southern Conference Correspondence, Rulings, Interpretations), Charles E. Jordan Papers, Duke University Archives; *Washington Post*, October 15, 1952.

33. William Friday, "Notes on the Meeting of the Trustees Committee on Athletic Relationships," May 6, 1953, Subgroup 1, Series 1, Subseries 2, Box 2 (Athletic Relationships, 1952–53), Gray Files, University of North Carolina Archives; *Washington Post*, May 10, 1953; Friday interview.

34. "Minutes of the Various Meetings Held at the Sedgefield Inn, Greensboro, North Carolina on May 7 and 8, 1953," May 14, 1953, Box 582 (Minutes, Atlantic Coast Conference, vol. 1), Byrd Presidential Records, University of Maryland Archives; *Richmond Times-Dispatch*, May 8, 1953; *Durham Morning Sun*, May 8, 1953; *Washington Post*, May 10, 1953.

35. Minutes of Regular Meeting, Southern Conference, May 8, 1953, Box 80 (Regular Meeting, Southern Conference, May 8, 1953), "Minutes of the Various Meetings Held . . . May 7 and 8, 1953," Byrd Presidential Records, University of Maryland Archives; *Raleigh News and Observer*, May 9, 1953; *Durham Morning Herald*, May 10, 1953.

36. Oliver K. Cornwell to "Gentlemen," May 14, 1953, Box 80 (Southern Conference, 1953), Minutes of Meeting, June 14, 1953, Box 582 (Minutes, Atlantic Coast Conference, vol. 1), Byrd Presidential Records, University of Maryland Archives; *Durham Morning Herald*, May 10, 1953; Corrie, *Atlantic Coast Conference*, 45–46.

37. William Friday to Gordon Gray, May 13, 1953, Friday to Gray, June 4, 1953, Subgroup 2. Series 2, Subseries 3, Box 10 (Atlantic Coast Conference, 1953–54), Gray Files, University of North Carolina Archives; Minutes of Atlantic Coast Conference Meeting, August 7, 1953, Report of the Committee on Constitution and By-Laws, October 1953, Box 582 (Minutes, Atlantic Coast Conference, vol. 1), *Southern Conference Constitution and By-Laws*, July 1, 1952, Box 109 (Southern Conference Presidents, 1952), Byrd Presidential Records, University of Maryland Archives; *Raleigh News and Observer*, May 6, 1953; *Charlotte Observer*, May 8, 1953.

38. Minutes of Atlantic Coast Conference Meeting, December 4, 1953, Box 582 (Minutes, Atlantic Coast Conference, vol. 1), Byrd Presidential Records, University of Maryland Archives; *Baltimore Sun*, December 5, 1953; Jack Falla, *NCAA: The Voice of College Sports, A Diamond Anniversary History, 1906–1981* (Mission, Kans.: National Collegiate Athletic Association, 1981), 135–36.

39. Harold W. Tribble to Hollis Edens, May 26, 1953, Box 6 (Atlantic Coast Conference), Edens Records, Duke University Archives; Tribble to Gordon Gray, May 26, 1953, Gray to Tribble, June 12, 1953, Subgroup 2, Series 2, Subseries 3, Box 10 (Atlantic Coast Conference, 1953–54), Gray Files, University of North Carolina Archives; Minutes of Meeting, June 14, 1953, Minutes of Atlantic Coast Conference Meeting, August 7, 1953, Minutes of Atlantic Coast Conference Meeting, December 4, 1953, Report of the Committee on Constitution and By-Laws, October 1953, Byrd Presidential Records, University of Maryland Archives; Corrie, *Atlantic Coast Conference*, 49–50.

40. Everett N. Case to Frank McGuire, May 14, 1953, Box 2 (Basketball, Varsity), Collection UA 15.007 (Department of Athletics Subject Files), North Carolina State University Archives; Meeting of Athletic Directors, May 25–26, 1953, Minutes of Meet-

ing, June 14, 1953, Minutes of Atlantic Coast Conference Meeting, December 4, 1953, Byrd Presidential Records, University of Maryland Archives; *Charlotte Observer*, May 9, 1953; *Raleigh News and Observer*, May 12, 1953, May 3, 1963; *Baltimore Sun*, December 5, 1953; Bud Millikan, telephone interview with the author, July 30, 2006; Jacobs, *Golden Glory*, 22.

41. Minutes of Meeting, June 14, 1953, Byrd Presidential Records, University of Maryland Archives; *Durham Morning Herald*, May 9, 1953; *Baltimore Sun*, May 9, 1953; *Raleigh News and Observer*, May 10, 1953.

42. Virginius Dabney, *Mr. Jefferson's University: A History* (Charlottesville: University Press of Virginia, 1981), 1–2, 44, 78, 80–82, 105, 185.

43. Chester Goolrick, "Mr. Jefferson's University," *Holiday*, February 1961, 51; Dabney, *Mr. Jefferson's University*, 92–96, 293–96.

44. Colgate W. Darden oral history, p. 1, RG 26-9, University of Virginia Archives; Guy Friddell, *Colgate Darden: Conversations with Guy Friddell* (Charlottesville: University Press of Virginia, 1978), 1–14, 30, 104–5; Dabney, *Mr. Jefferson's University*, 271–76, 327–30.

45. Darden oral history, pp. 10–11, Colgate W. Darden Jr. to Frank W. Rogers, November 29, 1951, RG 2/1/2.581, Box 3 (Athletics), "Report of the Athletic Committee of the Academic Faculty of the University of Virginia," October 10, 1951, RG 2/1/2.591, Box 2 (Athletics), President's Papers, University of Virginia Archives; Michael MacCambridge, ed., *ESPN College Football Encyclopedia* (New York: ESPN Books, 2005), 960; *University of Virginia, 1975–76 Basketball Handbook*, 62 (in author's possession); Friddell, *Colgate Darden*, 21, 22, 33; Dabney, *Mr. Jefferson's University*, 318–19.

46. Virginia Stokes to Mrs. Davis, n.d., Minutes of Meeting of the Athletic Council, May 30, 1953, Minutes of Meeting of the Athletic Council, September 25, 1953, RG 2/1/2.631, Box 4 (Athletics), President's Papers, University of Virginia Archives.

47. Minutes of the Board of Visitors Meeting, October 9, 1953, ibid.; Minutes of Atlantic Coast Conference Meeting, December 4, 1953, Byrd Presidential Records, University of Maryland Archives; *Washington Post*, October 10, 1953; *Cavalier Daily*, October 8, October 10, 1953; John S. Watterson, "Football at the University of Virginia, 1951–1961: A Perfect Gridiron Storm," *Journal of Sport History* 34 (Fall 2007): 375–87.

48. Report of the Committee on Constitution and By-Laws, October 1953, Minutes of Atlantic Coast Conference Meeting, May 6–7, 1954, Box 582 (Minutes, Atlantic Coast Conference, vol. 1), Byrd Presidential Records, University of Maryland Archives; Gene Corrigan oral history, p. 6, RG 26-178, University of Virginia Archives; *Raleigh News and Observer*, October 11, 1953; Corrie, *Atlantic Coast Conference*, 53; Jacobs, *Golden Glory*, 44; Gene Corrigan, interview with author, Charlottesville, Va., November 14, 2006.

Chapter 3

1. *Durham Sun*, December 28, 1958; *Durham Morning Herald*, December 28, 1958; *Winston-Salem Journal-Sentinel*, December 28, 1958.

2. *Charlotte Observer*, January 1, 1959; *Raleigh News and Observer*, December 25, 1994; Bill Beezley, *The Wolfpack: Intercollegiate Athletics at North Carolina State Univer-*

sity (Raleigh: North Carolina State University, 1976), 248; Alwyn Featherston, *Tobacco Road: Duke, Carolina, N.C. State, Wake Forest and the History of the Most Intense Backyard Rivalries in Sports* (Guilford, Conn.: Lyons Press, 2006), 12–13; Douglas Herakovich, *Pack Pride: An Illustrated History of N.C. State Basketball* (Cary, N.C.: Yesterday's Future, 1994), 38.

3. Harry T. Paxton, "The Basketball Bug Bites Dixie," *Saturday Evening Post*, March 10, 1951, pp. 31, 111–14; *Raleigh News and Observer*, December 25, 1994; Herakovich, *Pack Pride*, 38.

4. *Raleigh News and Observer*, December 28, December 29, December 30, 1958.

5. M. Chas. Mileham to Roy Clogston, January 23, 1958, Clogston to Mileham, January 25, 1958, Box 4 (Dixie Classic), Collection UA 15.007 (Department of Athletics Subject Files), University Archives, Special Collections Research Center, North Carolina State University, Raleigh; Charles H. Martin, "The Rise and Fall of Jim Crow in Southern College Sports: The Case of the Atlantic Coast Conference," *North Carolina Historical Review* 76 (July 1999): 253–84; Oscar Robertson, *The Big O: My Life, My Times, My Game* (Emmaus, Pa.: Rodale Press, 2003), 99; Bill Guthridge, interview with author, Chapel Hill, N.C., April 4, 2007.

6. *Raleigh News and Observer*, December 30, 1958; *Durham Sun*, December 30, 1958; *Durham Morning Herald*, December 30, December 31, 1958; *Cincinnati Enquirer*, December 30, 1958, January 1, 1959. Oscar Robertson gives a quite different description of fan behavior in his memoirs. He recalls that the crowd at Reynolds Coliseum during the Cincinnati–Wake game "was in a racist frenzy" and that it showered him with the crudest of racial epithets. See Robertson, *Big O*, 99–100. The newspapers in the Raleigh area and in Cincinnati that covered the Dixie Classic, however, did not report that prevailing conditions approached a "racist frenzy," though they made clear that the fans lustily booed Robertson at times. Bill Hensley, who was the sports information director at NC State in 1958, and Charlie Bryant, who was assistant coach at Wake Forest at the time, took strong exception to the claim that the crowd was in a "racist frenzy." Hensley also checked with others who played in or reported on the Classic, and their memories were consistent with his. Bill Hensley, email to the author, December 15, 2008, and Charlie Bryant, email to the author, December 16, 2008, in author's possession. This is not to deny the probability that some individuals in the crowd sullied the spirit of competition with racial slurs.

7. *Raleigh News and Observer*, December 31, 1958; *Durham Sun*, December 31, 1958; Robertson, *Big O*, 101.

8. *Raleigh News and Observer*, December 29, 1958, January 1, 1959; *Durham Morning Herald*, December 31, 1958, January 1, 1959; *Durham Sun*, January 1, 1959; *Charlotte Observer*, January 1, 1959.

9. *Durham Morning Herald*, January 2, 1959.

10. Furman Bisher, "Each Game He Dies," *Collier's*, January 31, 1948, pp. 22–23, 48; *Raleigh News and Observer*, February 25, 1951; Herakovich, *Pack Pride*, 20–21; Beezley, *Wolfpack*, 240–41.

11. Smith Barrier, *On Tobacco Road: Basketball in North Carolina* (New York: Leisure Press, 1983), 43–44; Ron Morris, *ACC Basketball: An Illustrated History* (Chapel Hill,

N.C.: Four Corners Press, 1988), 66; Paxton, "Basketball Bug Bites Dixie," 113; Featherston, *Tobacco Road*, 9; Herakovich, *Pack Pride*, 131; Beezley, *Wolfpack*, 167–68, 239–40.

12. Paxton, "Basketball Bug Bites Dixie," 111, 113; Herakovich, *Pack Pride*, 22; Barrier, *On Tobacco Road*, 44; Beezley, *Wolfpack*, 240–42.

13. Herakovich, *Pack Pride*, 19–24; Morris, *ACC Basketball*, 66; Beezley, *Wolfpack*, 242–44.

14. Beezley, *Wolfpack*, 245–47; Herakovich, *Pack Pride*, 25–29.

15. Barrier, *On Tobacco Road*, 48–50; Featherston, *Tobacco Road*, 17; Herakovich, *Pack Pride*, 28; Morris, *ACC Basketball*, 69.

16. Pamela Grundy, *Learning to Win: Sports, Education, and Social Change in Twentieth-Century North Carolina* (Chapel Hill: University of North Carolina Press, 2001), 192–97; Joe Menzer, *Four Corners: How UNC, N.C. State, Duke and Wake Forest Made North Carolina the Center of the Basketball Universe* (New York: Simon and Schuster, 1999), 33; Paxton, "Basketball Bug Bites Dixie," 111, 113; Barrier, *On Tobacco Road*, 46; Featherston, *Tobacco Road*, 10; Herakovich, *Pack Pride*, 130–31.

17. *Raleigh News and Observer*, February 25, 1951; Paxton, "Basketball Bug Bites Dixie," 112, 114; Menzer, *Four Corners*, 30–33; Featherston, *Tobacco Road*, 11–12; Herakovich, *Pack Pride*, 22–23; Morris, *ACC Basketball*, 68, 70. For the early history of basketball in North Carolina, the best source is Grundy, *Learning to Win*.

18. Menzer, *Four Corners*, 30; Barrier, *On Tobacco Road*, 51; Bud Millikan, telephone interview with author, July 30, 2006.

19. Norm Sloan with Larry Guest, *Confessions of a Coach: A Revealing Tour of College Basketball's Backstage* (Nashville, Tenn.: Rutledge Hill Press, 1991), 47; Tim Peeler, *Legends of N.C. State Basketball* (Champaign, Ill.: Sports Publishing, 2004), 9; Menzer, *Four Corners*, 35; Paxton, "Basketball Bug Bites Dixie," 113; Bill Hensley, interview with author, Charlotte, N.C., July 17, 2007.

20. Bisher, "Each Game He Dies," 23; Morris, *ACC Basketball*, 68–69; Bucky Waters, interview with author, Durham, N.C., April 4, 2007; Lou Pucillo, interview with author, Raleigh, N.C., March 17, 2008.

21. Morris, *ACC Basketball*, 68.

22. Bones McKinney with Garland Atkins, *Bones: Honk Your Horn If You Love Basketball* (Gastonia, N.C.: Garland Publications, 1988), 13, 39–78; Bynum Shaw, *The History of Wake Forest College: Volume 4, 1943-1967* (Winston-Salem: Wake Forest University, 1988), 46; Morris, *ACC Basketball*, 116–17; Barrier, *On Tobacco Road*, 93–97.

23. John Underwood, "Go Get 'em, Coaches!," *Sports Illustrated*, December 9, 1963, 90; McKinney, *Bones*, 40, 66; Morris, *ACC Basketball*, 116; Menzer, *Four Corners*, 67.

24. *Raleigh News and Observer*, February 21, 1954; McKinney, *Bones*, 77–78, 87; Barrier, *On Tobacco Road*, 103.

25. McKinney, *Bones*, 82–87; Morris, *ACC Basketball*, 40–41; Mike Douchant, *Encyclopedia of College Basketball* (Detroit: Visible Ink Press, 1995), 311; Jack Murdock, interview with author, Raleigh, N.C., March 18, 2008; Hensley interview.

26. John Roth, *The Encyclopedia of Duke Basketball* (Durham, N.C.: Duke University Press, 2006), 94–95, 185–86; Bill Brill, *Duke Basketball: 100 Seasons, A Legacy of Achievement* (Champaign, Ill.: Sports Publishing, 2004), 38–42; Red Auerbach with John Fein-

stein, *Let Me Tell You a Story: A Lifetime in the Game* (New York: Little, Brown and Co., 2004), 53–57.

27. *Greensboro News*, November 10, 1950; *Durham Morning Herald*, November 10, 1950, March 24, 1959; *Durham Sun*, November 9, 1950, March 24, 1959; *Duke Chronicle*, January 9, 1959; Roth, *Encyclopedia of Duke Basketball*, 112–13, 194–96; Brill, *Duke Basketball*, 42–44, 176.

28. William A. Link, *William Friday: Power, Purpose, and American Higher Education* (Chapel Hill: University of North Carolina Press, 1995), 66–75; Adam Powell, *University of North Carolina Basketball* (Charleston, S.C.: Arcadia Publishing, 2005), 36–37; Don Barton and Bob Fulton, *Frank McGuire: The Life and Times of a Basketball Legend* (Columbia, S.C.: Summerhouse Press, 1995), 43.

29. William Friday to Gordon Gray, July 31, 1952, Gray to John V. Connorton, August 19, 1952, Subgroup 2, Series 2, Subseries 3, Box 10 (Basketball, 1952–55), Gordon Gray to Carey H. Bostian, September 18, 1954, Subgroup 2, Series 1, Subseries 3, Box 5 (Basketball, 1950–55), Records of the Office of the President: Gordon Gray Files, University Archives, University of North Carolina, Chapel Hill; *Daily Tar Heel*, January 21, 1954; Barton and Fulton, *Frank McGuire*, 16–37, 44–45; Powell, *North Carolina Basketball*, 45.

30. Paul McMullen, *Maryland Basketball: Tales from Cole Field House* (Baltimore: Johns Hopkins University Press, 2002), 2–8; Kent Baker, *Red, White, and Amen: Maryland Basketball* (Huntsville, Ala.: Strode Publishers, 1979), 85–102; Morris, *ACC Basketball*, 52–53; Tom Young, interview with author, Virginia Beach, Va., June 27, 2008; Millikan, telephone interview with author.

31. Booton Herndon, "Eyes on the Buzzer," *Sports Illustrated*, March 14, 1955, pp. 28–31; Gary Cramer, *Cavaliers! A Pictorial History of UVA Basketball* (Charlottesville, Va.: Spring House Publishing, 1983), 45–50; Morris, *ACC Basketball*, 62–63, 278–79.

32. Morris, *ACC Basketball*, 38–39, 278–81.

33. Ibid., 59, 279–81.

34. *Raleigh News and Observer*, March 7, 1954; Pat Conroy, *My Losing Season* (New York: Dial Press, 2002), 139; Smith Barrier and Hugh Morton, *The ACC Basketball Tournament Classic* (Greensboro, N.C.: Greensboro Publications, 1981), 29–31; Morris, *ACC Basketball*, 278.

35. Peeler, *Legends of N.C. State Basketball*, 28–38; Herakovich, *Pack Pride*, 41–45; Morris, *ACC Basketball*, 33–36, 56–57, 279; Beezley, *Wolfpack*, 261.

36. John C. Prouty, *The ACC Basketball Stat Book, 1954 to 1993* (Huntingtown, Md.: Willow Oak Publishing, 1993), 286; Peeler, *Legends of N.C. State Basketball*, 36–37; Herakovich, *Pack Pride*, 45–47; Morris, *ACC Basketball*, 37, 40, 280; Barrier and Morton, *ACC Basketball Tournament*, 35–37.

37. John Sayle Watterson, *College Football: History—Spectacle—Controversy* (Baltimore: Johns Hopkins University Press, 2000), 227–36; Jack Falla, *NCAA: The Voice of College Sports—A Diamond Anniversary History, 1906–1981* (Mission, Kans.: National Collegiate Athletic Association, 1981), 136–40, 220–21.

38. Walter Byers to Gordon Gray, June 1, 1953, Everett N. Case to H. A. Fisher, June 24, 1953, Subgroup 2, Series 1, Subseries 3, Box 5 (NCAA Inquiry on Infractions, 1953), Gray Files, University of North Carolina Archives; Beezley, *Wolfpack*, 259–60.

39. Gordon Gray to Mr. Carmichael, June 4, 1953, Gray to J. W. Harrelson, June 4, 1953, Subgroup 2, Series 1, Subseries 3, Box 5 (NCAA Inquiry on Infractions, 1953), William Friday to Gray, Subgroup 2, Series 1, Subseries 3, Box 5 (Basketball, 1950–55), Gray Files, University of North Carolina Archives; Ronnie Shavlik to Dr. Fisher, June 9, 1953 [misdated 1952], UA 15.3 (Records of the Athletic Council), Box 7 (NCAA Infractions, 1951–54), North Carolina State University Archives; *Washington Post*, August 26, 1953.

40. Gordon Gray to Walter Byers, July 1, 1953, Gray to J. W. Harrelson, July 3, 1953, Case to Fisher, June 24, 1953, Subgroup 2, Series 1, Subseries 3, Box 5 (NCAA Inquiry on Infractions, 1953), Gray Files, University of North Carolina Archives.

41. Minutes of Atlantic Coast Conference, August 7, 1953, Gordon Gray to Chancellor Bostian, Chancellor Graham, and Chancellor House, June 2, 1954, Bostian to Gray, June 3, 1954, Subgroup 2, Series 2, Subseries 3, Box 10 (Atlantic Coast Conference, 1953–54), A. B. Moore to Gray, May 8, 1954, Subgroup 2, Series 1, Subseries 3, Box 5 (NCAA Inquiry on Infractions, 1954), Gray Files, University of North Carolina Archives; Roy Clogston to W. B. Brannin, October 9, 1953, UA 15.007 (Department of Athletics Subject Files), Box 3 (Clogston, Roy, 1952–54), North Carolina State University Archives; Bruce A. Corrie, *The Atlantic Coast Conference, 1953–1978* (Durham, N.C.: Carolina Academic Press, 1978), 46–48.

42. Carey H. Bostian to Walter Byers and Committee on Infractions, October 19, 1956, UA 15.007 (Department of Athletics Subject Files), Box 7 (National Collegiate Athletic Association, Investigations), North Carolina State University Archives; Bostian, "Report to President Friday on the Moreland Case," February 22, 1957, Subgroup 3, Series 1, Subseries 3, Box 63 (NCAA: Probation, Moreland Case, 1957), Records of the Office of the President: William C. Friday Files, University of North Carolina Archives; Furman Bisher, "A Scholarship for Jackie," in *The Grantland Rice Award Prize Short Stories*, ed. Robert Smith (Garden City, N.Y.: Doubleday, 1962), 111–24; Beezley, *Wolfpack*, 264–65; Herakovich, *Pack Pride*, 47–48.

43. Carey H. Bostian to Everett Case, March 16, 1956, UA 15.007 (Department of Athletics Subject Files), Box 2 (Basketball, Varsity), North Carolina State University Archives; Carey Bostian oral history, March 11, 1991, Item L-120, Southern Oral History Program, University of North Carolina Archives; *Raleigh News and Observer*, August 30, 1953; Rudolph Pate, "Carey Hoyt Bostian," *Popular Government* 25 (October 1957): 25–27; Alice Elizabeth Reagan, *North Carolina State University: A Narrative History* (Raleigh: North Carolina State University Foundation and North Carolina State University Alumni Foundation, 1987), 145–52.

44. Willis R. Casey, Harry E. Stewart, and Victor A. Bubas to Carey H. Bostian, October 18, 1956, UA 2.1 (Records of the Chancellor's Office), Box 19 (Moreland Case, National Collegiate Athletic Association), North Carolina State University Archives.

45. "Report to President Friday on the Moreland Case," February 22, 1957, Friday Files, University of North Carolina Archives; Bostian to Byers and the Committee on Infractions, October 19, 1956, North Carolina State University Archives.

46. *Raleigh News and Observer*, November 14, 1956; *Charlotte Observer*, November 15, 1956; Beezley, *Wolfpack*, 180–81.

47. Carey H. Bostian, "Report to President Friday on the Moreland Case," December 21, 1956, Subgroup 1, Series 1, Box 1 (Athletics: General, 1953, 1956–57), William C.

Friday to Reed Sarratt, February 12, 1957, Subgroup 3, Series 2, Subseries 3, Box 67 (National Collegiate Athletic Association, 1957–61), Friday Files, University of North Carolina Archives; *Raleigh News and Observer*, November 29, December 16, December 17, 1956.

48. James H. Weaver to C. H. Bostian, January 28, 1957, Oliver K. Cornwell, "Report to North Carolina State College of the Atlantic Coast Conferences Faculty Chairmen's Meeting," February 10, 1957, "Statement of Chancellor Bostian Concerning the Action of the Atlantic Coast Conference in the Moreland Case," n.d., Subgroup 3, Series 1, Subseries 3, Box 63 (NCAA: Probation, Moreland Case, 1957), Bostian, "Report to President Friday, December 21, 1956," Friday Files, University of North Carolina Archives.

49. Carey H. Bostian to James Weaver, January 25, 1957, "Excerpts from Interview with Jack W. Moreland," February 10, 1957, Subgroup 3, Series 1, Subseries 3, Box 63 (NCAA: Probation, Moreland Case, 1957), Weaver to William Friday, Subgroup 1, Series 1, Box 1 (Athletics: General, 1953, 1956–57), Friday Files, University of North Carolina Archives; Carey Bostian interview, July 17, 1981, UA 10.4, Box 3, North Carolina State University Archives; *Daily Tar Heel*, December 18, 1956; *Raleigh News and Observer*, December 20, 1956; Beezley, *Wolfpack*, 271.

50. Link, *William Friday*, 3–91; Arthur Padilla, *Portraits in Leadership: Six Extraordinary University Presidents* (Westport, Conn.: Praeger, 2005), 110–39.

51. Bostian, "Report to President Friday on the Moreland Case," February 22, 1957, Friday to Reed Sarratt, February 12, 1957, Friday Files, William C. Friday oral history, November 28, 1990, Item L-146, Bostian oral history, Item L-120, Southern Oral History Program, University of North Carolina Archives; Link, *William Friday*, 100–102; William C. Friday, interview with author, Chapel Hill, N.C., August 15, 2006.

52. Carey H. Bostian to B. Tartt Bell, November 19, 1956, UA 2.1 (Records of the Chancellor's Office), Box 19 (Moreland Case, Miscellaneous Letters), North Carolina State University Archives; Friday oral history, Item L-146, Southern Oral History Program, University of North Carolina Archives.

53. Carey H. Bostian to Roy B. Clogston, January 19, 1959, Subgroup 3, Series 1, Subseries 3, Box 63 (General, 1957–59), Friday Files, University of North Carolina Archives; *Raleigh News and Observer*, January 7, 1960; Herakovich, *Pack Pride*, 47–48; Bisher, "A Scholarship for Jackie," 124.

54. *Raleigh News and Observer*, February 25, 1957; Bisher, "Scholarship for Jackie," 117, 124; Herakovich, *Pack Pride*, 47–48.

55. Roy B. Clogston to Charles Creech, February 20, 1957, UA 15.007 (Department of Athletics Subject Files), Box 3 (Clogston, Roy, 1956–57), North Carolina State University Archives; Beezley, *Wolfpack*, 288–90; Herakovich, *Pack Pride*, 48–50.

56. "Odd Partners in Hot Basketball Act," *Life*, January 19, 1959, pp. 83–86; "Atlantic Coast," *Sports Illustrated*, December 8, 1958, p. 51; Morris, *ACC Basketball*, 282.

57. Remarks by Vic Bubas introducing Lou Pucillo, North Carolina Sports Hall of Fame, 1991, in author's possession (courtesy of Lou Pucillo); Peeler, *Legends of N.C. State Basketball*, 42–45; Herakovich, *Pack Pride*, 49–50; Pucillo interview.

58. *Raleigh News and Observer*, March 8, 1959; Peeler, *Legends of N.C. State Basketball*, 44–45; Morris, *ACC Basketball*, 285.

Chapter 4

1. *Winston-Salem Journal*, February 15, 1957; *Charlotte News*, January 17, 1957, March 4, 1958; *Charlotte Observer*, March 7, 1957; Ron Morris, *ACC Basketball: An Illustrated History* (Chapel Hill: Four Corners Press, 1988), p. 47.

2. *Raleigh News and Observer*, March 7, 1958; Smith Barrier and Hugh Morton, *The ACC Basketball Tournament Classic* (Greensboro, N.C.: Greensboro Publications, 1981), 6–8.

3. *Raleigh News and Observer*, March 8, March 9, 1957; *Charlotte Observer*, March 9, 1957; *Greensboro Daily News*, March 9, 1957.

4. *Winston-Salem Journal*, March 5, 1957; *Charlotte Observer*, March 7, 1957.

5. *Raleigh News and Observer*, March 7, 1957; Adam Lucas, *The Best Game Ever: How Frank McGuire's '57 Tar Heels Beat Wilt Chamberlain and Revolutionized College Basketball* (Guilford, Conn.: Lyons Press, 2006), 34, 121; Bones McKinney with Garland Atkins, *Bones: Honk Your Horn If You Love Basketball* (Gastonia, N.C.: Garland Publications, 1988), 90–91.

6. *Raleigh News and Observer*, March 8, 1957; Barrier and Morton, *ACC Basketball Tournament Classic*, 39–40.

7. *Raleigh News and Observer*, March 6, 1957; John C. Prouty, ed., *The ACC Basketball Stat Book, 1954 to 1993* (Huntingtown, Md.: Willow Oak Publishing, 1993), 334, 341, 347; Mike Douchant, *Encyclopedia of College Basketball* (Detroit: Visible Ink Press, 1995), 81; Morris, *ACC Basketball*, 281; McKinney, *Bones*, 100, 104.

8. Morris, *ACC Basketball*, 21–23, 281; Lucas, *Best Game Ever*, 20–24; Prouty, *ACC Basketball Stat Book*, 251, 264.

9. *Raleigh News and Observer*, March 9, 1957; *Greensboro Daily News*, March 9, 1957; McKinney, *Bones*, 104–5; Lucas, *Best Game Ever*, 120–23; Morris, *ACC Basketball*, 20–25; Prouty, *ACC Basketball Stat Book*, 334; Pete Brennan, interview with author, Duck, N.C., August 1, 2009.

10. *Raleigh News and Observer*, March 10, 1957; Barrier and Morton, *ACC Basketball Tournament Classic*, 40.

11. *Charlotte News*, February 26, 1957; Gerald Holland, "Dixie's Yankee Hero," *Sports Illustrated*, December 9, 1957, pp. 75, 77.

12. Richard J. Schaap, "Basketball's Underground Railroad," *Sports Illustrated*, February 4, 1957, p. 9; Don Barton and Bob Fulton, *Frank McGuire: The Life and Times of a Basketball Legend* (Columbia, S.C.: Summerhouse Press, 1995), 44–45; Morris, *ACC Basketball*, 123.

13. Holland, "Dixie's Yankee Hero," 82; Schaap, "Basketball's Underground Railroad," 9–10, 43; Lucas, *Best Game Ever*, 14.

14. Everett N. Case to H. A. Fisher, May 25, 1953, William Friday to Wallace Wade, June 22, 1953, Subgroup 2, Series 1, Subseries 3, Box 5 (Basketball, 1950–55), Records of the Office of the President: Gordon Gray Files, University Archives, University of North Carolina, Chapel Hill; *Richmond Times-Dispatch*, March 15, 1953; Scott Fowler, *North Carolina Tar Heels: Where Have You Gone?* (Champaign, Ill.: Sports Publishing, 2005), 3–4; Lucas, *Best Game Ever*, 12–15; Morris, *ACC Basketball*, 26–27. When the NCAA in-

quired about whether Rosenbluth had participated in a tryout at NC State, both Case (in his letter to Fisher) and Rosenbluth (in a conversation with William Friday) declared that there had been no workout. The *Richmond Times-Dispatch* reported in 1953 and Rosenbluth later recalled, however, that there had been a tryout during his visit to Raleigh. Given the fact that NC State was placed on probation in 1953 for holding illegal tryouts for prospects, those reports seem more plausible than the denials.

15. *Richmond Times-Dispatch*, March 15, 1953; Barton and Fulton, *Frank McGuire*, 45–46; Morris, *ACC Basketball*, 27.

16. Brennan interview.

17. Morgan Wootten, interview with author, University Park, Md., May 1, 2008.

18. Dean Smith with John Kilgo and Sally Jenkins, *A Coach's Life: My 40 years in College Basketball* (New York: Random House, 1999), 46; Morris, *ACC Basketball*, 122; Jeff Mullins, interview with author, Cornelius, N.C., July 16, 2007; Billy Packer, interview with author, Charlotte, N.C., July 16, 2007; Fred Shabel, interview with author, Philadelphia, Pa., June 12, 2008.

19. Frank Deford, "A Team That Was Blessed," *Sports Illustrated*, March 29, 1982, p. 60; Barton and Fulton, *Frank McGuire*, 140; Morris, *ACC Basketball*, 123; Lucas, *Best Game Ever*, 60; Smith, *Coach's Life*, 46; Holland, "Dixie's Yankee Hero," 77.

20. Barton and Fulton, *Frank McGuire*, 20–21, 38–41, 138–39, 151, 174; Lucas, *Best Game Ever*, 6–8; Holland, "Dixie's Yankee Hero," 83.

21. Daniel Klores, "Out of Bounds: Frank McGuire and Basketball Politics in South Carolina," *Southern Exposure*, Fall 1979, 104–11; Morris, *ACC Basketball*, 123; Frank Fellows, interview with author, Silver Spring, Md., February 19, 2007; Chip Conner, interview with author, Winston-Salem, N.C., May 21, 2007.

22. *Greensboro Daily News*, February 17, 1961; Art Chansky, *Blue Blood—Duke-Carolina: Inside the Most Storied Rivalry in College Sports* (New York: Thomas Dunne Books, 2005), 62, 78; Barton and Fulton, *Frank McGuire*, 67, 85, 138; Lucas, *Best Game Ever*, 67–69, 96–97.

23. *Daily Tar Heel*, January 21, 1954; *Raleigh News and Observer*, December 29, 1954; Morris, *ACC Basketball*, 28–31; Lucas, *Best Game Ever*, 103; Barton and Fulton, *Frank McGuire*, 67; Bill Hensley, interview with author, Charlotte, N.C., July 17, 2007; Charlie Bryant, interview with author, Raleigh, N.C., March 18, 2008.

24. Lucas, *Best Game Ever*, 125–28; Alwyn Featherston, *Tobacco Road: Duke, Carolina, N.C. State, Wake Forest and the History of the Most Intense Backyard Rivalries in Sports* (Guilford, Conn.: Lyons Press, 2006), 22.

25. Robert Cherry, *Wilt: Larger Than Life* (Chicago: Triumph Books, 2004), 48–50; Tex Maule and Jeremiah Tax, "The Magnetic Obsession," *Sports Illustrated*, March 25, 1957, pp. 33–36; Douchant, *Encyclopedia of College Basketball*, 79–83; Lucas, *Best Game Ever*, 130–36.

26. *Raleigh News and Observer*, March 23, 1957; *Charlotte Observer*, March 23, 1957; *Greensboro Daily News*, March 23, 1957; Lucas, *Best Game Ever*, 134–39; Fowler, *North Carolina Tar Heels*, 7–9.

27. Jeremiah Tax, "Cool 32 in Kansas City," *Sports Illustrated*, April 1, 1957, p. 59; Frank McGuire, "How We Became Champs," *Saturday Evening Post*, December 14, 1957, pp. 25, 88, 90; Deford, "Team That Was Blessed," 72; Fowler, *North Carolina Tar Heels*,

5–21; Cherry, *Wilt*, 52–56. In *Best Game Ever*, 141–78, Lucas provides a gripping detailed account of the championship game.

28. *Raleigh News and Observer*, March 24, 1957; *Charlotte Observer*, March 25, 1957; Deford, "Team That Was Blessed," 69; Barton and Fulton, *Frank McGuire*, 54; Lucas, *Best Game Ever*, 183–85; Douchant, *Encyclopedia of College Basketball*, 82; Brennan interview.

29. *Raleigh News and Observer*, March 25, 1957; *Charlotte Observer*, March 25, 1957; *Twin City Sentinel*, March 26, 1957; Holland, "Dixie's Yankee Hero," 75; Lucas, *Best Game Ever*, 179–80.

30. Andrew Doyle, "Turning the Tide: College Football and Southern Progressivism," in *The Sporting World of the Modern South*, ed. Patrick B. Miller (Urbana: University of Illinois Press, 2002), 101–25.

31. *Raleigh News and Observer*, March 25, 1957; *Charlotte Observer*, March 25, 1957; Holland, "Dixie's Yankee Hero," 75; Morris, *ACC Basketball*, 281.

32. Fred Hobson, *Off the Rim: Basketball and Other Religions in a Carolina Childhood* (Columbia: University of Missouri Press, 2006), 82–83; Deford, "Team That Was Blessed," 66.

33. *Raleigh News and Observer*, March 25, 1957.

34. R. B. House to Foy Roberson, February 22, 1955, Records of the Office of the Chancellor, Robert Burton House Series, Box 22 (Athletics, 1954–55), University of North Carolina Archives; *Daily Tar Heel*, January 8, 1955, February 16, 1956; *Raleigh News and Observer*, January 9, 1955; Morris, *ACC Basketball*, 212–13; Lucas, *Best Game Ever*, 98–99; William C. Friday, interview with author, Chapel Hill, N.C., August 15, 2006.

35. Minutes of Atlantic Coast Conference Meeting, December 7, 1956, Box 151 (Atlantic Coast Conference, 1956), Wilson H. Elkins Presidential Records, University Archives, University of Maryland, College Park; Minutes of Atlantic Coast Conference Meeting, May 3, 1957, RG 2/1/2.635, President's Papers, Box 3 (Athletics), University Archives, University of Virginia, Charlottesville; *Charlotte Observer*, March 25, 1957; Smith Barrier, *On Tobacco Road: Basketball in North Carolina* (New York: Leisure Press, 1983), 202–6; Barry Jacobs, *Golden Glory: The First 50 Years of the ACC* (Greensboro, N.C.: Mann Media, 2002), 46–48; Morris, *ACC Basketball*, 213–14.

36. Arthur Daley, "Sports Are Honest: A Defense," *New York Times Magazine*, March 4, 1951, p. 58; Roy Terrell, "The American Game," *Sports Illustrated*, December 9, 1957, pp. 26–29; John Sayle Watterson, *College Football: History—Spectacle—Controversy* (Baltimore: Johns Hopkins University Press, 2000), 242–43; Smith, *A Coach's Life*, 217; "MLB Attendance," http://bss.sfsu.edu/tygiel/hist490/mlbattendance.htm (accessed March 11, 2009).

37. Adam Powell, *University of North Carolina Basketball* (Charleston, S.C.: Arcadia Publishing, 2005), 51–55; Barrier and Morton, *ACC Basketball Tournament Classic*, 45; Morris, *ACC Basketball*, 282–85.

38. R. B. House to William Friday, April 15, 1957, House to Walter Byers, April 16, 1957, Byers to House, April 19, 1957, Box 22 (National Collegiate Athletic Association, 1953–57), House Series, University of North Carolina Archives; Schaap, "Basketball's Underground Railroad," 9–11, 43.

39. James H. Weaver to O. K. Cornwell, June 17, 1958, Subgroup 3, Series 2, Subseries 3,

Box 67 (National Collegiate Athletic Association, 1957–61), Records of the Office of the President: William C. Friday Files, C. P. Erickson to Frank McGuire, June 19, 1958, Box 10 (General: Gotkin, Harry, Correspondence, 1953–62), Records of the Office of the Chancellor: William Brantley Aycock Series, University of North Carolina Archives.

40. Walter Byers to C. P. Erickson, January 22, 1959, Byers to W. B. Aycock, January 15, 1960, Box 10 (General: Probation Data, 1957–61), Aycock Series, University of North Carolina Archives.

41. William Aycock oral history, April 11, 1990, Item L-118, Southern Oral History Program, University of North Carolina Archives; *Raleigh News and Observer*, February 26, 1957; James L. Godfrey, "William Brantley Aycock: University Administrator, 1957–1964," *North Carolina Law Review* 64 (January 1986): 215–18; William A. Link, *William Friday: Power, Purpose, and American Higher Education* (Chapel Hill: University of North Carolina Press, 1995), 57–58; Smith, *Coach's Life*, 58–59; Friday interview.

42. Harry Gotkin to W. B. Aycock, February 1, 1960, Box 10 (General: Gotkin, Harry, Correspondence, 1953–62), "A Memorandum of Statements Made by Chancellor William B. Aycock to Mr. Charles Gray," February 15, 1960, Box 10 (General: Student Audit Board, 1957–61), Aycock to Walter Byers, February 17, 1960, "North Carolina's Basketball Recruiting Policy," n.d., Box 10 (General: Probation Data, 1957–61), Aycock Series, "Confidential Report No. 27 by the N.C.A.A. Committee on Infractions," December 23, 1960, Subgroup 3, Series 2, Subseries 3, Box 67 (National Collegiate Athletic Association, 1957–61), Friday Files, University of North Carolina Archives.

43. Smith, *Coach's Life*, 53; Powell, *North Carolina Basketball*, 54.

44. Statement of W. B. Aycock, January 10, 1961, NCAA Confidential Report No. 27, Subgroup 3, Series 2, Subseries 3, Box 67 (National Collegiate Athletic Association, 1957–61), Friday Files, University of North Carolina Archives.

45. H. J. Dorricott to William B. Aycock, January 10, 1961, Box 10 (General: Probation Data, 1957–61), Aycock to Frank McGuire, April 28, 1961, Box 10 (General: UNC Department of Athletics, 1957–61), Aycock speech, "Control of Intercollegiate Athletics," May 2, 1961, Box 9 (National Collegiate Athletic Association, 1961), Aycock Series, University of North Carolina Archives; *Raleigh News and Observer*, January 11, January 24, January 25, 1961; *Charlotte Observer*, January 11, 1961; Smith, *Coach's Life*, 54–55.

46. Jeremiah Tax, "The Facts about the Fixes," *Sports Illustrated*, March 27, 1961, pp. 18–19; Ray Cave, "Portrait of a Fixer," *Sports Illustrated*, May 8, 1961, pp. 20–23; Tim Cohane, "Behind the Basketball Scandal," *Look*, February 13, 1962, pp. 84–93; Lou Brown, "I Worked with Basketball's No. 1 Briber," *Look*, February 27, 1962, pp. 71–85; Richard O. Davies and Richard G. Abram, *Betting the Line: Sports Wagering in American Life* (Columbus: Ohio State University Press, 2001), 103.

47. Brown, "I Worked with Basketball's No. 1 Briber," 71–84; Cohane, "Behind the Basketball Scandal," 85–88; Cave, "Portrait of a Fixer," 20–23; Tax, "Facts about the Fixes," 18–19.

48. Raymond E. Strong to Mrs. Marie Brown, March 30, 1961, W. B. Aycock to Charles Henderson, April 27, 1961, Henderson to Mr. and Mrs. Gunar E. Moe, May 4, 1961, Box 10 (General: New York Basketball Scandal, 1961), Aycock to Douglas Moe, September 24, 1962, Box 9 (Athletics), Aycock Series, University of North Carolina Ar-

chives; *Raleigh News and Observer*, May 4, 1961; *Charlotte Observer*, May 4, 1961; *Daily Tar Heel*, April 30, May 6, 1961.

49. *Raleigh News and Observer*, May 14, 1961; *Charlotte Observer*, May 14, 1961; Charley Rosen, *The Wizard of Odds: How Jack Molinas Almost Destroyed the Game of Basketball* (New York: Seven Stories Press, 2001), 165–216; Morris, *ACC Basketball*, 74–82.

50. *Raleigh News and Observer*, May 14, 1961, April 29, 1962, October 18, 1995; *Charlotte Observer*, August 6, 1959; John T. Caldwell to Coach Case, February 8, 1962, Box 26 (Athletic Department, 1961–62), Caldwell to Thomas F. Jones, December 1, 1966, Box 40 (Atlantic Coast Conference), Collection UA 2.1 (Records of the Chancellor's Office), University Archives, Special Collections Research Center, North Carolina State University Archives, Raleigh; Alice Elizabeth Reagan, *North Carolina State University: A Narrative History* (Raleigh: North Carolina State University Foundation and North Carolina State University Alumni Association, 1987), 168–202; Bryant interview.

51. "Text of Talk to Varsity Basketball Squad by Coach Everett Case, May 26, 1961," Box 24 (Athletics—Special Folder), Collection UA 2.1, North Carolina State University Archives; *Raleigh News and Observer*, May 14, 1961; *Charlotte Observer*, May 14, 1961.

52. *New York Herald Tribune*, May 23, 1961; "Scorecard," *Sports Illustrated*, May 29, 1961, p. 9; Barrier, *On Tobacco Road*, 91.

53. *Raleigh News and Observer*, May 14, May 15, 1961; *Durham Sun*, May 15, 1961; *The Technician*, May 15, 1961; *Daily Tar Heel*, May 19, 1961.

54. *Raleigh News and Observer*, May 16, May 17, 1961; Statement on "Intercollegiate Athletics" to Executive Committee of the Board of Trustees, May 22, 1961, Subgroup 1, Series 1, Box 1 (Athletics: General, 1963–64), Friday Files, Aycock interview, Item L-118, Southern Oral History Program, University of North Carolina Archives.

55. Minutes of Executive Committee of the Board of Trustees Meeting, May 22, 1961, Subgroup 2, Series 1, Subseries 3, Box 55 (Executive Committee Meeting, 5-22-61), Statement on "Intercollegiate Athletics," Friday Files, William C. Friday oral history, November 28, 1990, Item L-146, Southern Oral History Program, University of North Carolina Archives; *Raleigh News and Observer*, January 11, 1962; Link, *William Friday*, 104–9.

56. John T. Caldwell, Speech on "Intercollegiate Athletics," January 16, 1962, Subgroup 3, Series 1, Subseries 3, Box 63 (General, 1960–66, 1971), Friday oral history, Item L-146, Statement on "Intercollegiate Athletics," Friday Files, University of North Carolina Archives; *Charlotte Observer*, May 23, 1961.

57. *Raleigh News and Observer*, May 23, 1961, January 11, 1962, December 25, 1994; *Charlotte Observer*, May 24, 1961; *Durham Morning Herald*, May 23, May 24, 1961; "Report to the House of Representatives by Chancellor John T. Caldwell and President William Friday in Response to a Resolution of the House of Representatives," May 10, 1963, Subgroup 1, Series 1, Box 2 (Athletics: Dixie Classic Controversy, 1963), Friday Files, Friday oral history, Item L-146, University of North Carolina Archives; Roy Clogston to Joe Romoda, June 6, 1961, Box 3 (Clogston, Roy, 1960–62) Collection UA 15.007 (Department of Athletics Subject Files), North Carolina State University Archives.

58. *Richmond Times-Dispatch*, August 4, 1961; Smith, *Coach's Life*, 56; Barton and Fulton, *Frank McGuire*, 59.

59. *Raleigh News and Observer*, May 27, 1961; Frank J. McGuire to William B. Aycock, August 1, 1961, Box 10 (General: UNC Department of Athletics, 1957–61), Aycock Series, Aycock to John Umstead, August 2, 1961, Subgroup 3, Series 2, Subseries 3, Box 67 (Basketball, 1957–71), Friday Files, University of North Carolina Archives; Ray Cave, "McGuire Raises a Standard," *Sports Illustrated*, October 30, 1961, pp. 30–36.

60. Frank J. McGuire to William B. Aycock, August 1, 1961, Box 10 (General: UNC Department of Athletics, 1957–61), Aycock Series, University of North Carolina Archives; *Richmond Times-Dispatch*, August 4, 1961; Smith, *Coach's Life*, 57; Barton and Fulton, *Frank McGuire*, 63.

61. Smith, *Coach's Life*, 57–59; Friday interview.

62. Barrier, *On Tobacco Road*, 91; Smith, *Coach's Life*, 60.

Chapter 5

1. *Durham Morning Herald*, February 6, 1961; Ray Cave, "Duke's Red-hot and Blue Devil," *Sports Illustrated*, February 27, 1961, p. 41.

2. James H. Weaver, "Observations" [February 16, 1961], Subgroup 1, Series 1, Box 1 (Athletics: General, 1961–62), Records of the Office of the President: William Clyde Friday Files, University Archives, University of North Carolina, Chapel Hill; *Raleigh News and Observer*, February 5, February 17, 1961; *Durham Morning Herald*, February 6, 1961; Cave, "Duke's Red-hot and Blue Devil," 41.

3. Weaver, "Observations," Friday Files, University of North Carolina Archives.

4. *Raleigh News and Observer*, February 17, 1961; *Charlotte Observer*, February 17, 1961; Cave, "Red-hot and Blue Devil," 41.

5. Dean Smith, *A Coach's Life: My 40 Years in College Basketball* (New York: Random House, 1999), 55; Will Blythe, *To Hate Like This Is to Be Happy Forever: A Thoroughly Obsessive, Intermittently Uplifting, and Occasionally Unbiased Account of the Duke–North Carolina Basketball Rivalry* (New York: HarperCollins, 2006), 202; Alwyn Featherston, *Tobacco Road: Duke, Carolina, N.C. State, Wake Forest, and the History of the Most Intense Backyard Rivalry in Sports* (Guilford, Conn.: Lyons Press, 2006), 35–37.

6. *Durham Sun*, March 24, 1959; *Durham Morning Herald*, March 24, 1959; Les Woodcock, "A Decade of Records," *Sports Illustrated*, December 8, 1958, p. 94.

7. *Raleigh News and Observer*, May 6, 1959; Bucky Waters, interview with author, Durham, N.C., April 4, 2007; Bill Hensley, interview with author, Charlotte, N.C., July 17, 2007; Fred Shabel, interview with author, Philadelphia, Pa., June 12, 2008.

8. *Durham Morning Herald*, May 7, 1959; *Raleigh Times*, May 6, 1959; Ron Morris, *ACC Basketball: An Illustrated History* (Chapel Hill, N.C.: Four Corners Press, 1988), 130–34.

9. *Raleigh News and Observer*, May 5, 1996; Morris, *ACC Basketball*, 130–32, 134–35; Lou Pucillo, interview with author, Raleigh, N.C., March 17, 2008.

10. Jeff Mullins, interview with author, Cornelius, N.C., July 16, 2007.

11. *Durham Sun*, May 7, 1959; *Raleigh News and Observer*, November 20, 2004; Morris, *ACC Basketball*, 130–33; Mullins interview; Shabel interview.

12. Morris, *ACC Basketball*, 133; Waters interview; Mullins interview; Shabel interview.

13. Smith Barrier, *On Tobacco Road: Basketball in North Carolina* (New York: Leisure Press, 1983), 109; Shabel interview.

14. "Scouting Reports," *Sports Illustrated*, December 10, 1962, p. 44; Morris, *ACC Basketball*, 136; Jay Buckley, interview with author, Rockville, Md., August 22, 2007.

15. John Underwood, "Go Get 'em, Coaches!" *Sports Illustrated*, December 9, 1963, p. 83.

16. *Durham Sun*, May 7, 1959; *Raleigh News and Observer*, May 8, 1959; *Durham Morning Herald*, May 20, May 21, 1959; Roy Terrell, "Art Heyman: He Is Leading a Rout of the Tall Men," *Sports Illustrated*, December 10, 1962, p. 42; Morris, *ACC Basketball*, 84; Art Chansky, *Blue Blood: Duke-Carolina — The Most Storied Rivalry in College Hoops* (New York: Free Press, 2007), 64–65.

17. Cave, "Duke's Red-hot and Blue Devil," 41; Terrell, "Art Heyman," 41, 42; Shabel interview.

18. Pat Conroy, *My Losing Season* (New York: Dial Press, 2002), 132–33; *Newsday*, February 5, 1963; Barrier, *On Tobacco Road*, 109; Terrell, "Art Heyman," 41, 42.

19. Chansky, *Blue Blood*, 68; Waters interview.

20. Smith Barrier and Hugh Morton, *The ACC Basketball Tournament Classic* (Greensboro, N.C.: Greensboro Publications, 1981), 47–49; Jim Sumner, *Tales from the Duke Blue Devils Hardwood* (Champaign, Ill.: Sports Publishing, 2005), 46; Bill Brill, *Duke Basketball: 100 Seasons, A Legacy of Achievement* (Champaign, Ill.: Sports Publishing, 2004), 50.

21. *Raleigh News and Observer*, March 6, 1960; Morris, *ACC Basketball*, 82, 284; Barrier and Morton, *ACC Basketball Tournament Classic*, 47, 49.

22. John Feinstein, *Last Dance: Behind the Scenes at the Final Four* (New York: Little, Brown, and Co., 2006), 270–73; Cave, "Duke's Red-hot and Blue Devil," 41; Brill, *Duke Basketball*, 52; Morris, *ACC Basketball*, 94.

23. John Roth, *The Encyclopedia of Duke Basketball* (Durham, N.C.: Duke University Press, 2006), 121, 200, 268–69; John C. Prouty, *The ACC Basketball Stat Book* (Huntingtown, Md.: Willow Oak Publishing, 1993), 197, 203, 208; *Durham Sun*, February 6, 1961; "Scouting Reports," 44; Sumner, *Tales from the Duke Blue Devils*, 57–59.

24. Barrier and Morton, *ACC Basketball Tournament Classic*, 55; Sumner, *Tales from the Duke Blue Devils*, 53; Morris, *ACC Basketball*, 92.

25. Sumner, *Tales from the Duke Blue Devils*, 56–57; Morris, *ACC Basketball*, 85, 96–97.

26. *Raleigh News and Observer*, March 20, 1964; Morris, *ACC Basketball*, 98, 100.

27. Sumner, *Tales from the Duke Blue Devils*, 57–58; Morris, *ACC Basketball*, 98, 100, 288.

28. Alexander Wolff, "Birth of a Dynasty," *Sports Illustrated*, March 19, 2007, pp. 83–93; Sumner, *Tales from the Duke Blue Devils*, 58–59; Brill, *Duke Basketball*, 54; Morris, *ACC Basketball*, 100; Buckley interview.

29. Frank Deford, "A Lost Weekend in Carolina," *Sports Illustrated*, December 20, 1965, pp. 30–32; Roth, *Encyclopedia of Duke Basketball*, 244, 250–51, 340–41, 345–46; Brill, *Duke Basketball*, 55–56; Sumner, *Tales from the Blue Devils Hardwood*, 60–68; Morris, *ACC Basketball*, 101–13; Barrier and Morton, *ACC Basketball Tournament Classic*, 63–67; Prouty, *ACC Basketball Stat Book*, 47–49.

30. *The State*, December 1, 1966.

31. Harold W. Tribble to L. H. Hollingsworth, April 3, 1957, Box 12, Folder 708 (McKinney, Horace A.), RG 1.10 (Records of the President's Office: Harold W. Tribble), University Archives, Wake Forest University, Winston-Salem, N.C.; Bones McKinney with Garland Atkins, *Bones: Honk Your Horn If You Love Basketball* (Gastonia, N.C.: Garland Publications, 1988), 108; *Charlotte Observer*, March 26, 1957.

32. Harold W. Tribble to Coach Horace A. McKinney, March 29, 1960, Tribble to Reverend Horace A. McKinney, March 29, 1960, Box 12, Folder 708, Tribble Records, Wake Forest University Archives; "Horace Albert McKinney: Responsibility and the Desire for Perfection," *Sports Illustrated*, December 8, 1958, p. 112; Billy Packer, interview with author, Charlotte, N.C., July 16, 2007.

33. *Raleigh News and Observer*, March 27, 1957; Scouting Reports," *Sports Illustrated*, December 9, 1957, p. 46; Jack Murdock, interview with author, Raleigh, N.C., March 18, 2008; Charlie Bryant, interview with author, Raleigh, N.C., March 18, 2008.

34. *Raleigh News and Observer*, March 5, 1960; McKinney, *Bones*, 112.

35. Joe Menzer, *Four Corners: How UNC, N.C. State, Duke, and Wake Forest Made North Carolina the Center of the Basketball Universe* (New York: Simon and Schuster, 1999), 93–96; Packer interview.

36. *Old Gold and Black*, February 26, 1962; McKinney, *Bones*, 112–13, 116–17; Menzer, *Four Corners*, 76, 94.

37. *Old Gold and Black*, February 26, 1962; McKinney, *Bones*, 122, 125; Menzer, *Four Corners*, 107–8; Morris, *ACC Basketball*, 284.

38. Ray Cave, "Ohio State All the Way," *Sports Illustrated*, March 27, 1961, p. 20; *Raleigh News and Observer*, May 25, 1961; Billy Packer with Roland Lazenby, *Hoops!: Confessions of a College Basketball Analyst* (Chicago: Contemporary Books, 1986), 19–36; Morris, *ACC Basketball*, 285; McKinney, *Bones*, 134–40; Packer interview.

39. *Raleigh News and Observer*, November 26, 1961; *Old Gold and Black*, February 19, 1962; Menzer, *Four Corners*, 107–10; Barrier and Morton, *ACC Basketball Tournament Classic*, 55; Morris, *ACC Basketball*, 89, 92–93; McKinney, *Bones*, 142–43; Jim Savage, *The Encyclopedia of the NCAA Basketball Tournament* (New York: Dell Publishing, 1990), 213, 221.

40. "The Erupting Antics of 'Mr. Bones,'" *Life*, February 22, 1960, pp. 65–68; *Richmond Times-Dispatch*, January 23, 1960; Gene Warren, "Court or Pulpit, Ol' Bones Man of Action," *Sporting News*, March 7, 1964, pp. 33–34; McKinney, *Bones*, 127–29, 138; Mike Katos, interview with author, Philadelphia, Pa., June 12, 2008.

41. Menzer, *Four Corners*, 111; Morris, *ACC Basketball*, 287–89; Bryant interview; Packer interview.

42. *Winston-Salem Journal*, September 13, 1960; Menzer, *Four Corners*, 111; Warren, "Court or Pulpit," 33–34; Packer, *Hoops!*, 169–70; Hensley interview; Packer interview; Bryant interview.

43. Gene Hooks to Harold Tribble, September 27, 1965, Box 12, Folder 708, Tribble Records, Wake Forest University Archives; *Winston-Salem Journal*, September 29, 1965; *New York Times*, September 22, 2008; Packer, *Hoops!*, 38; McKinney, *Bones*, 99.

44. *Winston-Salem Journal*, April 10, 1964, September 29, 1965; *Raleigh News and*

Observer, April 12, April 16, 1964; *Old Gold and Black*, March 2, April 13, 1964; Murdock interview; Bryant interview.

45. *Old Gold and Black*, April 20, 1964; *Winston-Salem Journal*, April 23, 1964, September 29, 1965; email from Al Hunt to the author, November 12, 2007, in author's possession; Al Hunt, interview with author, Washington, D.C., November 1, 2007; Bryant interview.

46. Harold W. Tribble to Horace A. McKinney, March 10, 1959, Tribble to Gilmer Cross, May 12, 1964, Box 12, Folder 708, Tribble Records, Wake Forest University Archives; *Raleigh News and Observer*, May 8, 1964; *Old Gold and Black*, March 1, 1965; Morris, *ACC Basketball*, 289.

47. Horace A. McKinney to Dr. Tribble, September 27, 1965, Hooks to Tribble, September 27, 1965, Box 12, Folder 708, Tribble Records, Wake Forest University Archives.

48. Harold W. Tribble to Horace A. McKinney, January 5, 1966, Box 12, Folder 708, Tribble Records, Wake Forest University Archives; *Winston-Salem Journal*, September 29, 1965; *Raleigh News and Observer*, September 29, 1965; *Old Gold and Black*, October 4, 1965.

49. Dean Smith to Harry Gotkin, October 4, 1961, Box 10 (General: Gotkin, Harry, Correspondence), Records of the Office of the Chancellor: William Brantley Aycock Series, University of North Carolina Archives; Barrier, *On Tobacco Road* 140–41; Smith, *Coach's Life*, 61.

50. *Charlotte Observer*, August 6, 1961; Frank Deford, "Long Ago, He Won the Big One," *Sports Illustrated*, November 29, 1982, pp. 102–15; Ken Rosenthal, *Dean Smith: A Tribute* (Champaign, Ill.: Sports Publishing, 2001), 256.

51. John Feinstein, *A March to Madness: The View from the Floor in the Atlantic Coast Conference* (Boston: Little, Brown, and Company, 1998), 186; Morris, *ACC Basketball*, 266–67; Barrier, *On Tobacco Road*, 139; Smith, *Coach's Life*, 6–31.

52. Frank J. McGuire to William B. Aycock, May 14, 1958, Box 6 (Physical Education and Athletics), Aycock Series, University of North Carolina Archives; Don Barton and Bob Fulton, *Frank McGuire: The Life and Times of a Basketball Legend* (Columbia, S.C.: Summerhouse Press, 1995), 63; Dan Klores, *Roundball Culture: South Carolina Basketball* (Huntsville, Ala.: AM Press, 1980), 45; Barrier, *On Tobacco Road*, 140; Smith, *Coach's Life*, 31–46.

53. *Raleigh News and Observer*, December 1, 1961; Fred Hobson, *Off the Rim: Basketball and Other Religions in a Carolina Childhood* (Columbia: University of Missouri Press, 2006), 133–34; Morris, *ACC Basketball*, 268; Smith, *Coach's Life*, 61–65; Deford, "Long Ago, He Won the Big One," 108, 111.

54. W. B. Aycock to C. P. Erickson, January 5, 1962, Box 9 (Athletics), Aycock Series, University of North Carolina Archives; *Raleigh News and Observer*, December 1, 1962; Art Chansky, *Dean's Domain: The Inside Story of Dean Smith and His College Basketball Empire* (Atlanta: Longstreet, 1999), 53–54; Deford, "Long Ago, He Won the Big One," 112; Smith, *Coach's Life*, 66–68, 81–82; Morris, *ACC Basketball*, 289.

55. Smith, *Coach's Life*, 74–77; Morris, *ACC Basketball*, 288–89.

56. David Halberstam, *Playing for Keeps: Michael Jordan and the World He Made* (New York: Broadway Books, 1999), 77–78; Smith, *Coach's Life*, 70–71; Chansky, *Dean's*

Domain, 58–59; Rosenthal, *Dean Smith: A Tribute*, 13–17; Morris, *ACC Basketball*, 289; Deford, "Long Ago, He Won the Big One," 108, 111.

57. *Raleigh News and Observer*, March 5, 1966; Scott Fowler, *North Carolina Tar Heels: Where Have You Gone?* (Champaign, Ill.: Sports Publishing, 2005), 46–49; Morris, *ACC Basketball*, 104–5, 290; Rosenthal, *Dean Smith: A Tribute*, 17–19; Smith, *Coach's Life*, 71; Deford, "Long Ago, He Won the Big One," 111–12.

58. Dean Smith to C. P. Erickson, April 5, 1966, Box 15 (Athletics, Basketball), Records of the Office of the Chancellor: Joseph Carlyle Sitterson Series, University of North Carolina Archives; Smith, *Coach's Life*, 76, 82.

59. Tim Peeler, *Legends of N.C. State Basketball* (Champaign, Ill.: Sports Publishing, 2004), 11; Morris, *ACC Basketball*, 284–86; Prouty, *The ACC Basketball Stat Book*, 25–35.

60. *Raleigh News and Observer*, December 8, 1964; Douglas Herakovich, *Pack Pride: An Illustrated History of N.C. State Basketball* (Cary, N.C.: Yesterday's Future, 1994), 56–57; Mark Kriegel, *Pistol: The Life of Pete Maravich* (New York: Free Press, 2007), 94–95; Morris, *ACC Basketball*, 72, 286–88.

61. Kriegel, *Pistol*, 53–55, 84–86; Morris, *ACC Basketball*, 278–86.

62. Herakovich, *Pack Pride*, 59–62; Kriegel, *Pistol*, 94–99; Barrier and Morton, *ACC Tournament Basketball Classic*, 63–64; Peeler, *Legends of N.C. State Basketball*, 48–49; Prouty, *ACC Basketball Stat Book*, 45–47.

63. *Raleigh News and Observer*, January 2, 1965, May 1, 1966; Featherston, *Tobacco Road*, 53; Kriegel, *Pistol*, 87–118; Bryant interview.

64. Melissa Kean, *Desegregating Private Higher Education in the South: Duke, Emory, Rice, Tulane, and Vanderbilt* (Baton Rouge: Louisiana State University Press, 2008), 1–9; Hugh Davis Graham and Nancy Diamond, *The Rise of American Research Universities: Elites and Challengers in the Postwar Era* (Baltimore: Johns Hopkins University Press, 1997), 39; Thomas D. Clark, *The Emerging South*, 2nd ed. (Oxford: Oxford University Press, 1968), 297.

65. "The University of Maryland: Evaluation Report for the Commission on Institutions of Higher Learning of the Middle States Association of Colleges and Secondary Schools," November 1953, p. 33, Series 1, Box 7 (Middle States Association of College and Secondary Schools — Report 1953), Harry C. Byrd Papers, R. Lee Hornbake to Wilson H. Elkins, November 24, 1958, James E. Kinard to Hornbake, November 26, 1958, Box 597 (ACC Schools Scholastic Regulations), Wilson H. Elkins Presidential Records, University Archives, University of Maryland, College Park; W. B. Aycock to C. P. Erickson, May 2, 1963, Box 9 (Athletics), Aycock Series, University of North Carolina Archives; *Charlotte News*, December 18, 1965.

66. Mortimer M. Caplin to Edgar F. Shannon, May 18, 1960, Shannon to Caplin, May 20, 1960, Box 3 (Athletics: Atlantic Coast Conference), RG 2/1/2.641, Series 2, President's Papers, University Archives, University of Virginia, Charlottesville; Roy B. Clogston to Ken Alyta, May 12, 1960, Box 3 (Clogston, Roy), Collection UA 15.007 (Department of Athletics Subject Files), University Archives, Special Collections Research Center, North Carolina State University, Raleigh; *Greensboro Record*, May 6, 1960; *Raleigh News and Observer*, May 7, 1960.

67. Charles E. Jordan to James H. Weaver, November 17, 1961, Box 53 (Atlantic Coast Conference), Charles E. Jordan Papers, University Archives, Duke University, Durham,

N.C.; Minutes of Atlantic Coast Conference Meeting, May 1, 1964, Box 6 (Athletics: Atlantic Coast Conference), RG 2/1/2.671, President's Papers, University of Virginia Archives; *Raleigh News and Observer*, May 4, 1963, May 2, 1964.

68. Dean E. Smith to William Friday, August 14, 1961, Subgroup 3, Series 1, Subseries 3, Box 67 (Basketball, 1957–71), Friday Files, University of North Carolina Archives.

69. Middle States Association Evaluation Report, 51, 60, Byrd Papers, University of Maryland Archives; Bayard Webster, "The Fall and Rise of the University of Maryland," *Harper's Magazine*, October 1956, pp. 64–68; *Baltimore Sun*, January 18, 1955; *Washington Post*, January 18, 1955; George H. Callcott, *A History of the University of Maryland* (Baltimore: Maryland Historical Society, 1966), 360–62.

70. Wilson H. Elkins, "Institutional Responsibility for Football," n.d., Box 144 (Speeches), Elkins Presidential Records, University of Maryland Archives; *Washington Post*, May 19, 1955; Callcott, *History of the University of Maryland*, 368–77; George H. Callcott, ed., *Forty Years as a College President: Memoirs of Wilson Elkins* (College Park: University of Maryland, 1981), 14, 72–75; George H. Callcott, interview with author, University Park, Md., November 30, 2006.

71. Wilson H. Elkins to George C. Cook, December 13, 1954, Box 155 (Terrapin Club), Elkins Presidential Records, University of Maryland Archives; "How to Get Big-Time Football," *U.S. News and World Report*, January 28, 1955, p. 58; Webster, "Fall and Rise of the University of Maryland," 67; Callcott, *Forty Years as a College President*, 73–74.

72. Bud Millikan, telephone interview with author, July 30, 2006.

73. *Old Gold and Black*, December 6, 1955; *Raleigh News and Observer*, December 6, 1955; *Winston-Salem Journal*, December 6, 1955.

74. Harold W. Tribble to Pat Preston, November 8, 1956, Box 12, Folder 710 (Preston, Paddison), Tribble to J. Samuel Johnson, December 13, 1955, Box 8, File 492 (Student Demonstration, Dec. 1955, Messages of Support), RG 1.10, Tribble Records, Wake Forest University Archives; *Twin City Sentinel*, November 28, 1955; *Greensboro Daily News*, February 8, March 2, 1956; Bynum Shaw, *The History of Wake Forest College: Volume 4, 1943–1967* (Winston-Salem: Wake Forest University, 1988), 92–106; Hensley interview.

75. *Winston-Salem Journal*, May 7, 1964.

76. President's Report to the Trustees, January 10, 1964, H. W. Tribble to Confidential Files, January 13, 1964, Box 15, Folder 902 (Athletic Council, 1951–65), "Report of the Special Committee on Intercollegiate Athletics," August 22, 1964, Box 7, Folder 385 (Intercollegiate Athletics, Special Committee, 1964), Tribble Records, Wake Forest University Archives.

77. Report of the President to the Athletic Committee of the Board of Visitors on Athletic Policy at the University of Virginia, April 13, 1962, Box 4 (Athletics), RG 2/1/2.651, President's Papers, University of Virginia Archives; Gene Corrigan, interview with author, Charlottesville, Va., November 14, 2006; Ernest H. Ern, interview with author, Charlottesville, Va., December 8, 2008.

Chapter 6

1. *The State*, January 7, 1967; Ron Morris, *ACC Basketball: An Illustrated History* (Chapel Hill: Four Corners Press, 1988), 278–89.

2. *The State*, August 19, 1962, December 1, 1966, February 23, 1967; *Charlotte Observer*, August 19, 1962; *Augusta Chronicle*, June 23, 2002.

3. *The State*, December 1, 1966; Dan Klores, *Roundball Culture: South Carolina Basketball* (Huntsville, Ala.: AM Press, 1980), 45–72; Don Barton and Bob Fulton, *Frank McGuire: The Life and Times of a Basketball Legend* (Columbia, S.C.: Summerhouse Press, 1995), 77–84; John C. Prouty, ed., *The ACC Basketball Stat Book* (Huntingtown, Md.: Willow Oak Publishing, 1993), 45–52.

4. *Charleston News and Courier*, January 8, 1967; *The State*, January 8, 1967; *Florence Morning News*, January 8, 1967.

5. Frank Howard to Eddie [Cameron], February 8, 1967, with attached statement, Box 1 (Athletic Council, 1967–68), Edmund M. Cameron Papers, University Archives, Duke University, Durham, N.C; Robert C. Edwards to Walter T. Cox, February 20, 1967, Series 12, Folder 31 (Carolina Controversy, 1966–67), Records of the Office of the President: Robert C. Edwards, Special Collections, Clemson University, Clemson, S.C.; *The State*, February 8, February 9, 1967; Morris, *ACC Basketball*, 115.

6. *Charleston News and Courier*, February 10, 1967; *Raleigh News and Observer*, February 19, 1967; Morris, *ACC Basketball*, 91, 291.

7. Press Maravich to Bob Edwards, August 15, 1962, Series 11, Folder 45 (Athletics: Athletic Council, 1961–62), Edwards Records, Special Collections, Clemson University; Wright Bryan, *Clemson: An Informal History of the University, 1889–1979* (Columbia, S.C.: R. L. Bryan Co., 1979), 143; Jerome V. Reel, conversation with author, Clemson, S.C., September 20, 2007.

8. *The Tiger*, August 25, 1978; *Greenville News*, September 10, 1978; Bryan, *Clemson*, 135–44.

9. Alexander Wolff, "Ground Breakers," *Sports Illustrated*, November 7, 2005, pp. 58–67; Bryan, *Clemson*, 153–62; Darryl Hill, interview with author, College Park, Md., October 10, 2007.

10. Jim Sumner, "Looking Back—Clemson's Basketball Family in the 1960s," January 21, 2009, http://www.theacc.com/sports/m-baskbl/spec-rel/012109aaa.html (accessed July 17, 2009); *The Tiger*, May 14, 1969; Pat Conroy, *My Losing Season* (New York: Dial Press, 2002), 150–51; Prouty, *ACC Basketball Stat Book*, 25–68, 184; Morris, *ACC Basketball*, 90–91.

11. Mark Kriegel, *Pistol: The Life of Pete Maravich* (New York: Free Press, 2007), 65–68; Conroy, *My Losing Season*, 150; Morris, *ACC Basketball*, 108; Prouty, *ACC Basketball Stat Book*, 25–55.

12. "Report to the Ways and Means Committee by the Special Subcommittee Appointed to Study the Need for Multipurpose Athletic Facilities at the University of South Carolina and Clemson College," February 25, 1964, Box 2 (Building Program: Field House), Records of the Office of the President: Thomas F. Jones, 1963–64, University Archives, University of South Carolina, Columbia; Chick Jacobs, "Fike Field House," in *Clemson: Where the Tigers Play*, ed. Sam Blackman, Bob Bradley, and Chuck Kriese (Champaign, Ill.: Sports Publishing, 2001), 36–38; Conroy, *My Losing Season*, 146–48.

13. Robert C. Edwards to Bill Hornsby, February 18, 1969, Series 12, Folder 25 (Athletics: Basketball), Edwards Records, Edwards to Byron Harder Jr., February 28, 1969, Box 18 (Robert C. Edwards, 1967–68), Records of the Athletic Council, Special Collec-

tions, Clemson University; "Report to the Ways and Means Committee," Jones Records, University of South Carolina Archives; *Charleston News and Courier*, February 12, 1970; *Charlotte News*, February 17, 1969; *Charlotte Observer*, March 6, 1970; Prouty, *ACC Basketball Stat Book*, 57–68; Bryan, *Clemson*, 115.

14. *Washington Post*, January 8, January 16, 1964; Morris, *ACC Basketball*, 278–86.

15. Thomas F. Jones to Douglas M. Knight, December 19, 1963, Knight to Jones, December 30, 1963, Box 3 (Departments and Schools — Athletics), Jones Records, 1963–64, University of South Carolina Archives; Eddie Cameron to Marvin Bass, December 18, 1963, Box 3 (Athletics 1963–65), Douglas M. Knight Records, Duke University Archives; *Charlotte Observer*, December 17, 1963; *Durham Morning Herald*, December 17, 1963; *Gamecock*, January 10, 1964; Jeff Mullins, interview with author, Cornelius, N.C., July 16, 2007; Jay Buckley, interview with author, Rockville, Md., August 22, 2007.

16. "Final Part of Russ Benedict's Sportscast," January 13, 1964, Charles W. Noe to Thomas Jones, January 22, 1964, Box 3 (Departments and Schools — Athletics), Jones Records, 1963–64, University of South Carolina Archives; Barton and Fulton, *Frank McGuire*, 81.

17. *Washington Post*, March 13, 1964; Klores, *Roundball Culture*, 52–57; Barton and Fulton, *Frank McGuire*, 77–81.

18. Barton and Fulton, *Frank McGuire*, 81–82.

19. *The State*, March 29, 1962, January 30, 1974, July 16, 1981; Henry H. Lesesne, *A History of the University of South Carolina* (Columbia: University of South Carolina Press, 2001), 82, 99–102, 156–58.

20. Vic Bubas to Eddie Cameron, May 10, 1965, Box 2 (Basketball — USC/McGuire Controversy), Cameron Papers, Duke University Archives; James H. Weaver, Report on the Recruitment and Enrollment of Michael Grosso, n.d., Box 6 (Associations and Boards: Atlantic Coast Conference Commissioner Weaver), Jones Records, 1966–67, University of South Carolina Archives; *Greensboro Daily News*, November 21, 1966; *The State*, December 8, 1966; *Charleston News and Courier*, January 10, 1967.

21. Weaver, Report on Recruitment and Enrollment of Michael Grosso, Jones Records, University of South Carolina Archives.

22. Ibid.; James H. Weaver to Eddie Cameron, December 17, 1965, Bubas to Cameron, May 10, 1965, Box 2 (Basketball — USC/McGuire Controversy), Cameron Papers, Duke University Archives; *Daily Progress*, December 17, 1965; *Durham Morning Herald*, December 18, 1965; *The State*, May 6, May 7, 1966; Bruce A. Corrie, *The Atlantic Coast Conference, 1953–1978* (Durham: Carolina Academic Press, 1978), 86.

23. Eddie Cameron to Robert C. Edwards, February 3, 1966, Box 2 (Basketball — USC/McGuire Controversy), Cameron Papers, Duke University Archives; *Durham Morning Herald*, December 18, 1965; *Charlotte News*, December 18, 1965.

24. James H. Weaver to Thomas Jones, June 4, 1966, Jones to Weaver, June 21, 1966, Box 1 (Associations and Boards: Atlantic Coast Conference), Jones Records, 1965–66, University of South Carolina Archives; Paul F. Dietzel, *Call Me Coach: A Life in College Football* (Baton Rouge: Louisiana State University Press, 2008), 143; Lesesne, *History of the University of South Carolina*, 190.

25. James H. Weaver to ACC Presidents, Faculty Chairmen, and Athletic Directors, July 25, 1966, Box 6 (Associations and Boards: Atlantic Coast Conference, Miscella-

neous), Paul F. Dietzel to Commissioner Weaver and others, August 1, 1966, Box 1 (Athletic Affairs: Athletic Director Paul Dietzel), Jones Records 1966–67, University of South Carolina Archives.

26. NCAA Committee on Infractions, Confidential Report No. 45, December 21, 1966, Box 6 (Associations and Boards: National Collegiate Athletic Association Committee on Infractions), Weaver to ACC Presidents, Faculty Chairmen, and Athletic Directors, July 25, 1966, Jones Records, 1966–67, University of South Carolina Archives; Minutes of Duke Athletic Council Meeting, October 1, 1966, Box 2 (Meeting Minutes), Athletic Council Records, Duke University Archives; James H. Weaver to Herman Helms, June 2, 1966, Series 12, Folder 30 (Carolina Controversy, 1966), Edwards Records, Special Collections, Clemson University; *Gamecock*, November 4, 1966; *The State*, November 5, 1966.

27. James H. Weaver to Atlantic Coast Presidents, Faculty Chairmen, and Athletic Directors, November 3, 1966, Box 6 (Athletics—ACC), RG 2/1/2.701, President's Papers, University Archives, University of Virginia, Charlottesville; Mark Mulvoy, "The Off-Court Uproar in Dixie," *Sports Illustrated*, November 7, 1966, pp. 26–27; *Charlotte Observer*, November 7, November 24, 1966; *Greensboro Daily News*, November 21, 1966; *Charleston News and Courier*, November 24, 1966.

28. Robert C. Edwards to William W. Cobey, November 14, 1966, Series 12, Folder 31 (Carolina Controversy, 1966–67), Edwards Records, Special Collections, Clemson University; John T. Caldwell to Thomas F. Jones, December 1, 1966, Box 6 (Associations and Boards: Atlantic Coast Conference, Miscellaneous), Jones Records, 1966–67, University of South Carolina Archives; *Evening Star*, November 26, 1966.

29. Draft statement, n.d., Box 6 (Atlantic Coast Conference, Miscellaneous), Jones Records, 1966–67, University of South Carolina Archives; *Charlotte Observer*, November 1, 1966; *Raleigh News and Observer*, October 30, December 1, 1966.

30. *The State*, December 9, December 10, December 11, 1966; *Charleston News and Courier*, December 9, 1966.

31. Douglas M. Knight to Robert A. Dobson, December 21, 1966, Box 4 (Atlantic Coast Conference, 1965–69), Douglas M. Knight Records, Knight to H. Carson West, December 27, 1966, E. M. Cameron to J. C. Burris, December 28, 1966, Cameron to H. Filmore Mabry, January 5, 1967, Box 2 (Basketball—USC/McGuire Controversy), Cameron Papers, Duke University Archives; *The State* December 10, December 15, 1966.

32. NCAA Committee on Infractions, Confidential Report No. 45, Jones Records, University of South Carolina Archives; *The State*, January 9, 1967.

33. Thomas F. Jones to Frank McGuire, January 25, 1967, Box 1 (Athletic Affairs: Athletic Director Paul Dietzel), Jones to Todd Wilson, January 31, 1967, Box 1 (Athletic Affairs: Rules Violations—Letters Relating to ACC and NCAA Rulings), Jones Records, 1966–67, University of South Carolina Archives.

34. *The State*, January 10, 1967; *Charleston News and Courier*, January 15, 1967.

35. *Charleston News and Courier*, January 10, 1967; *Greensboro Daily News*, February 19, 1967; *The State*, March 29, 2009; Barton and Fulton, *Frank McGuire*, 86.

36. Paul F. Dietzel to E. M. Cameron, March 20, 1967, Box 1 (Athletic Council, 1967–68), Cameron Papers, Duke University Archives.

37. Ben S. Martin to Colgate W. Darden Jr., February 6, 1958, Series 2, Box 3 (Athlet-

ics, 1958), RG 2/1/2.635, President's Papers, University of Virginia Archives; Jerry Rad-cliffe, *The University of Virginia Football Vault: A History of the Cavaliers* (Atlanta: Whitman Publishing, 2008), 77–80.

38. Gene Corrigan oral history, March 5, 1994, RG 26-178, University of Virginia Archives; *Raleigh News and Observer*, March 9, 1957; Gary Cramer, *Cavaliers!: A Pictorial History of UVa Basketball* (Charlottesville: Spring House Publishing, 1983), 50–52.

39. *Charlotte News*, December 22, 1964; Cramer, *Cavaliers!*, 50–58; Morris, *ACC Basketball*, 282–87.

40. Virginius Dabney, *Mr. Jefferson's University: A History* (Charlottesville: University Press of Virginia, 1981), 422–25; D. Alan Williams, interview with author, Charlottesville, Va., December 9, 2007; Ernest H. Ern, interview with author, Charlottesville, Va., December 8, 2008.

41. Edgar F. Shannon Jr. to Richard N. Anderson Jr., February 6, 1961, Box 4 (Athletics, January–June 1961), University Coaches to President Shannon, January 31, 1962, Shannon to Billy McCann and others, April 7, 1962, Box 4 (Athletics, July 1961–June 30, 1962), RG 2/1/2.651, President's Papers, University of Virginia Archives; Gene Corrigan, interview with author, Charlottesville, Va., November 14, 2006.

42. Evan J. Male to Edgar F. Shannon Jr., January 31, 1961, Shannon to Male, February 7, 1961, Box 4 (Athletics, January–June 1961), "Report of the President to the Athletic Committee of the Board of Visitors on Athletic Policy at the University of Virginia," April 13, 1962, Box 4 (Athletics, July 1961–June 30, 1962), RG 2/1/2.651, President's Papers, University of Virginia Archives; Alan Williams interview; Ern interview.

43. "Report on the Athletic Department," 1957, Series 1, Box 3 (Athletics, 1957), RG 2/1/2.635, Pamphlet, "Operation Leadership," 1959, Series 1, Box 2 (Athletics—General, 1959), RG 2/1/2.641, President's Papers, University of Virginia Archives; *Washington Post*, November 22, December 2, 1965; Chris Graham and Patrick Hite, *Mad about U: Four Decades of Basketball at University Hall* (Waynesboro, Va.: Augusta Free Press, 2006), 47–48.

44. *Evening Star*, February 5, April 9, 1963; *Washington Post*, April 9, 1963; *Richmond Times-Dispatch*, February 5, April 9, 1963.

45. Jim Camp to Edgar F. Shannon Jr., February 23, 1964, Box 6 (Athletics—General, 1963–64), RG 2/1/2.671, President's Papers, University of Virginia Archives; Graham and Hite, *Mad about U*, 47; Morris, *ACC Basketball*, 94; Chip Conner, interview with author, Winston-Salem, N.C., May 21, 2007; Bill Millsaps, interview with author, Richmond, Va., December 10, 2007; Mike Katos, interview with author, Philadelphia, Pa., June 12, 2008; Corrigan interview; Ern interview.

46. Bill Gibson to Mr. and Mrs. Shannon, May 8, 1966, Box 6 (Athletics—Personnel), RG 2/1/2.691, President's Papers, University of Virginia Archives; Morris, *ACC Basketball*, 290–92; Katos interview.

47. Paul Saunier to Edgar F. Shannon Jr., April 13, 1961, Box 4 (Athletics, January–June 1961), RG 2/1/2.651, Marvin B. Perry Jr., to Steve Sebo, October 15, 1963, Box 6 (Athletics—General, 1963–64), RG 2/1/2.671, Saunier to Sebo, January 13, 1967, Sebo to Shannon, April 21, 1967, Box 5 (Athletics—General, 1966–67), RG 2/1/2.701, President's Papers, University of Virginia Archives; *Roanoke Times*, January 23, 1967; *Daily Progress*, April 28, 2007; Dabney, *Mr. Jefferson's University*, 427; Ern interview.

48. Bill Gibson, handwritten notes on Memorandum from Steve Sebo to All Head Coaches, April 5, 1967, Box 5 (Athletics—General), RG 2/1/2.701, President's Papers, University of Virginia Archives; *Roanoke Times*, January 23, 1967.

49. Chip Case, telephone interview with author, October 22, 1009; Barry Koval, telephone interview with author, October 27, 2009; Katos interview.

50. Account by unidentified reporter of interview with Bill Gibson, n.d., File 1633 (Bill Gibson), Media Relations Archives, University of Virginia; Cramer, *Cavaliers!*, 65.

51. *Richmond Times-Dispatch*, March 8, 1969; *Daily Progress*, March 8, 1969; *Roanoke Times*, March 11, 1969; *Durham Morning-Herald*, March 11, 1969; Cramer, *Cavaliers!*, 65.

52. *Cavalier Daily*, March 10, March 11, March 12, March 13, 1969.

53. *Richmond Times-Dispatch*, March 9, 1969; *Roanoke Times*, March 9, 1969; *Daily Progress*, March 10, March 19, 1969.

54. Minutes of the Athletic Advisory Committee, April 3, 1969, Box 9 (Athletics—3-2-2 Committee), RG 2/1/2.721, President's Papers, University of Virginia Archives; Account of interview with Gibson, File 1633, Media Relations Archives, University of Virginia; *Daily Progress*, March 12, 1969; *Cavalier Daily*, March 12, March 14, 1969; *Richmond Times-Dispatch*, March 14, 1969; Case interview.

55. *Cavalier Daily*, March 17, 1969; *Daily Progress*, March 19, 1969; Conner interview.

56. Kent Baker, *Red, White, and Amen: Maryland Basketball* (Huntsville, Ala.: Strode Publishers, 1979), 103–16; Prouty, *ACC Basketball Stat Book*, 5–15.

57. Paul McMullen, *Maryland Basketball: Tales from Cole Field House* (Baltimore: Johns Hopkins University Press, 2002), 17–24; Smith Barrier and Hugh Morton, *The ACC Basketball Tournament Classic* (Greensboro, N.C.: Greensboro Publications, 1981), 41–43; Baker, *Red, White, and Amen*, 17–26; Prouty, *ACC Basketball Stat Book*, 17–19; Tom Young, interview with author, Virginia Beach, Va., June 27, 2008.

58. *Washington Post*, December 26, 1952; McMullen, *Maryland Basketball*, 35–39; Morris, *ACC Basketball*, 52–53.

59. McMullen, *Maryland Basketball*, 23, 35–37; Fred Shabel, interview with author, Philadelphia, Pa., June 12, 2008; Young interview.

60. *Raleigh News and Observer*, March 10, 1958; Prouty, *ACC Basketball Stat Book*, 21–44.

61. *Evening Star*, February 5, 1963; Baker, *Red, White, and Amen*, 127–55; McMullen, *Maryland Basketball*, 38–39; Frank Fellows, interview with author, Silver Spring, Md., February 19, 2007.

62. Prouty, *ACC Basketball Stat Book*, 45–48; Gary Williams, interview with author, College Park, Md., June 26, 2006; Joe Harrington, interview with author, Leesburg, Va., March 20, 2007; Fellows interview.

63. "Scouting Reports," *Sports Illustrated*, December 6, 1965, p. 65; McMullen, *Maryland Basketball*, 33–38; Baker, *Red, White, and Amen*, 149–50; Gary Williams interview.

64. "Some Irate Alumni" to President Elkins, January 18, 1966, with handwritten note from Elkins to Mr. Cobey, Box 438 (Athletics—Director), Wilson H. Elkins Presidential Records, University Archives, University of Maryland, College Park; George H. Callcott, *A History of the University of Maryland* (Baltimore: Maryland Historical Society, 1966), 390–92.

65. *Washington Post*, January 3, 1966; *Baltimore Evening Sun*, March 30, 1967; George H. Callcott, ed., *Forty Years as a College President: Memoirs of Wilson Elkins* (College Park: University of Maryland, 1981), 75; McMullen, *Maryland Basketball*, 38–39; Baker, *Red, White, and Amen*, 150–51; Bud Millikan, telephone interview with author, July 30, 2006; Gary Williams interview; Fellows interview; Young interview.

66. Baker, *Red, White, and Amen*, 152; McMullen, *Maryland Basketball*, 39; Mullins interview; Young interview.

67. Baker, *Red, White and Amen*, 142–43; Billy Jones, interview with author, Orlando, Fla., May 12, 2008; Young interview; Gary Williams interview.

68. *Washington Post*, March 30, 1967; Baker, *Red, White, and Amen*, 156–61; Jim Kehoe, interview with author, Chesapeake Beach, Md., October 11, 2006; Fellows interview; Young interview.

69. *Raleigh News and Observer*, March 6, 1957; *Greensboro Daily News*, March 9, 1957.

70. James H. Weaver to Deryl Hart, February 13, 1961, Box 2 (Atlantic Coast Conference, 1960–63), J. Deryl Hart Records, Duke University Archives; *Duke Chronicle*, February 16, 1965; Pete Brennan, interview with author, Duck, N.C., August 1, 2009.

71. Douglas M. Knight to Lawrence K. Gessner, December 30, 1965, Knight to Gerald C. Lutton, January 5, 1966, E. M. Cameron to Lutton, January 7, 1966, Cameron "Memo to Duke Students," n.d., Box 3 (Athletics 1963–1965), Knight Records, Duke University Archives; "Scorecard," *Sports Illustrated*, December 20, 1965, p. 13.

72. David H. Wilcox Jr. to James Ralph Scales, January 2, 1971, Box 9, Folder 840 (Cheers at Games), RG 1.11 (Records of the President's Office: James Ralph Scales), University Archives, Wake Forest University, Winston-Salem, N.C.; *Daily Tar Heel*, January 20, 1954; *Duke Chronicle*, February 15, 1963; Bill Gilbert, "Little Pal on the Dead Run," *Sports Illustrated*, March 1, 1965, pp. 38–43; Curry Kirkpatrick, "One More War to Go," *Sports Illustrated*, March 2, 1970, pp. 12–15; Smith Barrier, *On Tobacco Road: Basketball in North Carolina* (New York: Leisure Press, 1983), 14; Morris, *ACC Basketball*, 115.

73. Charley Eckman and Fred Neil, *"It's a Very Simple Game": The Life and Times of Charley Eckman* (Baltimore: Borderlands Press, 1995), 126; *Washington Post*, March 11, 1967.

74. *Charlotte Observer*, March 2, 1963; Bones McKinney with Garland Atkins, *Bones: Honk Your Horn If You Love Basketball* (Gastonia, N.C.: Garland Publications, 1988), 95; Katos interview.

75. Office of the Commissioner to ACC Basketball Officials, January 10, 1969, Box 4 (Atlantic Coast Conference, 1965–69), Knight Records, Minutes of Atlantic Coast Conference Basketball Coaches Meeting, November 15, 1970, Box 2 (Big Four Athletic Directors, 1968–1971), Cameron Papers, Duke University Archives; *Raleigh News and Observer*, March 14, 1971.

76. *Raleigh News and Observer*, March 14, 1971; Dan Richards, *40 Years behind the Sports Desk* (San Jose: Writer's Showcase, 2002), 39–40; McKinney, *Bones*, 97; Morris, *ACC Basketball*, 275.

77. Eckman and Neil, *"It's a Very Simple Game,"* 15–93.

78. Ibid., 101, 125–28; *Duke Chronicle*, February 23, 1967; Gary Williams interview.

79. Bill Gibson to University Student Body, February 15, 1971, Box 8 (Athletics—

General, 1970–71), RG 2/1/2.741, President's Papers, University of Virginia Archives; Terry Sanford to David H. Scott, February 18, 1971, Box 20 (Athletics), Terry Sanford Records, Duke University Archives; J. R. Scales to William L. Faircloth, March 19, 1971, Box 6, File 449 (Basketball, Univ. SC disturbance), RG 1.11, Scales Records, Wake Forest University Archives; John T. Caldwell to Willis Casey, December 2, 1971, Box 55 (Athletics Department), Collection UA 2.1 (Records of the Chancellor's Office), University Archives, Special Collections Research Center, North Carolina State University, Raleigh; *Gamecock*, December 10, 1965; *Old Gold and Black*, March 12, 1971.

80. Jim Kehoe to S. H. Morrow, January 22, 1971, Box 22 (Men's Basketball—MD-SC 1971), Records of Athletics—Media Relations, University of Maryland Archives; *Washington Post*, February 18, 1972.

Chapter 7

1. *Baltimore Sun*, December 5, 1965.

2. Pamela Grundy, *Learning to Win: Sports, Education, and Social Change in Twentieth-Century North Carolina* (Chapel Hill: University of North Carolina Press, 2001), 181–83; Milton S. Katz, *Breaking Through: John B. McLendon, Basketball Legend and Civil Rights Pioneer* (Fayetteville: University of Arkansas Press, 2007), 11–57; Gena Caponi-Tabery, *Jump for Joy: Jazz, Basketball and Black Culture in 1930s America* (Amherst: University of Massachusetts Press, 2008), 81–105.

3. Charles H. Martin, "Jim Crow in the Gymnasium: The Integration of College Basketball in the American South," *International Journal of the History of Sport* 10 (April 1993): 68–86; Tom Graham and Rachel Graham Cody, *Getting Open: The Unknown Story of Bill Garrett and the Integration of College Basketball* (New York: Atria Books, 2006), 92–93, 117–18. Richard T. Culberson became the first black basketball player in the Big Ten when he joined the University of Iowa team as a transfer student in 1944. He played two seasons for Iowa, but the "gentlemen's agreements" continued to prevail in the Big Ten after World War II. Charles H. Martin, *Benching Jim Crow: The Rise and Fall of the Color Line in Southern College Sports, 1890–1980* (Urbana: University of Illinois Press, 2010), 73.

4. John Sayle Watterson, *College Football: History—Spectacle—Controversy* (Baltimore: Johns Hopkins University Press, 2000), 309–12; Martin, "Jim Crow in the Gymnasium," 70–71.

5. Charles H. Martin, "The Rise and Fall of Jim Crow in Southern College Sports: The Case of the Atlantic Coast Conference," *North Carolina Historical Review* 76 (July 1999): 253–84; Martin, "Jim Crow in the Gymnasium," 71.

6. Neil D. Isaacs, *All the Moves: A History of College Basketball* (New York: Harper and Row, 1984), 188–98; Mike Douchant, *Encyclopedia of College Basketball* (Detroit: Visible Ink Press, 1995), 45, 84; Martin, *Benching Jim Crow*, 69; Aram Goudsouzian, "The House That Russell Built: Bill Russell, the University of San Francisco, and the Winning Streak That Changed College Basketball," *California History* 84 (Fall 2007): 4–25; Aram Goudsouzian, *King of the Court: Bill Russell and the Basketball Revolution* (Berkeley: University of California Press, 2010), 30–54.

7. Wilt Chamberlain and David Shaw, *Wilt: Just Like Any Other 7-Foot Black Mil-*

lionaire Who Lives Next Door (New York: Macmillan Publishing, 1973), 49; Graham and Cody, *Getting Open*, 104, 158–60, 173.

8. Aram Goudsouzian, "'Can Basketball Survive Chamberlain?' The Kansas Years of Wilt the Stilt," *Kansas History* 28 (Autumn 2005): 150–73; Goudsouzian, "House That Russell Built," 11, 17–18; Goudsouzian, *King of the Court*, 32–45; Graham and Cody, *Getting Open*, 147.

9. Charles H. Martin, "Integrating New Year's Day: The Racial Politics of College Bowl Games in the American South," *Journal of Sport History* 24 (Fall 1997): 358–77; Martin, "Jim Crow in the Gymnasium," 73–74.

10. Russell J. Henderson, "'Something More Than the Game Will Be Lost': The 1963 Mississippi State University Basketball Controversy and the Repeal of the Unwritten Law," in *The Sporting World of the Modern South*, ed. Patrick B. Miller (Urbana: University of Illinois Press, 2002), 219–43; Bill Finger, "Just Another Ball Game," *Southern Exposure* 7 (Fall 1979): 74–81; Martin, "Jim Crow in the Gymnasium," 76–77.

11. Byrd's views on race and on integrating the University of Maryland are traced in a valuable study, Mark Tosso, "'The Curley Byrd Lays an Egg': H. C. Byrd and the Desegregation of the University of Maryland," Honors Thesis, Department of History, University of Maryland, May 2001 (courtesy of Keith W. Olson). The discussion of the Murray case is on 27–40.

12. *Baltimore Sun*, February 2, 1951, June 26, 1954; *Washington Post*, December 9, 1951; George H. Callcott, ed., *Forty Years as a College President: Memoirs of Wilson Elkins* (College Park: University of Maryland, 1981), 124; Hayward "Woody" Farrar, "Prying the Door Farther Open: A Memoir of Black Student Protest at the University of Maryland at College Park, 1966–1970," in *Higher Education and the Civil Rights Movement: White Supremacy, Black Southerners, and College Campuses*, ed. Peter Wallenstein (Gainesville: University Press of Florida, 2008), 137–65; George H. Callcott, *A History of the University of Maryland* (Baltimore: Maryland Historical Society, 1966), 351–53; Tosso, "Curley Byrd Lays an Egg," 70–76.

13. Gordon Gray to Joe R. Fletcher, December 7, 1954, Subgroup 2, Series 2, Subseries 3, Box 10 (General, 1954–55), Records of the Office of the President: Gordon Gray Files, University Archives, University of North Carolina, Chapel Hill; Alice Elizabeth Reagan, *North Carolina State University: A Narrative History* (Raleigh: North Carolina State University Foundation and North Carolina State University Alumni Association, 1987), 163–64, 187; William A. Link, *William Friday: Power, Purpose, and American Higher Education* (Chapel Hill: University of North Carolina Press, 1995), 82–84, 249–50; Peter Wallenstein, "Black Southerners and Nonblack Universities: The Process of Desegregating Southern Higher Education, 1935–1965," and Appendix 8, *Frasier v. Board of Trustees of the University of North Carolina*, in *Higher Education and the Civil Rights Movement*, ed. Wallenstein, 17–59, 270–74.

14. Colgate W. Darden Jr. to William J. Story Jr., March 3, 1952, RG 2/1/2.591, Box 27 (Segregation, 1952), Darden to Mrs. Roger Boyle, June 14, 1957, RG 2/1/2.635, Series 1, Box 23 (Segregation, 1957), Darden to Walter C. Rawls, August 6, 1958, RG 2/1/2.635, Series 2, Box 24 (Segregation, 1958), President's Papers, Colgate Whitehead Darden oral history, pp. 11–15, RG 26-9, University Archives, University of Virginia, Charlottesville; *Washington Post*, February 8, 1968; "ACC Basketball Tournament Program, 1968," 55 (in

author's possession); Virginius Dabney, *Mr. Jefferson's University* (Charlottesville: University Press of Virginia, 1981), 379–80.

15. Melissa Kean, *Desegregating Private Higher Education in the South: Duke, Emory, Rice, Tulane, and Vanderbilt* (Baton Rouge: Louisiana State University Press, 2008), 59–68, 139–50, 189–96; "Duke University: Allen Building Takeover, 1969," http://www.durhamcountylibrary.org/dcrhp/allen.php (accessed December 3, 2009); "ACC Basketball Tournament Program, 1968," 23.

16. *Old Gold and Black*, December 12, 1955, April 30, 1962, September 24, 1962; William H. Chafe, *Civilities and Civil Rights: Greensboro, North Carolina, and the Black Struggle for Freedom* (New York: Oxford University Press, 1980), 86; Bynum Shaw, *The History of Wake Forest College: Volume 4, 1943-1967* (Winston-Salem: Wake Forest University, 1988), 130–34. I am indebted to Edwin Wilson for providing the numbers of black students enrolled at Wake Forest.

17. George McMillan, "Integration with Dignity: The Inside Story of How South Carolina Kept the Peace," *Saturday Evening Post*, March 16, 1963, pp. 15–21; Wright Bryan, *Clemson: An Informal History of the University, 1889-1979* (Columbia, S.C.: R. L. Bryan Co., 1979), 153–62. For an analysis of McMillan's article, see M. Ron Cox Jr., "'Integration with [Relative] Dignity': The Desegregation of Clemson College and George McMillan's Article at Forty," in *Toward the Meeting of the Waters: Currents in the Civil Rights Movement of South Carolina during the Twentieth Century*, ed. Winfred B. Moore Jr. and Orville Vernon Burton (Columbia: University of South Carolina Press, 2008), 274–85.

18. "Voices from the Civil Rights Movement in South Carolina: Harvey B. Gantt," in *Toward the Meeting of the Waters*, ed. Moore and Burton, 358.

19. Henry H. Lesesne, *A History of the University of South Carolina, 1940-2000* (Columbia: University of South Carolina Press, 2001), 137–50, 228; Martin, *Benching Jim Crow*, 144.

20. Vernon Crook to W. B. Aycock, August 3, 1960, Aycock to Crook, August 5, 1960, Box 10 (General: UNC Department of Athletics, 1957–61), Records of the Office of the Chancellor: William Brantley Aycock Series, University of North Carolina Archives; *Raleigh News and Observer*, October 2, 1951; Martin, "Rise and Fall of Jim Crow," 265.

21. Carey H. Bostian to William Friday, January 9, 1959, Bostian to Claude W. Rankin, January 19, 1959, Subgroup 3, Series 1, Subseries 3, Box 63 (Basketball, 1957–65), Records of the Office of the President: William Clyde Friday Files, University of North Carolina Archives.

22. *Raleigh News and Observer*, October 17, 1957; Bill Beezley, *The Wolfpack: Intercollegiate Athletics at North Carolina State University* (Raleigh: North Carolina State University, 1976), 227; Martin, "Rise and Fall of Jim Crow," 265–67.

23. Ransom S. Averitt to Harold W. Tribble, January 31, 1963, E. Morris Hawks to Tribble, February 1, 1963, Box 7, Folder 384 (Integration, 1960–67), RG 1.10 (Records of the President's Office: Harold W. Tribble), University Archives, Wake Forest University, Winston-Salem, N.C.; Wilson H. Elkins to Charles Driesell, December 8, 1969, with enclosure, Box 440 (Athletics—Basketball, 1969), University Archives, University of Maryland, College Park; *Old Gold and Black*, February 4, 1963; Gregory J. Kaliss, "Un-Civil Discourse: Charlie Scott, the Integration of College Basketball, and the 'Progres-

sive Mystique,'" *Journal of Sport History* 35 (Spring 2008): 98–117; Martin, "Rise and Fall of Jim Crow," 265.

24. *Duke Chronicle*, November 20, 1964; Smith Barrier, *On Tobacco Road: Basketball in North Carolina* (New York: Leisure Press, 1983), 129.

25. Kean, *Desegregating Private Higher Education in the South*, 1–5; Barrier, *On Tobacco Road*, 129; William C. Friday, interview with author, Chapel Hill, N.C., August 15, 2006. For an excellent account of the experiences of the players who integrated the basketball teams at ACC and SEC schools, see Barry Jacobs, *Across the Line: Profiles in Basketball Courage—Tales of the First Black Basketball Players in the ACC and SEC* (Guilford, Conn.: Lyons Press, 2008), The quotation from Tate is on 155.

26. *Raleigh News and Observer*, May 5, 1962; *Diamondback*, October 22, 1964; Jacobs, *Across the Line*, 5; Darryl Hill, interview with author, College Park, Md., October 10, 2007.

27. *Washington Post*, April 9, 1964; Jacobs, *Across the Line*, 1–8; Billy Jones, interview with author, Orlando, Fla., May 12, 2008.

28. *Washington Post*, May 14, 1964; Jacobs, *Across the Line*, 5–14.

29. Paul McMullen, *Maryland Basketball: Tales from Cole Field House* (Baltimore: Johns Hopkins University Press, 2002), 27–32; John C. Prouty, *The ACC Basketball Stat Book* (Huntingtown, Md.: Willow Oak Publishing, 1993), 236; Jacobs, *Across the Line*, 14–19; Jones interview.

30. Billy Packer with Roland Lazenby, *Hoops!: Confessions of a College Basketball Analyst* (Chicago: Contemporary Books, 1986), 52–55; Joe Menzer, *Four Corners: How UNC, N.C. State, Duke, and Wake Forest Made North Carolina the Center of the Basketball Universe* (New York: Simon and Schuster, 1999), 140–43; Bones McKinney with Garland Atkins, *Bones: Honk Your Horn If You Love Basketball* (Gastonia, N.C.: Garland Publications, 1988), 68–69, 116; Billy Packer, interview with author, Charlotte, N.C., July 16, 2007.

31. Jacobs, *Across the Line*, 147–60; Packer, *Hoops!*, 56–59; Menzer, *Four Corners*, 143–47; Prouty, *ACC Basketball Stat Book*, 61, 65, 69, 346.

32. Dean Smith with John Kilgo and Sally Jenkins, *A Coach's Life: My 40 Years in College Basketball* (New York: Random House, 1999), 97–99; Scott Fowler, *North Carolina Tar Heels: Where Have You Gone?* (Champaign, Ill.: Sports Publishing, 2005), 65–67; Jacobs, *Across the Line*, 105–7; Menzer, *Four Corners*, 147–48.

33. Ken Rosenthal, *Dean Smith: A Tribute* (Champaign, Ill.: Sports Publishing, 2001), 27; Fowler, *North Carolina Tar Heels*, 67.

34. *Charleston News and Courier*, January 11, 1967; Bob Ottum, "Five Tall Strangers Shoot 'Em Up," *Sports Illustrated*, January 13, 1964, pp. 12–13; Preston Davis, "Cutting Down the Net: 100 Years of Basketball," *Davidson Journal* 37 (Spring 2008): 4–11; Prouty, *ACC Basketball Stat Book*, 200; McMullen, *Maryland Basketball*, 40–41.

35. Myron Cope, "Nobody Waits on This Lefty," *Sports Illustrated*, March 10, 1969, pp. 28–33; *University of Virginia 1975–76 Basketball Yearbook*, 14–15 (in author's possession); Terry Holland, interview with author, Greenville, N.C., March 20, 2008.

36. "Scouting Reports," *Sports Illustrated*, December 7, 1964, p. 53; Cope, "Nobody Waits on This Lefty," 33.

37. Joe Jares, "The Agony of Lefty Driesell," *Sports Illustrated*, March 8, 1965, pp.

32–35; Kent Baker, *Maryland Basketball: Red, White, and Amen* (Huntsville, Ala.: Strode Publishers, 1979), 268–69; McMullen, *Maryland Basketball*, 41; Joe Harrington, interview with author, Leesburg, Va., March 20, 2007.

38. *Charleston News and Courier*, January 11, 1967; "Scouting Reports," 53; Jares, "Agony of Lefty Driesell," 34; Cope, "Nobody Waits on This Lefty," 29–33; Baker, *Maryland Basketball*, 167.

39. Cope, "Nobody Waits on This Lefty," 33; Rosenthal, *Dean Smith*, 170; McMullen, *Maryland Basketball*, 42; Holland interview.

40. Jares, "Agony of Lefty Driesell," 32–35.

41. Rosenthal, *Dean Smith*, 27; Holland interview.

42. Jacobs, *Across the Line*, 108; Smith, *Coach's Life*, 99–100; Holland interview.

43. Smith, *Coach's Life*, 92–99.

44. *Durham Morning Herald*, May 4, 1966; *Daily Tar Heel*, May 4, 1966; Rosenthal, *Dean Smith*, 27–28; Smith, *Coach's Life*, 100–101; Jacobs, *Across the Line*, 109.

45. Holland interview.

46. *Charlotte Observer*, May 4, 1966; *Daily Tar Heel*, May 5, 1966; Jacobs, *Across the Line*, 115–16; Prouty, *ACC Basketball Stat Book*, 57–68, 266; Smith, *Coach's Life*, 116–17.

47. Jacobs, *Across the Line*, 51–74, 195–216, 241–68, 316–20; Prouty, *ACC Basketball Stat Book*, 198; Ernest H. Ern, interview with author, Charlottesville, Va., December 8, 2008.

48. Jacobs, *Across the Line*, 102, 320; Barrier, *On Tobacco Road*, 137; Len Elmore, interview with author, New York, N.Y., September 27, 2007.

49. *New York Times*, March 22, 1969; Kaliss, "Un-Civil Discourse," 106–8.

50. James H. Weaver to Robert C. Edwards, July 10, 1968, Box 18 (Robert C. Edwards, 1967–68), Records of the Athletic Council, Special Collections, Clemson University, Clemson, S.C.

51. Numan V. Bartley, *The New South, 1945–1980* (Baton Rouge: Louisiana State University Press, 1995), 145, 269; Thomas D. Clark, *The Emerging South*, 2nd ed.(Oxford: Oxford University Press, 1968), p. 94; Pete Daniel, *Lost Revolutions: The South in the 1950s* (Chapel Hill: University of North Carolina Press, 2000), 7, 39–60; David R. Goldfield, *Promised Land: The South since 1945* (Arlington Heights, Ill.: Harlan Davidson, 1987), 133; Jack Temple Kirby, *Rural Worlds Lost: The American South, 1920–1960* (Baton Rouge: Louisiana State University Press, 1987), xiv, 275–87; Jason Sokol, *There Goes My Everything: White Southerners in the Age of Civil Rights, 1945–1975* (New York: Alfred A. Knopf, 2006), 25, 46.

52. James W. Ely, Jr., *The Crisis of Conservative Virginia: The Byrd Organization and the Politics of Massive Resistance* (Knoxville: University of Tennessee Press, 1976), 136–39, 173–75; Goldfield, *Promised Land*, 137; Bartley, *New South*, 148–52, 445–46; Clark, *Emerging South*, 157–68.

53. David R. Goldfield, *Black, White, and Southern: Race Relations and Southern Culture, 1940 to the Present* (Baton Rouge: Louisiana State University Press, 1990), 169–73; James C. Cobb, *Away Down South: A History of Southern Identity* (Oxford: Oxford University Press, 2005), 212–22; Daniel, *Lost Revolutions*, 91–175.

54. Grundy, *Learning to Win*, 203–4.

55. Art Chansky, *Light Blue Reign: How a City Slicker, a Quiet Kansan, and a Moun-*

tain Man Built College Basketball's Longest-Lasting Dynasty (New York: St. Martin's Press, 2009), 170–71; Alwyn Featherston, *Tobacco Road: Duke, Carolina, N.C. State, Wake Forest and the History of the Most Intense Backyard Rivalries in Sports* (Guilford, Conn.: Lyons Press, 2006), 52; "ACC Basketball Tournament Program, 1968," 17, 23, 29, 35, 43, 49, 55.

56. Ron Morris, *ACC Basketball: An Illustrated History* (Chapel Hill: Four Corners Press, 1988), 97; Smith Barrier and Hugh Morton, *The ACC Basketball Tournament Classic* (Greensboro: Greensboro Publications, 1981), 7–8.

Chapter 8

1. Chip Conner Remarks at Memorial Service for Scott McCandlish, February 3, 2007, in possession of author (courtesy of Chip Conner); *Daily Progress*, November 23, November 26, 1969; Gary Cramer, *Cavaliers!: A Pictorial History of UVa Basketball* (Charlottesville: Spring House Publishing, 1983), 66–67; John C. Prouty, *The ACC Basketball Stat Book* (Huntingtown, Md.: Willow Oak Publishing, 1993), 64.

2. William A. Hobbs to William J. Gibson, December 30, 1969, Box 8 (Athletics—General, 1969–70), RG 2/1/2.731, President's Papers, University Archives, University of Virginia, Charlottesville; *Daily Progress*, November 23, November 26, 1969; Cramer, *Cavaliers!*, 67.

3. Email message from Chip Conner to the author, January 24, 2010 (in author's possession); Barry Parkhill, interview with author, Charlottesville, Va., November 13, 2006; Chip Conner, interview with author, Winston-Salem, N.C., May 21, 2007; Mike Katos, interview with author, Philadelphia, Pa., June 12, 2008; Chip Case, telephone interview with author, October 22, 2009; Barry Koval, telephone interview with author, October 27, 2009; Conner, Remarks at Memorial Service; Prouty, *ACC Basketball Stat Book*, 68.

4. *Raleigh News and Observer*, March 6, 1970; Michael E. O'Hara, *University of Virginia Men's Basketball Games: A Complete Record, Fall 1953 through Spring 2006* (Jefferson, N.C.: McFarland Publishers, 2008), 90–93; Smith Barrier and Hugh Morton, *The ACC Basketball Tournament Classic* (Greensboro, N.C.: Greensboro Publications, 1981), 77; Cramer, *Cavaliers!*, 67–69.

5. *Daily Progress*, November 29, 1970, February 26, 1971; Cramer, *Cavaliers!*, 72; Parkhill interview; Conner interview.

6. *Daily Progress*, November 29, December 6, December 14, 1970; *Raleigh News and Observer*, March 12, 1971; Jim Sumner, "Looking Back—Barry Parkhill Leaving a Legacy at Virginia," December 6, 2006, http://www.theacc.com/sports/m-baskbl.spec-rel/20606aab.html, copy in File #3843 (Barry Parkhill), Media Relations Archives, Department of Athletics, University of Virginia.

7. *The State*, January 12, 1971; *Richmond Times-Dispatch*, January 12, 1971; *Daily Progress*, January 18, January 19, 1971; Cramer, *Cavaliers!*, 72–74; Prouty, *ACC Basketball Stat Book*, 69–72; O'Hara, *University of Virginia Men's Basketball Games*, 95–100.

8. *Daily Progress*, December 8, 1970, January 18, February 28, March 18, 1971; *Raleigh News and Observer*, March 13, 1971; Cramer, *Cavaliers!*, 72–75.

9. *Raleigh News and Observer*, March 3, 1956, January 5, 1962, January 24, 1967;

Charleston News and Courier, January 6, 1967; Charlie Bryant, interview with author, Raleigh, N.C., March 18, 2008.

10. Curry Kirkpatrick, "One More War to Go," *Sports Illustrated*, March 2, 1970, pp. 12–15; Ron Morris, *ACC Basketball: An Illustrated History* (Chapel Hill: Four Corners Press, 1988), 187.

11. *Raleigh News and Observer*, October 16, November 25, 1966; *Washington Post*, October 16, 1966; Morris, *ACC Basketball*, 115, 118; Dean Smith with John Kilgo and Sally Jenkins, *A Coach's Life: My 40 Years in College Basketball* (New York: Random House, 1999), 85–86.

12. Frank Deford, "Chapel Hill's Tobacco Rogues," *Sports Illustrated*, February 20, 1967, pp. 24–26; Smith, *Coach's Life*, 87–91; Morris, *ACC Basketball*, 118–19, 291; Barrier and Morton, *ACC Basketball Tournament Classic*, 69–70.

13. *Raleigh News and Observer*, March 10, 1968; Smith, *Coach's Life*, 105–9; Morris, *ACC Basketball*, 124–26, 292.

14. *Durham Sun*, March 12, 1969; *Durham Morning Herald*, March 21, 1969; Curry Kirkpatrick, "Great Scott! And a Wealth of Carolina Blue," *Sports Illustrated*, December 16, 1968, pp. 32, 35; Joe Jares, "Voodoo Might Help," *Sports Illustrated*, March 24, 1969, pp. 18–21; Prouty, *ACC Basketball Stat Book*, 63; Morris, *ACC Basketball*, 128, 293.

15. Smith, *Coach's Life*, 124–26; Morris, *ACC Basketball*, 294–95.

16. Dean E. Smith to Orville Campbell, May 29, 1969, Box 15 (Athletics, May–June 1969), Records of the Office of the Chancellor: Joseph Carlyle Sitterson Series, University Archives, University of North Carolina, Chapel Hill; Joe Jares, "The Bvd Boys Shoot Down a Hex," *Sports Illustrated*, January 8, 1968, pp. 18–21; *Chapel Hill Weekly*, April 23, 1969; *Raleigh News and Observer*, April 24, 1969; *Charlotte Observer*, April 24, 1969; Smith, *Coach's Life*, 119; Morris, *ACC Basketball*, 294–95.

17. "Atlantic Coast," *Sports Illustrated*, December 4, 1967, p. 65; Jares, "Bvd Boys Shoot Down a Hex," 19; Morris, *ACC Basketball*, 128.

18. Bill Brill, *Duke Basketball: 100 Seasons, A Legacy of Achievement* (Champaign, Ill.: Sports Publishing, 2004), 56–57; Morris, *ACC Basketball*, 115–24, 291–92.

19. *Gastonia Gazette*, April 5, 1970; John Roth, *The Encyclopedia of Duke Basketball* (Durham, N.C.: Duke University Press, 2006), 118–20; Brill, *Duke Basketball*, 57–58; Morris, *ACC Basketball*, 130–37; Bucky Waters, interview with author, Durham, N.C., April 4, 2007.

20. Douglas M. Knight to Robert L. Dickens, March 26, 1969, Box 3 (Athletic Council, 1963–69), Douglas M. Knight Records, University Archives, Duke University, Durham, N.C.; *Raleigh News and Observer*, March 8, 1969; Alwyn Featherston, *Tobacco Road: Duke, Carolina, N.C. State, and Wake Forest and the History of the Most Intense Backyard Rivalries in Sports* (Guilford, Conn.: Lyons Press, 2006), 61.

21. Bucky Waters to Douglas Knight, March 12, 1969, Box 3 (Athletic Council), Knight Records, Duke University Archives; *Raleigh News and Observer*, March 8, 1969; *Durham Morning Herald*, March 13, 1969; Waters interview.

22. Jim Sumner, *Tales from the Duke Blue Devils Hardwood* (Champaign, Ill.: Sports Publishing, 2005), 83; Brill, *Duke Basketball*, 62–63; Roth, *Encyclopedia of Duke Basketball*, 352; Morris, *ACC Basketball*, 294–95.

23. John O. Blackburn, "Statement Released by the Chancellor for the President,"

August 18, 1972, Box 93 (National Collegiate Athletic Association, 1970–74), R. C. Waters to Carl James, April 12, 1973, Box 20 (Athletic Council, 1971–76), Terry Sanford to Waters, June 13, 1973, Duke University Press Release, September 11, 1973, Box 21 (Athletics — Basketball Coach, 1970–77), Terry Sanford Records, Duke University Archives; *Charlotte Observer*, February 17, 1972; Roth, *Encyclopedia of Duke Basketball*, 352; Brill, *Duke Basketball*, 63–66; Sumner, *Tales from the Duke Blue Devils Hardwood*, 85–86.

24. Douglas M. Knight to Frank L. Ashmore and others, November 29, 1968, Box 1 (Athletic Council, 1968–69), "Report of Academic Council Ad Hoc Committee on Duke Athletics," November 20, 1969, Box 1 (Athletic Program), Edmund Cameron Papers, Duke University Archives; William Johnson, "The Timid Generation," *Sports Illustrated*, March 11, 1968, pp. 68–78.

25. "Report of . . . Ad Hoc Committee on Duke Athletics," Duke University Archives.

26. "Statement by E. M. Cameron," November 28, 1969, "Comments concerning the Report Made to the Academic Council," January 22, 1970, Box 1 (Athletic Program), Roger L. Marshall to Alumni Officers and Program Leaders, December 5, 1969, Box 1 (Athletic Council, 1969–70), Cameron Papers, Terry Sanford to "Dear Colleague," August 11, 1970, Box 1 (Athletic Department Miscellaneous, 1969–1971), A. Kenneth Pye Records and Papers, Duke University Archives; Minutes of the Athletic Advisory Committee Meeting, January 7, 1970, Box 68 (Athletic Advisory Committee, 1969–70), RG 2/1/2.731, President's Papers, University of Virginia Archives.

27. Don Barton and Bob Fulton, *Frank McGuire: The Life and Times of a Basketball Legend* (Columbia, S.C.: Summerhouse Press, 1995), 86–91; Prouty, *ACC Basketball Stat Book*, 57–59.

28. Barton and Fulton, *Frank McGuire*, 87, 105.

29. Dan Klores, *Roundball Culture: South Carolina Basketball* (Huntsville, Ala.: AM Press, 1980), 93–110; *The State*, March 7, March 8, 2003; Curry Kirkpatrick, "The Toughest Kid on Anybody's Block," *Sports Illustrated*, January 4, 1971, pp. 21–27; Morris, *ACC Basketball*, 162–63.

30. *The State*, March 8, 2003; Kirkpatrick, "Toughest Kid on Anybody's Block," 22; Barton and Fulton, *Frank McGuire*, 93.

31. *The State*, March 7, 2003; Morris, *ACC Basketball*, 162; Barton and Fulton, *Frank McGuire*, 94–99; Kirkpatrick, "Toughest Kid on Anybody's Block," 27.

32. *Winston-Salem Journal*, April 24, 1968; *Raleigh News and Observer*, February 21, 1971; *The State*, March 7, 2003; Kirkpatrick, "Toughest Kid on Anybody's Block," 21; Barton and Fulton, *Frank McGuire*, 99–105.

33. *The State*, March 9, 2003; Kirkpatrick, "Toughest Kid on Anybody's Block," 27.

34. *The State*, March 9, 2003; Kirkpatrick, "Toughest Kid on Anybody's Block," 27; Barrier and Morton, *ACC Basketball Tournament Classic*, 80.

35. *Richmond Times-Dispatch*, March 15, 1971; *The State*, March 9, 2003; Barton and Fulton, *Frank McGuire*, 110; Morris, *ACC Basketball*, 295.

36. Kent Baker, *Red, White, and Amen: Maryland Basketball* (Huntsville, Ala.: Strode Publishers, 1979), 165; Morgan Wootten and Bill Gilbert, *A Coach for All Seasons* (Indianapolis: Masters Press, 1997), 39–41; Jim Kehoe, interview with author, Chesapeake Beach, Md., October 11, 2006; Morgan Wootten, interview with author, University Park, Md., May 1, 2008.

37. *Washington Post*, March 17, March 18, 1969; *Evening Star*, March 4, 1969; Jack Heise, interview with author, Gaithersburg, Md., March 1, 2007.

38. *Evening Star*, March 19, March 20, 1969; *Washington Post*, March 20, 1969; *Durham Morning Herald*, March 20, 1969; Paul McMullen, *Maryland Basketball: Tales from Cole Field House* (Baltimore: Johns Hopkins University Press, 2002), 46; Joe Harrington, interview with author, Leesburg, Va., March 20, 2007; Heise interview.

39. *Evening Star*, March 20, 1969; *Washington Post*, March 20, 1969; McMullen, *Maryland Basketball*, 54; Terry Holland, interview with author, Greenville, N.C., March 20, 2008; Harrington interview.

40. *Washington Post*, March 20, March 31, 1969.

41. Wilson H. Elkins Affidavit, August 12, 1969, Jim Kehoe to All Head Coaches, August 25, 1969, Box 440 (Athletics—Kehoe—AD—Recruiting Basketball, March 1969), Wilson H. Elkins Presidential Records, University Archives, University of Maryland, College Park; *Baltimore Sun*, August 23, 1969; Heise interview.

42. Kenneth Denlinger and Leonard Shapiro, *Athletes for Sale: An Investigation into America's Greatest Sports Scandal—Athletic Recruiting* (New York: Thomas W. Crowell Co., 1975), 69; Baker, *Red, White, and Amen*, 170; Holland interview; Harrington interview.

43. Sandy Treadwell, "Give Lefty a V, a V and . . . ," *Sports Illustrated*, January 25, 1971, p. 42; *Evening Star*, March 20, 1969; Baker, *Red, White, and Amen*, 173; Holland interview; Harrington interview.

44. Treadwell, "Give Lefty a V," 42; Baker, *Red, White, and Amen*, 169–74; Jack Zane, interview with author, Silver Spring, Md., February 9, 2007; Harrington interview; Kehoe interview.

45. "The Top 20," *Sports Illustrated*, November 29, 1971, 55; Baker, *Red, White, and Amen*, 174–76; Prouty, *ACC Basketball Stat Book*, 69–74.

46. Roy B. Clogston to E. M. Cameron, March 14, 1967, Marvin Francis to Athletic Directors, July 1, 1970, Box 2 (ACC Basketball Committee, 1969–71), Cameron Papers, Duke University Archives; Baker, *Red, White, and Amen*, 131; Morris, *ACC Basketball*, 212–15.

47. Smith Barrier, *On Tobacco Road: Basketball in North Carolina* (New York: Leisure Press, 1983), 205; Baker, *Red, White, and Amen*, 175, 190; Gene Corrigan Oral History interview, March 5, 1994, RG 26-178, University of Virginia Archives; Gene Corrigan, interview with author, Charlottesville, Va., November 14, 2006; Len Elmore, interview with author, New York, N.Y., September 27, 2007.

48. *New York Times*, March 11, 1974; Phil Taylor, "A Mad, Mad, Mad, Mad March," *Sports Illustrated*, March 19, 2007, n.p.; John Feinstein, *Last Dance: Behind the Scenes at the Final Four* (New York: Little, Brown, 2006), 33.

49. *Wall Street Journal*, April 11, 1967; *Los Angeles Times*, September 29, 1968; *New York Times*, March 10, March 11, March 14, March 15, 1974; Denlinger and Shapiro, *Athletes for Sale*, 79–104, 248–59.

50. *New York Times*, March 14, 1974; Wootten and Gilbert, *Coach for All Seasons*, 87–93.

51. Tom McMillen with Paul Coggins, *Out of Bounds: How the American Sports*

Establishment Is Being Driven by Greed and Hypocrisy—And What Needs to Be Done about It (New York: Simon and Schuster, 1992), 43, 58.

52. Peter Carry, "If You Want Tom, Easy Does It," *Sports Illustrated*, February 16, 1970, pp. 28–31; Lawrence Linderman, "The Tom McMillen Affair," *Playboy*, November 1971, p. 148; *Washington Post*, February 3, 1970; *Richmond Times-Dispatch*, November 29, 1970.

53. *Richmond Times-Dispatch*, November 29, 1970; Linderman, "Tom McMillen Affair," 158, 234; Carry, "If You Want Tom," 28–29.

54. *Richmond Times-Dispatch*, November 29, 1970; McMullen, *Maryland Basketball*, 54; McMillen, *Out of Bounds*, 48, 50–52; Tom McMillen, interview with author, Arlington, Va., January 25, 2007; Harrington interview.

55. *Richmond Times-Dispatch*, November 29, 1970; McMillen, *Out of Bounds*, 50–51; Linderman, "Tom McMillen Affair," 158, 238.

56. *Richmond Times-Dispatch*, November 29, 1970; McMillen, *Out of Bounds*, 30–35, 52–53; Linderman, "Tom McMillen Affair," 234, 238; Carry, "If You Want Tom," 30; McMillen interview.

57. *Baltimore Sun*, June 26, 1970; *Richmond Times-Dispatch*, November 29, 1970; McMillen, *Out of Bounds*, 53–54.

58. *Greensboro Record*, June 25, 1970; *Raleigh News and Observer*, June 26, June 30, 1970; *Washington Post*, June 24, June 26, 1970; *Evening Star*, June 26, 1970; *Charlotte Observer*, June 30, 1970; *Richmond Times-Dispatch*, November 29, 1970.

59. *Richmond Times-Dispatch*, November 29, 1970; Linderman, "Tom McMillen Affair," 238; McMillen, *Out of Bounds*, 54–56; McMillen interview.

60. *Washington Post*, September 11, 1970; Linderman, "Tom McMillen Affair," 239; McMillen, *Out of Bounds*, 56–57; Bill Guthridge, interview with author, Chapel Hill, N.C., April 4, 2007; McMillen interview.

61. *Washington Post*, November 28, 1971; Curry Kirkpatrick, "Sweating through the Dreads," *Sports Illustrated*, January 3, 1972, pp. 20–21; "Top 20," 55.

62. *Raleigh News and Observer*, March 12, 1972; Morris, *ACC Basketball*, 165–70; Baker, *Red, White, and Amen*, 181–88.

63. *Evening Sun*, January 11, 1971.

64. *Washington Post*, March 20, 1969; *Charlotte Observer*, April 4, 1969; Curry Kirkpatrick, "Po-Tential Almost Stole It," *Sports Illustrated*, December 10, 1973, pp. 22–25; Kathy Malin, conversation with author, Chapel Hill, N.C., March 29, 2001; Elmore interview; Harrington interview; Holland interview; McMillen interview.

65. Charles G. Driesell to Peter Lowry, June 24, 1970, Box 440 (Athletics—Basketball, 1970), Elkins Presidential Records, University of Maryland Archives; Bill Millsaps, interview with author, Richmond, Va., December 10, 2007.

66. *Raleigh News and Observer*, May 6, May 8, 1966.

67. Norm Sloan with Larry Guest, *Confessions of a Coach: A Revealing Tour of College Basketball's Backstage* (Nashville: Rutledge Hill Press, 1991), 39–48; Tim Peeler, *Legends of N.C. State Basketball* (Champaign, Ill.: Sports Publishing, 2004), 54–55; Barrier, *On Tobacco Road*, 177–79; Bill Hensley, interview with author, Charlotte, N.C., July 17, 2007.

68. Douglas Herakovich, *Pack Pride: The History of N.C. State Basketball* (Cary, N.C.: Yesterday's Future, 1994), 65; Sloan, *Confessions of a Coach*, 48–58.

69. "Report on the Maryland–N.C. State basketball game on January 7, 1967 played at Maryland," n.d., John T. Caldwell to Norman Sloan, January 10, 1967, Box 40 (Athletic Department), Collection UA 2.1 (Records of the Chancellor's Office), University Archives, Special Collections Research Center, North Carolina State University, Raleigh; Herakovich, *Pack Pride*, 66; Charlie Bryant, interview with author, Raleigh, N.C., September 23, 2008.

70. Frank Deford, "Tall, Stoned, and Gatoraded," *Sports Illustrated*, January 16, 1967, pp. 14–17; *Raleigh News and Observer*, November 14, 1979; Sloan, *Confessions of a Coach*, 7–8; Peeler, *Legends of N.C. State Basketball*, 56–57; Bryant interview.

71. Bill Beezley, *The Wolfpack: Intercollegiate Athletics at North Carolina State University* (Raleigh: North Carolina State University, 1976), 299–300; Peeler, *Legends of N.C. State Basketball*, 50, 64–66; Bryant interview.

72. *Raleigh News and Observer*, March 10, 1968; Sloan, *Confessions of a Coach*, 79–82; Peeler, *Legends of N.C. State Basketball*, 55; Herakovich, *Pack Pride*, 69; Morris, *ACC Basketball*, 292.

73. Beezley, *Wolfpack*, 302–4; Peeler, *Legends of N.C. State Basketball*, 67; Morris, *ACC Basketball*, 293–94; Prouty, *ACC Basketball Stat Book*, 67.

74. Peeler, *Legends of N.C. State Basketball*, 76; Herakovich, *Pack Pride*, 74; Morris, *ACC Basketball*, 159; Bryant interview.

75. Sloan, *Confessions of a Coach*, 83–85; Peeler, *Legends of N.C. State Basketball*, 77.

76. Tommy Burleson to Wolfpack Club Supporters, May 15, 1972, Box 55 (Athletics Department), UA 2.1 (Chancellor's Office Records), North Carolina State University Archives; Sloan, *Confessions of a Coach*, 84–85; Peeler, *Legends of N.C. State Basketball*, 77–78; Herakovich, *Pack Pride*, 74–75; Morris, *ACC Basketball*, 158.

77. David Thompson with Sean Stormes and Marshall Terrill, *Skywalker* (Champaign, Ill.: Sports Publishing, 2003), 19–20; Peeler, *Legends of N.C. State Basketball*, 51; Herakovich, *Pack Pride*, 88.

78. "Atlantic Coast Conference Investigation of Alleged Irregularities in the Recruitment of David Thompson," December 12, 1971, Box 2, Folder 98 (Case No. F54, NC State University, 1971–72), John Wesley Sawyer Papers, University Archives, Wake Forest University, Winston-Salem, N.C.; John T. Caldwell to Robert C. James, December 14, 1971, Box 59 (Investigation of Recruitment of David Thompson), Collection UA 2.1 (Records of the Chancellor's Office), North Carolina State University Archives; Thompson, *Skywalker*, 20; Sloan, *Confessions of a Coach*, 23; Herakovich, *Pack Pride*, 88.

79. John T. Caldwell to Warren S. Brown, September 28, 1972, Box 4, Folder 204 (North Carolina State University at Raleigh: NCAA Official Inquiry and Other Materials), Sawyer Papers, Wake Forest University Archives; Caldwell to Ralph E. Fadum, October 3, 1972, Caldwell to Brown, October 20, 1972, Box 59 (Athletics Council), Collection UA 2.1 (Records of the Chancellor's Office), North Carolina State University Archives; Beezley, *Wolfpack*, 305–14.

80. "Biographical Sketch of Coach Jack McCloskey, n.d., and attached untitled document, n.d., Box 12, Folder 706 (McCloskey, John W.), RG 1.10 (Records of the President's Office: Harold W. Tribble), Wake Forest University Archives.

81. John W. McCloskey to George C. Mitchell, January 14, 1970, McCloskey to "Dr." [James Ralph Scales], n.d., Box 7, Folder 577 (McCloskey, John W.), RG 1.11 (Records of the President's Office: James Ralph Scales), Wake Forest University Archives; Barry Jacobs, *Across the Line: Profiles in Basketball Courage: Tales of the First Black Players in the ACC and SEC* (Guilford, Conn.: Lyons Press, 2008), 164; Billy Packer, interview with author, Charlotte, N.C., July 16, 2007.

82. Morris, *ACC Basketball*, 157, 293–95; Prouty, *ACC Basketball Stat Book*, 332.

83. James Ralph Scales to John W. McCloskey, June 11, 1969, Scales to McCloskey, February 12, 1970, Box 7, Folder 577 (McCloskey, John W.), Gene Hooks to Scales, June 9, 1972, Box 12, Folder 957 (Athletics, 1967–68), RG 1.11, Wake Forest University Archives; Morris, *ACC Basketball*, 166.

84. Robert C. Edwards to Robert B. Hambright, February 18, 1970, Series 12, Folder 10 (Athletic Affairs, 1970), Records of the Office of the President: Robert C. Edwards, Special Collections, University Archives, Clemson University, Clemson, S.C.; *Charlotte Observer*, February 12, 1970; *Atlanta Journal*, July 22, 1970; Rick Telander, "The Descent of a Man," *Sports Illustrated*, March 8, 1982, pp. 62–69; Tates Locke and Bob Ibach, *Caught in the Net* (West Point, N.Y.: Leisure Press, 1982), 39, 41.

85. *Atlanta Journal*, July 22, 1970; *Richmond Times-Dispatch*, January 12, 1971; Telander, "Descent of a Man," 64; Locke and Ibach, *Caught in the Net*, 32–33, 43–44, 61.

86. Stephen H. Wainscott, "A Take-Charge Businessman: Robert Cook Edwards, 1958–1979," in *Tradition: A History of the Clemson Presidency*, ed. Donald M. McKale and Jerome V. Reel Jr., 2nd ed. (Macon, Ga.: Mercer University Press, 1988), 208–10; Locke and Ibach, *Caught in the Net*, 113–30; Prouty, *ACC Basketball Stat Book*, 69–87.

87. *Washington Post*, January 7, March 3, 1972; Cramer, *Cavaliers!*, 76–82.

88. Official Game Program, Virginia vs. William & Mary, December 16, 1972 (in author's possession); Cramer, *Cavaliers!*, 82.

89. *Roanoke Times*, December 26, 1971, April 30, 1972; *Daily Progress*, January 8, 1972; *Washington Post*, January 7, 1972; Gene Corrigan oral history, University of Virginia Archives; Corrigan interview.

90. Cramer, *Cavaliers!*, 82; Barrier and Morton, *ACC Basketball Tournament Classic*, 85.

91. *Daily Progress*, May 18, 1972; Conner interview; Parkhill interview. For those who neglected to read the preface, I should note that Wally Walker is my brother; this paragraph is based in part on conversations I had with him and other members of my family.

92. Minutes of Atlantic Coast Conference Meeting, May 2, 1969, Box 9 (Athletics—ACC, 1968–69), RG 2/1/2.721, President's Papers, University of Virginia Archives; *Raleigh News and Observer*, March 5, 1965, March 8, 1969, March 14, 1971, March 11, 1972; Barrier and Morton, *ACC Basketball Tournament Classic*, 7–8.

93. A. Kenneth Pye to E. M. Cameron, March 18, 1971, Box 20 (Athletics—Atlantic Coast Conference), Terry Sanford Records, Eugene Corrigan to Carl James and Bill Cobey, December 14, 1971, Minutes of Atlantic Coast Conference Meeting, February 9, 1972, Box 2 (ACC Basketball Committee, 1972), Cameron Papers, Duke University Archives.

94. *Durham Sun*, March 3, 1969; *Charlotte Observer*, March 6, 1970; *Daily Progress*, March 10, 1971; Smith, *Coach's Life*, 88–89.

95. Morris, *ACC Basketball*, 278–96; Smith, *Coach's Life*, 89.

96. *Winston-Salem Journal*, March 10, 1957; *Charlotte News*, March 13, 1957; *Raleigh News and Observer*, March 9, 1969; *The State*, March 9, 2003; Art Chansky, *Blue Blood: Duke-Carolina, The Most Storied Rivalry in College Hoops* (New York: St. Martin's Press, 2005), 112–13; Ken Rosenthal, *Dean Smith: A Tribute* (Champaign, Ill.: Sports Publishing, 2001), 20; Brill, *Duke Basketball*, 51; Feinstein, *Last Dance*, 113–14.

97. *Greensboro Daily News*, March 21, 1969; *Richmond Times-Dispatch*, March 22, 1969; Morris, *ACC Basketball*, 282–96.

98. Smith, *Coach's Life*, 155–56; Morris, *ACC Basketball*, 296; Barrier and Morton, *ACC Basketball Tournament Classic*, 85.

99. Curry Kirkpatrick, "Oh, Johnny, Oh, Johnny, Oh!," *Sports Illustrated*, April 3, 1972, pp. 31–37; *Richmond Times-Dispatch*, March 26, 1972; Morris, *ACC Basketball*, 170.

Chapter 9

1. *Raleigh News and Observer*, August 19, 1972.

2. Steve Sebo to Edgar F. Shannon Jr., July 25, 1967, Box 7 (Athletics—ACC, 1967–68), RG 2/1/2.711, President's Papers, University Archives, University of Virginia, Charlottesville.

3. K. N. Vickery, "The NCAA 1.600 Rule," n.d., Box 3 (Athletic Council, 1967–69), Athletic Council Records, University Archives, Special Collections, Clemson University, Clemson, S.C.; Everett D. Barnes and Francis E. Smiley to Chief Executive Officers of Member Institutions, January 28, 1966, Box 566 (National Collegiate Athletic Association, General File), Wilson H. Elkins Presidential Records, University Archives, University of Maryland, College Park; *Charlotte Observer*, April 26, 1966; Walter Byers with Charles Hammer, *Unsportsmanlike Conduct: Exploiting College Athletes* (Ann Arbor: University of Michigan Press, 1995), 67–77, 158–59.

4. John U. Munro to Robert Goheen, April 27, 1966, Box 18 (National Collegiate Athletic Association, 1963–69), Douglas M. Knight Records, University Archives, Duke University, Durham, N.C.; Goheen to Everett D. Barnes and the Council of the NCAA, April 13, 1966, Box 566, Elkins Records, University of Maryland Archives; Dan Jenkins, "It's One Point Six Pick Up Sticks," *Sports Illustrated*, March 21, 1966, pp. 30–31; *Charlotte Observer*, April 28, 1966.

5. Statement of Dr. Robert C. Edwards to the College Sports Information Directors of America, August 4, 1966, Series 12, Folder 9 (Athletic Affairs, 1966–69), Records of the Office of the President: Robert C. Edwards, Edwards to Hugh Germino, October 19, 1967, Box 7 (Atlantic Coast Conference, 1967), Athletic Council Records, Special Collections, Clemson University; *Roanoke Times*, November 13, 1969.

6. F. H. [Frank Howard] to Eddie [Cameron], August 3, 1966, Box 2 (Basketball—USC/McGuire Controversy), Edmund M. Cameron Papers, Duke University Archives; Howard to Atlantic Coast Conference Football Coaches and Athletic Directors, October 23, 1968, Box 8 (Athletics—General, 1968–69), RG 2/1/2.721, President's Papers, University Archives, University of Virginia; *Atlanta Journal*, November 19, 1969; *Greensboro Daily News*, November 20, 1969.

7. Robert C. Edwards to Walter T. Cox, May 12, 1967, Series 12, Folder 9 (Athletic Affairs, 1966–69), Records of the Office of the President: Robert C. Edwards, Special Collections, Clemson University; Edwards to John T. Caldwell, June 9, 1970, Box 215 (ACC and Minimum SAT Score of 800), Elkins Presidential Records, University of Maryland Archives; *Charlotte Observer*, April 28, 1966; *Atlanta Journal and Constitution*, April 2, 1967; *The State*, April 22, 1970; *Charlotte News*, April 27, 1970.

8. R. L. Dickens to E. M. Cameron, November 4, 1968, Box 1 (Athletic Council, 1968–69), Cameron Papers, Duke University Archives; Steve Sebo to Edgar F. Shannon, Jr., December 9, 1968, Box 8 (Athletics—General, 1968–69), RG 2/1/2.721, President's Papers, University of Virginia Archives; *Daily Progress*, November 23, 1969, November 27, 1970.

9. Minutes of the University of South Carolina Board of Trustees, May 2 and May 5, 1970, 45–46, University Archives, University of South Carolina, Columbia; Allan Kornberg to Terry Sanford, May 5, 1970, Box 20 (Athletics), Terry Sanford Records, Duke University Archives; John W. Sawyer to William Friday, May 5, 1970, Subgroup 1, Series 1, Box 1 (Athletics: General, 1970), Records of the Office of the President of the University of North Carolina (System): Willam Clyde Friday Files, University Archives, University of North Carolina, Chapel Hill; Minutes of University of Maryland Athletic Council Meeting, May 6, 1970, Box 439 (Athletic Council Minutes), Elkins Presidential Records, University of Maryland Archives; John T. Caldwell to ACC Presidents, May 21, 1970, Box 14, File 1071 (Atlantic Coast Conference, 1965–83), RG 1.11, President's Office: James Ralph Scales, University Archives, Wake Forest University, Winston-Salem, N.C.; *Atlanta Journal*, March 25, 1970; *Gamecock*, April 13, 1970.

10. John T. Caldwell to ACC Presidents and Chancellors, September 25, 1970, Box 14, File 1071, RG 1.11, Scales Papers, Wake Forest University Archives; Caldwell to ACC Presidents and Chancellors, October 22, 1970, Box 52 (ACC Study—Student Athlete Eligibility Requirements), Collection UA 2.1 (Records of the Chancellor's Office), University Archives, Special Collections Research Center, North Carolina State University, Raleigh; A. Kenneth Pye to President Sanford, October 30, 1970, Box 20 (Athletics—Atlantic Coast Conference), Sanford Records, Duke University Archives; "A.C.C. Meeting of Presidents—October 21, 1970—Raleigh, N.C.," n.d., Box 6 (Associations and Boards: Atlantic Coast Conference—Meetings), Office of the President: Thomas F. Jones, 1970–71, University of South Carolina Archives.

11. Paul F. Dietzel to Thomas F. Jones, September 24, 1970, Walter Byers to Jones, October 8, 1970, Box 6, Byers to Jones, October 7, 1970, Box 7 (NCAA), Office of the President: Thomas F. Jones, 1970–71, University of South Carolina Archives; *Gamecock*, October 26, 1970.

12. "Admission of Athletes with Grants-in-Aid in the ACC Institutions: A Confidential Report to the Chancellors and Presidents," Draft, December 8, 1970, Box 52 (ACC Study—Student Athlete Eligibility Requirements), Collection UA 2.1, North Carolina State University Archives; *Durham Sun*, October 23, 1970; *Greenville News*, October 23, 1970; *Greensboro Daily News*, October 24, 1970.

13. Introductory Remarks by Chairman Caldwell to ACC Institutional Heads, December 9, 1970, Box 52, Collection UA 2.1, North Carolina State University Archives; Minutes of Atlantic Coast Conference Meeting, December 11, 1970, Box 215 (Atlantic

Coast Conference, General File 1970), Elkins Presidential Records, University of Maryland Archives; *Daily Progress*, December 6, 1970; *Durham Sun*, December 11, 1970; *Roanoke Times*, December 12, 1970.

14. Minutes of the University of South Carolina Board of Trustees, December 12, 1970, March 29, 1971, pp. 237, 295, University of South Carolina Archives; John Caldwell to ACC Presidents, Draft, December 17, 1970, Box 52, Collection UA 2.1, North Carolina State University Archives; A. Kenneth Pye to Allan Kornberg, January 19, 1971, Box 20 (Athletics—Atlantic Coast Conference), Sanford Records, Duke University Archives; J. W. Sawyer to Dr. Scales, February 15, 1971, Box 14, Folder 1071 (Atlantic Coast Conference, 1965–83), RG 1.11, President's Office: James Ralph Scales, Wake Forest University Archives.

15. WSPA Editorial, April 22, 1971, Box 14, File 1071, RG 1.11, Scales Papers, Wake Forest University Archives; *Durham Morning Herald*, March 30, 1971; *Daily Progress*, March 31, 1971; *The State*, April 1, 1971; *New York Times*, April 10, 1971; Don Barton and Bob Fulton, *Frank McGuire: The Life and Times of a Basketball Legend* (Columbia, S.C.: Summerhouse Press, 1995), 112–13, 129–30; Tom Young, interview with author, Virginia Beach, Va., June 27, 2008.

16. Robert C. Edwards to Robert C. James, March 5, 1971, Edwards to James Ralph Scales, March 22, 1971, Series 13, Folder 18 (Atlantic Coast Conference), Office of the President: Robert C. Edwards, Special Collections, Clemson University; *Greenville News*, March 13, 1971; *Richmond Times-Dispatch*, March 14, 1971; *The State*, November 4, 1971.

17. *Washington Post*, August 8, August 10, 1972; *Greensboro Daily News*, August 8, August 10, 1972.

18. "Statement by R. C. Edwards . . . Concerning Court Decision on 800 Rule," August 8, 1972, Box 10 (Atlantic Coast Conference—Litigation, 1970–72), Athletic Council Records, Special Collections, Clemson University; *The State*, August 8, 1972; *Greensboro Daily News*, August 8, August 9, August 10, 1972; *Washington Post*, August 19, 1972.

19. *Raleigh News and Observer*, April 16, April 23, 1972; *Washington Post*, August 9, 1972; *The State*, August 9, 1972; *Charlotte News*, August 19, 1972; *Greensboro Daily News*, August 26, 1972; "ACC Opens the Door," *Sports Illustrated*, August 28, 1972, p. 9.

20. John T. Caldwell to Thomas F. Jones, December 1, 1966, Box 40 (Atlantic Coast Conference), Collection UA 2.1, North Carolina State University Archives.

21. Dean Smith with John Kilgo and Sally Jenkins, *A Coach's Life: My 40 Years in College Basketball* (New York: Random House, 1999), 218.

22. Bruce A. Corrie, *The Atlantic Coast Conference, 1953–1978* (Durham: Carolina Academic Press, 1978), 130–31, 139, 157–60; Barry Jacobs, *Golden Glory: The First 50 Years of the ACC* (Greensboro: Mann Media, 2002), 148.

23. Jacobs, *Golden Glory*, 212–14; Gene Corrigan, interview with author, Keswick, Va., March 20, 2010; John Feinstein, telephone conversation with author, March 6, 2010.

24. *America's Best Colleges: 2010 Edition* (Washington: U.S. News and World Report LP, 2009), 88–93.

25. Byers, *Unsportsmanlike Conduct*, 161–67, 297–313.

26. C. Fraser Smith, *Lenny, Lefty, and the Chancellor: The Len Bias Tragedy and the*

Search for Reform in Big-Time College Basketball (Baltimore: Bancroft Press, 1992), 46–50, 121–31, 187–222; Jacobs, *Golden Glory*, 194–95.

27. John Feinstein, "The Ordeal of Jim Valvano," *Sports Illustrated*, January 30, 1989, pp. 34–36; Alexander Wolff, "The Wolfpack Held at Bay," *Sports Illustrated*, March 12, 1990, pp. 28–29; *New York Times*, August 26, 1989; *Washington Post*, August 26, 1989; Tim Peeler, *Legends of N.C. State Basketball* (Champaign, Ill.: Sports Publishing, 2004), 114.

28. Peter Golenbock, *Personal Fouls: The Broken Promises and Shattered Dreams of Big Money Basketball at Jim Valvano's North Carolina State* (New York: Carroll and Graf, 1989), 37–40, 95, 175, 307; Joe Menzer, *Four Corners: How UNC, N.C. State, Duke and Wake Forest Made North Carolina the Center of the Basketball Universe* (New York: Simon and Schuster, 1999), 242–44; Marc J. Spears, "Washburn Traveled Long Road to Recovery," *Yahoo! Sports*, July 15, 2010, http://sports.yahoo.com/nba/news/?slug= mc-washburnlife071510 (accessed July 16, 2010); Byers, *Unsportsmanlike Conduct*, 305–6; Peeler, *Legends of N.C. State Basketball*, 112–14.

29. Ron Morris, *ACC Basketball: An Illustrated History* (Chapel Hill: Four Corners Press, 1988), 146–55; Douglas Herakovich, *Pack Pride: The History of N.C. State Basketball* (Cary, N.C.: Yesterday's Future, 1994), 82–83; Smith Barrier and Hugh Morton, *The ACC Basketball Tournament Classic* (Greensboro: Greensboro Publications, 1981), 89–91.

30. *NCAA News*, September 15, 1974, http://web1.ncaa.org/web_files/NCAANews Archive (accessed April 22, 2010); Morris, *ACC Basketball*, 149.

31. NCAA College Basketball Tournament Winners and Final Four Teams, http://www .fanbay.net/ncaa/fina14.htm (accessed April 22, 2010); ACC Men's Basketball Tournament History, http://www.mixx.com/stories/3988942/acc_tournament_history_past_ champions_and_mvp_winners (accessed April 22, 2010); *Washington Post*, April 23, 2010; Morris, *ACC Basketball*, 193, 217, 241.

32. Jacobs, *Golden Glory*, 14.

ESSAY ON SOURCES

When I first had the idea of writing a book on the early history of ACC basketball, the question that immediately arose in my mind was whether documentary evidence would be available on the topic. My initial trip to the University Archives at the University of Maryland, near my home, erased any doubts about the volume and the richness of primary sources. I found correspondence, minutes of meetings, reports of games, information on NCAA investigations, clippings, photographs, and other wonderfully illuminating material. It was at that point that I decided that a scholarly history of ACC basketball, based in part on archival research, was possible and, indeed, exceedingly promising. Subsequently, when I conducted research at the university archives of every other school that was a member of the ACC between 1953 and 1972, my experience at Maryland was repeated. I found an abundance of useful and fascinating documentary evidence that is on display in the notes of this book. The materials I cite were helpful in tracing various aspects of the ACC's history, but they were particularly valuable in understanding the relationship between academic and athletic objectives at every conference school in the period I cover.

Books and articles written by scholars and journalists were also essential for writing this volume. The work of the scholars cited in the notes placed my research in a broad context of the history of college athletics, southern history and culture, and the development of conference universities. The work of journalists who covered the ACC gave me information that is seldom available in archives about coaches, players, and individual games. Their reports of events they witnessed and principals they interviewed provided perspectives that would otherwise be impossible to obtain for a historian trying to reconstruct what occurred decades before. For the same reasons, I also benefited from the memoirs of former coaches. Memoirs must always be used with caution, but they offer unique and important insights. As with primary sources, even a cursory look at the notes in this book will reveal my indebtedness to other writers who have examined different segments of the rich and fascinating history of ACC basketball.

Finally, I am deeply grateful to the coaches, players, administrators, journalists, and scholars who gave generously of their time to talk to me. They provided information, judgments, contacts, and great stories. They shared their memories and knowledge in a frank and friendly way, and best of all, expressed great interest in my project. I extend my warm appreciation to the following for their encouragement, support, and assistance: Pete Brennan (Duck, N.C., August 1, 2009), Charlie Bryant (Raleigh, N.C., March 18 and September 23, 2008), Jay Buckley (Rockville, Md., August 22, 2007), George Callcott (University Park, Md., November 30, 2006), Chip Case (via telephone, October 22, 2009), Chip Conner (Winston-Salem, N.C., May 21, 2007), Gene Corrigan (Charlottesville, Va., November 14, 2006 and Keswick, Va., March 20, 2010), Len Elmore

(New York, N.Y., September 27, 2007), Ernie Ern (Charlottesville, Va., December 8, 2008), Thomas Fields (Silver Spring, Md., January 14, 2007), John Feinstein (via telephone, March 6, 2010), Frank Fellows (Silver Spring, Md., February 19, 2007), William Friday (Chapel Hill, N.C., August 15, 2006), Bill Guthridge (Chapel Hill, N.C., April 4, 2007), Joe Harrington (Leesburg, Va., March 20, 2007), Jack Heise (Gaithersburg, Md., March 1, 2007), Bill Hensley (Charlotte, N.C., July 17, 2007), Darryl Hill (College Park, Md., October 10, 2007), Fred Hobson (Chapel Hill, N.C., August 14, 2006), Terry Holland (Greenville, N.C., March 20, 2008), Al Hunt (Washington, D.C., November 1, 2007), Billy Jones (Orlando, Fla., May 12, 2008), Mike Katos (Philadelphia, Pa., June 12, 2008), Jim Kehoe (Chesapeake Beach, Md., October 11, 2006), Barry Koval (via telephone, October 27, 2009), Tom McMillen (Arlington, Va., January 25, 2007), Bud Millikan (via telephone, July 30, 2006), Bill Millsaps (Richmond, Va., December 10, 2007), Jeff Mullins (Cornelius, N.C., July 16, 2007), Jack Murdock (Raleigh, N.C., March 18, 2008), Billy Packer (Charlotte, N.C., July 16, 2007), Barry Parkhill (Charlottesville, Va., November 13, 2006), Lou Pucillo (Raleigh, N.C., March 17, 2008), Jerry Reel (Clemson, S.C., September 20, 2007), Fred Shabel (Philadelphia, Pa., June 12, 2008), Wally Walker (various times), Bucky Waters (Durham, N.C., April 4, 2007), Alan Williams (Charlottesville, Va., December 9, 2007), Gary Williams (College Park, Md., June 26, 2006), Ed Wilson (Winston-Salem, N.C., September 22, 2008), Morgan Wootten (University Park, Md., May 1, 2008), Tom Young (Virginia Beach, Va., June 27, 2008), and Jack Zane (Silver Spring, Md., February 9, 2007).

INDEX

Abdul-Jabbar, Kareem. *See* Alcindor, Lew

Adkins, Paul, 200

Aillet, Joe, 93

Alabama, University of, 116, 125, 311

Alabama College, 127

Alcindor, Lew, 193, 263, 284

Allen, Forrest C. "Phog," 20, 23, 25, 162

Allen, Noah Henry, 317

American College Testing Program (ACT), 310

American Council on Education, 85, 174, 283

Anderson, George "Butter," 64, 70, 72, 73, 138

Anderson, Willie, 317

Anlyan, William, 268

Appalachian Hall, 160

Appalachian State Teachers College, 150

Arkansas, University of, 127, 311

Association of American Universities, 34, 47, 56

Atlantic Coast Conference: first basketball game in, 1; national stature of, 7, 117, 261–62, 307–8; fan behavior, 7, 8, 136, 182–83, 188, 189–90, 217–23; league-wide balance, 7, 260–62, 306; and academic standards, 8, 54, 172–75, 318–20, 324; racial integration of, 8, 224–25, 230–41, 245–50, 252; creation of, 29–31, 42–62, 251, 309, 318, 324, 328; naming of, 53; organization of, 53–54; and bowl games, 54, 318; adds Virginia, 56, 58, 59; Weaver appointed as commissioner of, 60; penalizes NC State, 73, 87–89, 91–92; television coverage, 117–19, 252, 281; as drawing card for recruits, 139, 153, 211, 280–81; 800 rule, 175, 193–97, 240–41, 252, 270, 309–19, 321, 324, 326; penalizes USC, 193–97; and departure of USC, 199, 309, 312–16, 322; in postwar South, 251–54; attendance at games, 253; and growing pressure for national title, 254, 308; allows participation in NIT, 266; reprimands NC State, 298; and conference champions' record in NCAA tournament, 306–8; football and competition against teams of other leagues, 311–12, 318; success in expanded NCAA tournament, 328

Atlantic Coast Conference Basketball Tournament: as means of choosing champion, 55, 100–102, 305–7; attendance and popularity, 101, 253, 305; student tickets for, 305; decline in stakes and interest, 328

—individual tournaments by date: 1954 tournament, 84, 306; 1955 tournament, 84; 1956 tournament, 85, 102; 1957 tournament, 102–6, 151, 306; 1958 tournament, 178, 209–10, 289, 306; 1959 tournament, 98, 257; 1960 tournament, 121, 144; 1961 tournament, 124, 144, 155; 1962 tournament, 146, 150, 156, 170; 1963 tournament, 146, 157, 219; 1964 tournament, 157, 281; 1965 tournament, 149, 172; 1966 tournament, 149, 172, 240, 262; 1967 tournament, 262, 266; 1968 tournament, 262, 266, 294; 1969 tournament, 207, 262, 273; 1970 tournament, 257, 264, 273, 285, 294, 306; 1971 tournament, 264, 268, 274, 307; 1972 tournament, 289, 304, 308; 1974 tournament, 327

52; success under Millikan, 81, 183,
209–11; general admission standards,
174, 325; improves academic programs,
176–77, 289, 291; struggles to win in
ACC, 178, 211, 213–17; winning team
of 1964–65, 211–12; integration of, 225,
230–31, 238–39; success under Drie-
sell, 261, 275–80, 288–89; reprimanded
by NCAA, 277; students' pride in, 291;
and 800 rule, 313; academic ranking,
324; academic deficiencies in basket-
ball program of, 325; 1974 game with
NC State, 327; wins national cham-
pionship, 328
Maryland Medieval Mercenary Militia, 3
Mattocks, Tommy, 172
McAdoo, Robert, 308
McCandlish, Scott, 208, 256–57, 304
McCann, Billy, 200, 201, 202, 203
McCarthy, Brendan, 109
McCloskey, Jack, 241, 299–301
McComb, Ken, 161
McCracken, Branch, 20, 137, 228
McCray, Reuben, 11
McDuffie, Frank, Jr., 241, 245, 246
McDuffie, Sammie, 245
McFadden, Banks, 38, 146
McGuire, Al, 293
McGuire, Frank: and 1957 national cham-
pionship, 1, 112–17; and 1970–71 Mary-
land games, 2–4; rivalry with Case, 78,
80, 111–12, 120; background and per-
sonality, 78–79, 108–12, 161–62; hired
at UNC, 78–80; comments on ACC
tournament, 100, 273; and 1957 ACC
tournament, 100–106; and recruiting, 103, 106–9, 121–24, 192, 270–71;
popularity with fans, 106, 192; feud
with Weaver and Cameron, 111, 192,
195; resigns at UNC, 120, 132–33; and
NCAA penalties, 120–24, 134, 197–99,
320, 321–22; and 1961 fight with Duke,
136; on list of top coaches, 137; recruits
Heyman, 137, 141–42; hires Smith as
assistant coach, 163; success at South

Carolina, 182–83, 192, 261, 270–75;
hired at USC, 190–91; and Grosso controversy, 192–99, 270, 319; comment
on Cremins, 271; comment on Roche,
271; and USC departure from ACC,
316, 322
McKean, Ted, 207
McKinney, Horace A. "Bones": comments on Dixie Classic, 64; background and personality, 74–75, 150–51,
156–57; coaching ability of, 75–76,
151; comments on ACC tournament,
101; in 1956 ACC tournament, 102; in
1957 ACC tournament, 103–5; mocks
McGuire, 109; comments on television, 118; becomes head coach, 134,
150; and recruiting, 153–54; resignation of, 157–61, 299; rejects Clemson
job, 171; eases pressure on Tribble,
179; comments on Fike Field House,
188; protests calls, 219; recruits black
players, 240; and balance in ACC, 261
McLendon, John, 164, 225–26
McMillen, James, 286–87
McMillen, Jay, 211–12, 213, 216, 276, 284,
286, 288
McMillen, Margaret, 212, 284, 286–87
McMillen, Tom, 276, 280, 284–88, 291,
307, 327
McNeil, Charlie, 209, 210, 211
Mehaffey, Gene, 202
Meredith, James, 234
Miami, University of, 193, 323, 324
Michigan, University of, 148
Michigan State University, 63, 66–67, 113
Middle States Association of Colleges
and Secondary Schools, 176–77
Mikan, George, 70
Mileham, M. Charles, 65
Milford, Lee W., 36, 43
Miller, Chip, 208, 256
Miller, Larry, 166, 168, 262–63, 280, 307
Miller, Rich, 286
Millikan, Herman A. "Bud": hired at
Maryland, 40, 80; comments on for-